HISTORY OF THE LABOR MOVEMENT
IN THE UNITED STATES
VOLUME V

BY PHILIP S. FONER

History of the Labor Movement in the United States (5 vols.)
The Life and Writings of Frederick Douglass (5 vols.)
A History of Cuba and its Relations with the United States (2 vols.)
The Complete Writings of Thomas Paine (2 vols.)
Business and Slavery: The New York Merchants and the Irrepressible Conflict
W.E.B. Du Bois Speaks (2 vols.)
Paul Robeson Speaks
The Fur and Leather Workers Union
Jack London: American Rebel
Mark Twain: Social Critic
The Jews in American History, 1654-1865
The Case of Joe Hill
The Letters of Joe Hill
The Bolshevik Revolution: Its Impact on American Radicals, Liberals and Labor
American Labor and the War in Indochina
Helen Keller: Her Socialist Years
The Autobiographies of the Haymarket Martyrs
The Black Panthers Speak
The Voice of Black America: Major Speeches of Negroes in the United States, 1797-1973
    (2 vols.)
Women and the American Labor Movement: From Colonial Times to the Eve of World War I
The Spanish-Cuban-American War and the Birth of American Imperialism, 1895-1902
    (2 vols.)
When Karl Mark Died: Comments in 1883
Organized Labor and the Black Worker, 1619-1973
American Labor Songs of the Nineteenth Century
Labor and the American Revolution
We, the Other People: Alternative Declarations of Independence by Labor Groups, Farmers,
    Women's Rights Advocates, Socialists, and Blacks
Formation of the Workingmen's Party of the United States
The Democratic-Republican Societies, 1790-1800
The Factory Girls
The Great Labor Uprising of 1877
History of Black Americans: From Africa to the Emergence of the Cotton Kingdom
American Socialism and Black Americans: From the Age of Jackson to World War II
Inside the Monster: Jose Marti on the United States and American Imperialism
Our America: Jose Marti on Latin America and the Struggle for Cuban Independence
On Education: Jose Marti on Educational Theory and Pedagogy
The Black Worker: A Documentary History (with Ronald Lewis) (4 vols.)
Proceedings of Black State Conventions, 1840-1865 (with George Walker) (2 vols.)

HISTORY OF
THE LABOR MOVEMENT
IN THE UNITED STATES

VOLUME V: The AFL in the
Progressive Era, 1910–1915

BY PHILIP S. FONER

INTERNATIONAL PUBLISHERS, NEW YORK

LIBRARY OF CONGRESS CATALOGING IN PUBLICATION DATA

Foner, Philip Sheldon, 1910-
    The AFL in the progressive era, 1910-1915.

    (*His* History of the labor movement in the
United States; v. 5)
    Includes bibliographical references and index.
    1. American Federation of Labor—History.
2. Trade-unions—United States—History. 3. Strikes
and lockouts—United States—History. I. Title.
HD6508.F57 1975, vol. 5 [HD8055.A5]   79-26924
ISBN 0-7178-0570-0   331.88'0973s [331.88'32'0973]
ISBN 0-7178-0562-X pbk.

CONTENTS

HISTORY OF THE LABOR MOVEMENT

IN THE UNITED STATES

VOLUME V

PREFACE

In 1910 the American Federation of Labor was twenty-nine years old. It had already established the fact that it was the first truly stable national labor federation in U.S. history. Every attempt at national federation prior to the founding of the A.F. of L. had failed to achieve longevity. Only the American Federation of Labor had survived, and while not co-extensive with all unionization in the United States, it represented the vast majority of organized workers. By 1912, 2,483,500 American wage earners were organized, 1,843,158 of whom were members of the A.F. of L. Total membership of the A.F. of L.'s affiliated unions in 1912 was 74.1 percent of all unionized workers.

But in only two industries, liquor distilling and brewing, did the union membership rise to more than 40 percent of the total work force. In the skilled trades not more than 15 or 20 percent of the workers belonged to labor organizations. Less than 10 percent of the predominantly unskilled labor force in steel, oil, chemicals, and other mass production industries were organized. Clearly, the A.F. of L. represented only a small minority of the labor force.

In the third volume of my multivolume *History of the Labor Movement in the United States, The Policies and Practices of the American Federation of Labor, 1900-1909,* I sought to account for the unorganized status of the vast majority of American workers. To a major extent, it was due to the determined opposition of employers to unionism. However, added to this, were the policies adopted by the A.F. of L.: class collaboration (exemplified by participation in the leadership and framing of policies of the National Civic Federation); concentration on organizing the skilled

workers, and clinging to the craft union structure long after it was
largely outmoded as a form in unionizing the mass production industries; the exclusion of Blacks, women and foreign-born workers from
most of the craft unions; and the acceptance of a racist approach toward
Blacks, Chinese and Japanese workers, and those from Eastern Europe.
Despite the presence in the A.F. of L. of such industrial unions as the
United Mine Workers and the Brewers, the Federation was dominated
by craft unionism. Even the alternative proposal to industrial unionism—the creation of voluntary industrial departments, such as the
building trades department—fell far short of the mark, and failed to
eliminate jurisdictional conflicts. In short, while the A.F. of L. membership climbed in the years from 1900 to 1909, it failed to meet the
challenge posed by the rise of modern mass production industries, in
which the unskilled and semi-skilled, Blacks, women and recent immigrants were the majority of the workers.

Meanwhile, as was demonstrated in the fourth volume, *The Industrial
Workers of the World, 1905-1917*, the I.W.W. was attempting to meet this
challenge. By basing itself on industrial unionism and welcoming into its
ranks all workers regardless of race, sex, creed, color, nationality or skill,
the Wobblies made an enormous appeal to precisely those workers
neglected by the A.F. of L. The present volume covers the history of the
American Federation of Labor, and many of its affiliates, in the second
decade of the twentieth century. In discussing labor and Progressivism,
it has, however, been necessary to trace the origins before this period.
But the concentration is on an era of great labor militancy, an era which
produced "a transformation of workers' consciousness in America."

The focus in the present volume is not on inchoate dissatisfaction but
on organized resistance, on workers who belonged to trade unions, and
on their commitment to organize the unorganized, and the struggle for
change in their lives. Through these struggles, the organized workers
forged a link with large sections of the working class, and made it clear
that the U.S. ruling class had failed to extend completely its hegemony
over the working class. The volume demonstrates that the class collaboration promoted by the National Civic Federation and the foremost
leaders of the A.F. of L. on a national level failed to defuse the class
struggles on the local levels.

This work could not have been completed without the generous
assistance of numerous libraries and historical societies. I am indebted to
the American Federation of Labor for permission to use the incoming
correspondence of the A.F. of L. and the Letter Books of Samuel

Gompers. I wish to thank Dorothy Swanson and her staff at the Tamiment Institute, Elmer Bobst Library, New York University for kind assistance and cooperation, and the staffs of the Chicago Historical Society, Columbia University Library, Boston Public Library, Harvard University Library, Howard University Library, Library of Congress, New York Public Library, Bancroft Library, University of California, Berkeley, University of California, Los Angeles Library, University of Pennsylvania Library, Yale University Library, Kansas Historical Society, University of Wisconsin Library, State Historical Society of Wisconsin, Library of the U.S. Department of Labor, New York State Library, Detroit Public Library, Cleveland Public Library, Labadie Collection (University of Michigan Library), University of Maine, Farmington Library, Library Company of Philadelphia, Free Library of Philadelphia, Radcliffe College Library, Michigan Technological University Library, University of Alabama Library, Wayne State University Library, University of Chicago Library, Indiana University Library, University of Illinois Library, University of Maryland Library, and the National Archives. I also wish to thank the members of the library staff of the Langston Hughes Memorial Library, Lincoln University, Pennsylvania for cooperation and for assistance in obtaining materials through interlibrary loan from libraries, historical societies, and other institutions. Finally, I wish to thank my brother, Henry Foner, who read the manuscript and made useful suggestions.

Philip S. Foner

CHAPTER 1

The McNamara Case

On October 1, 1910, an explosion destroyed a printing plant of the Los Angeles *Times*, killing twenty-one *Times* employees. During April, 1911, following detective work coordinated by William J. Burns, the brothers John J. and James B. McNamara were arrested, accused of dynamiting the *Times* building, and indicted for murder. The enemies of labor seized upon the fact that J. J. McNamara was secretary-treasurer of a major trade union—the International Association of Bridge and Structural Iron Workers (BSIW)—and that J. B. McNamara was a trade unionist, to use the case for a general accusation that the labor movement resorted to murder in order to realize its aims. The "Crime of the Century," as the bombing incident was called, was a *"cause celebre"* in American labor history and had significant repercussions in the entire area of labor-capital relations.

The McNamara case is discussed at some length in work by Louis Adamic, Grace Hilman Stimson, and Graham Adams, Jr.,[1] but labor historians have paid relatively scant attention to it. It is either ignored, dismissed as just another example of labor violence, or treated as an interesting but isolated episode.[2]

The story of the McNamara case begins with the International Association of Bridge and Structural Iron Workers. By 1910, that union had gone through several years of bitter battle against a coalition of openshop forces. Included among them was the National Erectors' Association, founded on March 3, 1903, and a leading member of that Association was the American Bridge Company, a subsidiary unit of the giant United States Steel Corporation. From its inception in April, 1901,

U. S. Steel instituted a systematic procedure aimed at driving out of existence every labor organization of workmen in its various plants. By 1910, it had succeeded in virtually destroying the Amalgamated Association of Iron and Steel Workers, as well as the unions of the carpenters, moulders, machinists, bricklayers, masons, seamen, and longshoremen—in fact, all the organizations of workmen either in the plants it originally held or those it took over after its organization. With unionism in its plants all but defunct, U. S. Steel had proceeded to force down wages, lengthen the hours of work, and establish whatever working conditions it wished. The only remaining militant labor organization that still resisted the giant corporation's encroachments was the Bridge and Structural Iron Workers' union.[3]

With the support of U. S. Steel, the American Bridge Company refused to allow the union to do any erecting work within company property. Early in 1906, the union responded with a strike, which lasted for almost a decade and produced some of the most brutal tactics ever used in a struggle between capital and labor.[4] Shortly after the strike began, the National Erectors' Association entered the contest against the union, with the aim of completely destroying it and instituting the open shop. The Association hired Walter Drew, one of the nation's leading exponents of the open shop, to carry out its plan to destroy the ironworkers' union. It sent spies into the union, employed detective agencies to disrupt union activity, and stood ready to "lend its whole power and influence to the open-shop cause in any of the other building trades."[5]

Standard accounts of the McNamara case emphasize that the union had decided that any chances of success against the open-shop drive of the National Erectors' Association were doomed to fail if it employed only the ordinary union methods. Hence, according to this view, within a year after the strike against the American Bridge Company began, the International Association of Bridge and Structural Iron Workers launched a campaign of dynamiting, and from 1906 to 1911, union leaders were responsible for some 110 explosions. The damage done, on the whole, was not very great—usually less than several thousand dollars—and it has therefore been assumed that the intent was not to destroy building projects entirely, but rather to force employers to grant union demands in order to forestall greater destruction in the future.[6]

The scene now shifts to Los Angeles, where a determined campaign was being waged for the extinction of the labor movement. Led by Harrison Gray Otis, publisher of the Los Angeles *Times,* and the

Merchants and Manufacturers' Association (M & M), it aimed to convert Los Angeles into what one trade unionist described as "a city of slave owners, slave drivers, and chattel slaves."[7] Under Otis, the Los Angeles *Times*, with its tremendous circulation, became the spearhead of a twenty-year campaign against organized labor. It fully earned its reputation as the "most unfair, unscrupulous and malignant enemy of organized labor in America." By 1910, Los Angeles was being described as "Otistown of the Open Shop."[8]

Having fought off unionization, the Los Angeles employers were able to compete successfully with industries that had long been established in San Francisco, one of the most tightly organized union towns in the country. The employers there informed the labor leaders that unless the workers in Los Angeles were unionized, the San Francisco industrialists would either have to establish open-shop conditions or go out of business. It was precisely at this time that Los Angeles labor decided to launch a new campaign to unionize the city. The San Francisco unions voted to take immediate steps to aid their sister unions in Los Angeles, and a decisive effort to organize the open-shop city was begun.[9]

On one side were ranged the M & M, the Chamber of Commerce, and the National Association of Manufacturers, with Harrison Gray Otis' *Times* as the coordinator and publicist of the open-shop alliance. On the other side were the Los Angeles unions, supported by the militant unions of San Francisco, the AFL, the International Moulders' Union, and the International Association of Bridge and Structural Iron Workers. The union allies decided that the strongest point of attack would be through the iron workers' union, which was among the few well-organized unions in the city. In addition, the Founders' and Employers' Association had just rejected the union's demands: a minimum wage of $4.00 for an eight-hour day, and extra pay for overtime. On June 1, 1910, the metal workers struck, and by the 10th, fifteen hundred of them had abandoned their jobs. The M & M pledged both money and moral support to the employers, and by the end of June it had collected $350,000 to smash the strike. Unions throughout California voted to assess themselves enough to be able to send from eight to nine thousand dollars weekly to Los Angeles.

Although the unionists had refrained from violence, Los Angeles Mayor Alexander announced that the police would act against any pickets who blocked the streets illegally, and the Superior Court issued a series of injunctions against the strikers which, if obeyed, would have crippled any action the workers might have taken. On June 22, 1910, in an editorial entitled "Common Peril," the Los Angeles *Times* declared: "These are days of common peril in Los Angeles. A foreign foe is at the gates and threatens all alike. . . . The call comes to drop all little disputes and devote all attention to the enemy. . . ."

On July 16, an anti-picketing ordinance was enacted by unanimous vote of the Good-Government Council. It prohibited "loitering, picketing, carrying or displaying banners, signs, or transparencies, or speaking in public streets in a loud or unusual tone for certain purposes." The penalty was fifty days in jail or a fine of $100, or both.[11]

The union members kept right on picketing and the police arrested them by the score, eventually booking 472 people. But few strikers deserted, and the passage of the anti-picketing ordinance without a dissenting vote only served to reawaken labor's interest in politics.

A boycott of "scab beer" was begun when the brewers rejected demands for increased wages for the bottlers and drivers, who were the lowest-paid workers on the West Coast. It was so successful that by September, the brewers were ready to sign. In the first nine months of 1910, the Central Labor Council grew from 62 unions with 6,000 members to 85 unions with 9,500 members. Twenty-five hundred unaffiliated union men brought labor's strength to 12,000.[12] On September 23, after five days in Los Angeles, James Wilson, president of the Pattern Makers' League of North America, reported to the AFL Metal Trades Department:

> There is a determination on the part of the men that speaks well for the success of the movement that we are now engaged in in this city. . . . It is only time when victory will be achieved.[13]

Then, on October 1, 1910, the Los Angeles *Times* building was destroyed by an explosion and resulting fire which left twenty-one dead. The next morning, the *Times*, printed in an auxiliary plant, flashed the provocative headline: "UNIONIST BOMBS WRECK THE 'TIMES.'" Upon learning of the incident, Otis had immediately concluded that the labor unions were responsible, and he brought to bear all his talent for inflammatory journalism. The publisher editorialized:

> O you anarchist scum, you cowardly murderers, you leeches upon honest labor, you midnight assassins, you whose hands are dripping with the innocent blood of your victims, you against whom the wails of poor widows and the cries of fatherless children are ascending to the Great White Throne, go mingle with the crowd on the street corners, look upon the crumbled and blackened walls, look at the ruins wherein are buried the calcined remains of those whom you murdered.[14]

A wave of hysteria swept through Los Angeles as unexploded bombs were discovered near the homes of H. G. Otis and F. J. Xeehandelaar, leader of the M & M. Several sticks of dynamite were also found near the Alexander Hotel annex and the Hall of Records, then in the process of construction by the anti-union Llewellyn Iron Works. On Christmas Day, the Llewellyn factory itself was partially wrecked by an explosion. All this kept the city in a state of excitement and terror, and the employers sought to use the hysteria to defeat the continuing metal trades' strike.[15]

But George Gunrey, secretary-treasurer of the Strike Committee, kept assuring AFL headquarters in Washington that "we are still making progress and moving along to our ultimate success." The committee, he reported, had met with Mayor Alexander, who urged that the strike be called off "as the Merchants and Manufacturers would never give in." "We told him," Gunrey wrote, "that as far as we were concerned the strike was just started and that we had no power to call it off as that was up to the men and it was as much as our lives were worth to ask them to call it off." The mayor then mentioned "the explosion," and evidently hinted that it was connected with the strike, but the committee "assured him that we were ready at all times to aid the authorities in any investigation they might make and we also were open for investigation."[16]

The investigation was already under way. With the posting of sizable rewards for the discovery of the perpetrators of the *Times* explosion, a nationwide hunt had begun. The M & M, the Chamber of Commerce, and the municipal authorities each hired detective agencies to track down the dynamiters. The city employed William J. Burns, a notorious anti-labor detective,* who was already investigating a wave of dynamitings which had, since 1906, smashed machines, bridges, building frames, and supplies in more than one hundred explosions throughout the country as part of the ongoing war between the Bridge and Structural Iron Workers and the Erectors' Association. Burns told Mayor Alexander that his evidence had convinced him that the *Times* bombing was the latest incident in this war and was planned, as were all the others, at the union's international headquarters in Indianapolis.[17]

Burns soon identified the union's chief dynamiters as James B. McNamara and Ortie McManigal. He insisted that McNamara was the

---

*Although it is generally noted in histories of the McNamara case that Burns was engaged by the city of Los Angeles, Louis Adamic claims that he was hired by the National Erectors' Association. (*My America*, New York, 1942, p. 31.)

man who had wrecked the *Times* building and that McManigal had set the dynamite at the Llewellyn plant. He charged further that they had received their orders and payment from John J. McNamara, secretary-treasurer of the BSIW, and from H. S. Hockins, who was on his payroll. Burns' operatives trailed J. B. McNamara and McManigal to Detroit, where they were suspected of planning to destroy the new two-million railroad station. On April 14, 1911, Burns' son, Raymond, along with police officers from both Detroit and Chicago, arrested the suspects. Dynamite, percussion caps, and alarm clocks were found in their valises.

Upon being told that they were wanted for a recent bank robbery in Chicago, for which they had valid alibis, the prisoners waived extradition and voluntarily accompanied their captors to Chicago. On the train, McNamara began to suspect that he had been arrested in connection with the *Times* explosion, and, according to Burns, he futilely offered his captors $30,000 for an opportunity to escape. In Chicago, in a proceeding that was only quasi-legal at best, the prisoners, instead of being booked and jailed, were taken to the home of Chicago Police Sergeant William H. Reed for questioning and held in private captivity.[18]

Burns was certain he could persuade McManigal to confess by convincing him that the detective knew everything and that the union would, in the end, let McManigal take the blame for the *Times* disaster and die. Burns later revealed that this strategy enabled him to get McManigal to tell everything he knew and to promise to help the prosecution to the limit of his ability.[19] Beginning on April 13 and continuing until the following morning, McManigal gave an amazingly detailed account of his career as a dynamiter. His statements implicated John J. McNamara, Frank Ryan, president of the BSIW, H. S. Hockin, and other union leaders in a dynamite conspiracy against the National Erectors' Association. According to McManigal's signed confession, it was J. B. McNamara who actually placed the bomb in the *Times* building on his brother's instructions.[20]

With McManigal's confession in his hands, Burns was ready to proceed against J. J. McNamara. As soon as he had reached Chicago, Burns had telegraphed Los Angeles for extradition papers and for policemen to serve them. When they arrived, he went to Indianapolis and obtained a warrant for J. J. McNamara's arrest from the governor of Indiana. (Walter Read of the Erectors' Association seems to have been helpful in this project.) Burns and two detectives then went to the BSIW office, where they arrested J. J. McNamara in the midst of an executive board meeting, and charged him with murder in connection with the *Times* bombing and with implication in the Llewellyn bombing. McNamara was immediately rushed to police court where he was arraigned before Judge James A. Collins, who denied McNamara's request for a lawyer and released him, instead, to the Los Angeles police for extradition. Within half an hour after his arrest, McNamara found himself in an automobile heading for Los Angeles. On the afternoon of the same day—April 22—James B. McNamara and McManigal were turned over to two Los Angeles police officers. On the 26th, the three men entered jail in Los Angeles.[21]

The day after the arrest of J. J. McNamara, the Los Angeles *Times* ran a headline reading: "THE DYNAMITERS OF THE TIMES BUILDING CAUGHT. Crime Traced Directly to High Union Labor Officials."[22] Obviously, for Otis, the case had been tried and decided before the trial began.

J. J. McNamara had been arraigned in a police court, which did not have jurisdiction in extradition cases. He had been refused the right to consult a lawyer, had been subjected to extradition proceedings even though he was not a fugitive from justice, and had been conveyed out of the state by automobile. The fact that Burns had subverted due process did not trouble the Los Angeles *Times,* or most of the rest of the nation's press. But it did make the whole procedure look like kidnapping. Moreover, it was this act, together with the fact that a third man, McManigal, had confessed and implicated the McNamaras, that caused so many people to believe that this was another frame-up. It was too reminiscent of the Haywood-Moyer-Pettibone case, a few years earlier, in the aftermath of the murder of the ex-governor of Idaho. These men had also been abducted—from Colorado—to stand trial on the basis of the confession of an informer named Harry Orchard. In that case, Clarence Darrow had successfully defended the accused and had completely exposed the frame-up.*

Here, too, there was a kidnapping and an informer—all the earmarks of another frame-up. The AFL pointed out that the "unlawful and un-American kidnapping of McNamara formed one of the chief factors of fixing in the minds of working people of our country that he was innocent." The labor movement feared, with justification, that the illegal removal of the McNamaras would set a precedent that could be used

*For the Haywood-Pettibone-Mayer case, *see* Philip S. Foner, *History of the Labor Movement in the United States,* Vol. IV, New York, 1965, pp. 40-59.

extensively in the future. The McNamara case was thus tainted by this virtual kidnapping, and many people quickly concluded that a prosecution and a detective agency capable of such reckless action was also capable of fabricating the entire case.[24]

The fact that the McNamaras asserted their innocence, and that J. J. was a distinguished union official with a reputation for integrity, only served to strengthen the belief that Burns had manufactured the evidence against them. "That I am innocent of any infraction of the law in word or deed needs no emphasis from me, for the truth is mighty and will prevail right speedily," J. J. McNamara wrote to Gompers, "and for it I shall be content to wait." During a visit by the AFL president to the brothers in the Los Angeles jail, J. J. McNamara again asserted his innocence. The brothers seemed determined to plead innocent and to take their chances in a prolonged legal fight.[25]

For his part, Gompers testified from his personal knowledge of the man that John J. McNamara was "a painstaking, conscientious, and efficient official, conservative and thoroughly in sympathy with the higher aims of organized labor." And the executive officers of eight other international unions* with headquarters in Indianapolis added:

> We know John J. McNamara. He is an industrious, reliable, painstaking and courteous gentleman. He is a graduate of an Indianapolis law school, thus making manifest his ambition to tread the paths that lead to higher planes of activity. In every way so far as we know he is a model citizen.[26]

The background of the case also served to strengthen the argument that the McNamaras were victims of a frame-up. Centrally involved was the publisher of the Los Angeles *Times,* Harrison Gray Otis, whose hatred of the labor movement was intense and who, it was generally believed in labor circles, would not stop at any limits in his effort to destroy the trade unions. It was not surprising, then, that many in the labor and liberal movements saw the case as a product of Otis' anti-labor prejudice. Some of them even charged that Otis himself had ordered the destruction of the *Times* building. Others held him indirectly responsible, arguing that the building's destruction had actually been caused by a leaky gas jet, and that the time bomb was apparently designed to do minimum damage to the property, but had been accidentally placed near

---

*The organizations were the International Typographical Union, the Bricklayers, Masons and Plasterers, the United Mine Workers, the Journeymen Barbers, the Teamsters, the Bookbinders, the Carpenters and Joiners, and the Locomotive Firemen and Enginemen.

the leaking gas. Witnesses were said to be ready to prove that the gas odor had been so bad that some employees had been forced to leave the plant the night of the explosion.[27]

Then, of course, the Erectors' Association, the American Bridge Company, and U. S. Steel had their own reasons for encouraging the prosecution of the McNamaras and their elimination from the labor scene.[28] There was also an important political factor involved in the prosecution of the labor leaders. The McNamara case was being fought against the background of the 1911 Los Angeles mayoralty campaign, which was reaching its climax at the same time. The metal trades strike had aroused the political consciousness of Los Angeles labor. "The political end of the situation is being given a great deal of attention," Gunrey wrote to AFL Secretary-Treasurer Frank Morrison on February 10, 1911. "We feel reasonably sure that by coupling the Labor Union Party with the Socialist Party, also coupling the Afro-American League of this city, which had already joined hands with us,* and with what recruits we can gain from the unskilled laborers by organizing them into the Unskilled Labor Organization, I think we can win the city of Los Angeles at the coming Municipal Election."[29] By the time the McNamara trial began, it appeared likely that the Socialist candidate, Job Harriman, was headed for victory. With the threat of a Socialist victory in Los Angeles, it was reasonable to assume that the McNamara case had been manufactured in order to intimidate the moderate, middle-class voters into rejecting the Socialists.[30]

Finally, additional grave doubt was cast on the entire procedure by the repeated strong hints by Burns that many prominent AFL leaders, including Gompers, were implicated in the dynamiting. "The whole affair smacks of well-laid prearrangement . . . to strike at the men having the confidence of the working people," Gompers declared. And he wrote John Mitchell of the United Mine Workers on January 5, 1911: "The information which has come to me from Los Angeles is to the

*On January 5, 1911, Gunrey wrote to Morrison: "We are in touch with the leadership of the Afro-American League, an organization that practically includes all the colored people in Los Angeles. We held a joint committee meeting and formed a temporary organization. . . . We believe this is a move in the right direction, and it is up to Organized Labor to support the colored wage earner, and when he once realizes that, he will be with us politically and otherwise. This organization of colored people has been used in this city from time to time . . . as a strikebreaker, and they are getting tired of the game, and now believe that their lot should be cast with us. They also hold the balance of power politically in this city. . . ." (Geo. Gunrey to Frank Morrison, Los Angeles, January 12, 1911, *AFL Corr.*)

effect that a great conspiracy has been and is still afoot to fasten upon the union workmen any and all crimes which may be committed in Los Angeles."[31]

When all this is taken into account, it is not surprising that when the McNamaras were indicted, the national labor leadership asserted their innocence. "I have investigated the entire case and I am more convinced than ever that there is a 'Frameup' and a plot behind these arrests," Gompers declared. Standing with the AFL president in declaring the McNamara case a fraud was the Socialist Party and its press, as well as prominent public spokespersons. During April, 1911, the Party's National Executive Committee pledged support to the BSIW and called on party locals throughout the country to form joint defense groups with the unions. The Party also released a pamphlet which placed the McNamara case in the context of a nationwide class struggle:

> It concerns the labor movement. . . . It is not an isolated incident. It is just one more battle in the long struggle between Organized Wealth and Organized Humanity. . . . In California especially within the last two or three years, the Labor Unions and the Socialist Party have been making a steadily winning fight against the hitherto unbridled exploitation of labor by capital. These capitalists are growing desperate.[32]

The Socialists believed that employer desperation provided the explanation for the initiation of the attack on the McNamaras. "The opponents of unionism, fixing the stigma of crime on them, hope to smash unionism," observed the New York *Call*. "They hope, through accomplishing their execution, to beat all workers into meekness, to terrorize them into submission, and thereby render it easier to exploit them."[33]

Added to the formal organization statement was the powerful voice of Eugene V. Debs, the Party's leader, who declared in the Socialist weekly, *Appeal to Reason:* "I want to express my deliberate opinion that the *Times* and its crowd of union-haters are the instigators if not the actual perpetrators of that crime and the murder of twenty human beings." And Debs cried out: "Arouse ye hosts of labor and swear that the villainous plot shall not be consummated."[34]

A temporary united front developed around the McNamara case between the Socialists and the AFL leadership. The basis for unity lay in their conviction that the McNamaras were innocent of any involvement in the *Times* explosion.

Even though the McNamaras were members of the AFL, the IWW, too, rallied to their defense, calling "the whole thing" a "frameup" by the Merchants and Manufacturers Association for the purpose of destroying labor organizations."[35]* But the IWW suggested only one defense tactic—the "general strike." "Strike! Strike!" appealed William D. ("Big Bill") Haywood, the IWW leader. "Fold your arms for one day, the day the McNamaras go on trial, is all that will be necessary."[36]

On June 18, 1911, 80,000 working men and women met in mass meeting in Chicago to voice their protest "against the efforts of the United States Steel Corporation to hang J. J. McNamara and wreck union labor." The resolutions adopted summed up the approach of most trade unions and Socialists to the McNamara case. They read:

> Whereas, on April 22, 1911, the latest outrage of organized capital against organized labor was committed by the unlawful kidnapping of J. J. McNamara from his office at Indianapolis and carrying him, without due process of law, three thousand miles to Los Angeles, there to be tried on the charge of having murdered men he never saw and never knew; and whereas, the charge is made against McNamara in name, but against union labor in fact; therefore, be it resolved, by the trade unionists and Socialists of Chicago, that the arrest and kidnapping of J. J. McNamara is in violation of the fundamental law of the United States and of common right and justice; and be it further resolved, that we affirm our faith in J. J. McNamara and pledge to his defense our moral and financial support; and be it further resolved, that a copy of these resolutions be given to the press and a copy sent to J. J. McNamara and his brother in jail in Los Angeles.[37]

The BSIW asked Clarence Darrow to conduct the defense, but the Chicago labor lawyer, who was in ill health, delayed his decision. Meanwhile, BSIW President Frank Ryan engaged Job Harriman, the California Socialist, as the principal attorney for the defense. However, Gompers believed that it was essential that Darrow undertake the defense, and he visited Chicago to plead with him to defend the

*Bruce Roger, a Wobbly, warned, however, that should the facts prove that the bomb had indeed been set by a member of the BSIW, the view that the affair was a "frame-up" would backfire." "What then?" he asked. "Shall we join with the masters in hounding to the gallows and death a member of the working class, who, acting individually, and smarting under some form of capitalist tyranny, set with his hand the deadly fuse?" Should not the IWW be prepared, under such a development, he went on, to applaud "his brave and courageous deed?" To this, the editor of the *Industrial Worker* replied: "The workers have nothing to gain by violence, although it is surprising that there are not more acts of vengeance on the part of men who are driven by the lash of hunger. The following are the words of Francesco Ferrer: 'That which violence wins for us today, another act of violence may wrest from us tomorrow.'—Ed." (*Industrial Worker*, Nov. 17, 1910.)

Francisco Ferrer (1859-1909), Spanish philosophical anarchist and founder of the Escuela Moderna in Barcelona where he introduced reform principles in education, was executed by government authorities after being convicted on flimsy evidence for complicity in insurrection. His execution stirred world-wide protests.

McNamaras. (The defense plans had originally included McManigal until he repeated his confession to District Attorney Fredericks and thereafter remained on the side of the prosecution.) Darrow finally gave his reluctant consent, but estimated that $350,000 would be needed. Gompers promised to get it. Darrow then announced that it was his duty "to combat the powerful forces of society in the courts," and that he would administer the defense in the McNamara case.[38] He assembled a highly competent staff including pro-labor Judge Cyrus F. McNutt of Indiana, Job Harriman, Lecompte Davis, and Joseph Scott, the latter two being local lawyers of excellent reputation.

District Attorney Fredericks accepted aid from both the M & M and the NAM. As for the Erectors' Association, he came to consider it as one of his clients.[39]

On May 5, 1911, when the defendants were arraigned, they pleaded "not guilty." In a "Call to Labor," issued the next day, the AFL Executive Council assumed responsibility for the McNamara case and began soliciting money for the defense. While conducting the campaign for the defense, it emphasized that no member of organized labor sympathized with crime. "Indeed," it went on, "organized labor is opposed to, and is a standing protest against violence and crime committed by anyone or by any force or authority." But even as organized labor was horrified by the destruction of human life and property in Los Angeles, workers could also "feel the great outrage which has been committed against the accused men." The McNamaras, the AFL insisted, had been targeted by a detective agency "well known to have no hesitancy or scruples in manufacturing evidence and charges against others"—one that had long been known to have spies in factories and organizations "to misdirect the grievances of workmen into violent channels." The McNamaras were the "innocent victims of capitalist greed," victims of an alliance made up of the National Erectors' Association, the M & M of Los Angeles, and the editor and proprietor of the Los Angeles *Times,* Harrison Gray Otis. Thus, the accused men would have "the most formidable power and influences with which to contend. How a fair trial under such circumstances can be accorded them is difficult to understand." Still, their only hope was an adequate defense, and this would require funds.[40]

To raise the $350,000 needed for the defense required an enormous effort, but the AFL organized a permanent Ways and Means Committee "so that an ample opportunity for defense may be assured." The Committee appealed to all national and international unions, city central bodies, and local and federal unions for a 25 cents per capita contribution for the defense of the McNamaras: "The great need of the hour is money with which to meet the heavy drains incident to the collection of evidence and other expense, made necessary to cope with the corporate wealth and unlimited means behind the prosecution."[47]

McNamara defense committees were set up in cities and towns throughout the country. The defense fund was literally deluged with contributions. Only the American Federation of Musicians refused to respond. (C. L. Bagley, president of Los Angeles Local 47, convinced that the brothers were guilty, persuaded his national union to refrain from assisting the defense.)[42] Thousands of workers wore pins and buttons sold by the McNamara Ways and Means Committee, reading "McNamara Brothers Not Guilty," and "Justice for the McNamaras. Kidnapped. AFL." Large audiences came to see a film produced under labor auspices that portrayed the injustice of the case, titled "A Martyr to his Cause," and subtitled "Incidents in the Life and Abduction of the Secretary-Treasurer of the International Association of Bridge and Structural Iron Workers." The premiere was held at the American Theatre in Cincinnati where it was seen by an estimated 50,000 people.[43] It began with John McNamara, "a young man of 17 or 18 years of age," leaving home, bidding his father and mother goodbye. "He kisses his mother affectionately, shakes his father's hand, and promises the latter to be a good boy and to play fair in all that he does." Then the film carried McNamara through his career as a structural iron worker, foreman, and secretary-treasurer of the International Association of Bridge and Structural Iron Workers, his arrest in the union's Indianapolis office, his illegal extradition, and his arrival and confinement in Los Angeles. The script for the final two scenes reads:

HIS MESSAGE TO ORGANIZED LABOR

Scene 19: Cell. Mac, seated in his cell, is writing. As he finishes, flash on sheet, the following:

TO THE BROTHERHOOD OF ORGANIZED LABOR:

In this second attempt to crush and discredit the cause we represent I realize fully the desperation of the enemies of labor arrayed against us, but I am of good heart, for it will fail. That I am innocent of any infraction of the law in word or act needs no emphasis from me, for the truth is mighty and will prevail right speedily; and for it I shall contentedly wait.

I send to all brothers and friends of union labor the world over my earnest and affectionate greetings, with the assurance there is no villainy of which we are afraid. I am also confident that it is not asking too much of the public to suspend judgment in these matters until opportunity for a full and fair defense has been afforded.

J. J. Mc.

(Back to picture) Mac with head bent low, reads the paper, then dissolve into Scene 20: The home fireside. Close-up of mother, alone, weeping over a letter from her son.[44]

Labor Day, 1911 was named "McNamara Day" throughout the United States. In Cleveland, St. Louis, Indianapolis, New York, Chicago, Philadelphia, Atlanta, Seattle, San Francisco, Portland, Oakland, San Diego, and Los Angeles, large and enthusiastic crowds marched, demanding the McNamaras' release. Twenty thousand marched in open-shop Los Angeles (and some rode on horseback) near the jailhouse, vowing their commitment to defeat the frame-up. They carried signs and banners with the declaration: "If the McNamaras die, 20,000 will know the reason why."[45]

At other rallies, signs and banners read: "This is the BIG CLASS WAR"; "The carpenter of Nazareth was crucified. They would hang the ironworker of Indianapolis"; "Who Obeys the Law? The Working Class. Who Breaks the Law? The capitalist class." Small wonder that Burns wrote: "A social revolution seemed at hand."[46]

The trial of the McNamaras was scheduled to begin on October 11, 1911. During the preceding days, McNamara Defense Committees staged meetings, demonstrations, and parades "in order to show the ruling class . . . the organized workers are on the alert."[47] In New Orleans, the Joint McNamara Committee, which included the Central Trades and Labor Council and the Socialist Party, brought thousands of workers together "to protest the frame-up." Speaker after speaker emphasized that the McNamara case was "simply the fight of organized capital against organized labor." P. A. Cooley, a member of the Executive Board of the Structural Iron Workers, offered an additional explanation. He related the "six-year fight of the Structural Iron Workers against the United States Steel Corporation, and declared that the organization was the only one of many that had succeeded in winning out against that corporation. Hence the attack on the leadership."[48]

The day before the trial opened, Gompers told 15,000 people in Philadelphia that he had just come from Los Angeles where the McNamaras had assured him of their innocence, and that when he had left J. J. McNamara, the latter took his hand and, looking him in the eye, declared: "Sam, I want to send a message by you to organized labor and all you may meet. Tell them we're innocent—that we are the victims of an outrageous plot." After Gompers had concluded the speeches with the declaration that the McNamaras were being tried on "charges we know to be absolutely false," thousands paraded through the streets, carrying signs which included the widely-publicized slogan: "If the McNamaras Die, 20,000 Will Know the Reason Why."[49]

Sixty correspondents were present in Los Angeles on October 11 to report developments to all the important American papers and to others in London, Paris, and Berlin. By October 15, Darrow knew that the prosecution had gathered masses of damaging evidence. Three days later, he learned that U. S. Attorney General George Wickersham had other evidence secured through a federal subpoena sactioned by President William Howard Taft. He now believed that an acquittal was entirely out of the question. There were twenty-one separate indictments against the two brothers, and Darrow later wrote:

> The situation looked hopeless to me, for even though we might get a disagreement, or "Not guilty" in the first case, there were all the others, which would make endless trials possible. . . . I knew that the State would never submit to defeat so long as there was any hope for them to win.[50]

Meanwhile, the trial proceeded, day after day, mired in the preliminary procedure of jury selection. By October 25, the first venire of 125 talesmen had been exhausted—and only six of them had been seated on the jury. By November 7, the jury box was finally filled. Throughout these weeks, the labor movement stood solidly behind the McNamaras. In November, the AFL convention intensified its fund raising by assessing all officials one week's pay. The delegates sent a message to the McNamaras assuring them that the AFL believed in their innocence and would continue to give them both moral and financial support. Gompers repeated his statement that the case was a plot to wreck organized labor.[51]

But Darrow was suffering from anxieties, doubts, and depression. All of his attempts to gather favorable evidence and witnesses had failed. Defense witnesses and relatives of the McNamaras alike were so thoroughly harassed by detectives that they were evicted from their quarters and fired from their jobs. Burns operatives infiltrated the McNamara defense staff in Los Angeles, and by means of a dictaphone, the prosecution was able to record conversations held in the McNamaras' jail cells.

It was at this juncture, in the middle of November, that Lincoln Steffens arrived in Los Angeles. The noted "muckraker"* had heard of the case while in London. He tells us in his famous autobiography of a talk with Keir Hardie, who had read of the McNamara case in the English press. The British labor leader convinced Steffens that he should go to Los Angeles and find out just why conservative organizations like

*For the role of the "muckrakers," *see* next chapter.

labor unions would hire dynamiters in their struggle against capital. So Steffens journeyed to California to write a series of articles for syndicated papers. He assumed that the McNamaras were guilty, and he determined to concentrate on the reasons that lay behind the act of violence. After obtaining permission from Judge Walter Bordwell to visit with the prisoners, he did so and told them of his intention to explain, through his newspaper articles, the conditions leading labor to the use of dynamite. "Justifiable dynamiting" was to be his defense of the McNamaras, and he wanted the prisoners' agreement to help him uncover the facts of labor's case against capital.

Steffens later recalled that J. B. McNamara responded favorably to this fantastic proposition, since the muckraker was doing what the brothers wanted done above all: "to force attention to the actual conditions of labor" that led trade union leaders to resort to violence. But J. J. McNamara was skeptical and asked Steffens, "Have you seen Darrow about this?" However, both brothers finally consented, subject to Darrow's approval. When Steffens did see Darrow, the defense lawyer was stunned by the proposition suggesting that the McNamaras had actually set off the dynamite.* Nevertheless, apparently convinced that the defense was on extremely shaky ground, he instructed Steffens to stand by and watch the progress of the case.[53]

That weekend—November 19-20—Darrow and Steffens went to visit publisher E. W. Scripps at his ranch near San Diego. After supper, Darrow reviewed the distressing state of the case for the defense, and out of the conversation came a suggestion by Darrow for a possible settlement out of court. With Scripps' strong encouragement, Steffens formulated a plan to transform Darrow's desire into reality. All that was needed, he believed, was to convert the Los Angeles capitalists to the principles of scientific Christianity** and to convince the heads of

*Whether or not Darrow shared Steffens' belief that the "boys" were really guilty is difficult to determine accurately. Most historians of the case believe he stated as much privately even before Steffens appeared on the scene. Darrow certainly said so openly in retrospect.

**Steffens' theory of scientific Christianity, which he was now to put to the test, was based on the belief that evil results not from bad men, but from bad conditions, and that the big business men, not the officials actually govern every city. Since he was convinced that the "big bad men of business"—sinners, just like any others—were never asked to do good, they therefore never did good. To improve society, all one had to do was to ask its commanders to be magnanimous and show them that magnanimity paid. Steffens had previously asked the "big sinners" for help for people, and they had never failed to deliver: "I had been looking for a chance to try it more openly in a more spectacular situation which all men could see." The McNamara case gave him that "chance"—"to try out Christianity as a working principle—among sinners." (Lincoln Steffens *The Autobiography of Lincoln Steffens*, New York, 1931, pp. 525, 670-71.)

industry in the open-shop city that the best way to end the continuing war with labor was to sponsor a "deal" between the prosecution and defense in the McNamara case. In return for letting the prisoners off with prison terms—or possibly even letting them go free—labor could be convinced that it should cease its costly war, and all would be peace and harmony.[54]

Steffens went directly to Meyer Lissner, the Los Angeles reform leader, with the proposal that the business leaders should approach the case in a spirit of reconciliation, have the McNamaras released, and call a conference of business and labor leaders to put Los Angeles firmly on the path to progress. Steffens offered to demonstrate the practicability of his scheme by converting the most difficult men on a list drawn up by Lissner, and even agreed to accept the challenge of securing the support of publisher Otis. Unable to meet with Otis, he conferred with his son-in-law, Harry Chandler. Surprisingly, he won over both Chandler and Otis, and the latter gave his support to the idea of a settlement when Steffens presented it to him. Chandler agreed to negotiate with District Attorney Fredericks and to inform Otis when the bargain had been completed, while Steffens was to negotiate with Darrow.

A representative group of business leaders then met and endorsed the compromise. They resolved "that arrangements be made for a meeting between citizens representing labor for the purpose of considering such methods as may be practicable for bringing about an improvement of relations existing between the employer and the employee in the community."[55]

The plan to be submitted to District Attorney Fredericks, with the approval of the Los Angeles businessmen, included the proposal that the McNamaras should go unpunished and that further pursuit of other suspects should be abandoned. But Fredericks balked. Although willing to settle out of court, he refused to even consider any proposal involving no punishment for the McNamaras. As Grace Hilman Stimson points out, "The National Erectors' Association . . . had heard of the Los Angeles negotiations and was pressing for uncompromising terms."[56] The district attorney therefore demanded that the McNamaras plead guilty, that James receive a life sentence and John a shorter term in prison, possibly ten years.[57]

The proposal, modified to meet the district attorney's conditions, was then placed before the two defendants. James McNamara at first opposed any settlement which involved his brother's pleading guilty. He himself was prepared to hang, if necessary, to save his brother's life, but he would not have John, as a union official, plead guilty and cast a shadow over organized labor. Darrow, however, while insisting that no one must die, made it clear that settlement out of court was possible only if both brothers pleaded guilty. James then agreed.[58] Darrow immediately wired Gompers to send somebody to represent the AFL, without disclosing just what was involved. Edward N. Nockels, secretary of the Chicago Federation of Labor, made the trip. At first, he balked as Darrow sadly outlined the deal involving pleas of guilty by the McNamaras. But after the status of the case was pointed out to him in detail, and he heard Darrow insist that it was hopeless to expect anything but a guilty verdict, Nockels was convinced that "under all the circumstances . . . it was for the best."[59]

Steffens and Darrow had entertained the hope that only J. B. McNamara, charged with actually setting the explosion, would have to plead guilty. But they soon came to realize that this would not work. They realized, too, that the open-shop Los Angeles capitalists had more in mind than a desire to accept the "Golden Rule" when they agreed to Steffens' proposition. Their problem was that a mayoralty election was set for December 5; that Job Harriman, the Socialist candidate, was a seeming victor; and that Harriman would be an uncooperative mayor in the struggle to keep Los Angeles an open-shop town, since he was allied with the city's labor movement.

They were also convinced that if the trial was still in progress on election day, considering the widespread belief that the McNamaras were innocent victims of a frame-up, Harriman was certain to win. Even if the trial ended before the election with a guilty verdict, public opinion would still be much the same. Only a confession of guilt by the McNamaras *before* the election could insure a Harriman defeat and a victory for the businessmen's candidate, the incumbent Mayor Alexander.

It is clear, then, that the defense's bargaining power was very limited. Then an incident occurred that completely undermined it. Darrow was charged with an attempt at jury-bribing. He was supposed to have been seen publicly passing the bribe money to Bert Franklin, chief of the detectives hired by the defense. In the wake of this episode, any chance of getting the preliminary plan accepted by District Attorney Fredericks went out the window.[60]

On Friday, December 1, 1911, both McNamaras came to court. J. J. McNamara was not on trial and had not been in the courtroom before. Everyone suspected that something important was about to happen.

Lecompte Davis quietly informed the court that the defense desired to change its plea. James B. McNamara then pleaded guilty before Judge Bordwell to "the crime of murder." At 5:45 p.m. on the night of September 30, 1910, he had placed in Ink Alley, a part of the *Times* building, a suitcase containing sixteen sticks of dynamite, set to explode at one o'clock the next morning. "It was my intention," he said, "to injure the building and scare the owners. I did not intend to take the life of anyone. I sincerely regret that unfortunate men lost their lives. If the giving of my life could bring them back, I would gladly give it...." His brother, John J. McNamara, pleaded guilty as an accessory to the dynamiting of the Llewellyn Iron Works.[61]

The McNamaras had carried out their part of the agreement by pleading guilty. But they soon discovered that the prosecution and the judge had reneged on two aspects of the agreement. At the request of the district attorney, Judge Bordwell, on December 5, sentenced J. B. McNamara to life imprisonment rather than death, but instead of the expected ten years, he sentenced John McNamara to fifteen. Moreover, instead of a kindly, humane statement from the bench, as had been promised to Steffens, Bordwell bitterly denounced both prisoners as vicious criminals, and would not admit any extenuating circumstances for their crime.[62]

On December 9, 1911, James and John McNamara were taken under heavy guard from the Los Angeles jail. The next morning, escorted by twelve armed guards, the brothers entered San Quentin prison.

On the day following the confession of guilt, the streets of Los Angeles were strewn with "Harriman for Mayor" buttons flung into the gutters by thousands of voters overcome with feelings of anger and disgust. The election returns on December 5 made it clear that the McNamara confessions were the deciding factor in turning a Socialist victory into a disastrous defeat. Alexander was reelected by a 35,000-vote majority. The *Times* gloated in its editorial the following day:

> The voice of the people is the voice of God. Yesterday in Los Angeles, God's people spoke: and the enemies of God stand confused. Scoffing, anarchistic Socialism has been crushed—as far as this city is concerned—with the same swift, merciless annihilation that the heel of a giant crushes the head of a reptile.[63]

At a station in New Jersey, an Associated Press reporter boarded a Pullman car and awakened Samuel Gompers in his berth. The aged labor leader's eyes moistened as he read the dispatch. "I am astounded. I am astounded," he repeated, insisting that right up to that moment, he had believed the brothers to be innocent. "The McNamaras have betrayed labor," he declared.[64]

In a statement issued from AFL headquarters entitled "To the American Public on the McNamara Case," the seven union officials who had made up the McNamara Ways and Means Committee declared solemnly that they had had no knowledge of the brothers' guilt until the news of the confessions appeared in the press, and that they were justified in believing that it was a gas explosion that had wrecked the *Times* building and in accepting the word of the McNamaras that they were not guilty. They continued:

> Organized labor of America has no desire to condone the crimes of the McNamaras. It joins in the satisfaction that the majesty of the law and justice have been maintained and the culprits commensurately punished for the crime.
>
> And yet it is an awful commentary upon existing conditions when any one man among all the millions of workers can bring himself to the frame of mind that the only means to secure justice for labor is in violence, outrage and murder.[65]

Labor leaders everywhere joined in repudiating the McNamaras, and the complaint was widely voiced that they had not received the heaviest possible punishment—death.[66] The position of the Socialist Party and its organs, however, was quite different. While conceding that the crimes committed by the McNamaras should be unqualifiedly condemned, the movement would not "retract one word from its defense of the McNamaras in the case." The Socialists had fought "for a fair trial of labor officials against the lawless acts of General Otis and his associates and representatives in their efforts to predetermine the verdict," and would do it again if it faced a similar situation: "If today there should be a similar kidnapping on a similar charge, the Socialists would plunge into the fight."[67] "The conference has nothing to hide and no apologies to make," the Socialist McNamara Defense Fund of New York City declared in its final report. In the future, as in the past, "we shall stand ready to assert the solidarity of the working class, to condemn murder whether the murderers be propertied or the propertyless element of society, and to resist to the best of our ability all attacks on the interests of the working class."[68]

In the midst of the fierce chorus of denunciation with which labor leaders and the labor press repudiated the McNamara brothers, here and there a voice was raised in their defense. Those who did so emphasized two points in urging the American people to temper their judgment of the McNamaras, even while condemning their acts. First, an actual state of war existed between the forces of capital and labor; and secondly, the crimes of the McNamaras paled into insignificance when compared with the crimes constantly being committed by capitalism. "Big Bill" Haywood of the IWW, who spelled out the second argument in detail, asserted at the close of his presentation: "I am with the McNamaras and always will be."[69] Debs, too, viewed the McNamaras' actions as the answer to "government by injunction, anti-picketing ordinances and other capitalist devices to stay the march of labor." But in a perceptive letter to a friend after the McNamaras' confession, Debs struck at an even deeper aspect of the case:

> The McNamaras are the product of capitalism. They have not been taught in the refinements and delicacies of things. If you want to judge McNamara you must first serve a month as a structural ironworker on a skyscraper, risking your life every minute to feed your wife and babies, then be discharged and blacklisted for joining a union. Every floor in every skyscraper represents a workingman killed in its erection. It is easy enough for a gentleman of education and refinement to sit at his typewriter and point out the crimes of the workers. But let him be one of them himself, reared in hard poverty, denied education, thrown into the brute struggle for existence from childhood, oppressed, exploited, forced to strike, clubbed by the police, jailed while his family is evicted, and his wife and children are hungry, and he will hesitate to condemn these as criminals who fight against the crimes of which they are the victims of such savage methods as have been forced upon them by their masters.[70]

In time, more and more Americans began to understand that in the context of the sharp class struggle that characterized American society, some unionists were bound to conclude that political and economic action were inadequate means of attaining labor's objectives. Having acquired a bitter distrust of the government and courts as a result of long experience, these unionists had no substantial reasons to feel that their beliefs would be respected in any court of law or by any government agency. Quite naturally, then, they did not turn to these bodies when they could not secure their demands from the corporations they were battling. Instead, they came to believe and accept the idea that violence was a legitimate weapon in the class struggle.[71]

There is still another aspect of the case which is too often ignored by historians. As Herbert Shapiro has pointed out, "a more careful look at the [McNamara] case indicates that *agents provocateurs* may well have played a significant role in leading the Iron Workers Union to its sabotage campaign." These company agents were in a position to influence the choice of alternatives made by union leaders, and there is a good deal of evidence, according to Shapiro, that "agents played a major role in organizing and implementing terroristic acts." He concludes that McManigal may well have been an agent working for Burns, noting that even prosecutor John D. Fredericks in Los Angeles had had doubts about McManigal's genuineness, and that, upon meeting McManigal, he had promptly asked him if he was a Burns agent, a question to which there is no recorded reply. Shapiro is convinced, too, that Herbert S. Hockin, one of the national leaders of the Iron Workers' Union, was also a Burns agent working as an *agent provocateur*, inciting the iron workers to acts of violence.[72]*

In 1957, in an interview with George H. Shoaf, formerly of the *Appeal to Reason*, John J. McNamara never once admitted any guilt in connection with the *Times* explosion. With respect to the confession, he insisted that Darrow had isolated the brothers from news of the outside and had convinced them that the public was against them. Had they known the state of the workers' solidarity, he said, they would have fought to the end: " . . . We would never have allowed ourselves to be coerced into confession to the crime charged against us." McNamara maintained that Darrow had convinced them that the situation was "ominous," that the brothers were safer in jail than outside, that "a fair and unbiased jury would be impossible to secure," that there had been threats to lynch them, and "that in the interest of public safety it would be best if we acted on his advice, pleaded guilty and accepted lenient sentences."** He continued:

> Neither Jim nor I wanted to plead guilty. We wanted the case to go to trial. I am sure we could have stated our case so plainly, and presented facts sufficient to justify any militant action we may have taken, that a fair-minded public instead of condemning us would have understood and been sympathetic. But Darrow and Steffens overruled us, and we went to hell.[73]

Ironically, it was precisely because he believed that he could get the American people to understand why the use of dynamite had been resorted to by the McNamaras that Steffens had worked out the deal in the first place. Moreover, initially, Steffens felt he had accomplished a

---

*Shapiro concluded that access to the records of the Burns Detective Agency would be most helpful in fully resolving this issue of the role of agents in the McNamara case, but the agency has thus far refused to open its file for the purpose of historical research.

**In 1931, J. B. McNamara told Esther Lowell, a reporter for the *New Masses*, that in the deal worked out, "J. J. McNamara was promised release in three years and three months, J. B. in seven years." (Esther Lowell, "California Prefers Hanging," *New Masses*, May, 1931, p. 6.)

great deal. He released a statement by J. J. McNamara accepting the settlement as a possible road to progress, in which he declared:

> You don't want us to strike, you don't want us to organize, we cannot afford individually to go to law.... What are we to do? If my act ... brings this question fairly before the world and leads to any answer except the war we have, I shall feel that, though I may be in prison, I shall be serving my cause.[74]

There was good reason for Steffens' initial reaction. The McNamara case was not a clear-cut frame-up, and while the trial seemed to have ended with a one-sided compromise, the defense had succeeded in saving the brothers from the death penalty. Yet, even though the death sentence was avoided, the prison terms were severe, and J. B. McNamara died an inmate of the California prison system.* For other reasons, too, Steffens came to have doubts about the success of his class reconciliation policy. He was disturbed by the hatred of the McNamaras that was being expressed in most circles, especially in the churches, and he bemoaned the fact that Christians had seemed to have rejected Christianity. In his autobiography, Steffens states that the "contract" between the capitalists and himself was all but reneged on by the employers.[75] A conference to reconcile labor and capital was never held. On the contrary, not only did the employers display no desire to accept unionism after the agreement had been worked out, but they had united to smash the iron workers' strike. Los Angeles continued to be known as the open-shop city.** In addition, part of the agreement called for the dropping of charges against

---

*On December 11, 1926, after fifteen years in San Quentin, J. B. McNamara wrote to Fremont Older, the California reform publisher: "I have faith in the rank and file and that faith will stand me well in hand in the next six years or so." (Lincoln Steffens Papers, Columbia University Special Collections, Rare Book Room.) Ten years later, "America's oldest political prisoner," as he was then called, was still in jail. His release, however, was urged by the AFL convention meeting in Tampa. Reporting this action, the *Daily Worker*, organ of the Communist Party, noted: "For 25 years he [J. B. McNamara] has suffered without breaking, in the California state prison." And it added: "McNamara went to jail to save other labor leaders from a like fate." It cited the deal made by Steffens with the "biggest capitalist politicians and masters of industry in California," in which, it asserted the latter "promised faithfully" that if the McNamaras confessed, "all other attempts to convict other labor leaders would be dropped." But the promise was never kept. (*Daily Worker*, Nov. 28, 1936.)

J. B. McNamara died of cancer in San Quentin on March 12, 1941, at the age of 59, after spending 30 years in prison. His last words to his friends were: "I will find my freedom only in the liberation of the working class. Whether that occurs while I am in San Quentin prison or out is of minor importance to me." (*People's World*, March 10, 1941.) At the time of his death, J. B. McNamara was a member of the Communist Party.

**Most unions suffered severe losses in membership during the early months of 1912, and the Central Labor Council and the Councils of the Metal Trades and the Building Trades were badly crippled.

any individuals other than the McNamaras, but this pledge, too, had not been kept. Instead, a federal trial took place of members of the Iron Workers' Union who had been arrested on charges stemming out of the dynamiting incidents, and convictions of thirty-eight of them were secured.[76] According to both Steffens and current newspaper accounts, charges were also to have been dropped against two labor radicals— Matthew Schmidt and David Kaplan—who had been indicted along with the McNamaras. This pledge, too, was violated. Efforts to locate Kaplan and Schmidt continued and they were finally arrested, brought back to California, and sentenced to long prison terms.[77]

The most immediate sequels to the McNamara case, however, were Clarence Darrow's trials on the juror bribery charge. A second trial resulted from the jury's inability to reach a verdict in the first proceedings. Darrow was not willing to defend the McNamaras as legally innocent, but he insisted on explaining that the real cause of the explosion at the *Times* lay in the workings of an oppressive system. He warned the jury that the McNamara incident was not the end of industrial terrorism. "These acts of violence," he declared, "will occur over and over again until the human race is wise enough to bring more justice and more equality to the affairs of life than has ever obtained before." During the second trial, Darrow gave a clear answer to the question of who was ultimately responsible for deaths caused by industrial terror:

> It is the men who have reached out their hands and taken possession of all the wealth of the world; it is the owners of the great railroad systems; it is the Rockefellers, it is the Morgans, it is the Goulds, it is that paralyzing hand of wealth which has reached out and destroyed all the opportunities of the poor; and their acts are protests against their wrongs.[78]

The second trial in 1913 ended with the jury in disagreement, and eventually the charges were quietly dropped.

Long before this, Lincoln Steffens had reached the conclusion that "Christianity will not work; I may have to admit it."[79] Yet a question remained that still had to be answered. "What are we Americans going to do," Steffens asked, "about conditions which are bringing up healthy, good-tempered boys like the McNamara boys to really believe, as they most sincerely do—they and a growing group of labor—that the only recourse they have for improving the conditions of the wage-earner is to use dynamite against property and life?"[80]

The Survey, a social work journal, submitted Steffens' question, somewhat reworded, to a group of social workers, philanthropists, college professors, and others, and it devoted its entire issue of November 30, 1911 to the answers it received. They differed considerably, but there was general and significant agreement that actual class warfare existed in the United States and that the conditions leading to that warfare had to be changed.[81] While conducting this symposium, the editors of *The Survey* joined with social reformers in a series of conferences in New York City to decide what else might be done. Out of these conferences there emerged, in time to be printed in *The Survey's* symposium issue, a petition to President Taft urging him to support an inquiry into the causes for violence in industry. Among the signers of the appeal were Lillian Wald, Jane Addams, Henry Morgenthau, Paul Kellogg, Louis Brandeis, Irving Fisher, E. A. Ross, and Rev. John Haynes Holmes, all nationally known as reformers.

The signers applauded the settlement of the McNamara case and found that the public had said "no" to violence. But they went on to state that while the avenue of political action was open in this country, there was genuine reason to doubt that the channel of economic action was likewise open. Economic freedom, they maintained, was undermined by such measures as labor espionage and injunctions. The signers pointed to the chasm that might lie ahead, and they repeated Lincoln's statement that "a house divided against itself cannot stand." They expressed the desire to have light shed "on the larger lawlessness which is beyond the view of the criminal court."[82]

President Taft recommended to Congress the creation of an inquiry into industrial relations. The request was caught up in the electoral politics of 1912, and Congressional approval was delayed until Woodrow Wilson took office in 1913 and could submit his own nominees to conduct the inquiry.[83]

The United States Industrial Commission, which was designated to perform this task, was presided over by Frank P. Walsh. It devoted some attention to the McNamara case, but it went into many other labor struggles and played an important role in educating public opinion about the realities of the labor-capital conflict.

The McNamara case occurrred in the midst of the emerging Progressive movement and had a profound effect on developments during the Progressive era. We shall now turn our attention to this movement and this era, and analyze the role of organized labor in their emergence and development.

CHAPTER 2

Labor and the Progressive Movement: I

The political activities of organized labor after 1900 took place in a period generally called "The Progressive Era." The reform movements that characterized this era drew their strength from agrarian and middle-class elements and laborites. Their roots lay deep in the Greenback-Labor, anti-monopoly, and Populist movements of the 1870s, 1880s, and 1890s, in which these classes had united temporarily to found a third party of national dimensions aimed at ending big business domination over the economic and political life of the nation. William Jennings Bryan's defeat in the election of 1896 sounded the death knell of Populism, and the capitalists and their allies were confident that they no longer had to fear such radical movements—that the people were tired of the decades of agitation against the monopolists and wanted only an end to the warfare.

THE MUCKRAKERS

But the ideas planted by the earlier radical movements lived on. They received new impetus through the widely-read exposés of a whole school of writers: journalists, college professors, reformers, ministers, and public officials. In the decade between 1903 and 1912, over two thousand articles exposing the evils in American society appeared in such magazines as *McClure's, Collier's, Munsey's, Everybody's, Frank Leslie's, Cosmopolitan, Independent,* and *American Magazine.* These magazines sold for ten or fifteen cents a copy, instead of the twenty-five and thirty-five cents charged by the older magazines, and the articles of exposure, supplemented as they were by editorials, cartoons, and serials, opened the eyes of millions of Americans to the rapid spread of corruption and social injustice which had accompanied the development of monopoly capitalism. Thomas W. Lawson exposed the Money Trust (1902), Ida M. Tarbell, the Oil Trust (1903), Charles Edward Russell, the Beef Trust (1905), Ray Stannard Baker, the railroads (1906) and the alliance between corrupt labor leaders and the trusts at the expense of the unorganized workers and the public (1903–1904), David Graham Phillips, the Senate (1906), Burton J. Hendricks, the operations of life insurance companies (1906), and Lincoln Steffens, the ties between business, the underworld, and the system of political power. In *The Shame of the Cities* (1904), originally published as a series of articles in *McClure's, The Struggle for Self-Government* (1906), and *The Upbuilders* (1909), Steffens demonstrated how "the Sovereign Political Power of Organized Business" was responsible for nationwide corruption. He wrote of the big business man:

> I found him buying boodlers in St. Louis, defending grafters in Minneapolis, originating corruption in Pittsburgh, sharing with the bosses in Chicago, and beating good government with corruption in New York. He is a self-righteous fraud, this big business man. He is the chief source of corruption. . . .[1]

During these same years, the Hearst press, and to a lesser extent the Pulitzer newspapers, concentrated on such exposures, reaching and influencing millions of readers. In addition, a chain of Socialist periodicals—*The Appeal to Reason, The Comrade, Wilshire's Magazine,* the *International Socialist Review,* and such Socialist newspapers as the New York *Call,* the Chicago *Daily Socialist,* and the Cleveland *Citizen*—published similar exposés, but, unlike the writings of the non-socialist capitalist muckrakers, theirs went to the heart of society's problems and contained both more basic criticism of that society and a proposal to solve its problems by changing the system.

A stream of realistic and naturalistic literature merged with the flood of journalistic exposure. In his novel, *The Octopus* (1901), Frank Norris portrayed the wheat growers in the coils of the Southern Pacific Railroad, and in *The Pit* (1903), he followed them into the den of the grain speculators in Chicago. In *The Jungle,* the most famous book to emerge from this era, which was originally serialized in *The Appeal to*

Reason, the Socialist Upton Sinclair* combined a picture of the exploita
tion of the Bohemian immigrant workers in the Chicago stockyards with
a vivid depiction of the disease-breeding filth of the meat packing
industry. Another Socialist, Jack London, in *The Iron Heel* (1908),
dramatically pictured the control of American life by the capitalist
oligarchy and predicted that it would use force to prevent the working
class, led by the Socialists, from taking office and power once elected.
During these years, too, Theodore Dreiser probed incisively into the
effect of the social system on morals, human relations, and human
character in works like *Sister Carrie* (1900), *Jennie Gerhardt* (1911), *The
Financier* (1911), and *The Titan* (1914).[2]

Muckraking magazines carried a number of articles dealing with labor
issues, especially child labor, women workers, industrial safety, convict
labor, and the evils of home work in tenement factories. In his novel, *The
Jungle,* Upton Sinclair vividly portrayed the life of workers in the
Chicago meat packing industry.** In the main, however, the problems
facing laboring people were not of concern to the muckrakers. The only
one to deal extensively with organized labor was Ray Stannard Baker,
and, as Leroy Henry Shramm points out, "Baker's attitude was and
remained ambivalent: unions were necessary, but potentially dangerous." The truth is that Baker saw powerful labor as a greater threat than
the giant corporate interests.[3]

While organized labor was critical of the muckrakers' failure to
concern themselves to any great extent with the wages and working
conditions of American labor, it leaped to their defense when they were
attacked by President Theodore Roosevelt. On April 14, 1906, Roosevelt fastened the title of "muckrakers" upon the journalists who wrote
of corruption in American life. He drew the term from Paul Bunyan's
Pilgrim's Progress, in which one of the figures was the man with the

---

*In addition to Upton Sinclair, Socialists among the muckrakers included such leading
figures as Jack London, Charles Edward Russell, Rheta Childs Dorr, Gustavus Myers,
John Reed, William English Walling, John Spargo, W. J. Ghent, A. M. Simons, Reginald
Wright Kauffman, and Robert Hunter. Through the writings of these men and women and
the analysis they presented of the reasons for corruption and social injustice, the Socialists,
as Louis Filler points out, became "the outstanding educational force" to be found "in
every field where reform was in progress." (*Crusaders For American Liberalism,* Yellow
Springs, Ohio, 1939, p. 124.)

**Sinclair wrote his book as a tract for socialism, seeking to expose the oppression of the
working class, but the American consumer took the book as a warning that the quality of
meat must be improved. "I aimed at the public heart," Sinclair wrote, "and by accident I hit
in the stomach." *The Jungle* was important in mobilizing public support for a federal meat
inspection act.

muckrake, "who could look no way but downward." The "muckraking" journalists, Roosevelt charged, concentrated so much on exposing the "small percentage of evil" in American society that they failed to see the predominant good.* The *International Woodworker* voiced the opinion of most trade union journals in criticizing Roosevelt:

> It is not because the muckrake men were stirring up the filthy things below that prompted President Roosevelt to rush to the rescue for which he received the approbation of all plutocratic corruptionists, bribe takers, and bribe givers, together with other evil doers, official and unofficial, who were quaking in their boots lest they might be the next to have their methods exposed in the light of "publicity" by the muckrakers.

Their "real offense," the union journal insisted, was that, because of them, the people were learning how the giant corporations were extending their influence into every corner of national life, corrupting it as they proceeded, and how the great industrial and public utility corporations, Wall Street, the trusts, and monopolies ran the two major parties. "The System," as the muckrakers called the alliance between big business and government, pervaded every facet of American life, and it was because they dared to expose this truth that they had brought the president's wrath down upon themselves.[4]

"THE SYSTEM"

One magazine writer in 1905 described the governing institution in the United States as "government of the corporations and privileged interests, under political machines and their tools and their beneficiaries, for the enormous enrichment of the privileged few and for the perpetuation of machine-rule." This description was clear to all who were familiar with the operations of "The System."

1. It operated in the nomination and election of candidates. As one journalist pointed out in *Frank Leslie's* in 1903:

> In a presidential or congressional election, the great corporations pick the candidates and the party to whom they feel they can look for favors; then they contribute enormous sums to carry the election. Frequently a definite bargain is made with the National Committee that something shall be done or another one not done. It is a cold matter of business. Commercial acumen which has

*Roosevelt was alarmed by the fact that the literature of exposure was producing an "enormous increase in the socialist progaganda . . . [and] building up a revolutionary feeling. . . ." (E. E. Morison, *The Letters of Theodore Roosevelt*, Cambridge, Mass., 1951, vol V, p. 183.)

built up vast fortunes in a generation or two, like those of the Standard Oil crowd or Carnegie's coterie of young men, can usually pick a winner or make a winner, in a national campaign.

Other writers demonstrated that the same power existed in municipal and state elections. The boss and the machine, responsible to the big business groups who financed the campaigns, selected candidates who would serve the needs of the powerful corporations.

2. "The System" operated full-time in Congress. In the Senate, there was little need for pressure to be applied for big business to gain its ends. The upper house was filled with oil magnates, mine owners, and, directors of banks and railroads—all elected by state legislatures controlled by these corporations. The atmosphere was one of an exclusive businessmen's club—the Senate was actually called "The Millionaires' Club"—and senators were almost as widely known by the particular economic interests they represented as by the state from which they came.

The House of Representatives was, of course, more dependent on popular vote. Occasionally, then, a progressive measure might be permitted by the party leaders to pass the House, with the understanding that it would be lost or smothered in the Senate. In the main, however, such bills were referred to committees and by them to sub-committees, from which they were never to emerge. Committees and sub-committees, in such cases, were not called by their chairmen, or, if called, could not muster a quorum. Extended and delaying hearings were granted. "Jokers" were added to the bills that effectively emasculated them. "Uncle Joe" Cannon, the Speaker of the House, always loyal to the interests of the corporations, drew up the membership of important committees so that they would be a graveyard of all progressive measures.

3. In state and city governments, big business control was even more direct. Describing the situation in New Jersey, a writer pointed out:

> The legislation proposed for the people was all scrutinized at the [Camden & Amboy Railroad] Company's offices in Trenton and allowed to go through if the company were favorable or indifferent, but its disapproval doomed it to certain defeat. It selected the governor of the State, picked out the men who were to go to Congress and named United States Senators. So absolute was its control of all the departments of the state government that the state itself became known among the people of other states as the State of Camden and Amboy. It went into the cities and controlled councils and mayors with the same iron hand.[5]

For the same reasons, Delaware was known as "the State of Dupont"; California as "the state of the Southern Pacific Railroad"; New York as "the State of Wall Street," and Pennsylvania as "the State of Standard Oil and U. S. Steel."

Burton J. Hendricks charged in 1910 that under "Boss" Thomas C. Platt, the Republican Party in New York "became simply the intermediary through which the corporations assumed the functions of government." At election time, corporations handed over generous sums to the state committee. These were distributed to the various districts in order to elect the party's candidates to the legislature. In turn, successful candidates recognized their obligations to those who had sent them to Albany. Corporations told Platt which bills they wished to have killed, and Platt passed the word on to his legislative henchmen. Through the patronage, big business was also assured of friendly administrative action in the various state departments. During the 1906 campaign, Timothy L. Woodruff, Platt's lieutenant, admitted to a group of labor leaders that the party had not been able to listen to workingmen up to then because 95 percent of its campaign contributions came from corporations.[6]

The great majority of city governments were controlled by bosses and machines operating in behalf of powerful corporate interests. The latter paid handsomely in bribes to get control of franchises, city contracts, and other forms of public privileges. In Chicago, Philadelphia, New York, St. Louis, Memphis, etc., the story was everywhere the same. The orgy of plunder by the Tweed Ring in New York was only a tame example of municipal misgovernment when compared with the revelations during the opening decade of the 1900's. The politicians, servants of the corporations, handed over to their control huge slices of the city's wealth in the form of gas, electric, and transit franchises, and various other types of concessions. No limit was imposed by statute on the duration of such grants. Consequently, they were almost always given in perpetuity—or in some cases for 999 years. Towns, cities, and states signed away for all time rights which would become more and more valuable as time went on. These and other similar concessions to corporate wealth were pushed through state legislatures and municipal councils with scarcely a dissenting vote.[7]

By the turn of the twentieth century, the political boss had become an institution in American political life. But the real bosses were the interests which stood behind him, with the power to buy and sell. The carefully documented exposures of the Muckrakers made it abundantly clear that the ousting of "the System" would not be an easy task. In most regions of the country, the state and city machines of both old parties were so well oiled and so well entrenched, and the business groups controlling the bosses and the machines so accustomed to dominating America's political life, and so determined to protect their valuable privileges, that it seemed that a miracle would be required to make headway against this corrupt alliance.

THE PROGRESSIVE PROGRAM

The Progressive movement set out to accomplish this miracle. In the name of the people, it sought to mobilize the political power of the people in order to wrest political control from the old-line, business-dominated politicians and their corrupt organizations. This attempt to democratize the political machinery and make government more responsive to popular will was essential if substantial economic and social betterment were to be secured. It was an open secret that the elected representatives of the people were, in fact, the hired representatives of one or more business corporations. Unless greater political democracy was first achieved, the Progressives insisted, economic reform and social justice were impossibilities. Thus, the "Progressive revolt" revolved around two poles: political and economic reform. Both were inextricably intertwined, and neither could be viewed in isolation from the other.

In general, the Progressives advocated the institution of such measures, originally advanced by the Populists, as the direct primary, to restore to the people the choice of their elected representatives; a limitation on campaign contributions to end big business control of the nomination and election of hand-picked candidates; the regulation of lobbyists; rules to limit the power of the Speaker of the House and to prevent the smothering of bills in committees; the election of United States senators by direct popular vote instead of by the state legislatures; a full airing of legislative actions through the publication of debates and votes; a system of initiative and referendum to enable the voters to legislate directly when necessary; a law for the recall of officials who betrayed their trust; the Australian (or secret) ballot; prohibition of the granting of unlimited franchises; and public ownership of public utilities. The specific demands of the various movements varied in certain respects from locality to locality.* But the central idea of liberating the nation from the corrupt alliance of big business and machine politics, which was undermining representative government, and of restoring political and economic democracy to the people, was fundamental to the Progressive impulse.

Political reform, however, was only one of the great issues to which the American people were increasingly directing their attention during the Progressive era. One particular concern which stood out was social reform, or the protection of the individual from the evils of industrialism and its corollary, urbanism. The American people were coming more and more to realize that the rushing industrialization and urbanization which had been brought about by the expansion of American business during the previous half century had been accomplished at a great cost in human suffering. These vast economic forces, inspired by the drive for ever-increasing profits, had thrown great masses of the population— "the other half," in the words of Jacob Riis—into conditions of hardship and urban squalor from which they were helpless to extricate themselves. To Progressives, these conditions made a mockery of the American Dream and cried out for correction by the organized efforts of society. To be sure, progressive-minded Americans were attempting to combat the evils of industrialism and urban life through private means: settlement houses, patterned after the pioneering work done during the

*The reform movement in Wisconsin (known as the "Wisconsin Idea"), under the leadership of Republican Governor Robert M. La Follette, placed major emphasis on the direct primary, reform in the method of railroad taxation, reduction of railroad rates, regulation of public utilities, a Corrupt Practices Act to make it difficult to use large sums of money to influence nominations and elections, an anti-lobby measure to limit the power of lobbyists, an inheritance tax, and a graduated income tax. The movement in Iowa (known as the "Iowa Idea"), under the leadership of Republican Governor Albert B. Cummins, stressed the direct primary, regulation of the railroads, and tariff reform. The Missouri movement, under the leadership of Democratic Governor Joseph W. Folk, emphasized such reform measures as effective regulation of the railroads and public utilities, an anti-lobby law, a direct primary law, the initiative and referendum, and labor and social legislation. In Oregon, W. W. U'Ren and his People's Power League advocated a thoroughgoing series of reform measures: the Australian ballot, registration of voters, initiative, referendum, and recall, direct primary, direct election of United States senators, a corrupt practices act, and a presidential preferential primary. The "Oregon System," as it came to be called, had a profound effect throughout the country. In the early movement for Progressive reform in Oregon, U'Ren was legislative agent of the AFL, the Knights of Labor, and the Farmers' Alliance and Grange in that state. (*Direct Legislation Record*, vol. III, March 1896, p. 16; vol. V, March, 1898, pp. 19-20.)

The reform movements in other states differed only in detail from those described above. However, some reformers were identified chiefly with national issues; others were concerned mainly with local or state problems. Some devoted their energies toward correcting the social evils of the time, while others concentrated on fighting corruption in business and government.

'nineties by Jane Addams in Chicago and Lillian Wald in New York City, were appearing in scores of the nation's big cities and mobilizing the energies of thousands of scores of eager young "social workers" in the task of assisting society's unfortunate, especially the immigrant masses. But private efforts were not enough, and it was primarily by invoking the power of government in social affairs that progressives hoped to achieve effective solutions to the problems of industrialism and urbanism.[8]

In 1963, Gabriel Kolko published *The Triumph of Conservatism*, in which he harshly criticized historians for labelling "the period from approximately 1900 until the United States intervention in the war," as the "Progressive era." Kolko argued that so-called progressivism actually represented "the triumph of conservatism," that the Progressives were really conservatives all along, concerned about preserving the existing distribution of wealth and power. What progressivism really amounted to, he maintained, was "political capitalism"—the conscious and successful attempts by the largest and most powerful business interests to use the federal government in order to achieve a measure of stability in the economic and social order that private efforts had failed to bring about.[9]

Since the revisionism of Kolko (and, to a lesser extent, of James Weinstein),[10] a number of historians have begun to speak of the "so-called Progressive era," and, in "An Obituary to the Progressive Movement," Peter Filene states flatly: "The Progressive movement never existed."[11] But historians have nonetheless continued to refer to the "Progressive era." At the same time, they have been calling for a clearer understanding of the role played by organized labor. The need for this is clear. Whatever their differences, recent historians of the Progressive era have generally agreed that the reform impulse which swept across the nation during the first decade and a half of the twentieth century was a response to the impact of industrialism on American society, that the Progressive movement was the result of an attempt to cope with this rapid transformation of American social and economic institutions, and that the reform movement was most vigorous in the urban areas most affected by the industrial change and growth. All of these historians have emphasized the role of the urban middle classes in the reform movement and have credited them with whatever results were achieved by the movement for social and economic reforms. The urban working class, the group most affected by the transformation of American society, and the role of organized labor have received only scant attention in studies of the Progressive era.*

Then, in 1962, J. Joseph Huthmacher suggested that organized labor was deeply interested in the "bread and butter reforms" of the Progressive movement, that the urban workers supported Progressive candidates with their ballots, and that the social workers, the unions, and middleclass reformers often worked together.[12]

In a case study of the state of New York, published three years later, Irwin Yellowitz emphasized that "organized labor had a strong interest in the work of the Progressives. . . ." His work investigated the relationship between labor and the social progressives—those who believed that social justice was the prime object of Progressivism—and disclosed that the labor unions and social progressives were actively, if not successfully, seeking to carry out the reforms desired by the workers and the lower class. Yellowitz called for studies of this relationship in other states and in cities as well.[13] Since 1965, the role of organized labor in politics during the Progressive era has become a subject of increasing interest among historians. By now it is clear that the history of the Progressive era cannot be fully written until this important phase of the story is included.

LABOR AND DIRECT LEGISLATION

A major contribution of organized labor to the Progressive impulse lay in initiating and advancing the cause of direct legislation, perhaps the key demand of the entire Progressive movement. The first to bring the idea of the initiative and referendum to popular attention was James William Sullivan, national lecturer for the AFL on Direct Legislation.** In 1894, a newspaper declared editorially: "The man who has done most for the Referendum and Initiative in this country is Mr. J. W. Sullivan, now national lecturer for the American Federation of Labor on Direct Legislation. He has been an indefatigable educator concerning this new

*In his study of modern American reform, Eric Goldman makes no mention of organized labor's role prior to the New Deal era (*Rendezvous With Destiny*, New York, 1953). Richard Hofstadter mentions it only once in his study of the reform movement (*The American Political Tradition*, New York, 1948, p. 239). George E. Mowry has only one paragraph on labor in his study of the years 1900–1912 (*The Era of Theodore Roosevelt, 1900–1912*, New York, 1958, p. 11). Samuel P. Hayes devotes only a few pages, most of which are of a general nature, in his study of the response to industrialism in the period from 1880–1914 (*The Response to Industrialism, 1880–1914*, Chicago, 1957, pp. 63–69).

**In March, 1897, the *Direct Legislation Record* called Sullivan "the father of the Direct Legislation movement in the United States." (Vol. IV, p. 19.) The same issue contained a biographical sketch of Sullivan.

system."[14] Sullivan, a member of the Typographical Union, began investigating direct legislation in 1883 and five years later, he went to Switzerland to study it first-hand. Returning after a year's stay, he began a campaign to interest the trade unions in the movement; at first, he emphasized the importance of having labor organizations adopt the initiative and referendum in their own operations.* In 1892, Sullivan published *Direct Legislation by the Citizenry Through the Initiative and Referendum*, in which he discussed the Swiss system of direct legislation and called upon the labor movement in the United States to take the lead in establishing it in this country. As he saw it, direct legislation offered the workers a quick and effective way of solving their basic problems. In a chapter entitled "The Way Open to Peaceful Revolution," he wrote:

> Today in the United States, in scores, nay, hundreds of industrial communities the wage-working class is in the majority. . . . If the wage-workers, a majority in a direct vote, should demand in all public work the short-hour day, they would get it. . . . Further, the wage workers might vote anti-Pinkerton ordinances, compel during strikes the neutrality of the police, and place judges from their own ranks at least in the local courts.

Eventually, he went on, "the labor organizations might supply the framework of a political party such as had almost elected Henry George mayor of New York in 1886,"** and with "the wage workers now in political ascendancy," could use direct legislation to get "the full product of their labor."[15]

In 1893, Sullivan became a national lecturer for the AFL on Direct Legislation. In articles in the *American Federationist* and in lectures to workers and others throughout the country, he helped to make the cause of direct legislation a living force. The following account in the New York *Voice* of August 11, 1894 provides an illustration of his work and its effect:

> Haverhill, Mass., Aug. 10 (Special Correspondence to *The Voice*): It was but a few months since Mr. Sullivan came up from New York to lecture on the Swiss plan of the Initiative and Referendum. . . . His address set men of Haverhill on fire and for several weeks they thought of nothing else and

---

*As a result of Sullivan's activity, the initiative and referendum were established for legislation and elections in a number of trade unions. (*Direct Legislation Record*, vol. IV, 1897, pp. 66–68; vol. V, March, 1898, pp. 15–16; September, 1898, pp. 64–65.) In 1899, however, Sullivan abandoned this aspect of the work, observing: "It is to be remembered that in the trades unions there is no need of Direct Legislation as in the state with its subdivisions. The Unions confer no franchises, have nothing to do with corrupt legislators, and have no machine bosses." (*Ibid.* vol. VI, June 1899, p. 27.) Events were soon to disprove his optimistic portrayal of trade union democracy.

**Sullivan had campaigned for Henry George in the 1886 election. (For a discussion of the United Labor Party in that campaign, *see* Foner, *op. cit.*, vol. II, pp. 119–29.)

labored for nothing else. By effective organization and pressure, they have forced the Mayor and the Board of Aldermen to pass without an opposing vote a measure prepared by Mr. Sullivan, for the adoption of the Australian ballot and the Initiative and Referendum. Thus those who have actually achieved the initiation of the Initiative and the Referendum are the group of men and women who comprise the Central Labor Union, with the coadjutors, mostly workers in the shoe factories of Haverhill, Mass. On the whole, it must be considered one of the most notable steps democracy has taken in this country for many years. The thing was done by the people, the people who work by day in shoe shops, but who think while they work, and think right, and who act when they are not at work.

The contagion of this victory has already spread. The Massachusetts branch of the American Federation of Labor has just been holding its annual session in Boston, and has put itself definitely on record in favor of direct legislation. It arranged to inaugurate a campaign, under the supervision of Mr. Sullivan, to educate the people on the subject.

As a representative of the AFL, Sullivan attended frequent conferences of Direct Legislation Leagues in various states and helped rally labor support for their campaigns for the initiative and referendum. The Direct Legislation League of New Jersey publicly acknowledged this assistance:

A most valuable aid to the League has been the action of the labor organizations. A number of the local unions sufficient to show that the opinion is general if not unanimous have formally approved the League's principles. Among the other central bodies taking such action are the Essex Trades Council, the State Typographical Union, and the New Jersey Branch of the American Federation of Labor. Much is due to J. P. McDonnell of the Paterson *Labor Standard** and John G. McCormack of the Trenton *Potters' Journal* for the instructions their papers have given on the subject.[16]

Next to Sullivan, the most active labor figure in the movement for direct legislation was Henry Sterling, a member of the International Typographical Union's Boston local. In January, 1900, Sterling read a paper on direct legislation at a meeting of the Boston Central Labor Union, and in the same year, he became chairman of the Joint Committee for Direct Legislation of the Boston Central Labor Union, the Building Trades Council, and the Massachusetts State Federation of Labor. In that capacity, Sterling sent thousands of letters and petitions on direct legislation to trade unions all over the country "to unify the union sentiment in favor of the measure." "In the labor union," he declared, "lies the latent potential power to secure the adoption of Direct Legislation in three-fourths of the States in the Union." Under Sterling's

*For the career of J. P. McDonnell, Socialist editor of the Paterson *Labor Standard*, see Foner, *op. cit.*, vol II, pp. 30-31.

leadership, the Massachusetts State Federation of Labor instituted in 1901 the practice of obtaining pledges from candidates for the state legislature on direct legislation. "Organized labor," declared a letter sent by the Federation's committee headed by Sterling, "is very earnest in urging that the Legislature submit the measure to a vote of the people. In your district are many trade unionists, and we respectfully but urgently request that you state your position on the matter in order that we may inform our members."[17]

In 1894, the AFL unions in Los Angeles raised the demand for the initiative and referendum among a series of proposals they wished to see incorporated in a new city charter. In 1902, largely as a result of continual pressure from organized labor through the Los Angeles Council of Labor and its representatives in the Los Angeles Direct Legislation League, Los Angeles became "the first city in the country to provide the recourse of direct legislation."[18]

The initiative and referendum were the subject of frequent debates and resolutions at the annual AFL conventions. At the 1901 session, Gompers analyzed the reasons that impelled labor's interest in direct legislation. He pointed out that under the boss and machine domination of government in the interests of big business, labor was unable to secure legislation it desired or defeat bills which were aimed against it: "So that we workers may have an opportunity of petitioning for favorable or vetoing vicious legislation . . . are some of the causes upon which the American Federation of Labor predicates its demand for direct legislation for initiative and referendum."[19]* At its next convention, a resolution was adopted which stressed "the need for an increase of power in voters, to be attained by the adoption of the referendum and initiative."[20] Special attention was directed to the manner in which the referendum had been secured in Winnetka, Illinois, and it was recommended that the same procedure be followed throughout the country. The Winnetka System, called the "Rule-of-Procedure Systems," provided for the adoption of direct legislation without any change in the written constitution of the state or of the city charter by the passage of a bill by the municipal government. The referendum had been instituted by the labor

---

*Although Gompers favored the use of the referendum in the political arena, he ceased to advocate its use in the trade unions. In 1897, he had recommended that AFL officers be elected by referendum, as they were in the Cigarmakers' International Union, but in 1900, when Max Hayes, the Socialist delegate of the Cleveland Federation of Labor, introduced a resolution calling for election by referendum, Gompers opposed it in debate and vote and helped secure its defeat. Evidently it was necessary to use the referendum to defeat machine domination of government, but its use to defeat machine domination of the AFL was quite another matter. (*See Proceedings,* AFL Convention, 1900, pp. 13-16, 32-35.)

unions of Winnetka by questioning candidates for mayor and aldermen as to where they stood on the issue, and then supporting those who pledged to advocate the measure when in office. The plan was enthusiastically endorsed by the AFL, and a special issue of the *American Federationist* was published in January, 1902, describing the Winnetka System in detail. Accompanied by an "address" suggesting a similar procedure for the trade unions in all municipalities, the special issue was distributed to AFL affiliates throughout the country.

From 1902 through 1903, the unions, in cooperation with reform bodies, conducted vigorous campaigns in all cities throughout the country and in Canada along the lines of the Winnetka System. By the end of 1903, direct legislation—including, in many cases, the initiative and referendum—had been adopted in Detroit, Buffalo, Waco (Texas), Toronto, and a score or more of other cities.[21]

Meanwhile, the various state federations of labor were conducting state-wide campaigns to give the people of the various states an opportunity to vote on a constitutional amendment for the initiative and referendum. In Missouri, Massachusetts, Connecticut, New York, Texas, Illinois, Kansas, Michigan, and other states, the trade unions were active, in conjunction with Direct Legislation Leagues, in questioning candidates for the legislatures as to their position on direct legislation. In Missouri, the campaign was especially effective. A leader of the Missouri Direct Legislation League reported:

> The labor unions are very strong and influential here and support our movement to a man. They are a unit in our favor. They are all pledged to the initiative and referendum and are exceedingly eager to secure it. They will question candidates to the Legislature if they will use their influence and vote for the Direct Legislation Amendment.[22]

Having secured the adoption of constitutional amendments incorporating direct legislation in several states, organized labor turned to the national legislative scene. In 1904, the AFL and the National Grange jointly sponsored a national program for the initiative and referendum which called for the questioning of candidates for Congress as to whether or not, if elected, they would vote to install the system in the national government. The program "proposing the adoption of the initiative and referendum" by Congress opened with a statement citing the need for it in the United States:

> That the few are the ruling power in this country is evidenced by the laws enacted—laws which grant *special privileges*. One form of these is private monopolies in transportation, such as railroads and the telegraphs; and private

monopolies in raw materials, such as coal, iron, salt, etc.; and private monopolies in manufacture and trade secured through the monopolies in transportation and raw materials.... So rapid is the increase in the monopolies in raw material and transportation rates that if the system continues a while longer it will result in monopoly in every line of manufacture and trade. The remedy of the rule of the corporations is for the people to guard their sovereignty by establishing a right to a direct vote on public questions through the initiative and referendum.

Recognizing that an act of Congress providing for a general initiative and referendum would be unconstitutional, the AFL proposed a plan which provided for the advisory initiative and referendum "until the people take to themselves the final power in legislation by a constitutional amendment for the optional referendum and direct initiative." The proposal took the form of a resolution to be adopted by both houses of Congress as rules of procedure. This resolution provided that whenever 75,000 voters presented to the House and the Senate any bill, constitutional amendment, or other form of question as to national policy regarding interstate commerce or ten other areas of national policy,* the petition had to be received, read twice, referred to a committee for consideration, and reported back, together with such amendments, substitutes, or recommendations as were deemed desirable. The House, after considering the subject and agreeing with the Senate, but without an enacting clause, would refer the original bill as initiated to the voters, and also such alternative measure or recommendation as had been agreed upon. If, in a majority of the congressional districts and a majority of the states, a majority of the votes should be cast for the measure, an enacting clause would be incorporated and a vote upon it taken in Congress. Each measure initiated by petitions was to have precedence over all other measures, except appropriation bills and bills immediately necessary for the preservation of the public peace, health, or safety; it was to be reported to the Speaker of the House for submission not later than one year from the time it was filed.

The resolution for an advisory referendum on laws of Congress and measures passed by a house or both houses also provided that whenever

---

*The term "national policy concerning interstate commerce" was defined as follows: "that is concerning railways, telegraphs, telephones, currency, or other instrument of interstate commerce, or a corporation or individual whose business it is to operate any of the instruments of interstate commerce." The ten other areas of national policy were: "(1) trial by jury or any modification of the law of injunction; (2) dependencies; (3) hours and conditions of labor; (4) immigration; (5) postal savings bank; (6) direct election of senators, president and vice-president of the United States; (7) the civil service, including the election of fourth-class postmasters; (8) direct nominations; (9) direct initiative and optional referendum, and (10) proportional representation."

500,000 voters requested it in writing, such laws or measures would be submitted to a vote of the people for the purpose of instructing their representatives. The balloting was to take place not later than the following general election occurring more than sixty days after the filing of the petition.[23]

Gompers was convinced that neither the advisory initiative nor the advisory referendum was in conflict with any part of the United States Constitution. As he saw it, they were simply regulations setting forth how a certain class of petitions to Congress might be inaugurated, filed, and considered by Congress, then referred to an advisory vote of the people through the machinery of the referendum. He conceded that the will of the people as expressed through such an advisory vote would not be binding on the members of Congress, but he believed that they would feel a moral obligation not to depart from it. Gompers was certain, and rather naively so, that this moral obligation would make the system effective.[24]

Various state federations of labor and state granges, especially those in Missouri, Massachusetts, Pennsylvania, and Illinois, promoted the campaign for the advisory initiative and referendum on Congressional legislation. Speaking to the 1905 AFL convention, Gompers reported:

> Success has crowned the action of the State Federation of Missouri. Nine of the sixteen Congressmen elected answered in the affirmative, and in writing, as also did the newly-elected Missouri Senator. In Illinois, the newly-elected Senator, in a letter, gave this pledge: "I favor any principle—I care not what it may be called—that enlarges the power of the people on all questions, State and National, that affects the well-being of citizens!"[25]

Although the national campaign was not successful, it helped popularize the demand for the initiative and referendum. By this time, that demand had become a key issue in the nationwide "Progressive Revolt." But it was organized labor that first raised it. As far back as 1894, Gompers had declared that "all lovers of the human family, all who earnestly strive for political reform, economic justice, and social enfranchisement must range themselves on the side of organized labor in this demand for direct legislation."[26] The adoption of the initiative and referendum in many communities throughout the country was the result of just such an alliance of organized labor and other Progressive forces.* To be sure, the triumph of the initiative and referendum in these

---

*By 1912, the initiative and referendum had been adopted in South Dakota, Utah, Oregon, Montana, Oklahoma, Missouri, Arkansas, Colorado, Arizona, California, Washington, Nebraska, Idaho, and Ohio. (Charles A. Beard, *Contemporary American History, 1877-1913*, New York, 1917, pp. 284-86.)

communities did not bring with it, as some of the labor advocates of direct legislation had predicted, the solution of most of the problems facing the American people. Nonetheless, it was an important step forward in American democracy, and labor's contribution to its realization was truly a significant one.

LABOR AND THE RECALL

Organized labor also played a significant role in initiating and advancing the movement for recall of elected officials. This progressive demand first appeared in the Los Angeles City Charter of 1903 as a result of several years of agitation led by the Los Angeles Council of Labor. In 1898 and 1900, the Council of Labor and the Socialist Party of the city worked together to nominate members of the Board of Freeholders who would pledge themselves to incorporate the initiative and referendum and recall in the proposed instrument. The Board was charged with the responsibility of writing a new city charter. In 1902, the Council of Labor and its spokesman, Dr. John R. Haynes, head of the Los Angeles Direct Legislation League, were successful in having the charter revision committee incorporate proposals for the initiative, referendum and recall. With the help of the Los Angeles Union Labor Party, the only political party in the city to espouse direct legislation, the friends of direct legislation won a signal triumph in the 1902 charter election. Despite the cry of conservatives that the recall was "revolutionary," Los Angeles adopted the charter by a huge majority, including the amendments providing for direct legislation. In January, 1903, the California legislature approved the amendments to the Los Angeles City Charter. The action represented a triumph for the California State Federation of Labor and the Direct Legislation League, which worked together to achieve it.[27]

A year later, the nation's attention was focused on the movement in Los Angeles to recall a member of the City Council, a campaign in which organized labor played a decisive role. The Los Angeles City Council voted to give the city's printing charter to the highest bidder, the Los Angeles *Times,* spearhead of the open shop throughout the West Coast and a bitter foe of organized labor in general and of the Typographical Union in particular. The cry of "Recall!" immediately went up, and J. P. Davenport, one of the councilmen who had voted for the award, was selected for a test action. The Typographical Union led the campaign for Davenport's recall; its members in his ward (the sixth) started the move to secure signatures for this purpose. "It is fitting," notes Grace H. Stimson, "that a trade-union was in the forefront of a movement to make practical application of a charter provision which organized labor had itself helped to promote."[28] This was the first recall petition ever circulated in the United States.[29]

When the necessary number of signatures had been obtained, the City Council set the recall election. Dr. Arthur D. Houghton was selected as the candidate to oppose Davenport in the recall election. Davenport made several frantic efforts to prevent the election through court intervention, but, after a few early victories, the final decision went against him. During the campaign, the Los Angeles *Times* and the *Daily Journal,* the two most powerful papers in the city, the street railway companies, the gas company, the liquor interests, the Republican Party, and the property owners and business men of the sixth ward all supported Davenport. The trade unions, assisted by the Direct Legislation League, the Good Government League, and several smaller newspapers campaigned for Dr. Houghton. The pro-Davenport forces made trade unionism the issue. The *Daily Journal* cried out on September 15, 1904:

> The man who votes tomorrow against J. P. Davenport votes for the supremacy and arrogance of labor unionism in Los Angeles. Like a snake, it is hiding in the grass because the people of Los Angeles have such a hearty contempt for its vile practices that only by dissembling and masking its real purpose can it hope to gain a point.

Houghton defeated Davenport by a vote of 1,837 to 1,083, carrying all but one of the sixteen precincts in the sixth ward, including Davenport's own precinct. "The results of yesterday's election in the Sixth Ward," wailed the Los Angeles *Times* on September 17, "is nothing short of a disgrace to the ward and an affront to the city at large." This lament from the arch foe of organized labor and other progressive forces was enough to verify the significance of the election result. The effect was tremendous. Dr. Stimson writes:

> The recall election on September 16, 1904 made not only local but national political history. For the first time in the United States a public official was recalled from office by vote of the people. . . . Houghton's backers readily give credit for the victory to the labor unions, which had planned and carried out a systematic campaign. . . .
>
> The success of the movement to recall Davenport greatly enhanced the popularity of direct legislation. Within several years a number of communities in California had written, the initiative, referendum and recall into their charters, and cities in other states were beginning to take note of these democratic processes. In Los Angeles, proponents of better government

found that the mere threat of recall was sufficient to deter councilmen from voting for unpopular measures. After the Davenport affair, two of the other city legislators who had awarded the printing contract to the *Times* were defeated when they sought renomination. Most pleasing to the unionists who had worked indefatigably in the recall campaign, however, was the failure of the *Times* to win later city contracts. In 1905, the Council with little discussion simply awarded the contract to the lowest bidder, and through the rest of the decade the *Times* was unable to influence the Council in its behalf.[30]

In 1910 and 1911, the recall issue again aroused nationwide interest, and once again organized labor played an important part in the movement. On June 16, 1910, Congress passed an act to enable the territories of Arizona and New Mexico to form constitutions and state governments. Constitutional conventions were to meet in the two territories in the fall of 1910 to draw up constitutions for the states. The New Mexico convention, dominated by conservative elements, drew up a conservative organic instrument of government. However, the situation in Arizona was different. There, the trade unions spearheaded the movement for a progressive constitution. On July 13, 1910, the Arizona *Republican* featured the following announcement: "Representatives of the workingmen's unions in Arizona, in convention in Phoenix yesterday, labored and brought forth a new political party, and named it The Labor Party of Arizona." The following day, the Arizona *Republican* carried the text of a telegram sent to Gompers by J. C. Provost, head of the convention which had organized the Labor Party:

> The Labor Party of Arizona extends its appeal for aid to the American Federation of Labor in this campaign for a working-class constitution, regardless of the attitude of the federation officials who still expect us to accept promises of those old-line party politicians by whom labor has been repeatedly betrayed. Enlightened labor has gone into this campaign in its own behalf and in its own interest.

The unions, led by the Typographical Union, the Western Federation of Miners, the Blacksmiths' Union, and the Carpenters' and Joiners' Union, had organized the Labor Party of Arizona for the express purpose of electing progressive candidates to the Constitutional Convention.[31] Its declaration of principles stated:

> We, the representatives of Labor of the Territory of Arizona in conference assembled, in order to secure and perpetuate the blessing of liberty; to secure just and rightful government; and to promote our mutual welfare and happiness, hereby declare and affirm that we have organized ourselves into the Labor Party of Arizona, and do ordain and establish the following code of principles and platform and that we further demand their incorporation in the Constitution of the State of Arizona.

All political power is inherent in the people and government is instituted for their protection, security and benefit, and they have the right to alter or reform the same whenever the public good may require it.

As measures to strengthen labor in its struggle for better conditions, we advocate and pledge ourselves and our elected delegates to the Constitutional Convention to the following program.[32]

Twenty-seven demands were included in the Labor Party's program, and they merit listing here, since they represented the most advanced platform of the entire Progressive movement: (1) the initiative, referendum, and right of recall; (2) universal and equal male and female suffrage; (3) a maximum workday of eight hours; (4) election of United States senators by popular vote; (5) two-year terms for all state, county, and municipal officers; (6) the right of the state to engage in industrial pursuits; (7) a law to end the abuse of the injunction; (8) government by enacted law; (9) the state to defray the expense for the defense in criminal cases as well as for the prosecution; (10) an employers' liability law; (11) the power to declare laws uncontitutional to reside only in the people by referendum vote; (12) abolition of the fee system in all courts; (13) a child and female labor law restricting the hours and conditions of employment; (14) requirement of six months' residence to qualify citizens to become voters; (15) no private detectives or police to be permitted to give testimony; (16) no law to be passed in any way limiting the franchise of the citizens, nor any fee system to be permitted in the registration, primary, or election laws; (17) the amendment of the constitution only by a majority vote of the electors on the initiative of the legislators or the people; (18) an honest registration law; (19) the secret ballot; (20) the direct primary; (21) a thoroughgoing and effective corrupt practices act, including publishing of campaign funds and contributions before elections; (22) a state-guaranteed banking law; (23) a state industrial commission with qualified inspectors for each industry; (24) the absolute freedom of speech, press, and peaceable assemblage; (25) exclusion of measures passed by the referendum from the governor's power of veto; (26) no competitive convict labor; and (27) compulsory education to the age of sixteen.[33]

"Labor Party Busy At Work," read a headline in the Arizona *Republican* of July 19, 1910. The Party nominated a ticket composed of 21 candidates, eighteen of whom were members of the Democratic Party and had pledged to support the Labor Party's program, while three were independents.[34] In the campaign to elect its delegates to the Constitutional Convention, the Labor Party organized committees in each county, held meetings in union halls and at social gatherings, and distributed pamphlets and leaflets throughout the territory. In its leaflet addressed "To the Farmer," the Labor Party urged the farmer "to align yourself with *Labor* from all the industries . . ., join it hand to hand and get back control of your government through the Initiative, Referendum and Recall. Have incorporated in the Constitution such provisions as will give you control over your law-making and judicial representatives."[35]

On September 12, 1910, Arizona voted overwhelmingly for the Democratic candidates to the Constitutional Convention, many of whom had pledged to support the key demands in the Labor Party's platform, and all of whom were advocates of the initiative, referendum, and recall. The Arizona *Republican* acknowledged that the aggressive campaign waged by the Labor Party had played a large part in the Democratic victory.[36] It even characterized the Constitutional Convention as a gathering "in the interest of labor."[37] This was not an exaggeration. The convention was controlled by pro-labor delegates, all of whom were advocates of direct legislation and social legislation for labor. "With four men out of the five [of the Committee on Labor] carrying union cards," the Arizona *Republican* commented on October 14, 1910, "it is probable that labor will get an 'even break.'"

The convention produced a constitution that was extremely progressive and especially friendly to labor. It contained provisions for the initiative, referendum, and recall, including the recall of judges; for the eight-hour day; regulation of employment of children and women; provisions for safety of workers in hazardous occupations; an employers' liability law, and the abolition of convict labor. "These things," the Labor Party declared in endorsing the constitution, "should commend it to all those who believe with Lincoln that labor is superior to capital and that people are of more importance than property."[38]*

Despite the threat of Congressional and presidential disapproval of the proposed constitution, the people of Arizona voted overwhelmingly on February 9, 1911 to accept the document as written. The instrument thereupon went to Congress, where the inclusion of the recall of elected officials immediately provoked a heated dispute. The conservatives in Congress and President Taft asserted that they were ready to accept the Arizona document provided that the recall features did not apply to

---

*In his first annual message to Congress, President Abraham Lincoln declared in part: "Labor is prior to, and independent of capital. Capital is only the fruit of labor, and could never have existed if labor had not first existed. Labor is the superior of capital, and deserves much the higher consideration." (Philip S. Foner, editor, *Abraham Lincoln: Selections from His Writings*, New York, 1944, p. 82.)

judges. The Progressives, pointing out that this demand was especially important to labor as a result of its experiences under the Sherman Act,* took up the cudgels for the constitution as adopted by the people of Arizona.[39]

Organized labor in many cities petitioned Congress to adopt the Arizona constitution without any change. An especially effective campaign along this line was conducted by the labor movement in Ohio. Since delegates to a constitutional convention were scheduled to be elected in the fall of 1911 to draw up a new constitution for Ohio, the trade unions and Progressive reformers believed that if Arizona's constitution was approved by Congress, it would help the movement to incorporate the initiative, referendum, and recall in the new constitution for Ohio.[40]

In May, 1911, the Arizona Constitutional Petition League of Typographical Union No. 63 of Toledo, Ohio was organized. It sponsored a petition to be presented to Congress calling for "the approval and adoption" of the Arizona constitution as passed by its people on the ground that "they only have the right to decide upon a constitution under which they are to govern themselves." The petition movement gained the support of all the unions in Toledo as well as of the Central Labor Council. Thousands of signatures were obtained to the petition, which was presented to Congress on June 28, 1911. In addition, the Ohio State Federation of Labor, the Ohio State Grange, and the Ohio Direct Legislation League united to support the petition movement. As a result, petitions were sent from various parts of Ohio to Congress in favor of the Arizona constitution.[41]

The bill providing for Arizona's admission as a state passed Congress on August 11, 1911 but was vetoed four days later by President Taft because of the inclusion of the recall-of-judges provision. Immediately, the trade unions in various parts of the country petitioned Congress, demanding that the bill be passed over Taft's veto.[42] Meanwhile, a compromise was worked out under which Arizona would withdraw the "obnoxious provision" from its constitution with the understanding that it would restore it once it became a state. On this basis, Taft signed the bill and Arizona became a state. Shortly thereafter, the recall-of-judges provision was incorporated as part of Arizona's constitution. "Never before has organized labor been so successful in creating public

*The Sherman Anti-Trust Act of 1890 stipulated that combinations in the form of a trust "or otherwise," acting in restraint of interstate commerce, were illegal. Court decisions included organized labor among the "or otherwise," and held that unions were liable under the Sherman Act.

opinion as now," a contemporary labor paper boasted joyfully as it noted the successful conclusion of the battle for the inclusion of the recall provision in Arizona's constitution.[43]

Arizona was not the only territory to be influenced by the Progressive impulse. Oklahoma, which achieved statehood just as the Progressive era was gathering momentum, became a laboratory for Progressive experimentation. On June 16, 1906, President Roosevelt signed an enabling act to admit Oklahoma Territory and Indian Territory to the Union as one state. An election was to be held on November 4, 1906 to elect 112 delegates to a convention which would write a constitution for the new state. Oklahoma thus had an opportunity to write a constitution which would reflect the chief planks of the Progressive program.

An alliance of organized labor, farmers, and social reformers set out to do precisely that. Although it was largely agricultural at this time, Oklahoma did possess an extensive body of organized labor. In 1907, there were over 21,000 unionists in 303 unions. Of this number, one-third were miners in coal fields in the western part of the state. Other large bodies of organized workers were in the Railroad Brotherhoods and the construction trades.[44] The Twin Territories Federation of Labor, composed of AFL unions, was organized in 1903 and worked closely with the Railroad Brotherhoods and the Farmers' Educational and Cooperative Union of America (popularly referred to as the Farmers' Union).[45] These three forces joined in the drive for a progressive state constitution.

They were joined by Oklahoma's leading social reformer, Kate Barnard, a young Catholic social worker from Oklahoma City, who had become convinced that the only way to eliminate poverty and achieve social justice was through the organization of labor and the use of union-made products. Barnard formed and became secretary of the Oklahoma chapter of the Women's International Union Label League.* In January, 1907, she also founded Federal Union No. 12374 for unskilled laborers in Oklahoma City and was elected its representative to the Oklahoma City Trades and Labor Assembly. As a member of both the Trades' Assembly and the Farmers' Union, Barnard became an important force in the labor-farmer-social reformer campaign to gain control of the constitutional convention and write a progressive state constitution.[46]

The delegates to the Oklahoma Constitutional Convention met from November 20, 1906 to March 15, 1907. The majority were members of

---

*The League began in Muncie, Indiana early in 1899 and spread into many communities. It sought to educate women buyers to purchase only products carrying union labels.

the unionist-farmer-social reformer coalition. The convention wrote a document described by Samuel Gompers as the "most progressive constitution now existing on the American continent." On September 17, 1907, the people of the Twin Territories overwhelmingly accepted the constitution. Reflecting the "prevailing progressive spirit," it included the initiative, referendum, recall, and the Australian ballot. But there were also specific gains won by the unions. The miners received an eight-hour day, an elected chief mine inspector, and the prohibition of the employment in the mines of girls, women, and boys under sixteen. All workers won a victory when the fellow-servant doctrine was abrogated,* when no limits were placed on damage suits resulting from industrial injuries, and when an elected commissioner of labor was authorized to inspect the railroads and other industries for safety hazards. The social reformers gained the demands urged by Kate Barnard: prohibition of the use of convict-lease labor and of the employment of children under fifteen years of age in hazardous occupations, and the establishment of compulsory education.

Thus, while the western radical agrarians were mobilizing their forces behind the movement for greater democracy, organized labor was conducting a similar drive in various communities throughout the country. Certainly as far as direct legislation not normally considered part of labor's demands was concerned—the Australian ballot, the initiative, referendum, and recall—it was organized labor that provided the initial impetus and the major sustaining drive behind the movement. But in several states, organized labor in alliance with the social Progressives was also able to win victories for specific "bread-and-butter" reforms of the Progressive movement from which all workers, organized and unorganized, benefitted.

*The fellow-servant rule prevented recovery by an injured employee who had knowledge of the danger which led to his injury. The employee's fear of losing his job because of refusal to work on a dangerous machine or in the face of other hazards did not matter. In a decision handed down in England, the doctrine was set down that "a master is entitled to carry on his business in a dangerous way 'if the servant is foolish enough to agree to it.'" (C. B. Labatt, *Commentaries on the Law of Masters and Servants*, Rochester, N. Y., 1904, p. 62.)

CHAPTER 3

Labor and the Progressive Movement: II

In analyzing the political activities of organized labor, historians have traditionally concentrated on the role of national bodies, such as the AFL, to which they have devoted most of their attention in discussing labor's attitude toward various presidential candidates. An analysis of organized labor's participation in municipal politics is essential in order to round out the picture of its political activities. This is especially true of the Progressive era.

LABOR AND MUNICIPAL REFORM

During the 1820s and 1830s, when the American labor movement was in its infancy, several farsighted individuals had stressed the importance of workers' participation in shaping the developing city governments along lines that would serve labor's needs.[1] But aside from leading the movement to institute the system of free public education,* it was not until the beginning of the twentieth century that organized labor paid any considerable attention to the character of city government. To the degree that labor was interested in political issues, its eyes were focused mainly on national affairs. Except for the Union Labor Party movement in New York City, which ran Henry George for mayor in 1886, and similar developments in other cities at that time,** organized labor did not concern itself to any great extent with municipal problems.

In 1902, the Connecticut State Federation of Labor called upon the

*See Foner, *op. cit.*, vol. I, pp. 86, 123, 216–17, 247.
**See *ibid.*, vol. II, pp. 119–31, 148–56.

trade unions in every municipality to play an active role in the various reform movements aimed at ending boss domination of city governments. "Organized labor holds the balance of voting power in nearly all the cities and should exercise it," went its appeal.[2] The response was not enthusiastic. In the eyes of most workers, government by reformers was hardly any improvement over government by a corrupt boss and machine—and in some ways it was worse. They had sound and compelling reasons for this feeling:

1. There were actually two groups of reformers in the Progressive movement: civic reformers and social reformers. The former emphasized honest, efficient government and were indifferent to the social injustices of industrialized America, while the social reformers, backed by consumers' leagues, campaigned to end social injustice through social reform measures aimed at ending the specific conditions which produced poverty, ill health, or the demoralization of the working woman. In most cities, the reform movement was headed by the civic reformers who came from the wealthy so-called respectable elements of society. Their objective was to purify city government, end graft, replace corrupt officials with "good" men,* and institute honest, efficient, businesslike city government. These reformers, however, either refused or failed to recognize that the corrupt politicians were bribed by wealthy business men, particularly the seekers of public utility franchises. Behind the corrupt bosses were the real forces responsible for the evils the reformers were supposed to be combatting. But since many of the "respectable" elements wanted special privileges from government themselves, they were not inclined to expose this connection. Indeed, it was not unusual to find that when reformers replaced corrupt officials with "good" men, all that happened was that the most flagrant types of graft were replaced by a more subtle and infinitely more important species of corruption— namely, the tendency of the "good" men, once in office, to serve the business interests from which they themselves came, regardless of the interests of the people as a whole. Some of the worst franchise grabs in the history of municipal governments were engineered by "good" city officials who had ousted the more disreputable grafters in a reform uprising.[3] It often turned out that the same men who were responsible for corruption were behind the reform forces. As Gustavus Myers wrote in 1910:

*This movement was nicknamed "Goo-goo" for ("good government"), and its enthusiastic supporters, mostly the "respectable" elements, were called "Goo-goos."

The very men who cheated cities, states and nation out of enormous sums in taxation; who bribed, through their retainers, legislatures, common councils and executive and administrative officials; who corruptly put judges on the bench; who made government simply an auxiliary to their designs; who exacted tribute from the people in a thousand ways; who forced their employees to work for precarious wages and who bitterly fought every movement for the betterment of the working classes—these were the men who made up those so-called "reform" committees—just as today they constitute them.

If there had been the slightest serious attempt to interfere with their vested privileges, corruptly obtained and corruptly enhanced, and with the vast amount of increment and graft that these privileges brought them, they would have instantly raised the cry of revolutionary confiscation. But they were very willing to put an end to the petty graft which the politicians collected from saloons, brothels, peddlers, and the small merchants.[4]

2. The outlook of many reformers rarely extended beyond the needs of the upper and middle classes. In 1911, Charles O. Pratt, the transit workers' spokesman in Philadelphia, rejected an appeal for support from the wealthy reformer, Rudolph Blankeberg, who was running for mayor, on the ground.

> ... that the best that oppressed Philadelphia can expect from your hand in the way of reform would be an academic, perfectly polite dilletante expression of the vital city problems, with municipal action directed at the sinful or weak poor, and complete protection afforded the sinful and powerful rich.[5]

This judgment was based on past experience with reformers, who ignored the needs of the great mass of the laboring classes, particularly the daily problems with which the workers were preoccupied. Thus, the "respectable" elements never understood the needs and problems of the new immigrants who were becoming members of the community in increasing numbers. The machine bosses, through their ward heelers, took special pains to win the support of these immigrants, guiding them through the early confusing days of house- and job-hunting, advising and encouraging them, helping them in time of stress, offering them camaraderie in their social clubs, participating in their family celebrations or funerals, and hastening them through the naturalization procedure— all to gain their votes. One commentator observed:

> The Tammany workers were "Big Brother, little sister, and general fixer" to their slum constituents. To them the poor looked for jobs as watchmen, laborers, and chauffeurs, for permits to sell newspapers, black boots, roast peanuts or keep chickens, for assistance in gaining admission to hospitals, for intercession with the landlord when the rent was overdue, for passing the hat to save the destitute from Potter's Field, or for intervention in the courts when a youth had run afoul of the law.[6]

As John D. Bueneker has demonstrated, some middle-class reformers did seek to serve the needs of the immigrant working class and did win their votes as a result, but all too often reformers made no effort in this direction. On the contrary, they dismissed the immigrants as tools of the machine bosses and blamed the corrupt state of municipal government on the increasing flow of foreign-born workers into the cities. Amos Pinchot, one of the few reformers who recognized that the boss and the machine gained a great deal of their power through their social and human functions wrote: " . . . so long . . . as we reformers refuse to attack the sources of Tammany's power, Tammany is perhaps a little bored with us, but, on the whole, the Tiger feels safe and happy."[7]

Another example of the failure of the reformers to understand the needs of the working people (and of their indifference to these needs) was the stress they placed on getting rid of the saloon. Indeed, the "Sunday-Saloon-Closing" movement became a key issue for many reformers, and they devoted much of their time to seeking to enforce laws for this purpose. To be sure, some union organizers and officers also opposed the saloon, fearing "the dulling effect of alcohol on working-class consciousness." At the 1909 AFL convention, Gompers declared: "The time has come when the saloon and the labor movement must be divorced."* Nevertheless, union members were overwhelmingly against prohibition, partly because it would deprive thousands of union men of their jobs, and partly because they felt it discriminated against the poor, since the rich would always be able to obtain all the liquor they wanted. But a major reason was that the saloon was the "poor man's club," and that the alcohol it dispensed was only a part of the role it played in working-class and immigrant cultures.[8] The reformers, however, showed no understanding of the social function of the saloon in the lives of the workers. They never bothered to ask if the miserable shack or tenement that a worker called home was the place where he wanted to spend his Sundays. Nor were they interested in the fact that for tired toilers, too poor to pay for any other form of social life,

---

*The IWW took the same position. "We are out to make the workers think," insisted the *Industrial Worker*, "and we think that sober men think better than drunkards." Wobblies closed down saloons, often by force, especially during strikes. (Joyce L. Kornbluh, *Rebel Voices: An I.W.W. Anthology*, Ann Arbor, Michigan, 1964, pp. 257-58, 270-71; Ronald M. Benson, "Sober Workmen," unpublished paper delivered at Organization of American Historians, April 11-14, 1979, pp. 10-11.)

Other advocates of temperance in labor circles during this period included Warren Stone of the Brotherhood of Locomotive Engineers, L.E. Sheppard of the Conductors; D. B. Robertson of the Locomotive Firemen, John Mitchell of the United Mine Workers, and John B. Lennon, AFL Treasurer.

the saloon offered relief from the monotony and agony of everyday existence. "The saloon exists in our town," wrote one worker, "because it supplies a want—a need. It offers a common meeting place. It dispenses good cheer. It ministers to the craving for fellowship. To the exhausted, worn-out body, to the strained nerves—the relaxation brings rest." Brand Whitlock, the Ohio Progressive pointed out: "The saloon is a part of our whole economic system, and . . . the only way to get rid of the saloon is to reform economic conditions. The saloon gratifies not only what our economic conditions make a physical necessity but it gratifies also what our economic conditions make a social necessity."[9] But the "respectable" elements in the reform movement were themselves responsible for these "economic conditions" and they were not interested in this logical approach to the problem of the saloon. Similarly, in their crusade against prostitution, these elements were not interested in the fact that the miserable wages they paid working girls forced many of them into a life of prostitution.*

Workers who led dull, monotonous lives at the machine and came home to miserable hovels were starved for amusement and entertainment. The churches, the schools, and the libraries failed to meet this problem. The machine bosses stepped into the breach with processions, picnics, and other forms of entertainment. The reformers sneered, but they did nothing to meet the needs of the working people. As the Philadelphia *Press* pointed out in 1902:

> Politicians owe no small share of their power to the various means through which they supply these lacking needs of the working people. . . . Reform will always be at a disadvantage in its contest with the Machine until it realizes that the city itself ought to furnish many of these needs. While the politician meets this need, he will always have the advantage over a program of city reform which consists of nothing more than closing down saloons and houses of prostitution, reducing the illicit vote and convicting repeaters and bribe takers. Reform must beat the politician on his own grounds by adding to all

*"What is the relation between insufficient wages and the victims of the redlight district?" Mary E. McDowell asked in 1908. And she answered: "It is the aid to wages which is got from this oldest trade in the world." On March 18, 1913, Ms. McDowell wrote to Julius Rosenwald, head of Sears and Roebuck: "It is time to change the public mind from the vice question to the real, fundamental needs of the thousands of helpless girls, 82% of whom are actually helping to maintain their families." (Mary E. McDowell Papers, Chicago Historical Society.) Ms. McDowell sharply criticized Rosenwald for his statement before the State White Slave Commission in which he said flatly that "low wages have no connection with prostitution." Acting Governor Baratt O'Hara agreed with McDowell. He pointed out that the Commission had demonstrated that more than 60,000 women in Chicago were receiving $5 or less per week, were "absolutely underfed," and never had "a full meal." "Is it any wonder women do wrong?" he asked. (New York *Call*, March 8, 1913.)

this: public baths in every ward, gymnasiums for youths and adults of both sexes, public bakeries, a supply of hot water and facilities for washing which bathhouses can give, music in every square through the summer, more parks and more recreation in them, lectures in school rooms now empty, concerts and opportunities for feeling the color and light which there is in life, in art, in social contact and knowledge. Until these come and are made a part of the reform civic program, the politician will be at an advantage in corruptly furnishing what the people want because we do not have a reform movement under which the municipality will furnish it honestly.[10]

3. Many reformers were not interested in including labor in the alliance of the groups that made up the reform movement. "Go to the people with your program," Lincoln Steffens urged the reformers. "Be sure to appeal especially to the plain people"[11] Frank Moss, in a speech entitled "A Basis for Municipal Reform," delivered in 1902, voiced the same appeal when he said:

> The basis for municipal reform must be found in winning the patriotism and appealing to the ideals of the great laboring element in our midst; in enlisting the plain people; in obtaining the cooperation of the trade unions. You will never beat the corruptionists by banding together only the so-called "better classes," the church members and church workers, and going to the polls with that backing alone.

Four years later, a group of Chicago municipal reformers conceded that winning labor's support was the key to victory for their cause: "If we can get the labor men with us as they ought to be, we will sweep the city and forever silence the corrupt opposition."[12]

But the "better classes" were not interested in having organized labor as an ally. Even many of the Muckrakers, much as they wanted to end corruption in American life, were frightened by the prospect of an alliance with organized labor to accomplish this, and they were especially alarmed at the prospect of uniting with the more militant elements in the labor movement. In the minds of most middle- and upper-class reformers, militant unionism meant mob violence and in many respects was a greater danger to the nation than the trusts. There was continual talk among the reformers of protecting the "public interest" from both the unions and the trusts.[13] Then again, the "respectable" reformers were not eager to give the unions and their leaders respectable status by accepting them into the civic reform fold. They knew, too, that once labor was part of the movement for "civic righteousness," embarrassing questions would be asked—such as why the bribe-giving businessman should not be punished as well as the bribe-taking politician; why the "respectable" leaders of the reform movement, who were speaking out in favor of more efficient city government in which laws would be enforced, did not themselves obey the laws against foul conditions in the tenements and factories which they owned; why the reformers, who spoke out so heatedly against houses of prostitution, did nothing to raise the wages of the working girls who were compelled to supplement their meager earnings with a life of vice just in order to make ends meet; why the reformers did not demand that the Sunday-closing law be enforced against the clubs for the wealthy, which were the "gilded saloons of the rich," as well as against the corner saloons—and a host of similar questions. Small wonder, then, that many reformers showed little interest in following Steffens' and Moss' advice.

We have already observed that in too many cities, corrupt trade union officials were often in the pay of politicians and were part of the established political machines. No appeals from reformers, no matter how concerned they may have been with labor's special problems, would have persuaded these officials to abandon their connections with the boss and the machine and join the reform cause.[14] Nevertheless, the absence of labor representation in many of the municipal reform movements was no indication of a lack of interest on the part of workers in ending boss rule of city governments. Indeed, in many cities where the reform movements advanced a program that was clearly in the interest of the working people and discarded the outlook which so often antagonized workers, organized labor played a vital role in them, even overruling the opposition of union officials tied to the machine.[15]

In the early 1890s, the Detroit Trades Council and its affiliates vigorously supported Mayor Hazen Pingree, the first important Progressive mayor in the country, in his battle for a municipal electric light plant, a three-cent fare on the street railways, reduction of gas and telephone rates, and assistance to unemployed workers instead of imprisoning them as vagrants. In an article in the *American Federationist* of October, 1895, entitled "Detroit in the Van," J. W. Sullivan emphasized the role that the Detroit trade unions were playing in mobilizing public support for Pingree's progressive administration. He pointed out that the cost of lighting performed by the city was about half of that under private management; that gas had been brought down in price to eight cents per thousand cubic feet; and that the three-cent fare was providing workers with excellent transportation at the lowest cost in the country. All this, he declared, was "a matter of financial interest to every workingman."[16]

Later, in Jersey City, the Council of Trades' Unions and its affiliates were active in helping to secure the election in 1901, and the reelection for several terms thereafter, of Mark Fagan, a reform mayor. The trade unions backed him in his battle against the political bosses and the corporations, and helped him achieve his program for new schools, free baths and dispensaries, a modern park system, improved fire, health and street-cleaning services, a progressive tax program under which corporations would pay their share of taxes, and municipal control of the street railways.[17]

LABOR AND REFORM IN TOLEDO

It was in two Ohio cities—Toledo and Cleveland—that great battles for progressive reform were waged, and there, too, organized labor was a potent force in the reform movements. Two factors are worth noting at the outset: (1) the leadership and rank-and-file of the labor movement in these cities were especially alert to the value of having progressive municipal government; and (2) the leaders of the reform movements— "Golden Rule" Samuel M. Jones, Brand Whitlock, Tom L. Johnson, Newton D. Baker, Fred C. Howe, and Peter Witt—believed in trade unionism and in the value of having organized labor's support in the battle for reform.[18]

In 1897, the sixty Toledo trade unions united to support "Golden Rule" Samuel M. Jones for Mayor. Although he ran on the Republican ticket, Jones was a liberal industrialist who had instituted the eight-hour day among drillers of his oil wells, and, as president of the Western Oil Men's Association, had gotten a resolution unanimously passed by the organization favoring the eight-hour day. (This was probably the first organization of employers on record to take such a stand.) Jones was a firm believer in trade unionism,* although he felt that in its battle against the employers, organized labor should put its main stress on enlightening the majority of the population with respect to the moral evils inherent in the existing social and economic structure of society. Even before he became mayor, Jones antagonized the Republican machine by enthusiastically welcoming trade union support for his campaign, and, once in office, he infuriated the Republican boss by consulting trade

*However, Jones was critical of unions which organized only skilled workers. He appealed to all unions to abandon "all distinctions of 'skilled' and 'unskilled' in organizing. A few men are 'skilled' for the simple reason that there is only opportunity for a few to be skilled; the great mass of the working world must forever remain 'common labor'. . . . The cause of labor is a unity as the cause of humanity is one. In the recognition of the principle of solidarity is the hope of labor, the hope of the nation and the hope of the human race." (Samuel M. Jones to Gompers, June 2, 1900, *AFL Corr.*)

union leaders rather than corporation spokesmen on the needs of the city.[19] Consequently, in the next election, the Republican machine demanded that Jones accept party dictation as a condition for being renominated to succeed himself. He refused, and ran instead on an independent ticket, sponsored by the trade unions of Toledo. An AFL spokesman wrote to Gompers from Toledo:

> We are running Mayor Jones on an independent ticket, and he is going to poll more votes than the Republican and Democratic nominees for Mayor. After we elect him we are going after their nominees for Governor. We are going to show them that Labor cannot be turned down at will. Mayor Jones' platform is the AFL platform, equal rights to all, special privileges to none.* He refused the Republican nomination when they asked him to pledge himself to the party and said that he would be Mayor for all the people. These are the kind of men we have got to stand by.[20]

Jones was reelected mayor by a landslide in a campaign that was featured by attacks upon him as the candidate of the "Anarchist element in the city."[21] Thereupon, the trade unions turned their attention to the gubernatorial campaign. After both the Republican and Democratic parties had nominated reactionaries as their candidates for governor, the trade unions invited Mayor Jones to run as an independent campaign on a platform drawn up by the unions, which raised five demands:

> 1st. Self-government through nomination of candidates by the people through the direct primary and direct making of laws by the people through the initiative and referendum.
> 2nd. Public ownership of all public utilities. The extension of the principle now operating in the public ownership of the Post Office, to the operation of Mines, Highways, Steam and Electric Railroads, Telegraphs, Telephones and Water and Lighting Plants.
> 3rd. Union wages, hours and conditions or better for skilled labor, and an eight-hour day, with a living wage, for unskilled labor, on all public work.
> 4th. Abolition of the contract system, that glaring evil of the competitive system, on all public work, and the substitution of direct employment. Immediate cessation of the present system of exploiting prison labor for the benefit of the profit-mongers and to the injury of free labor.
> 5th. It is the imperative duty of the State Legislature to deal with the question of unemployment, to the end that provision may immediately be made that no citizen of Ohio, who is willing to work, shall be driven into pauperism, crime or insanity, for want of work.[22]

*Jones' platform called for (1) public ownership of all public utilities; (2) no granting of any new or extension of any existing franchises; (3) abolition of the contract system of doing the work of city improvement; (4) substitution of the day labor plan by a minimum wage of $1.50 for an eight-hour day; and (5) the employment of organized labor in all public work. (Samuel Jones, *The New Right*, New York, 1899, p. 112.)

Jones accepted the invitation and a petition campaign was launched to place his name on the ballot. All five members of the committee which sponsored the petition were trade unionists: three were AFL officials and two were officers of the Railroad Brotherhoods.[23] An AFL leader wrote to Gompers from Toledo:

> The Independent movement has been launched. It is my firm belief that Jones will be elected, and should this prove true, what a triumph this would be for labor! I think it would be a good idea if you should run a notice in the next issue of the *Federationist:* "Samuel M. Jones, Candidate for Governor, Independent ticket, upon the AFL platform. The Unions and R.R. organizations have sponsored him, are endorsing and campaigning for him."[24]

Asserting that "there is no relief to the laborer in either old parties," Ohio unions enthusiastically endorsed Jones, and their members campaigned for him.[25] The Chicago *Record* reported:

> His [Jones'] campaign workers are trade union volunteers. They talk from curbstones and speak on street corners. They hold meetings with working people during the noon hour and attend Republican and Democratic meetings to ask questions of the partisan speakers. The slogan of the Jones voters, heard from one end of Ohio to the other, is as follows:
> "Rattle my bones over the stones;
> I'm only a voter whom nobody owns,
> And that is the reason I'm voting for Jones."[26]

Although he had only a hastily prepared organization and the press was "united in suppressing news of his comings and goings and in minimizing his campaign,"[27] Jones made a respectable showing. (He carried the two large cities of Toledo and Cleveland by sizable majorities.) The organization which had sponsored and supported him in the gubernatorial campaign remained in existence after the election and was active in reelecting Jones when he ran again for mayor of Toledo in 1901 and 1903 on an independent ticket.[28]

As mayor of Toledo until his death in 1904, Jones put in operation many of the demands raised by organized labor in the city. He established the eight-hour day and a minimum wage for city employees; introduced kindergartens and free concerts and opened public playgrounds; provided municipal work for the unemployed; vetoed the council's grant of renewal of the street railway franchise to a private corporation; took away clubs from the police and replaced them with canes; broke up the system of arresting on suspicion and holding those so arrested without charge—a practice which had been used effectively to break strikes; refused to help the street railway company in its efforts to break the union; and, by threatening to withhold police support to strikebreakers, helped the union maintain its organization and win a new agreement with improved conditions.[29]

The era of "Golden Rule" Jones in Toledo, characterized by the special role of organized labor in the reform movement, laid one of the foundations for the emerging "Progressive Revolt." And upon Jones' death while still in office, organized labor, in unity with progressive reform forces, rallied behind Brand Whitlock, Jones' trusted legal advisor, and elected him mayor in November, 1905 on a reform and anti-monopoly platform.[30]

Immediately upon taking office, Whitlock took the canes away from the police and, as he wrote in 1910, "since that time they have carried nothing in their white gloved hands."[31] He also made it clear as soon as he assumed office that the police were not to be used to help the employers break strikes and that the mayor's office was not to be viewed as an agency of the open-shop drive. In the Pope-Toledo automobile strike of 1907, Whitlock let the company know that he did "not intend to use the police department as a strike-breaking factor."[32]

Whitlock fought the street railway company and, after a long, stubborn battle, extracted a lower fare and better operating conditions from management. He destroyed a scandalous ice monopoly perpetrated by a group of "outstanding" citizens. And he continued Jones' policy of establishing playgrounds, public baths, public concerts, and other social services. In 1907, Whitlock was reelected mayor by a plurality of more than 6,500 votes. He gave credit to the "working men" for the victory. "The feeling toward me of the working men, of the poor, of the outcast almost now brings tears to my eyes," he wrote directly after the election.[33] Two years later, he was again elected in a campaign featured by the most bitter calumny heaped upon the reform administration by the conservative forces and by a vigorous campaign in its behalf by the labor forces in the city.[34]

LABOR AND REFORM IN CLEVELAND

In January, 1901, the United Trades and Labor Council of Cleveland distributed a petition among its affiliated unions urging the nomination of Tom L. Johnson as the Democratic candidate for mayor. Within a few days, thousands of trade unionists had signed the petition, and the sheets, added to the petitions distributed by other reform elements in the city, made up a mammoth roll. Johnson was nominated on a platform which was epitomized by the slogan: "Home rule; three-cent fare; and just taxation." A key demand was for municipal ownership of all public utilities.[35]

Like "Golden Rule" Jones, Johnson was a successful businessman who had accumulated a substantial fortune before he joined the reform movement. He became a champion of Henry George's single-tax program, took an active part in the United Labor Party's 1886 campaign to elect George mayor of New York, and studied the progressive reforms achieved in Detroit under Mayor Pingree, particularly the establishment of the three-cent fare. He antagonized conservative industrialists who denounced him as a "traitor" to his class because he had aligned himself with the labor party in New York, and had defied the employers' associations by recognizing the unions and introducing higher wages and shorter working hours in the steel mills and on the street railways he owned. On February 25, 1901, the Cleveland *Plain-Dealer* reported that Johnson was considered by the Chamber of Commerce as a "dangerous candidate" for mayor because the trade unions had participated actively in the petition movement to secure his nomination, and because of "his popularity with his employees and with workingmen everywhere."

In the campaign, Johnson defied the conservative business interests by coming out publicly in favor of union labor. "If I were a laboring man," he declared, "I should join a union. . . . I believe in labor unions as a means of bringing together and uplifting the laboring classes." He denied that trade unions and trusts were identical—a common charge made by too many middle-class progressives: "A man in a trust does not trust his partner, but the union men strike and starve together for their rights."[36] When the Republican candidate, in an effort to swing the labor vote, played up the fact that Johnson was a millionaire, a group of trade unionists, all of whom were Johnson's former employees, replied:

> Whereas, Tom Johnson has always been a friend of union labor indicated by his attitude toward his former employees, shortening the working hours of said employees from a working day of fifteen hours at $1.75 per day to a day of ten hours, at $2 per day; and
> Whereas, by fair and impartial management of his line he compelled a decrease of hours and an increase of wages upon the lines of the other three companies. . . .
> Whereas, we have full confidence in his ability to obtain for the people of Cleveland a 3-cent fare, therefore be it
> Resolved that we unanimously endorse Tom Johnson, our former employer, for mayor; and be it further resolved, that we ask the cooperation and assistance of all union men in Cleveland in electing a friend of workingmen to the office of chief executive of our city.[37]

On March 13, the Cleveland unions officially endorsed Johnson and his program.[38] On April 1, 1901, Johnson was elected mayor by a plurality of 6,033 votes over his Republican opponent. During the first of his three administrations, he threw open the city parks to the people, removing the "Keep Off the Grass" signs and establishing playgrounds and ball fields in them in the summer and skating rinks in the winter; opened public bathhouses; dedicated the northwestern corner of the public square to free speech; educated the people in municipal problems by conducting regular discussions with them in a huge tent which was moved from place to place throughout the city; brought natural gas into Cleveland, thereby reducing the rates for gas; broke the street-paving combine monopoly; introduced a more equitable tax system under which corporations would assume a larger share of the taxes; and took steps to introduce the three-cent fare. Although his three-cent fare program was enjoined in the courts and his tax victory over the public service corporations was wiped out in the state legislature, Johnson did more in less than two years to introduce progressive government in Cleveland than had been accomplished in the city's entire history up to that time.[39] "There is scarcely a municipality in the country that does not need a Tom Johnson house-cleaner," observed a labor paper.[40]

So important was organized labor's support for Johnson that when he ran for reelection, the Republicans tried desperately to split the labor vote by nominating Sol Southeimer, a leader of the Cigarmakers' Union No. 17 and president of the United Trades and Labor Council, as its candidate for vice-mayor. But the maneuver failed. At an emergency meeting of the Council, Southeimer was given an ultimatum "either to give up his office as United Trades and Labor Council president or get off the Republican ticket as candidate for vice-mayor." The issue was then referred to his own union. Since the constitution of the central labor body specifically stated that no one but a regular delegate could hold office or take part in the deliberations of the organization, the local union met immediately to take action on the case. During the discussion, Southeimer was called a "flopper": "He had once made speeches against the trusts and corporations . . . [and] by accepting the nomination on the Republican ticket, had shown a complete change of heart, had defied the union, and was no longer fit to represent the cigarmakers in the United Trades and Labor Council." Refusing to bow to labor's demand that he resign, Southeimer was withdrawn by the cigarmakers' local as its delegate to the United Trades and Labor Council.[41]

Endorsed by the trade unions of Cleveland, Johnson was reelected by a 5,985 plurality.[42] Directly after his reelection, Johnson began the campaign for a municipal electrical power system for Cleveland. Local 39 of the International Brotherhood of Electrical Workers headed the trade union committee established by the United Trades and Labor Council to further the campaign. Its members were especially active, circulating literature throughout the city exposing the efforts of the powerful public service corporations to bribe the councilmen to vote against the municipal electric lighting system. The victory for Johnson's program not only established the Cleveland Municipal Plant, but also forced the Cleveland Electric Illuminating Company to reduce its rates.[43]

As opposition to his program became more and more pronounced in the state legislature, Johnson decided in 1903 to run for governor on the Democratic ticket. In the campaign, Johnson's attitude toward organized labor and trade union support for his program was made a key issue by the Republicans. They played up the fact that Peter Witt, a former molder appointed by Johnson as city clerk, had been blacklisted by the foundry employers' association as a "dangerous radical," and that he had worked closely with Max Hayes, Socialist leader of the Cleveland Typographical Union. Indeed, "Socialism" was said to be the aim of the Johnson-trade union alliance in Cleveland. Mark Hanna, the Republican boss of the state and senator from Ohio, stumped the rural areas charging Johnson and his allies with seeking to establish a Socialist government in Ohio, and Johnson himself as being secretly the real head of the Socialist Party. "Says Johnson is Socialist" read the headline in the Cleveland *Plain-Dealer* of September 30, 1903. And the story went on: "With all the emphasis at his command, Senator Hanna twice today publicly charged Mayor Tom Johnson with being the national leader of the Socialist Party of the United States." "I beg of you." Hanna told an audience in Sandusky, "to rise and kill the attempt to float the flag of Socialism over Ohio." Later, in Lima, he declared: "Vote for the Tom Johnson socialistic ticket and you vote for the absolute destruction and ruin of your American institutions and for utter chaos in this country." It meant nothing that the Socialist *Cleveland Citizen*, edited by Max Hayes, kept repeating regularly that "Tom Johnson is NOT A Socialist, and no Socialist will charge him with being of that faith. Mr. Johnson is an individualist and defender of the competitive capitalist system. . . ."[44] The attacks had their effect, and with the public service corporations flooding the state with money to buy votes, Johnson's defeat was a foregone conclusion.

On April 28, 1908, the Cleveland *Plain-Dealer* banner-headlined the news: "Cleveland's entire street railway system now in control of the Municipal Traction Company. . . . Within ten days 3-cent fare will be put into effect." The day before, the city of Cleveland had taken over all the street railways, climaxing Johnson's battle to establish municipal ownership and the three-cent fare. "Cleveland is leading the world in the solution of municipal problems," wrote Lincoln Steffens. "The victory that she has just won marks the greatest advance in municipal government in the United States."[45] It is therefore tragic that after this victory for municipal progress, the Johnson administration turned against the most important force that had helped to make it possible—organized labor—and in so doing paved the way for its defeat.

Throughout Johnson's war to take over the Cleveland Electric Railway Company and make it part of a city-owned system operating on a three-cent fare basis, the unions had supported him to the hilt. They assumed, therefore, that when the Municipal Traction Company took over the older company on that historic day, April 27, 1908, it would also take over the agreement Cleveland Electric had with Local 268 of the Amalgamated Association of Street & Railway Employees of America and respect the workers' seniority rights, especially since A. B. Du Pont, administrator of Municipal Traction, had so assured A. L. Behnes, the Amalgamated Association's International vice-president.[46] But having achieved his long-sought goal, Johnson appeared to have lost interest in the relations between the municipally-owned corporation and the union. He left the entire matter in Du Pont's hands, and the latter quickly proved himself to be viciously anti-union. He rejected the union's request for the continuation of the old agreement which provided for an increase of two cents an hour in wages, free rides for employees, and strict observance of seniority rights. "We will not recognize the old Cleveland agreement," Du Pont announced on April 30. "The Municipal Traction Company and not the Cleveland Electric is employing the men."[47]

Union men with twelve to fifteen years' seniority were discharged and replaced by younger men at much lower wages. The workers were required to pay their own fares, where Cleveland Electric had permitted its men to ride to and from work free of charge.[48]

Cleveland's trade unions were furious. The United Trades and Labor Council reminded Du Pont that without union support, municipal ownership and operation would never have come into existence, and that the Municipal Traction Company's anti-union practices were hardly the appropriate reward for organized labor's activity in its behalf. But Du

Pont refused to budge. Warned that the union street car workers would strike to enforce their former agreement, he replied casually: "I do not expect a strike. Even if one is called, not 10 percent of the men will respond."[49]

Meeting at the United Trades and Labor Council's headquarters, the members of Local 268 debated the question of calling a strike against the Municipal Traction Company. The strike vote was overwhelmingly carried—1,452 to 128—but, concerned lest they embarrass the Johnson administration and the cause of municipal ownership, the workers decided to hold off strike action until the outcome of an appeal directly to Mayor Johnson. The union leaders then met with Johnson, who stated that he would see to it that the union was recognized and that the men obtained free rides. He then suggested that the strike leaders get together with Du Pont to settle their differences. When the men replied that they could not even get to talk with Du Pont, Johnson declared that he had hoped that he could be present at such a conference, but unfortunately he had to leave Cleveland to attend a convention. "We will all have lost our jobs before then," the men protested. Johnson then urged that the issues in dispute be submitted to a three-man arbitration board. He was certain the men's grievances could and would be settled, and concluded with the appeal: "Now at the beginning of such a bright era for Cleveland, let us not dispute over minor matters."[50]

The men assured the mayor that the existence of their union and their seniority rights were hardly "minor matters," but that they were prepared to accept his offer of arbitration. "Street Car Men Ready to Arbitrate Wage Contract" read the headline in the Cleveland *Plain-Dealer* the next day, May 4, 1908. But the arbitration board never met. Johnson had left the city, and Du Pont continued to discharge union conductors and motormen and replace them with non-union men at lower wages. On May 15, 1908, Local 268 voted again on the question of striking. "With scarcely a dozen dissenting voices," the *Plain-Dealer* reported, "1,300 angry street car men, members of the old Cleveland Electric union, voted for an immediate strike in two stormy meetings at United Trades and Labor Council headquarters."[51] The following morning, 1,350 conductors and motormen walked off their jobs. Du Pont immediately introduced strikebreakers, imported from New York, into the battle, and the police escorted scabs to and from their jobs. The strikers fought back and bitter warfare raged in the streets of Cleveland between the strikers and the police.

The United Trades and Labor Council unanimously endorsed the strike, praised the strikers, and condemned the Municipal Traction Company for having provoked the struggle. The Council pointed out that the union had done everything possible to avoid the strike; it therefore went "on record as endorsing the action of the street railway union and call upon all union men and their sympathizers to refrain from riding on the cars of the Municipal Traction Company until a satisfactory settlement is arrived at." "Walk ten miles, if necessary, but walk," the Council told all union men in the city. The Socialist Party of Cleveland supported the strikers, along with the trade union leaders.[52]

Despite this support, the strike was smashed and the strikers, having been beaten into submission, applied to return to work. Twelve hundred of them were turned down by the Municipal Traction Company, and the few who were rehired lost their seniority. Local 268 was to all intents and purposes destroyed.

Tom Johnson did nothing either to prevent the strike or halt Du Pont's strikebreaking and union-busting role during and after the struggle. He defended himself then and later (and was similarly defended by many Progressive reformers) by charging that the strike was instigated and financed by private public service corporations, particularly the financiers who controlled Cleveland Electric, for the sole purpose of discrediting municipal ownership.[54] Although it is true that the private corporations welcomed and encouraged the strike, the fact is that the battle grew out of the workers' legitimate grievances and Johnson's failure to prevent his commissioner from carrying through his anti-union policies. *The Motorman and Conductor,* official journal of the Amalgamated Association, denied that the corporations had financed the strike or that it had been called for the purpose of discrediting Johnson's street-railway program:

> That the strike was financed by outside parties is absolutely false. It was financed by the treasury of the Amalgamated Association. Neither was it a fight against any three-cents franchises. It was a fight against the Municipal Traction Company on account of the treatment it accorded to its employees.

The union could not remain quiet, the journal continued, while its members were being discharged and persecuted in various ways, simply because these anti-labor practices were being perpetrated by a municipally-owned company charging three-cent fares, much as it sympathized with the objectives of removing public franchises from the control of private corporations and political bosses, and of providing working people with a reduced cost of transportation: "The primary purpose of the Association is to establish and maintain to its membership, the best possible conditions of employment, and to protest against the loss of such conditions."[55]

Johnson's conflict with organized labor was doubly tragic for the Progressive cause in Cleveland. For one thing, he alienated all of the trade unions at a time when he needed wide support in order to realize his complete program. For another, his conduct led directly to the defeat of municipal operation of the street railways. The defeated strikers, hoping to get back their jobs if the Cleveland Railway regained operation of its lines, began circulating petitions for a referendum election to be held on the advisability of continuing city ownership of the street railways. This action was based on the Schmidt Act, passed by the Ohio legislature, which provided that if 15 percent of the voters signed petitions, a referendum had to be held on all franchise grants to public service corporations. Over 23,000 signatures were obtained for the referendum election. Held in October, 1908, the election resulted in a defeat for the city-owned plan by the close vote of 38,249 to 37,644—a plurality of 605 out of 76,000 votes cast.[56] It was immediately pointed out that by antagonizing organized labor, Johnson had paved the way for the defeat of his most cherished project, for even though not all trade unionists were ready to reject the city-owned plan because of the anti-union policy pursued by the Municipal Traction Company, enough of them were affected to determine the outcome.[57]

In the fall of 1909, Johnson was defeated for reelection as mayor. He left office on January 1, 1910, a broken man, his health seriously impaired. He died on April 10, 1911. At his funeral, the trade unions came out in full force to pay their respects. Except for his stand during the street railway strike of 1908, labor had regarded Tom Johnson as its friend. As one worker, waiting at Euclid Square for the funeral procession to pass, told a reporter for the Cleveland *Plain-Dealer:* "No work today? Well I should say not. There is one thing that I insisted on doing and that was coming down here and paying my respects to a man who had lived like a man, and who was my friend, although he never heard of me."[58]

"It was he [Johnson]," wrote Eugene V. Debs, "who set the masses to thinking about the wrongs of which they are the victims."[59] And they gave Johnson the backing that enabled him to make Cleveland "the best governed city in America," and the necessary support during the "Nine Years' war with Privilege," as Johnson described his administrations, to bring cheaper and better services to the community and expanded government activities to meet the needs of the common people.

LABOR AND MUNICIPAL OWNERSHIP: CHICAGO

On April 8, 1906, three hundred delegates assembled at Chicago's Brand Hall. They represented 53 labor unions and eight civic societies identified with the labor movement or friendly to it: two turner societies, two single tax leagues, and four municipal ownership leagues. An organization was formed under the name of the Chicago Progressive Alliance, and a six-point platform was adopted: (1) an end to inequalities in taxation; (2) municipal ownership of street railways; (3) a law requiring the suspension of business on primary and election days; (4) the nomination of all candidates for elective offices by direct primaries; (5) initiative and referendum; and (6) abolition of the injunction abuse. The first two demands were, at that time, of special importance to Chicago labor.[60]

The struggle for tax reform in Chicago was led by the Federation of Teachers, an affiliate of the Chicago Federation of Labor. In 1902, Margaret Haley and Catherine Goggin of the Teachers' Federation discovered that the reason there was not enough money to keep Chicago's schools open the entire year and pay the teachers was because the street car companies and other public service corporations were dodging taxes they were obligated to pay. Although these franchises were listed as worth millions on the stock market, they were assigned no value on the city's tax rolls. By means of circulars and public meetings, the Teachers' Federation relentlessly pursued the issue. It attacked the Board of Equalization and forced it to tax the Chicago utilities corporations on the actual value of their franchises. At the same time, the Federation sued the companies for the taxes they had avoided paying. After a long battle, the suit was won in the face of fierce opposition from the city's business interests, from the taxing authorities, from the city government, and from the school board itself. This resulted in adding some six or seven hundred thousand dollars to the city's annual income, of which the schools received about $250,000.* *The Public,* a progressive Chicago weekly, noted:

> In the progress of the fight, the Chicago Teachers' Federation came to be a representative body of acknowledged force in the community; and as its intelligence regarding despotic tendencies expanded, it came more and more

---

*The Chicago Federation of Teachers also exposed the methods by which previous school boards had leased school lands to the Chicago *Tribune* and the Chicago *Daily News,* thereby depriving the school fund of valuable income. Naturally, it earned the bitter enmity of these papers in the process. (*See* "Chicago School Lands," *The Public,* vol. IX, December 15, 1906, pp. 754–55.)

to be a local agency of democratic progress. What had at first seemed to its members to be arbitrary or corrupt school management, was revealed to them as a phase of the despotic tendencies (whether corrupt or not) in all public affairs. Against these tendencies this organization had ever set its face, and with such effect that the victories won in Chicago for municipalization of public utilities are directly traceable to its work.[61]

While this last point may be something of an exaggeration, it is nevertheless true that the Federation of Teachers did play a significant role, along with other sections of organized labor, in the movement for municipal ownership. In Chicago, this movement was directed mainly at the traction companies and was spearheaded by the Public Ownership League, organized in 1902 with Clarence Darrow as chairman of its executive committee. In the autumn election of 1902, the League placed Darrow on the ballot as candidate for the lower house of the state legislature, running on a municipal ownership platform. Although at this point organized labor as a whole did not yet participate actively in the League, a number of trade unions helped circulate the petitions to run Darrow and helped to elect him to the legislature. Darrow's 11,000 votes were nearly double those of the other two successful candidates.

Already popular with Chicago labor for his general activity in the Progressive cause and for his legal defense of the trade unions since the days of the Pullman strike of 1894, Darrow's popularity rose considerably after the election when he helped to win an arbitration award for the workers of the Union Traction Company who were trying to organize into the AFL's Association of Street Railway Employees. The award ordered the company to dissolve its company union and granted the workers a substantial wage increase of more than $100 per year per man.

Plans were immediately initiated to organize a Union Labor Party for the mayoralty elections scheduled for April, 1903, with Darrow as candidate for mayor and with public ownership of public utilities as the platform. Darrow, however, refused to accept the nomination on the ground that it would split the progressive vote and guarantee the election of the Republican candidate. The Union Labor Party replaced him with another candidate, but its appeal to labor was seriously limited by the absence of a popular nominee.

The bitterness in trade union circles over Darrow's abandonment of the Union Labor Party did not diminish labor's interest in his efforts in the state legislature to achieve immediate municipal ownership. The Chicago Federation of Labor sent petitions to the legislature in support of the Mueller Bill, which Darrow was actively seeking to have passed. The bill provided, among other things, that any city could own and operate street railways if the voters in a referendum election approved the measure by a three-fifths majority. In May, 1903, the bill passed the legislature and was signed by the governor.[62]

It was to take another year before the Mueller Act was voted on in Chicago. Meanwhile, organized labor intensified its activity in behalf of municipal ownership. On September 21, 1903, the Chicago Federation of Labor went on record in favor of IMO (immediate municipal ownership) and elected delegates to the IMO convention held in the city under the sponsorship of the Public Ownership League. Henry Demarest Lloyd, the noted Chicago reformer, welcomed the trade union delegates to the convention, declaring: "The presence of the representatives of organized labor in our midst will influence the traction situation in a decisive manner. It spells victory for the forces seeking municipal ownership."[63]

However, not all union leaders in Chicago were pleased with the steps taken by the Chicago Federation of Labor in favor of immediate municipal ownership. Union racketeers like "Skinny" Madden of the Steamfitters' Union, union adherents of the policy of not antagonizing big business by advocating radical programs, and union officials who were part of the Democratic machine and occupied soft jobs on the city payroll as building inspectors, bridge inspectors, or members of some bureau or other, mobilized their influence against municipal ownership. Although they had been unable to prevent the Chicago Federation of Labor from endorsing the program, they did succeed in stopping a number of the affiliated unions from lending it their support.[64]

In November, 1903, an issue arose which united nearly all of organized labor behind municipal ownership and sharply reduced the ability of the conservative union officials to disrupt activity for the program. On November 12, 2,200 employees of the Chicago City Railway, which operated all the lines on the South Side, quit work in a strike for union recognition and increased wages. Even before the strike began, strikebreakers had been imported from other cities and they were thrown in the moment the union motormen and conductors quit work. Protected by the police, the strikebreakers began to move the cars through the streets. The strikers fought back, stoning every car that moved.

The union, through its representative, Clarence Darrow, offered to arbitrate, but the company refused. On November 22, five thousand strike sympathizers paraded to a meeting at Tatersall's attended by fifteen thousand workers. With the entire executive committee of the

Chicago Federation of Labor seated on the platform, along with representatives of most of the important unions, the meeting heard and cheered speeches supporting the strikers, denouncing attempts by the mayor and the City Council to grant the company a new franchise, and calling for immediate municipal ownership. The Chicago *Tribune* reported on November 23, 1903: "Municipal ownership—not in twenty years, but at once—and the swift ousting of the Chicago City Railway from its possession of the streets was the doctrine spread through the ranks of 15,000 workingmen yesterday afternoon at Tatersall's." The meeting adopted a resolution demanding abandonment of all negotiations with the company for extension of its franchise and called upon the mayor and the City Council "to at once remove from the cars the police force and place them in the position that they are paid to fulfill, that of protecting the property and interests of all the citizens, instead of operating the street cars of a law-breaking corporation, and to institute proceedings at once to take over the lines operated by this company and place them immediately under municipal ownership and operation." Ward clubs were to be organized by the Chicago trade unions to make sure that no franchises were given away and to advance the entire movement for immediate municipal ownership and operation.[65]

Three days later, the strike was settled—but the trade unions did not forget the demands voiced at the great mass meeting on November 22. The Chicago Federation of Labor intensified its campaign for immediate municipal ownership and joined with other groups in demanding that the city officials order a referendum on the issue. On April 5, 1904, by overwhelming majorities, the voters of Chicago approved the Mueller Act and instructed the city not to grant any more franchises, but to proceed without delay to acquire ownership of the street railways.[66]

A year later, in the mayoralty election of 1905, the Chicago Federation of Labor endorsed Edward F. Dunne, the Democratic candidate and a prominent advocate of city ownership and operation of the street car lines, and rallied trade union support behind his candidacy. Dunne was elected and began the battle to achieve the program of city ownership of the street-car lines. It proved easier, however, to elect a municipal ownership mayor than to put the plan into operation against the combined opposition of a City Council dominated by conservative businessmen, a state legislature controlled by conservative members from the rural districts, state and federal courts in the hands of former corporation lawyers, and behind them all, "the titanic force of money and corruption" represented by the traction companies. The corporations poured huge sums into buying newspapers, party bosses, Council members, state legislators, and even judges. Conservative reformers opposed to municipal ownership joined the alliance of Chicago's financial and business interests against Mayor Dunne and his allies.[67]

In the face of this powerful coalition, Dunne was indecisive and confused. Despite this, however, the Chicago Federation of Labor endorsed him for reelection in 1907, stating that his "clean, straightforward and consistent record in favor of municipal ownership" merited labor's support. (The Federation also condemned those members of the City Council who had sabotaged the municipal ownership program.)[68] But the Democratic Party bosses deserted Dunne and made a deal to support the Republican candidate in order to inflict a death-blow on municipal ownership. Dunne was defeated.

"If Chicago wants IMO of street cars, or other things, Illinois will have to change its laws, its customs, its judges," observed the *Chicago Daily Socialist*.[69] Still, the long struggle for municipal ownership was not entirely in vain. Fearful of a possible resurgence of the movement, the private traction companies were compelled to improve the service on the street-car lines. Under an agreement between the city and the private companies, the city was to receive 55% of the net earnings above 5% income on the valuation of their properties as fixed by a commission of experts. For the year ending February 1, 1908, the private companies paid the city more than a million and a half dollars as its share of their net earnings.[70] Moreover, a basic principle had been established. As one contemporary newspaper pointed out:

> Under the persistent agitation for municipal ownership of Mayor Dunne and the progressive elements in Chicago, among whom organized labor was an essential force, the traction companies of the city have been forced to recognize that the public has some rights which public service corporations are bound to recognize. As a result of the agitation for municipal ownership, the traction companies themselves have been forced to make concessions which would have seemed incredible ten years ago. If the people of Chicago can influence great corporations to recognize their rights, there is no reason why the people in other cities cannot compel similar corporations holding valuable franchises to like action.[71]

LABOR AND MUNICIPAL OWNERSHIP: NEW YORK

Although Cleveland and Chicago were the storm centers in the nationwide agitation in American cities for municipal ownership, the battle in New York also attracted considerable attention. There the demand "for a municipal system of rapid transportation" was raised by the trade unions as early as 1896,[72] but the issue did not attract mass support until almost a decade later. In the summer of 1904, the Municipal Ownership League of New York was formed, with the Central Federation of Labor as one of the founding bodies. Soon municipal ownership clubs were being set up in many of the assembly districts. Many of the clubs in Brooklyn were started by the Central Labor Union, and President Michael J. Flaherty reported on December 20, 1904:

> We have obtained several thousand signatures since the summer when we organized our first Municipal Ownership Club. We have organized several districts, and a committee of five appointed by the Central Labor Union, is still at work. Whenever we obtain one hundred signatures in any one Assembly District we form an organization.[73]

On December 18, 1904, a committee appointed by the Central Federated Union to present labor's position on municipal ownership recommended that the trade unions in New York go on record in favor of a municipal gas and lighting plant and municipal ownership and operation of the rapid transit system. The report, read by Alfred J. Boulton of the Stereotypers' Union, emphasized three reasons for this recommendation:

> First—the saving of dollars each month by humble families, who measure in dimes the difference between comparative comfort and positive privation.
> Second—the providing of facilities and opportunities for the working people to enjoy the advantages of distant high schools, colleges, museums, art galleries, menageries, parks and pleasure resorts, which are now practically denied to them through the greed of our transportation companies.
> Third—Municipal Ownership would dry up the most prolific fountains of legislative corruption, official bribery and debauchery of the franchise. It would be a staggering blow to the corporation-owned political machines, which are the mere agents of their corporate masters in nominating candidates and controlling legislation.[74]

Within two months, a fourth reason was added. The union-busting role of August Belmont against the workers of the Interborough Rapid Transit Company, the breaking of their strike, and the establishment of the open shop on the subway lines—all served to intensify trade union support for municipal ownership of the rapid transit system. "Possibly as you walk down town from Harlem or are half-suffocated in a trolley car because of the strike in the subway," read a leaflet distributed by the Central Federated Union, "you will begin to realize some of the advantages of municipal ownership of public utilities."[75]

In the spring of 1905, as the mayoralty election approached, the Municipal Ownership League decided to nominate an independent candidate against the candidates of the corporate interests which controlled both political parties. To no one's surprise, the nomination went to William Randolph Hearst. Hearst's New York *American* was practically the official organ of the Municipal Ownership League, and his employees were influential in many of the local municipal ownership clubs. Hearst was making an important contribution to the municipal ownership cause at this time by exposing and blocking various proposed gas and franchise grabs in the state legislature, by condemning Belmont's open shop policies on his subway lines, and by publicizing the municipal ownership movement when nearly every other paper was condemning it as an unAmerican assault on private property.[76] To be sure, Hearst was interested in municipal ownership, as in all issues he promoted, only to the extent that he could use it to increase circulation of his newspapers and promote his own political ambitions. If the movement also boosted the political prospects of any other figure who was active in it and thereby threatened Hearst's ambitions, he withdrew his support. In Chicago, for example, the Hearst press was indispensable in achieving the election of Mayor Dunne on a municipal ownership platform, but when Dunne loomed as a rival to Hearst's ambition to secure the Democratic presidential nomination, he stopped supporting the mayor in his battle against the powerful alliance that opposed his program, and his newspapers were silent when Dunne ran for reelection. Likewise, Hearst did little to help Tom Johnson in his struggle for municipal ownership in Cleveland because he regarded Johnson as a rival for the Democratic presidential nomination. In short, Hearst did a great deal to promote the municipal ownership cause when it coincided with his personal interests, and abandoned it whenever it conflicted with them.[77]

Hearst ran for Congress in 1902 and was endorsed by many labor groups—the New York City letter carriers, the hatters, the printers, the metal workers, and the steamfitters. He was elected by a huge plurality and represented a working-class district in the House of Representatives. But while his newspaper continued to demand labor legislation, he did nothing in Congress to further this cause. Indeed, he rarely even occupied his seat in the House, a fact which convinced some observers that he was only interested in furthering his own interests.[78]

But at the time of the 1905 mayoralty campaign in New York City, Hearst's opportunistic role had not yet become clear to the forces favoring municipal ownership, and they believed that in the Congressman-publisher, they had a candidate who would wage an effective battle for the cause. Although the Central Federated Union did not formally endorse Hearst, many trade unions did and campaigned vigorously for his election. The campaign itself was a minor miracle. To all appearances, there was little prospect for victory for a hastily organized movement against the established political machines, well supplied with funds by the public service corporations. Yet so vigorous was the fight for municipal ownership, and so popular was the demand among the people that thousands, especially in the ranks of the working class, broke with Tammany and supported the Municipal Ownership League. When the votes were tabulated, the results showed that Hearst had been beaten by a margin of only 3,474 votes in a total vote of approximately 609,000. But on the basis of the best evidence available, it is clear that the election was stolen from Hearst by the Democratic machine. Thousands of Hearst ballots were thrown into the East River by Tammany henchmen and replaced by ballots marked for McClellan, the Democratic candidate. Election boxes were seen floating in the river. Efforts to obtain a legal hearing at which the Municipal Ownership League could present evidence of fraud in the election were unsuccessful. Irwin Yellowitz notes:

> Hearst had appealed to the lower middle class and the working class by his attacks on the entrenched wealth and power represented in the trusts and political machines, and by his promise to return government to the people. He had truly "come, in the minds of a great mass of poor men, to stand for the rights of the poor," and they swung to his support with a vengeance.[80]*

After the mayoralty campaign of 1905, Hearst organized the Independent League of New York, with public ownership as its leading demand. While the organization was dominated by Hearst and his personal employees, it attracted progressives who were resentful of big business domination of the old parties and favored public ownership. At a state convention, the Independence League nominated Hearst for governor on a public ownership platform. Later, the Democratic convention also nominated Hearst as its gubernatorial candidate to run against Charles Evans Hughes, the Republican nominee.

At first, there was less labor support for Hearst in the gubernatorial campaign than there had been when he ran for mayor.[81] Indeed, there was

---

*In addition to municipal ownership of street railways, Hearst promised an end to graft, 55¢ gas, new schools, and improvement in the pay and working conditions of city employees. He promised that he would resign if he could not keep his pledge. (*New York Times,* Nov. 3, 1905.)

so much pressure for an independent labor party that the Central Federated Union in New York City was forced to yield to the pressure and decided in favor of independent political action. On August 10, 1906, the Independent Labor Party was officially organized. As one labor leader pointed out: "Both the Republican and Democratic parties are more or less divided, and as far as this city is concerned, labor has the best chance it has had of taking independent political action since the campaign of Henry George for mayor in 1886."[82]

But as the campaign developed, more and more trade unionists came out for Hearst, and interest in the Independent Labor Party waned. In part this was due to the work of Hearst supporters who were active in getting resolutions passed by trade unions favoring his candidacy.[83]

On September 29, 1906, August Belmont, who was known as a Democrat, warned President Roosevelt that the "labor vote" would decide the election: "Hearst appeals to the labor vote, and has a record with them which will ensure to him the support of a substantial portion of that element. Mr. Hughes has no record of this kind at all, and I am satisfied—and all to whom I have spoken on the subject agree with me—that it is of great importance that Mr. Hughes should place himself in a favorable attitude toward labor." Belmont advised the president that he should have Hughes emphasize labor issues, such as slum housing, child labor, and "sweat shops."[84] Roosevelt relayed the suggestion to Hughes and attempted to implement it by securing labor support for the Republican campaign in New York. But he could find no labor leader of stature who would speak out in support of Hughes. " . . . I have been astounded and indeed alarmed to find that most of the men who I wanted to get hold of and send to you," Roosevelt wrote to Hughes, "were against us." Even Republican labor leaders feared that to oppose Hearst would alienate them from their membership.[85] The Republicans were reduced to inducing Richard Croker, abdicated boss of Tammany, to appeal to labor to vote against Hearst and public ownership. Croker wrote from Ireland:

> I hope the workingmen's organizations will work together and not be misled by wild talk of trusts. The workingmen's organizations are themselves combines and trusts. I oppose trusts which would injure the public, but I am in favor of workingmen standing by their employers and encouraging capital to develop and extend labor. If Mr. Hearst wins and carries out his ideas he will paralyze labor by forcing capitalists to invest in bonds and stocks instead of labor.[86]

Although Hearst and the public ownership he espoused were defeated (749,002 to 691,105), he carried every borough in New York City.

Since Tammany, under the leadership of Charles F. Murphy, sabotaged his campaign, Hearst's ability to carry New York City so convincingly was clearly due primarily to the labor vote.[87]

In both the mayoralty campaign of 1905 and the gubernatorial campaign of 1906, the issue of public ownership aroused more interest than it had in any previous election. In both campaigns, the labor movement supported Hearst, not because it regarded him as a consistent champion of its interests, but because the movements he led at this time gave expression to labor's own demand for public ownership of public utilities.

LABOR AND MUNICIPAL OWNERSHIP: CONCLUSION

In Seattle, Buffalo, Detroit, and other cities, the trade unions were active in the campaign for municipal ownership of public utilities and were affiliated with the Municipal Ownership Leagues in their communities.[88] In Los Angeles, moreover, the trade unions were the leaders in the successful movement for municipal ownership. Early in 1906, union delegates and other interested individuals organized the Public Ownership Party on a platform which stressed, in addition to municipal ownership, direct legislation, free school books, increased educational facilities, and the eight-hour day at fair wages on public works.[89] Although the party was not successful in its 1906 campaign, it made the issue of municipal ownership so important in Los Angeles politics that it was to be raised again and again until it was finally achieved. Trade union activity for the demand was a crucial factor in the eventual outcome. The electrical workers' local, for example, was credited with being largely responsible for the establishment of municipal power and light—"the largest municipally-owned electrical system in the world." "We spoke from soap boxes in the streets," the union declared after the final victory. "We appointed a committee of our members to draw up resolutions asking the Street Railway Commission . . . to appraise the portion of the Southern California Edison Co. that was within the city limits. By dint of hard work, the City Council which was very favorable to us managed to bring this about. . . ."[90]

Paying tribute to organized labor's contribution to the general Progressive impulse through its role in the municipal ownership movement, a New Jersey newspaper declared in April, 1906:

> Involved in the municipal ownership issue is the transcendentally important one of the abolition of privilege, a proposition which concerns the entire

nation. The machines composed of party leaders and the privileged interests have not developed from the nation down through the states and thus to the municipalities. The movement has progressed in just the opposite direction. Local leaders have become state bosses and then, in time, have come to wield a dangerous power through the House committees and the Senate as a whole. Since bossism has followed principally from the endeavor of the corporations to control municipal franchises, it is apparent that municipal ownership is more than a local issue. Hence it is worth noting at this time that the trade unions in many cities have made a significant contribution to the state and national progressive upheaval by their persistent work in the movement for municipal ownership.[91]

Municipal ownership did not succeed in breaking the alliance between corrupt politicians and the powerful business interests. Nor did it strike at the main corporate power in America's economic and political life. Nevertheless, the movement revealed an awakening social awareness on the part of vast numbers of the population and compelled recognition of the principle that, as the Central Federation of New York put it, "public utilities belong to the people, to be used by the people to accommodate the people and not to make money for the few."[92]

LABOR'S PROGRESSIVE PROGRAM

We have already seen enough of organized labor's contributions to conclude that it deserves an important place among the generators of the Progressive movement and a central political role in its development. What did labor accomplish as a result of these contributions? To answer this question, we must first understand that the labor forces combined in their proposals both the demands common to the entire Progressive movement and those specifically applicable to organized labor. This was illustrated as early as 1899 in the platform adopted by the trade unions of Ohio, which raised the demands for the direct primary, the initiative and referendum, public ownership of all public utilities—and for union wages and hours on public work, abolition of the contract labor system, and work for the unemployed. This trend continued. Thus, in 1906, the Central Federated Union of New York drew up a platform which it submitted to the reform forces in the state. It included proposals for direct primaries, the initiative and referendum, direct nomination and election of all candidates, including United States senators, abolition of private ownership of public utilities—and specific labor planks such as amendment of the Sherman Anti-Trust Act and abolition of "government by injunction."[93] In the same year, the Chicago Progressive Alliance, organized by the trade unions of Chicago, demanded the direct primary, initiative and referendum, public ownership of public utilities, equalization of taxation—and abolition of "the abuse of the writ of injunction by certain corporation stalking horses, who have by various devices obtained place on the bench in Federal and State courts."[94] Also in 1906, the Boston Progressive Alliance, organized by the trade unions in that city, adopted a declaration of principles which it determined to require all candidates for local office desiring labor's endorsement to sign. This called for public ownership of steam electric railroads, gas, electric light, and other public services, adoption of laws which would punish bribe takers and bribe givers alike, direct nomination of all candidates by the people "to supersede the present unfair and corrupt methods of nomination by cliques and party bosses," initiative, referendum, and recall, election of United States senators and state and county judges by the people—and

> Recognition of labor organizations in legitimate efforts to regulate wages, working hours and conditions surrounding the employment of wage earners, limitation on the use of injunctions in labor disputes and the enactment of legislation more clearly safeguarding the rights of members of labor organizations as to trial by jury; operation of all public works on union principles, and the equalizing of wages of both sexes in municipal and state employment when performing equal work.[95]

Many of the demands raised by organized labor, in common with other reform groups, were achieved during the Progressive period. By 1915, every state was using the direct primary in some form or other, while at least two-thirds had adopted it on a state-wide basis. By 1912, twenty-nine states had devised methods by which the voters could, in practice, choose United States senators, despite the wording of the federal constitution. The initiative and referendum were accepted by twenty-two states between 1898 and 1918, while the recall spread to a dozen states before the close of the era.[96] In addition, the Progressive period witnessed the institution in many cities of reduced street railway fares, more equalized taxation, better school facilities, public baths, playgrounds, municipal hospitals, medical and dental care, clinics, free meals for underprivileged school children, evening schools, free libraries, and free lectures, and in many states of workman's compensation laws, protective legislation for woman and child labor, and more effective factory inspection laws.[97]

But for Black workers, the benefits derived from these reforms meant very little. The major reforms of the Progressive movement did not take place in the South, where most Blacks were concentrated, and even in the

North, Progressive reformers showed little interest in the special problems facing Blacks, such as job discrimination, inadequate housing and school facilities, etc.[98]* In the main, labor, both organized and unorganized, generally gained from the Progressive programs. But organized labor expected more from the Progressive movement—particularly support for its demands for the right to organize and strike and the outlawing of "government by injunction." Unfortunately, in many states, the trade unionists were not represented in the leadership of the Progressive movement and the agrarian, middle-class, and professional elements who held the leadership were not interested in advancing these specific labor demands. They were prepared to support labor's demands for the enactment of social welfare legislation, and they gave the labor movement invaluable assistance in securing such legislation in states which had never enacted such laws or had failed to enforce those which had been adopted.** But there were clearly defined limits beyond which the Progressives were not willing to go.

This point is well illustrated by what happened in California. There the Progressives learned from bitter experience that they could not afford to ignore the labor forces, and after at first concentrating on moral reform and remaining indifferent to labor and social reform, they began a campaign to include labor issues in their platforms and place labor men on their slates.[99] In 1910, Hiram Johnson was elected governor with the full support of the labor movement, led by the California State Federation of Labor. In previous legislatures, organized labor had failed to achieve its program of labor legislation, but after the election of the Progressive governor, the California State Federation of Labor proposed forty-nine bills to the legislature. Thirty-nine of them were passed by the 1911 legislature, among which were many which had previously failed to obtain passage. These included the "Full-Crew Law," which provided that railroad trains must be properly manned and carry a full crew for safe operation, a law which the Southern Pacific Railroad had theretofore repeatedly succeeded in defeating. Another measure which

*The outstanding exposé of exploitation of and discrimination against Blacks in the South during the Progressive era was the series of articles by Ray Stannard Baker, "Following the Color Line," which appeared in *McClure's Magazine.*

**In Vermont, an alliance of the State Federation of Labor and the Workingmen's Political League, and Progressive reformers secured the enactment of labor legislation for the first time in the state's history, particularly laws protecting woman and child labor through adequate factory inspection. (Winston Allen Flint, *The Progressive Movement in Vermont,* Washington, D. C., 1941, p. 107.) For a somewhat different development in Connecticut, *see* Frederick M. Heath, "Labor and the Progressive Movement in Connecticut," *Labor History,* vol. XII, Winter, 1971, pp. 52-67.

had up to that time been blocked by the railroad's lobbyists provided that railroad employees should not remain on duty for a period of longer than sixteen continuous hours. The "pay-check" law provided for regular payment of laborers in money or its equivalent. Under the old system, employers of unskilled labor had made a practice of issuing "pay-checks" to their men that were redeemable at the pleasure of the employer—if at all. The Sailors' Enticement Law, too, had been previously defeated, but was enacted by the 1911 legislature. It repealed the law which made it a misdemeanor for any person to entice a sailor to leave his ship. Child labor legislation, the protection of electrical workers, an employers' liability act, and an eight-hour law for women were among the other laws passed. Statutes dealing with such issues as workmen's compensation and the establishment of public exchanges were also enacted. In response to labor pressure, a compulsory arbitration bill was defeated. Later, inquiries were authorized into the treatment of working women and children and into the conditions of workers in migrant labor camps.[100]

But defeated were bills that would legalize peaceful picketing and provide jury trials in contempt cases arising out of labor disputes, as well as two labor-endorsed anti-injunction measures. While the labor legislation of the Johnson administration, especially that of the first years, was viewed as representing important victories for organized labor in California, the entire record of the administration revealed that Progressives set distinct limits on the concessions to the labor movement. Employers still retained the ability to weaken labor's right to organize and strike.

Labor had succeeded in convincing the Progressives that they would have to accord a new and important emphasis to the needs and problems of the urban working class. But many Progressive reformers still viewed the trade union movement unsympathetically, lumping the unions with the trusts as twin evils in American society. In keeping with this outlook, they considered the closed shop an expression of the monopolistic power of labor which had to be fought as vigorously as the monopolistic power of the corporations. While the repercussions of the McNamara case undoubtedly moved a number of Progressives to understand that the best way to combat tendencies toward violence in trade union circles was by demonstrating that government could meet the vital needs of the working class, others reacted to the same events by accepting the view that labor and violence were inseparable one from the other, and that unionism had to be curbed.[101]

AFL LEADERSHIP AND THE
PROGRESSIVE MOVEMENT

Although the AFL had helped to initiate and further the demand for direct legislation, its leaders sought to separate this activity from the general Progressive upheaval of the period. Until 1910, Gompers never even mentioned the Progressive movement in connection with the demand for direct legislation. Finally, in the March, 1910 issue of the *American Federationist*, he endorsed the "spirit of democracy" emerging in many of the states in which the Progressives were active and which was resulting in the "initiative, referendum and direct nominations."[102] Actually, however, the AFL leadership showed little interest in the fundamental Progressive doctrine that the powers of government must be expanded for the welfare of the people and that there should be much more extensive legislation than had been enacted up to that time. Government still occupied a minor role in the scheme of things as viewed by the AFL leaders, and they were primarily concerned with those governmental policies and actions which inhibited organization and minimized the economic power of the unions. Their horizon was limited largely to the factory gates, and they were not too concerned with following the workers beyond those gates into their homes and communities. They sought mainly to secure legislative action against governmental obstacles to organization and collective bargaining, emphasizing that once this was secured, the unions, and not the government, would be able to achieve higher wages, shorter hours of work, and better working conditions.[103]

However, it was precisely in those areas that were most important to the AFL leadership that the Progressive reformers did the least work and showed the least interest. To the AFL leadership, this came as no surprise because they had long since concluded that the agrarian and middle-class reformers either had no sympathy with organized labor or did not understand its problems. They could see little benefit to be derived by organized labor from a movement that was cool to the demands for the right to organize and for freedom from "government by injunction."

There were, of course, other reasons for the lack of enthusiasm toward Progressivism in AFL headquarters. By exposing the control of both major parties by big business, the Progressives strengthened the arguments of those labor elements who criticized the Federation's reliance on these very parties in political action. Moreover, the Progressive movement advanced the whole principle of independent political action, since in those communities where neither of the major parties were prepared to incorporate Progressive demands in their platforms, new parties appeared to advance the program. "Golden Rule" Samuel M. Jones voiced the opinion of many Progressives when he wrote to Gompers that "there is no choice for the people between the two old parties."[104]*

Recognizing that organized labor's criticism of the reformers' attitude toward several of its key demands was justified, a number of leaders of the Progressive movement emphasized that the more the labor forces sought to influence the growth of Progressivism, the more they could assure that its program would include these issues. George L. Record, leader of the Progressive forces in New Jersey, called on the AFL to enter the Progressive fold, build a political alliance between organized labor and the reformers, and, by sheer strength of numbers, achieve a dominant influence in the movement. "The toiler, who has the votes, should have the government," he declared in an appeal to the AFL in April, 1908. "Ten years of government by such men as you have in your labor bodies all over the country would bring about the millennium. Now get busy and organize your forces." Once this was done, he predicted, the unions "could have everything they wanted politically."[105]

This was only one of many appeals directed to the AFL by those Progressive leaders who understood the importance of achieving close and cordial relations between organized labor and the reformers. Samuel M. Jones wrote to Gompers: "If the cause of human liberty, which is the cause, as I understand it, of organized labor, can be advanced by aiding the work we are doing in Ohio, I will be much gratified to have you openly endorse it and even help it along with a few speeches."[106] "It would be most helpful to us," Tom Johnson wrote to Gompers from Cleveland, "if you would publicize what we are doing, and, if you can spare the time, come here to address meetings of unions in behalf of the cause."[107] From Mayor Dunne of Chicago, Gompers received an appeal urging him to address meetings being held to support the municipal ownership program. "We expect to have thousands of your members at these meetings," Dunne wrote, "and it will be most helpful to our effort to compel adherence to the will of the voters expressed at the last election in favor of municipalization of the street car system."[108]

Gompers remained silent on these requests. But in a pamphlet written

*Gompers was suspicious of many reform organizations on the ground that they were sponsored by advocates of independent political action. He was cold to the American Association for Labor Legislation, even though he served as a nominal vice-president for a number of years, regarding it as made up of intellectual "third party agitators." (*American Federationist,* June, 1915, p. 430.)

by a Toledo business man to discredit Mayor Jones and public owner-ship in Ohio, Gompers underscored the following paragraph as repre-senting his own thinking:

> The full grown workingman is no baby—no ward of the state. What he wants is just laws and a fair show. That granted, he can take care of himself, and only in case of such disaster as no economic system can provide against, will he have occasion to ask alms of anybody. He needs not more govern-ment, but less.

With this approach, Gompers indicated in his pencilled comments in the margin next to the printed paragraph, "I am in full agreement."[109]

In the summer of 1910, it will be remembered, the Labor Party of Arizona was organized to give effective expression to labor's demand that the constitution drawn up for that state would be a progressive document. Its program of twenty-seven demands, as we have seen, represented one of the most advanced platforms of the entire Progressive movement. In a memorandum to the AFL Executive Council, Secretary Frank Morrison condemned the Labor Party and its platform as repre-senting a dangerous trend that had to be combatted—"the tendency to depend upon the government for all types of assistance, which if allowed to grow will sap the self-reliant spirit of the American working class. When you take into consideration the moving spirit of the new Labor Party are Socialists, its program is not surprising.* But certainly legiti-mate trade unionists should have nothing to do with this type of program."[110]

Fortunately, the majority of legitimate American trade unionists in the cities and states were shaping such programs throughout the Pro-gressive era. Unlike the AFL leadership, they had reached the conclu-sion that the government must be freed from the influence of big business and that its powers must be extended to serve the social and economic needs of the people. They sought to effectuate these aims by participat-ing actively in the Progressive movement, both as initiators of numerous Progressive demands and as a powerful force, together with other reform groups, in the campaign to reshape America in a progressive image.

---

*Actually, although there were Socialist trade unionists at the convention which organized the Labor Party of Arizona, the majority were not Socialists. Furthermore, the Socialist Party of Arizona nominated its own ticket for delegates to the Constitutional Convention. (Arizona *Republican*, Aug. 25, 26, 1910.) The national leadership of the Socialist Party not only did not support the Arizona Labor Party but tried to do everything possible to prevent its growth. Job Harriman was asked by the Socialist Party National Executive Committee to go to Arizona and help destroy the newly-formed labor party there and thus avert "the formation of a labor party as a rival to the Socialist Party." ("Minutes of the *Weekly Bulletin*, September 3, 1910.)

CHAPTER 4

The Political Policies and Practices of the AFL, 1910–1912

Starting in the cities, the Progressive movement surged outward to the states and the national government, where a long period of struggle ensued between the "Progressives" and reactionary "stand-patters." By 1910, the Progressive movement was at full tide across the entire country, demanding effective legislation to democratize governmental machinery and for economic and social reform.

PROGRESSIVES IN CONGRESS

In Congress, the reform forces fought to break the reactionary blockade that had been erected against all progressive legislation. During the first session of the 61st Congress, from March to August, 1909, the AFL once again concentrated on its anti-injunction campaign. However, since Cannon and the Republican Old Guard still had a firm grip on the machinery of Congressional appointments, these bills ended up on the legislative scrap heap. Meanwhile, the insurgent Republicans of the Taft administration, led by La Follette of Wisconsin, Norris of Nebraska, Cummins and Dolliver of Iowa, Beveridge of Indiana, and Fowler of New Jersey, launched a revolt against the Old Guard's dictation. Together with progressive Democrats, including the twelve union-card-holding congressmen, they conducted a fight in both houses of Congress for tariff reform, a graduated income tax, conservation, postal savings, and more stringent regulation of railroads. While organized labor was interested in most of these issues,[1] for it, the most significant battle waged by the Progressives was the campaign to overthrow "Cannonism"—the dictatorial rule of the House of Representatives by Speaker Joseph Cannon.

In 1909, about twenty of the leading insurgents met in Gompers' office and agreed upon the changes in the rules for which they would press in the special session of Congress. The prinicipal provision was that any member of the House might move to discharge a committee from further consideration of a bill, that such motions must be recognized in the order in which they were entered, and that they could be adopted by majority vote. This effort was defeated at the time, but in the second session of the 61st Congress, in March, 1910, the long-contested war against the Speaker's despotic control over procedure and committee appointments was carried to a successful conclusion. A combination of Democrats and insurgent Republicans put through a resolution, introduced by George W. Norris of Nebraska, enlarging the Committee on Rules, providing for the election of the committee by the House, and excluding the Speaker from membership. Although Cannon retained the office—a motion to declare the speakership vacant failed—his power was considerably reduced.[2]

On June 17, 1910, House Resolution 808 was passed, marking an important victory for the Progressive forces, especially for organized labor, against the abuse of smothering bills in committee. It provided, as did the earlier proposal, that any member could make a motion to discharge any committee from further consideration of a bill, and that such motions had to be recognized in the order in which they were received. If the motion prevailed, this automatically brought the bill before the House, where it could be debated and voted on.[3] Unfortunately, the resolution was passed too late in the session to be of much value until the next session of Congress convened.

Organized labor did not immediately obtain any concrete results from the new atmosphere in Congress. The committees appointed by Cannon were still functioning, still refusing to advance the bills advocated by the labor movement, and still opposing all efforts to report out a bill granting relief from the injunction abuse. Toward the end of the session, the AFL conceived a new method of getting around the Republican blockade. The twelve union-card-holding congressmen, known as the "Labor Group" in Congress, met with Gompers and Morrison,[4] and thereafter, William Hughes of New Jersey, a member of the group, introduced a rider to the Civil Supply Bill which provided funds for anti-trust prosecutions by the federal government under the Sherman Act. This rider prohibited the use of these funds for "the prosecution of any organization or individual for entering into any combination or agreement having in view the increasing of wages, shortening of hours, or bettering the conditions of labor, or for any act done in furtherance thereof *not in itself unlawful.*"

On June 4, 1910, the bill, with the rider included, passed the House. In the Senate, however, it was amended by striking out the Hughes amendment. When the bill, as amended by the Senate, was returned to the House, all the Senate amendments were disapproved by unanimous consent and the measure went to a conference committee. Finally, on June 23, the Hughes rider came to a vote in the House and was rejected by a vote of 138 to 130, with 105 congressmen not voting. It was subsequently revealed that it was the National Association of Manufacturers' lobby that had maneuvered to achieve this outcome. "Colonel" Mulhall, the chief NAM lobbyist, had succeeded in getting thirteen congressmen—Democrats and Republicans—either to vote against the Hughes amendment or to stay away from the House when the vote was taken, and this margin was sufficient to defeat the rider.[5] "No action of Congress nor any vote ever taken in Congress," Gompers commented bitterly, "has shown such a transparent disregard for the rights and welfare of the workers as this record vote displays for all the world to see." He sought some comfort in the assurance that "The defeat of the Hughes amendment will serve to more thoroughly arouse the workers to the absolute necessity of a more active, intelligent and united action on the political field."[6]

SENTIMENT FOR INDEPENDENT POLITICAL ACTION

The truth is, even though Gompers refused to recognize it, that many workers had already come to the conclusion that the only way to achieve a "more active, intelligent and united action on the political field" was by abandoning the policy of begging the major parties for concessions and fighting for labor's just demands through its own political party. On February 11, 1910, the Central Federated Union of New York, the AFL's city central labor body, went on record in favor of a labor party after hearing Delegate Morris Braun of the Cigarmakers' Union declare, in a fiery speech, that the time had come for such action. "I am tired of being assessed continually to try to get legislation passed in the interests of the working class," he declared, "and when we get it we find that it is either a trick bill or not enforced at all. I am tired of bending the cringing knee before the lawmakers of capital, and begging them for mercy. Petitioning will only get us kicks or promises—that and nothing more." He pointed to the Taff-Vale decision in England and told how the courts of that country had decided that it was a crime to strike or boycott. "What was its effect?" asked Braun. "It simply taught the workers that lobbying on the outside of the house of Parliament would avail them nothing. They stopped lobbying and walked into the house and passed laws in their own interests for themselves." And he concluded:

> We have had enough tomfoolery in this country. We should learn to send men of our class to the House of Congress, and make laws for ourselves. Then you will get what you want. I am therefore in favor of calling on the president of the American Federation of Labor to urge the holding of a conference of all the national and international presidents of the various unions of this country, affiliated with that body, to take up the matter of forming an Independent Labor Party.

The vote on the motion was taken, and the delegates voted over-whelmingly in favor of the proposal.[7] A few weeks later, the Chicago Federation of Labor passed a similar resolution and came out strongly for a labor party.[8] And in Philadelphia, the unions affiliated with the AFL took the initiative in March, 1910 in organizing a state-wide labor party. The action flowed out of the general strike in Philadelphia, when all the AFL unions walked out to support the cause of the car men who had struck when the Rapid Transit Company discharged 173 union members.* The strikebreaking role of the city and state governments, acting as open agents of the corporations, aroused the trade unionists to the need to use their political as well as economic power. As one group of unionists put it:

> It is the duty of labor to see to it that the votes of labor are no longer cast for the kind of men who are prepared and who are willing to sell the interests of labor and of all who put them into office as soon as they obtain the coveted goal, and who give to corporations the power to abuse the privileges granted them by the people. Labor should vote its own men into office. If it does not, it has only itself to blame for the consequences.[9]

On March 24, at a meeting of delegates from all the trade unions of Philadelphia, the United Labor Party was born. A month later, a platform was adopted and plans were set up to establish organization in every part of the state. Pennsylvania's independent political party of labor, organized by the AFL unions, urged ballot reform; the initiative and referendum; equal suffrage for men and women regardless of race; municipal and government ownership of public utilities; a graduated income tax; an inheritance tax; postal savings bank and parcel post systems; equal wages for women performing the same work as men;

*The Philadelphia general strike of 1910 is discussed below.

government ownership of railroads; the curtailment of writs of injunction; the abolition of trusts; direct election of United States senators; abolition of strikebreaking and of the state constabulary; the enforcement of the state's eight-hour day law; the abolition of laws restraining free speech and press; and the enactment of new laws to improve working conditions in the state.[10]

On August 15, 1910, the Central Labor Federation of New York City officially announced the establishment of an independent labor party to be called the Federated Labor Party of New York City. The Party's platform included provisions for impartial enforcement of the state's eight-hour laws; a child labor law; a compulsory education law; an employers' liability and compensation law; municipal ownership of public utilities; the establishment of postal savings banks; enactment of an anti-injunction law by Congress; a national eight-hour law; the direct election of United States senators, the president, and all judicial officials; and the extension of employers' liability and compensation laws to include all forms of employment.[11]

But the rising tide of labor sentiment for independent political action made little impression on the national leaders of the AFL. The "reward-your-friend-and-punish-your-enemy" policy, Frank Morrison declared in a public interview, was still labor's best political weapon: "It has accomplished a great deal. Our influence in the national lawmaking body is gradually but surely increasing." The Congressional elections of 1910, he predicted, would see far-reaching results for the AFL's political action program. "We have nearly 1,500 district organizers in the country and the machinery in all of the districts necessary to put this political action program into effect."[12]

THE ELECTION OF 1910

However, the AFL did little in the Congressional elections beyond publicizing the voting records of the congressmen on the Hughes amendment. It circulated more than a quarter of a million copies of an eight-page booklet entitled "Record Vote of Congressmen For and against Labor," which listed the votes in the House for and against the Hughes amendment. It detailed the names of all House members and how they had voted and recorded those who voted for the amendment as having "voted for labor's rights," and thereby merited labor's support in the election; those who voted against it were recorded as having "voted against labor's rights," and therefore should be defeated. A "satisfactory explanation to their constituents" was demanded from those who were listed as "not voting."

Several other pieces of literature went out from AFL headquarters to all parts of the country prior to the election. In the main, they were appeals to all workers to vote and mentioned neither political party. The final appeal, dated November 2, simply urged the workers "to be partisan to a principle, rather than to a party. Stand by those who have done their duty; be always everlastingly alert, so that all may say that labor knows its political as well as its economic duty."[13]

So innocuous and meaningless was the advice offered to workers by the AFL leadership in the 1910 campaign that even some of the more conservative elements in the Federation were disgusted. One sign of this was the publication during the campaign of a series of articles by Arthur Henderson, chairman of the British Labor Party, in the *International Molders' Journal,* edited by John P. Frey. The articles stressed the fact that the conditions that had led British labor to form its own party were similar to those facing American labor and pointed out the gains achieved by the British trade unions as a result of this independent political action. Henderson emphasized that the British trade unions had gone into politics as an independent force after the infamous Taff-Vale decision, under which the railway employees and miners were mulcted out of a total of $840,000 in damage suits, and he referred to the Danbury Hatters' suits as the same type of oppression* that could only be met effectively by similar action. The articles were reprinted in a number of trade unions and prompted the Socialist Cleveland *Citizen* to ask if the Molders' Union would have its "charter revoked or be reorganized and policed by a Federation organizer" for having so vigorously challenged the AFL's traditional political policy.[14]

The Seattle *Union Record,* official organ of that city's Central Labor Council, not only publicized Henderson's articles, but featured a series entitled "Labor Parties of the Past," which told the story of independent political action by American workers from the 1870s to the twentieth century. The study took issue with the AFL's repeated assertion that

*In its decision in the Danbury Hatters' case, delivered on February 3, 1908, the Supreme Court unanimously declared that the Sherman Anti-Trust Act applied to organizations of labor, and that the Lowe Company of Danbury, Connecticut could sue the United Hatters of North America for three times the amount of damage it had suffered by reason of the union's boycott of the company's products. Judgment of $240,000 was obtained against the members of the union in 1909, and the Supreme Court gave it its approval, ordering a collection of the full amount with additional penalties and interest. (For the history of the case, *see* Philip S. Foner, *History of the Labor Movement in the United States,* vol. III, New York, 1964, pp. 39, 309-10, 313-14, 341-42.)

past labor movements in this country had declined immediately after venturing into politics, and especially into independent political activity. It contended that when the labor movement had conducted its political activity without, at the same time, neglecting the economic struggles, it had prospered, and that its decline was the result of a failure to organize industrially, thus isolating itself from the workers. The study was sharply critical of the current AFL political policy. It conceded that events in the industrial area had compelled the AFL to retreat from its long-standing opposition to "political action by unions," and to advocate that "its members take part in politics." This was certainly advance, it agreed, but it would net labor very little so long as the AFL continued to rely on the two major political parties:

> That kind of politics will never produce a party that can be relied on by labor.... What is needed is what the workers of Great Britain have achieved: a labor party, organized on a permanent basis and financed by the trade unions, through which labor can elect a group of Congressmen and legislators that represent the workingmen, and know to whom they owe their election and why.[15]

These discussions in the trade union press, like the actions by AFL unions in New York, Chicago, and Pennsylvania that same year, revealed how much more politically alert the Federation's members on the city and state levels were than the national leadership. Although the AFL Executive Council did nothing in the campaign beyond publicizing the voting records of congressmen and urging the membership to vote, for which it spent a total of $3,148.78,[16] many affiliated unions worked closely with the insurgent Republicans and Democrats to defeat Old Guard candidates.[17]

The election returns in 1910 were more heartening for labor than those of 1906 and 1908. Many reactionary Republicans were defeated, and, for the first time in over a decade, the Democrats obtained a majority in the House of Representatives. The House elected in November, 1910 was made up of 299 Democrats and 160 Republicans. Fifteen members of the House held paid-up union cards of membership—eleven Democrats, three Republicans, and one Socialist.[18]

LABOR VICTORIES

On the eve of the opening session of the 62nd Congress, on March 4, 1911, the press headlined the startling news that Samuel Gompers had issued a warning that unless labor's demands were now realized, a political party of the workers would arise in the United States. He directed this warning at the Democratic Party, stating: "Unless the Democratic Party shall take hold of the interests of the masses, as against the interests of the classes, wherever they clash, it is not going to be the party of the future for the mass of the people. I feel that the time has come when we shall have a constructive, progressive, radical labor party, unless the Democratic Party shall perform its duties."[19] In a letter to the AFL Executive Council on March 3, 1911, Gompers explained the reasons for the statement which must have alarmed most of that body's members. The organized workers, he pointed out, had engaged in a long period of agitation in political campaigns and before Congress for redress of labor's grievances. They had, in the main, followed the advice of the AFL to avoid the pitfall of an independent political party and had concentrated on the policy of rewarding labor's "friends" and punishing its "enemies." But thus far, they had reaped few gains from this procedure. Still, they had held on to the hope that once the Old Guard Republicans—the main political enemy of labor—were defeated and the Democratic Party gained control of Congress, the long years of agitation would finally produce results. "Now," he added, "if, after the victory in the Congressional elections of last autumn, the Democrats do not act, it will be almost impossible to prevent the dissatisfaction with the old parties from expressing itself in a great demand for a radical labor party. By pointing this out to the Democrats before the new session of Congress begins, we can make them understand that they can prevent this new party from rising by proving that there is no need for it."[20] Up to this point, Gompers had been able to head off the demand for a labor party by maneuvers and bureaucratic control, but the movement was achieving such a magnitude that he needed the assistance of the Democratic Party.

Gompers' warning was not lost on the Democrats, who were also aware of the sentiment for independent political action in the labor movement and knew that they would be the chief losers in the event of the formation of a labor party. With the change of the political complexion of the House of Representatives, the long reign of Speaker Cannon was ended. (He was replaced by Champ Clark of Missouri, whom Gompers considered a true friend of organized labor.) The new chairman of the labor committee, "in which the labor movement was intensely interested,"[21] was William B. Wilson, former secretary-treasurer of the United Mine Workers, while three other trade unionists were also assigned to that body. For the first time in labor's memory, the committee reported speedily and favorably to the House proposals curtailing the application of the Sherman Act to unions and the use of injunctions in labor disputes. By May 6, six bills had been introduced into the House providing for trial by jury in contempt cases growing out of labor disputes.[22]

By the time the 62nd Congress had completed its session on March 3, 1913, more legislation in which labor was interested had been enacted than during any previous Congress. The AFL listed twenty-seven measures in which it had been interested which had become laws during this session. The major setback was in the area of legislation exempting labor organizations from prosecution under the Sherman Anti-Trust Act. A bill to accomplish this was passed by both houses of Congress, but it was vetoed by President Taft, who denounced it as class legislation of the most vicious type. The House passed the bill over Taft's veto, but before it could come up in the Senate, the 62nd Congress had expired.

Even though labor's most important demand still remained unfulfilled, the AFL was jubilant. Gompers felt that his warning to the Democratic Party had brought results and that the political policies inaugurated by the Federation in 1906 had been justified. The fear of a labor party had been greatly reduced. "Labor's efforts have been rewarded by effective and tangible results," Gompers said gleefully. "The future looks bright. . . ."[23]

There were other reasons for rejoicing. One was the unanimous decision of the U. S. Circuit Court of Appeals on April 10, 1911, reversing the judgment of the lower court in the Danbury Hatters' case. A month later, the Supreme Court ruled in the contempt cases against Gompers, Mitchell, and Morrison, by reversing Judge Wright's decision and dismissing the case.* This victory, however, was tempered by the court's ruling that although there were not sufficient grounds for Justice Wright's action, the men could still be punished for contempt by proper proceedings. "Thus it seems that there has been a considerable number of premature congratulatory messages sent," Gompers wrote to the Executive Council on May 17, 1911.[24] As we shall see, Gompers' words of caution were justified.

---

*On December 23, 1908, Judge Daniel T. Wright found Gompers, Mitchell, and Morrison guilty of contempt in refusing to abide by the injunction issued in the case of the boycott of the Bucks' Stove and Range Company. Morrison was sentenced to six months in the United States jail in the District of Columbia, Mitchell to nine months, and Gompers to ten months. For the details of the Bucks' Stove and Range Company case and the sentencing of the three AFL leaders, see Philip S. Foner, *History of the Labor Movement in the United States,* vol. III, pp. 338-42, 361-63.

A further cause for rejoicing lay in the amount of labor legislation passed in various states during 1911. Legislation on employers' liability, child labor, the eight-hour workday for women, workmen's compensation, improved conditions in hazardous trades, and the abolition of convict labor were passed in California, North Carolina, Kansas, Vermont, New Jersey, Massachusetts, and other states.[25] The AFL *Weekly News Letter* emphasized that the trade unionists had played an important part in securing these laws. On April 22, 1911, it reported: The trade unionists of this country are becoming live to the influence which they can assert along legislative lines."

At the same time, however, the AFL went to great pains to make it clear that nothing that had happened in 1911 had caused it to change its belief that political action should occupy a minor place in the scheme of the labor movement. On the eve of the 1912 presidential campaign, and at the very peak of the general "progressive temper," Gompers hammered away at "the fact that the well-being of the wage workers . . . has been promoted more by union activity than by any legislation thus far accomplished"—a fact which none of the critics of the AFL's political program would have denied—and insisted that organized labor must continue to set minimum political objectives, such as legislation limiting governmental policies and acts which inhibited organization and restricted the economic power of the unions. Referring to the growth in progressive sentiment in favor of increased social legislation, Gompers warned the AFL membership not to "be deluded by fanciful political programs that assume to transport the labor movement to some Utopian land of promise. Strive for the better day *today*. Material and actual results constitute the ethics of trade unionists."[26]

This sentiment was voiced at a time of increasing agitation throughout the nation on the part of pressure movements by labor and general reform groups for housing laws, child labor laws, minimum wage and hours laws, for a living wage for workers which would provide enough to secure education and recreation, for the maintenance of families during periods of illness and old age, for safe and sanitary homes in healthful surroundings, for workmen's compensation for victims of industrial accidents and diseases, and for social insurance to cover old age and unemployment. But the AFL leaders still clung to the issues they had raised years earlier. The national leadership was still thinking in terms of 1906, while the majority of the membership was engaged in achieving a labor program that was far in advance of the earlier platform and more in keeping with the broader needs of the working class.

THE NATIONAL CONVENTIONS OF 1912

The specific demands submitted by the AFL to the major parties for incorporation into their 1912 platforms differed only slightly from those spelled out in Labor's "Bill of Grievances" of 1906. They were: (1) exemption of unions from the anti-trust laws; (2) prohibition of labor injunctions and the guarantee of trial by jury in contempt cases; (3) restriction of the sale of convict-made goods; (4) restriction on immigration; (5) guarantee of the right to quit work and provision of adequate safety measures for seamen; (6) the creation of a separate department of labor of cabinet rank; (7) guarantee of the right of petition for federal workers; (8) legislation providing workmen's compensation for government employees; and (9) the demand for a constitutional amendment to be submitted for ratification by the states for the "absolute suffrage of women co-equal with men."[27]

The AFL showed no concern for the broader social programs which various labor groups and reformers in general were seeking to incorporate into the party platforms. At the National Conference of Social Work held in Cleveland in June, 1912, a number of labor leaders joined political reformers and social workers in presenting a report which was to be submitted to the major political conventions. This report stressed the need for governmental regulation of substandard working and living conditions and set forth a "platform of social standards" which included demands for the establishment of an eight-hour day and six-day week, with special standards of work for women and children; the establishment of decent standards of sanitation, health, and safety in industry, with compensation for injury; decent housing for every family; prohibition of child labor under 16 years of age; regulation of factory work for women; government aid to the unemployed; old age and unemployment insurance; and a living wage for all "who devote their time and energy to industrial occupations."[28] The AFL paid no attention to this far-reaching social program for American labor. In addition, the significant comments by the AFL leadership and the *American Federationist* on the platforms of the major parties dealt almost exclusively with their declarations on the labor injunction and contempt proceedings. In outlining the AFL's political program for the year, the Executive Council once again emphasized the fact that labor's essential gains in the future would primarily be, as they had been in the past, the product of economic action. Labor, it declared, did not expect nor want more from government in the form of ameliorative functions than to be allowed to operate without restrictions on the economic front.[29]

Of the nine proposals submitted by the AFL Executive Council, through Gompers, the Republican Party would pledge itself only to a workmen's compensation act, an act to restrict immigration, and one ending the involuntary servitude of seamen. It made a particular point of rejecting the demands to amend the Sherman Anti-Trust Act and limit the issuance of injunctions in labor disputes, reaffirming its intention of upholding at all times, the authority and dignity of the courts, both state and federal, and their powers to enforce their processes and protect life, liberty, and property, which, it affirmed, must be preserved inviolate.[30] The AFL had not expected any significant action on labor's demands from the Republican Party and had simply gone through the motion of presenting them for the sake of the record. Therefore, the labor planks adopted by the 1912 Republican convention in Chicago, where the Old Guard was in full control, as well as its renomination of Taft as the Republican standard bearer, came as no surprise.[31]

Gompers appeared next before the Platform Committee of the Democratic National Convention in Baltimore to present labor's demands. He informed the committee that he was speaking not only for the two million organized workers, but "also for the workers who are not members of labor unions." (It was a common practice for Gompers to claim to speak for the vast body of unorganized workers on political matters, even when the AFL was doing little to bring them into the trade unions.) Gompers reminded the Platform Committee that for thirty years he had not been identified with any political party, that he had been a Republican during his early manhood, but that "for more than twenty years I could not play with them. It seemed to me that they did not play fair with the masses of our people." It was now necessary for the Democratic Party, he asserted, to prove that it was the party, "not merely in declaration, not merely mouthing the sentences, but in truth representing the great mass of our people as against predatory wealth, as against the combinations of those who own the land and control the machinery and the products of labor.... We have gone to the Republican Party with these requests and they have turned a deaf ear to us."[32] But, significantly, Gompers did not repeat his warning of the previous year that "the time has come when we shall have a constructive, progressive, radical labor party, unless the Democratic Party shall perform its duty." The AFL leaders had already made up their minds that the Federation would support the Democratic Party, and so they felt no need to play with fire by raising the specter of a labor party.[33]

The Democratic platform pointed with pride to the legislation of interest to labor that had been passed by the House of Representatives, under the Party's control, during the Congressional session that began in March, 1911. It then reaffirmed its labor planks of 1908 which pledged the Party to enact legislation exempting labor unions from prosecution under the Sherman Anti-Trust Act; limiting the use of injunctions in labor disputes; creating an independent department of labor in the Cabinet; and strengthening and extending the operation of the civil service laws. The most important sentence in the labor plank read:

> That there should be no abridgement of the right of the wage earners and producers to organize for the protection of wages, and the improvement in labor conditions, to the end that such organizations and their members should not be regarded as illegal combinations in restraint of trade.[34]

Gompers came to the Democratic convention determined to line up support for the nomination of Champ Clark of Missouri as the presidential candidate, and he urged William Jennings Bryan to get behind the Speaker of the House, who, as indicated above, was considered by the AFL to be a friend of organized labor.[35] The AFL regarded the move to nominate Woodrow Wilson, governor of New Jersey, as the Democratic standard bearer with a notable lack of enthusiasm. In February, 1912, AFL trade unionists in Des Moines, Iowa had sent a long memorandum to the Executive Council urging it to support Clark as the Democratic presidential candidate and particularly to oppose Wilson's nomination. It called attention to the reactionary, anti-labor views Wilson had expressed prior to his election as governor of New Jersey. It pointed out that in his *History of the American People,* he had denounced the railroad strikers of 1877, had condemned the Pullman Strike of 1894 and praised President Cleveland's action in breaking the strike, had attributed the violence in strikes to foreign agitators who had brought their doctrines to America and had infected American workingmen with them, had referred to the immigrants from Southern Europe as being "even less desirable than the Chinese," and had deplored the "dictation of labor organizations." The Iowa unionists also stressed the fact that Wilson was in the good graces of the House of Morgan, as indicated by the fact that his candidacy was being boomed by *Harper's Weekly,* which was controlled by J. P. Morgan. They pointed out that his criticism of Bryan, his expressed hope that something might be done "to knock Mr. Bryan once and for all into a cocked hat," and his reference to the supporters of Bryan as the "alien element"—all showed him to be clearly unworthy of labor's support.[36]

There was considerable substance to these charges, even though they did not tell the whole story of Wilson's relations with organized labor prior to his being considered for the Democratic presidential nomination. In the main, his treatment of labor in this multi-volume *History of the American People*, published in 1902, was, as one historian has noted, "very conservative."[37] He did condemn the great railroad strikes and declared that such struggles had to be crushed by "sheer authority"; he did praise Cleveland's strikebreaking role in the Pullman Strike; he did slander the immigrants from Southern Europe, and attribute strike violence exclusively to the work of "foreign agitators," while ignoring the force and violence used by employers to smash the labor movement.[38] But he also attributed the growth of the trade union movement to the concentration of capital in the hands of "small groups of men who seemed to be in a position to control at their leisure the productive industries of the country"—a development which forced "the workingmen of the industrial East . . . to organize themselves for the protection and advancement of their own special interests."[39] He also criticized court actions against the right to organize, noting that " . . . the courts were forced to execute, sometimes very harshly, the law against conspiracy, fitting formulas originated in an age gone by to circumstances more difficult to form their judgments upon than any a past age had produced."[40] In general, Wilson revealed in his *History* that he regarded both capital and labor as threats to the traditional American liberty and freedom, and that of the two groups, he regarded the trade unions as the greater menace since they were dominated by "class interests" and engaged in violence.[41]

In 1902, Wilson was elected president of Princeton University, and while his role in attempting to abolish the exclusive fraternity cliques gained him a reputation as a liberal reformer, his attitude toward organized labor during his university presidency caused him to be viewed as a supporter of the open shop. In his "Credo," published in 1907, and again in his 1909 address to the Princeton graduating class, he placed himself on record against trade unions on the grounds that they were injurious to the best interests of individual workers. "The labor of America," he told the Princeton graduates as he concluded his vicious attack on organized labor, "is rapidly becoming unprofitable under its present regulation by those who have determined to reduce it to a minimum. Our economic supremacy may be lost because the country grows more and more full of unprofitable servants."[42] In the same year, in reply to an invitation to speak at a banquet of the Anti-Boycott Association, he wrote: "I am a fierce partisan of the Open Shop and of everything that makes for individual liberty."[43]

These statements endeared Wilson to the conservative Democratic businessmen, many of whom were his intimate friends, who were grooming him for governor of New Jersey as the first step on the road to the White House.[44] (Wilson himself later conceded that he had obtained all his information about trade unions from "those who do employ labor on a large scale.")[45] But organized labor in New Jersey did not share the enthusiasm of the business groups for the Princeton University president, and when he was proposed in 1910 as Democratic candidate for governor, the labor movement in the state opposed his nomination. Branding him as the "tool or agent of Wall Street interests," and as a man who had "publicly shown his antagonism to organized labor," the State Federation of Labor urged "every trade unionist and wage earner in the State of New Jersey to oppose his nomination, and if nominated by the interests of Wall Street, to do their utmost to defeat him and teach the financial interests of Wall Street, New York that the honest voters and trades unionists of the State of New Jersey are perfectly capable of selecting their own Governor."[46]

"Evidently," Wilson wrote to George Harvey, "the cue is to be to ... quote me as the enemy of organized labor; but no doubt I could take care of myself on those heads if nominated with the proper unanimity."[47] His method of "taking care of himself," after his nomination, was to claim that he had been misrepresented. In a public statement, he declared:

> I have always been the warm friend of organized labor. It is in my opinion, not only perfectly legitimate, but absolutely necessary that labor should organize if it is to secure justice from organized capital, and obtain legislation that will impose full legal responsibility upon the employer for his treatment of his employees and for their protection against accident, to secure just and adequate wages, and to put reasonable limits upon the working day ... for there is a sense in which the condition of labor is the condition of the nation itself.
> . . .
> I am much more afraid that the great corporations, combinations, and trusts will do the country deep harm than I am that labor organizations will harm it.[48]

But the New Jersey trade unionists were not impressed, and the secretary of the State Federation of Labor announced sarcastically that "the fact that Wilson was seeking the governorship accounted for his rapid change of heart."[49]

Handbills flooded the state quoting from Wilson's Baccalaureate Address of 1909, in which he had attacked the "restrictive practices of unions." On the other hand, the pro-labor acts of Wilson's Republican opponent, Vivian M. Lewis, were extolled, and the leaflets, distributed in bulk to the trade unions for circulation among their members, told the laboring man to vote for Lewis.[50] Wilson sought to counter this effective Republican campaign strategy by repeating over and over that he was a true friend of organized labor whose views had been misrepresented; that he had only criticized certain phases of trade union activity, and was certain that organized labor wanted this kind of friend rather than a hypocritical endorser of everything it did. He proposed that a workable employers' liability law be enacted—"one that would work without being worked."* A good workmen's compensation law was a key demand of the New Jersey trade unions.[51]

The State Federation of Labor, however, stood by its resolution. In a statement to the press, the Executive Council called upon the workers in the state to "abide by the resolution adopted by the State Federation of Labor opposing the candidacy of Woodrow Wilson for Governor."[52] But Wilson did succeed in winning over a section of the labor vote as a result of his campaign activity and pledges. In any event, he certainly went to the governor's mansion with a better understanding of the labor movement and its significance in politics.[53]

Wilson's fight against bossism in New Jersey during his administration as governor made him a national figure. As far as labor specifically was concerned, he kept his pledge to enact a forward-looking workmen's compensation act, and he also supported fifteen other measures proposed by the New Jersey State Federation of Labor. These included a fire escape law, a child labor law, a law regulating employment agencies, and a factory inspection law.[54] However, he refused to sign the amendments to one of his "seven sister" anti-trust bills exempting trade unions and farmers' organizations from prosecution as conspiracies in unreasonable restraint of trade, a stand which, in the eyes of the national AFL, was more important in evaluating his presidential prospects from the standpoint of organized labor than his support of social legislation.[55] As far as Gompers was concerned, Wilson's opposition to these amendments, along with his earlier views on organized labor, indicated that "he did not understand labor problems" and was not suited to occupy the White House.[56]

However, the New Jersey Federation of Labor did not share Gom-

---

*In his inaugural address as governor, Wilson explained what he meant by this expression: "We must have a workingman's compensation act which will not put upon him the burden of fighting powerful composite employers to obtain his rights, but which will give him his rights without suit directly, and without contest, by automatic operation of law, as if a law of insurance." (Newark *Evening News*, Jan. 18, 1911.)

pers' views and, aware that the AFL Executive Council was campaigning for Champ Clark, it adopted a resolution declaring that because efforts were being made to place Wilson in a "false position as to his attitude towards organized labor . . . organized labor would be derelict in its duty if it allowed to pass this opportunity to show appreciation for services rendered the workers of New Jersey." Then, after listing the benefits it had received under Wilson, the resolution concluded by commending him "for his unremitting and untiring efforts in assisting to bring about better conditions for the wage earners of New Jersey...." Printed in pamphlet form, this resolution was distributed to all the delegates at the Democratic convention and helped to bring about Wilson's nomination on the 46th ballot, thus ending the longest balloting at any Democratic convention since the Civil War.[57]

Although Wilson's nomination was a disappointment to Gompers,[58] the AFL endorsement of the Democratic Party would have followed automatically had not the situation been complicated by the unexpected appearance on the political scene of a third party—the Progressive Party.

The new party movement emerged out of an attempt long in preparation by the insurgent Republicans to bring about the nomination of a progressive Republican candidate to succeed Taft. Senate Robert M. La Follette was the initial leader of this insurgent group, but by the end of 1911, to La Follette's surprise and chagrin, the leadership of the movement was taken over by ex-President Theodore Roosevelt. With the country on the verge of rebellion against the *status quo* in the political and economic life of the nation, Roosevelt, who did not underestimate the extent of the industrial and agrarian unrest, set out to adjust the Republican Party to the changed economic conditions and thus keep the unrest from flowing into more radical channels.[59] As the election of 1912 approached, he abandoned support of his old protegé, Taft, and threw his hat in the ring for the Republican presidential nomination. Roosevelt secured the support of most of the delegates from those states in which primary elections were held, but Taft, who controlled the Party machinery, was supported by a majority of the delegates from the states which selected delegates by the usual boss-dominated methods. There were, however, 252 contested seats, and if these cases had been decided in Roosevelt's favor, he would have won the nomination. But they were not, and when the Republican convention decided them in Taft's favor, Roosevelt announced plans for the formation of a new party. At a special convention held in August, 1912, the new third party was launched as the Progressive ("Bull Moose") Party with Roosevelt as its presidential candidate.

Although the Progressive platform called for a wide range of reforms relating to government (such as the direct primary and the referendum, initiative, and recall of elected officials), it gave particular attention to labor's demands in an effort to attract the labor vote. The worker was to be protected in case of industrial accident, with the burden shifted from the family to industry in the event of injury, industrial disease, or death. Minimum safety and health standards were to be fixed by law and wages, hours, and conditions of work publicized. Child labor was to be abolished, and the 8-hour day was to prevail for women and young persons, as well as for all industries that worked 'round the clock. One day in seven was to be set aside for rest. Mimimum wage legislation for women in industry was to be enacted. Industrial research laboratories were to be established, as were continuation schools for industrial education. A scheme of social insurance, including unemployment insurance and old age pensions, was to be devised and adopted. If a state or federal law was declared unconstitutional by the courts, this decision was to be submitted to the vote of the people. Contract convict labor was to be abolished, and a department of labor established in the president's cabinet. The platform said nothing about revising the Sherman Anti-Trust Act to exclude labor from prosecution under its provisions, but on the subject of injunctions, it had the following plank:

> We believe that the issuance of injunctions in cases arising out of labor disputes should be prohibited when such injunctions would not apply when no labor disputes existed. We also believe that a person cited for contempt in labor disputes, except when such contempt was committed in the actual presence of the court, or so near as to interfere with the proper administration of justice, should have a right to trial by jury.[60]

Apart from that of the Socialist Party, the Progressive Party's platform was the most advanced of the party platforms in the 1912 campaign.* Had La Follette been the presidential nominee on this platform, he would undoubtedly have gained widespread labor support and made it difficult for the AFL leadership to endorse the Democrats, other progressive planks, the exemption of unions from prosecution for he had earned the admiration of many workers as a champion of organized labor. In 1908, as head of the Wisconsin delegation to the Republican National Convention, he had drawn up and presented a

---

*The Socialist Party platform included every one of the Progressive planks—in fact, the Socialists claimed that January 9, 1909, devoted considerable space to the problems and the Socialist Party"—but, in addition, it demanded public works for unemployed workers, complete abolition of injunctions in labor disputes, removal of trade unions from the operation of the Anti-Trust Law, and called on class-conscious workers "to break the fetters of wage slavery and fit themselves for a future society." (Ira Kipnis, *The American Socialist Movement, 1897–1912*, New York, 1952, p. 366.)

minority report to the Resolutions Committee which demanded, among other progressive planks, the exemption of unions from prosecution under anti-trust laws and the prohibition of the issuance of injunctions in labor disputes. The report was overwhelmingly rejected as "socialistic," but the trade union press hailed the Wisconsin Progressive as a true friend of organized labor.[61] *La Follette's Weekly Magazine,* launched on January 9, 1909, devoted considerable space to the problems and demands of organized labor, and many of its articles and editorials were reprinted in the labor press.[62]

In 1910, La Follette introduced a bill in the Senate, proposed by the Sailors' Union of the Pacific, which sought to protect liberty of contract for American seamen, to provide better living conditions aboard ship, to prevent the undermanning of vessels, and to do away with the "crimping" and "shanghaiing" of American sailors. The basic purpose of the legislation was to liberate seamen from what amounted to virtual slavery. Under the existing law, seamen were bound to their ship by contract, and if they quit their ships before the contracts expired, no matter what the cause, they not only forfeited all of their wages, but were also liable to imprisonment as well. In 1898, the White Act was passed which limited the penalty for desertion in various ports to loss of wages and clothing, but the provisions of that law were not enforced.

Andrew Furuseth, the leader of the Sailors' Union, devoted all his time and energy from 1894 to 1911 to lobbying for new legislation. He made little progress until he secured La Follette's support. La Follette in the Senate (and William B. Wilson in the House) led the battle on behalf of the seamen. In 1911, a measure sponsored by La Follette failed to pass, but in 1912, it passed both the House and the Senate. However, President Taft vetoed the measure and the problem was carried over to the new administration. La Follette continued to lead the Congressional battle for decent conditions for seamen.[63]

In 1911, La Follette took up the cause of the workers employed in the Post Office Department, whose right to organize was being bitterly opposed by the Postmaster General. The Department was penalizing and discharging these workers for forming their own unions and seeking to affiliate with the AFL. It expected little opposition from Congress, but La Follette took up the struggle of the railway mail clerks and sent every clerk a list of questions, assuring them that all answers would be kept confidential. He was quickly swamped with mail in which the railway mail clerks described acts of intimidation, coercion, and other forms of tyranny on the part of superintendents and other officials of the railway mail service, and in which they expressed their desire to organize and join the AFL. Early in August, 1912, La Follette delivered a speech in the Senate in behalf of his amendment to the Post Office Appropriations Bill which would have prevented the discharge or other penalizing of postal employees for forming unions of their own choosing. He emphasized that he had received 15,000 letters from mail clerks and that many of them had been opened by the Post Office Department, a method of espionage that he characterized as similar to that in operation in Czarist Russia. The speech aroused widespread comment; the amendment passed the Senate and became part of the law governing the removal of employees from the civil service.[64]

By the time the national political conventions met, La Follette was clearly the outstanding Senatorial champion of organized labor. His nomination as the Progressive presidential candidate would have struck a responsive chord among many trade unionists.[65] On the other hand, Roosevelt was heartily disliked in some labor circles and distrusted in most. His sudden conversion to sympathy for organized labor and its problems when he resumed political activities in 1910 could not erase his past record in the White House. As president, he had furthered the open-shop movement by his action in the Miller case;* had done nothing to halt the use of injunctions in labor disputes or to advance the movement to amend the Sherman Act to eliminate trade unions from its effects; had issued an executive order which forbade a federal employee from petitioning for redress of grievances; and had helped break the Chicago teamsters' strike. Labor, therefore, understandably refused to respond to Roosevelt's blandishments. When the former president called upon the trade unions of New York to vote Republican in the 1910 gubernatorial election "and stand with us, for we are fighting the wage worker's battle," a labor mass meeting answered him by pointing out that no one who had "only recently begun to pose as the champion of the working-man" should advise labor on how to vote. The meeting thereupon endorsed John A. Dix, the Democratic candidate for governor.[66]

Roosevelt was, as Professor Eric F. Goldman puts it, "progressivism incarnate" for the vast majority of reformers. The movement he led quickly assumed the character of a religious crusade, attracting not only the great majority of the insurgent republicans from the Western states,

*In 1903, Roosevelt reinstated William A. Miller, an employee in the bindery department of the Government Printing Office who had been discharged after he had been dropped from the Bookbinders' Union for anti-union activities. In his action, Roosevelt came out in favor of the open-shop principle. (See Philip S. Foner, History of the Labor Movement in the United States, vol. III, pp. 51–52.)

but also a whole host of social workers and social reformers, along with politicians who had previously not been associated with reform movements. The reformers saw at last a chance for the realization of their dreams. The reason for this, as Professor Richard Hofstadter points out, was that "the Progressive mind was easy to please."[67]

Labor, however, was harder to please. The labor planks of the Progressive platform notwithstanding, organized labor felt that Roosevelt was not really sympathetic to labor's fundamental right to organize. The Western Federation of Miners identified him as a "pawn in the game" which the "industrial autocrats" were playing.[68] Certainly, the fact that a large part of the Progressive Party's financial support was derived from the contributions of the heads of great corporations lent substance to labor's suspicions.[69] "The prophet of the common people in this instance has more millionaires in his train than anyone who before lifted a strange banner," the Boston *Globe* commented editorially on August 4, 1912. Roosevelt regarded these millionaires as "sufficiently high-minded and far-sighted to see that in the long run privilege spells destruction not only to the class harmed by it, but the class possessing it." To Roosevelt and his capitalist supporters, the Progressive Party was a means of staving off "revolution."[70] As George W. Perkins, a former partner of J. P. Morgan and a substantial contributor to the Progressive Party's campaign fund, put it: "Federal legislation is feasible, and if we unite to work for it now we may be able to secure it. Whereas, if we continue to fight against it much longer, the incoming tide may sweep the question along either to government ownership or to Socialism."[71]

But many trade unionists were unwilling to trust capitalists who assumed a progressive air only to stave off more radical movements, and the fact that the Progressive platform had, at Perkins' insistence, eliminated all references to the Sherman Anti-Trust Act and the need to amend it in labor's interest, was proof that the capitalist forces exercised a powerful, if not dominant influence over the new party.[72] Furthermore, the more advanced elements in the labor movement were antagonized by the color line drawn by the new party and its lilywhite set-up in the South.[73]

THE 1912 CAMPAIGN

Nevertheless, as the campaign progressed, Roosevelt made headway in winning labor support for the Progressive Party. This was partly because of the wide publicity that the labor planks of the party's platform was receiving, partly because the Progressives kept Perkins out of active participation in the campaign, and partly, too, because Roosevelt made effective use of the tariff issue in appealing to workers in industries receiving huge benefits from protection, who, according to Roosevelt, would bear the brunt of unemployment and reduced wages when a Democratic administration removed it.[74] But his most effective argument was his presentation of Wilson's earlier statements on organized labor which, Roosevelt charged, proved that the Democratic candidate was an enemy of the trade union movement.[75]

This was not an easy argument for the Democrats to answer, even though Gompers had been won over. On July 9, 1912, a few weeks before the Democratic convention, Wilson met with Gompers and other AFL leaders in Trenton. "In that meeting," Gompers wrote later, "I felt my prejudices disappearing before the sincerity and obvious humanitarianism of the man. . . . I left Trenton very much relieved."[76] Nevertheless, Gompers did not endorse Wilson. The August, 1912 issue of the *American Federationist* treated the Democratic Party more favorably than the Republicans, but no preference was shown for any presidential candidate. "They [the workers]," Gompers wrote, "will keep in mind the failure of the one [the Republican Party] and the response and good faith of the other [the Democratic Party], and, at the right time, in a most effective manner, manifest their own interest by the exercise of their great privilege, the franchise."[77] But this rather lukewarm endorsement did not satisfy the Democratic Party. On August 10, 1912, John W. Kern, who had been chairman of the Democratic Platform Committee, wrote to Gompers urging that the Executive Council issue a public statement pointing out why the Democratic Party merited labor's support in the election. He reminded Gompers that the labor plank in the Democratic platform "was written by yourself and adopted by the Committee on Resolutions without the dotting of an 'i' or the crossing of a 't.' "[78] Gompers did not reply for more than a month, and when he did, he sent Kern a copy of the Special Campaign Issue of the AFL's *Weekly News Letter* which officially announced the 1912 position of the Federation, as agreed upon by the Executive Council.[79] Most of the issue was devoted to an analysis of the labor provisions of the three party platforms: the Republican Party was accused of having "totally ignored the questions of Labor's Demands"; the Democrats were praised for having reaffirmed the "favorable platform planks of 1908"; and the labor section of the Progressive Party platform was characterized as "equally outspoken and favorable." Workers were cautioned that "parties and candidates are to be judged by their actions in preference to their declarations." On this score, the Republicans clearly merited no support from organized labor: "So long as it has had entire control of the legislation and the administration, it was quite impossible to get from it any consideration, much less action, on any fundamental question affecting the rights, interests of and justice due to the toilers of our country." The publication reminded the workers that the Democratic-controlled House of Representatives, which had convened in March, 1911, had passed twenty-eight measures desired by labor, while the Republican Senate had rejected seventeen of them. In conclusion, the Executive Council commended the friends of labor in Congress for their services, regardless of party affiliation: "We cannot express too great an appreciation of the work done in the interests of labor and humanity by the fifteen trade union members in the House of Representatives, by the Democratic members of both House and Senate as well as the assistance rendered by the Progressive Republicans."[80]

While this statement, signed by the AFL Executive Council, helped promote the Democratic cause, it certainly did not do much to counter the appeal of the Progressives, especially since it kept Wilson's name completely in the background. It seemed obvious that if the Democratic candidate was to win any substantial labor support, he would have to erase the image created by his past statements, which the Progressives were doing their utmost to fix in the minds of the workers, and to advance a positive program of his own. His campaign speeches offered him the opportunity to accomplish this, but a study of his early campaign speeches indicates that he did not seem to realize this. To be sure, in his acceptance speech, he referred to the working people as the "backbone of the nation," and said: "The welfare, the happiness, the energy, the spirit of the men and women who daily work in our mines and factories, on our railroads, in our offices and marts of trade, on our farms and on the sea, is the essence of our national life."[81] But there was nothing here that could not have been uttered by any other candidate for the presidency, including Taft.

Then, on August 28, 1912, Wilson met Louis D. Brandeis, the "People's Lawyer," for the first time. This meeting represented a turning point for Wilson, for, as Professor Arthur S. Link, the leading Wilson scholar points out, it "was to have momentous consequences for the presidential campaign and for the whole course of domestic reform during the Wilson administration."[82] Brandeis helped to shape many of the ideas that went into the "New Freedom," but his influence on Wilson's ideas on labor and the labor movement was especially significant.

Brandeis emphasized that the movement for greater political democracy, expressed in such demands as the direct primary, initiative, referendum, and recall, were meaningless unless they were accompanied by industrial democracy. Without industrial democracy, he maintained, political democracy was a mockery. Industrial democracy required that "the employees must have the opportunity of participating in the decisions as to what shall be their conditions and how the business shall be run." This, in turn, could best be achieved by the organizing power of labor. Hence, labor's right to organize and bargain collectively was the key to the achievement of industrial democracy which, in turn, would give substance to political democracy. Brandeis further emphasized that the state should remain neutral in the class struggle and should not enact social legislation in favor of labor, unless the concentrated power of business threatened to destroy unionism. Then "the state must in some way come to the aid of the workingman if democratization is to be secured."[83] Thus, according to Brandeis, labor's demand for the right to organize and bargain collectively meant much more than hours, wages, and working conditions, for without the first two pre-conditions, the others would have no substantial power behind them to insure their enforcement. This principle was, of course, in substantial agreement with the approach of the national leadership of the AFL, especially as enunciated by its chief spokesman, Samuel Gompers.* Actually, Brandeis endorsed some of the criticisms of AFL policy made by militant unionists, especially of its failure to organize the mass of the unorganized workers, and he differed with the leaders of the AFL on the question of "scientific management" and the Taylor system, which he supported and they opposed.** But in the main, he supported the trade union outlook of the Federation's leadership.[84]

*Too much reliance on social legislation, Brandeis said, "would destroy the labor unions, the great protection of the workingman against the trusts." (*New York Times*, Sept. 19, 1912.)

Gabriel Kolko maintains that Brandeis was really "anti-labor in fact as well as principle," defending the right of labor to organize but only in open shops, and urging the incorporation of trade unions so that they might be sued, thereby forcing them to act conservatively. (*The Triumph of Conservatism, A Reinterpretation of American History, 1900-1916,* New York, 1963, pp. 207-08.)

**Frederick Winslow Taylor advocated scientific management not only as a means of restoring full control of production to management and of speeding up workers, but also as a weapon to eliminate unionism. (*See* Philip S. Foner, *History of the Labor Movement in the United States,* vol. III, pp. 43-44.)

Brandeis' influence on Wilson's campaign appeal to labor soon became evident. At their first meeting, he pointed out to Wilson that the key weakness in the Progressive Party's platform was its failure to pledge support for labor's demand for the right to organize and bargain collectively. Therefore, the social legislation promised by the third party was "welfare" assistance to labor which, in the absence of strong trade unions, would, like all other forms of paternalism, produce little of lasting value for the workers. The Democratic position, he insisted, must be to couple the right to organize with the need for social legislation wherever it was required to protect labor from the overwhelming power of industry. The basic principle was expressed in the idea: "Our industrial freedom and civic freedom go hand in hand and there is no such thing as civic freedom in a state of industrial absolutism."[85]

Following his meeting with Brandeis, Wilson began to emphasize two principles in his campaign speeches which clearly reflected the attorney's influence: organization of labor, and legislation to protect labor from the "heartlessness" of industry. In his speech in Minneapolis on September 18, he discussed at length the need to conserve the human resources of America, and particularly advocated improvement of working conditions in the factories. "I say," he declared, "that property rights as compared to the vital red blood of the American people must take second place. . . . What is the use of having industry if we die in producing it?"[86] "What I am interested in," he said in another speech, "is having the government of the United States more concerned about human rights than about property rights. Property is an instrument of humanity; humanity isn't an instrument of property." "I tell you solemnly, ladies and gentlemen," he declared in a speech in Newark, New Jersey, "we cannot postpone [social] justice any longer in the United States."[87]

On September 26, Wilson spoke in Fall River, Massachusetts. Many workers in the shoe factories of Massachusetts had been impressed by the labor planks in the Progressive Party platform, and support for Roosevelt was especially strong in these areas. In his Fall River speech, Wilson placed major emphasis on labor's right to organize, asserting unequivocally that it should be granted that right and stressing that it was a key feature of the "New Freedom." The Democratic platform, he went on, recognized that right, while the Progressive platform ignored it. The former demanded revision of the Sherman Anti-Trust Act to exclude trade unions from its provisions, while the latter was silent on this issue:

The right to organize on the part of labor is not recognized by the laws of the United States, and nowhere in the third-term platform* is it promised that the right will be granted. Any employer can dismiss all his workmen for no other reason than that they belong to a union. So the thing is absolutely one-sided. I believe we ought to hold a brief for the legal right of labor to organize.[88]

The idea that the law was "one-sided" in dealing with the right of workers to join unions was stressed in other speeches by Wilson, and he called for a change in the law to recognize and safeguard labor's right to organize. He also criticized the courts and judges for making the "one-sided" nature of the law even worse by their decisions. He called upon judges to understand the world in which they lived as far as labor-capital relations were concerned. They had not, he maintained, "opened their eyes to the modern world," and they must begin immediately to recognize a new concept in two important areas: in recognizing the right of labor to organize, and in the protection of the worker in matters of health and injury.[89]

Wilson also criticized Roosevelt's emphasis on the need for social legislation in order to keep labor from seeking more radical solutions: "We shall never get very far in the settlement of these vital matters so long as we regard everything done for the workingman, by law or by private agreement, as a concession yielded to keep from agitation and a disturbance of our peace." On the contrary, he declared, these laws were needed in order to give substance to American democracy, and they were owed to the workers by society as a whole: "Organization cannot accomplish what society as a whole can accomplish through appropriate legislation."[90]

In addition to influencing Wilson's course during the campaign, Brandeis also wrote and spoke in behalf of the Democratic candidate. On September 17, he spoke before the convention of the Massachusetts State Federation of Labor and criticized the Progressive Party as a pretended friend of labor. He asserted flatly that labor could hope for nothing from this new party with its platform that stood "for the perpetuation and extension of private monopoly in industry." The proposals for social legislation in the new party's platform were admirable, he conceded, but he then went on to characterize them as really worthless, even if enacted into law, because there was no guarantee of labor's right to organize: "Unless the right to organize is preserved and developed, all the laws

*Wilson did not refer to the Progressive Party by name; the reference to the third-term party is to the fact that Roosevelt had been president previously for nearly two terms.

advocated in the New Party platform, even if upheld by the courts, would be little better than dead letters." And he went on:

> Nowhere in that long and comprehensive platform, neither in its nobly phrased statement of principles, nor its general recommendations, nor in its enumeration of specific measures, can there be found any pledge to secure the right of labor to organize, without which all other grants and concessions for improvement of the condition of the workingmen is futile.[91]

The Democrats supplemented Wilson's and Brandeis' speeches with literature directed at winning the labor vote. One widely distributed pamphlet, entitled *Which Party Can Labor Trust?*, praised the pro-labor legislative program of the Democratic House elected in 1910. It branded the Republican Party as "antagonistic to labor" and condemned Roosevelt for having "failed to secure remedial legislation in the interest of labor" during his presidential administration.[92] Another pamphlet, entitled *What Democrats Have Done for Labor*, and featuring on its cover a picture of William B. Wilson, the trade unionist chairman of the House Committee on Labor, carried a summary of the legislation of interest to labor that had been adopted by the Democratic-controlled House.[93]

Gompers made only a few speeches in the campaign, for, as he explained later: "Experience in the previous presidential campaign [of 1908] after the attacks were made against my associates, and particularly against me, indicated that I could best help in the campaign by counsel and assistance rather than conspicuous service that would focus attacks upon me."[94] This policy, however, did not prevent the *New York Times* from calling for "popular wrath" against the Democratic Party because its labor plank represented a virtual vote of confidence in the AFL in general, and in Gompers in particular.[95]

In the October *American Federationist*, Gompers condemned the Republican platform and nominee, praised Wilson and the Democratic platform, and declared that although the Progressive platform and Roosevelt's labor pronouncements were highly gratifying to labor, it had been unable to obtain legislative protection while Roosevelt was president. In the next issue—the final one before the election—Gompers endorsed Wilson's candidacy, noting casually that the Progressive platform contained favorable provisions for labor, but making no mention of Roosevelt.[96]*

*There is no record of any expenditures made by the AFL for political activity during the 1912 presidential campaign. (*See* U. S. Congress House of Representatives, 63rd Congress, 1st Session, *Hearings Before the Committee on the Judiciary,* Serial 14, part 1, Washington, 1914, p. 2423.)

With Taft labelling Wilson a radical, asserting that "the coming of social justice involved a forced division of property, and that means socialism," and predicting that a Democratic victory would introduce "class legislation designed to secure immunity for lawlessness in labor disputes on the part of the laborers,"[97] the Democratic candidate grew in popularity with the workers and many of them rallied to his slogan of the "New Freedom."

The election returns resulted in a Democratic landslide which far exceeded the wildest hopes of the AFL leaders. The popular vote was: Wilson, 6,293,019; Roosevelt, 4,119,507; Taft, 3,484,956; Debs, 901,-873. Not only was Wilson elected—the first Democratic chief executive since Cleveland in the 1890s—but the Democrats, for the first time in many years, gained domination of both houses of Congress by comfortable majorities. And seventeen of the newly-elected Congressmen were members of trade unions! The victory represented the high peak of the reform movement which had been steadily gaining momentum and volume ever since the beginning of the century. As Professor Arthur S. Link remarks, "The country was now overwhelmingly progressive in temper."[98]

Although it was obvious that a good many workers had voted for either Debs or Roosevelt,[99] Gompers was quick to claim that the AFL deserved a large part of the credit for the Democratic victory. "We did not go into the open this time but we made our fight just the same," he declared in a press interview directly after the election.[100] Later, in 1914, testifying before the House Judiciary Committee, Gompers was asked what party labor had supported in 1912. He replied: "The labor interests opposed particularly the reelection of Mr. Taft, and in order to accomplish that as best we could, we aided in every way we could the election of Mr. Wilson."[101]

One thing, at least, was certain: the newly-elected president had clearly and unequivocally pledged himself to support organized labor's key demands, and had acknowledged that they were at the foundation of his "New Freedom" program. It looked as if a new era had indeed dawned for American labor.

CHAPTER 5

The Fruits of Victory

The Democratic victory in the 1912 presidential election was a fortunate stroke indeed for the AFL leadership. The demand for an independent labor party had been gaining more and more support in AFL unions. At the 1912 convention, held after the election, the agitation for such a party was evident in an impressive body of resolutions from affiliates urging the Executive Council to call a convention of labor and its friends to lay the foundation for a new political organization. The Gompers administration conceded that the demand for an independent labor party was greater than ever before, but it countered with the argument that there was actually less need for it than at any time in the past. After many years of fighting against seemingly hopeless odds in the legislative field, it contended, the unions at last had a friendly face in the White House, and a party in power that was definitely prepared to do something concrete for labor's claims. "You have a Democratic House, you are going to have a Democratic Senate, and you have been promised that all these laws of which labor has complained are going to be remedied," Gompers argued. "The people who have confidence in the Democratic Party, I believe, can afford to wait patiently on their promises."[1]

BEGINNING OF THE WILSON ADMINISTRATION

This argument was effective in convincing all but the Socialists to adopt a "wait-and-see" attitude. But Gompers was well aware that only results would satisfy the forces in the Federation who were clamoring for a labor party. "If the Administration fulfilled its pledges in good faith," he wrote, "the political policies which I helped to inaugurate would have proved themselves."[2] On February 12, 1913, Gompers requested a meeting with Wilson to discuss this very problem. He and Frank Morrison met with the president-elect, and they were assured by Wilson that "they would not be disappointed with the labor program he would outline in his inaugural address."[3] In that address, Wilson stressed the need to fulfill the pledges his party had made to labor during the campaign and called for a broad program of social legislation:

> This is no sentimental duty. The firm basis of government is justice, not pity. These are matters of justice. There can be no equality of opportunity, the first essential of justice in the body politic, if men and women and children be not shielded in their lives, their very vitality, from the consequences of great industrial and social processes which they cannot alter, control or singly cope with. Society must see to it that it does not itself crush or weaken or damage its own constituent parts. The first duty of law is to keep sound the society it serves. Sanitary laws, pure food laws, and laws determining conditions of labor which individuals are powerless to determine for themselves are intimate parts of the very business of justice and legal efficiency.[4]

Morrison, who attended the inauguration, was jubilant. "You said to Mr. Gompers and myself," he wrote to the president, "that you thought we would be satisfied with your address. I am satisfied and will do what I can to have Congress enact the legislation necessary to secure the splendid reforms which you have clearly outlined in your address." The AFL secretary expressed confidence that the enactment of these laws by Congress would "gradually eliminate from our present civilization the many inequalities and injustices which weigh heavily upon many of our people."[5]

Wilson's early appointments, in the main, heightened the feeling of elation at AFL headquarters. Most important was the appointment of William B. Wilson as Secretary of the new Department of Labor.* The comment of the *New York Times* that the appointment of the former secretary-treasurer of the United Mine Workers was made at the "instigation of Samuel Gompers," and that of the New York *Herald* that the department should be called "the new department of union labor," were

---

*Agitation for a Department of Labor was begun soon after the Civil War by William H. Sylvis. The movement was taken up by the Knights of Labor, and that effort led to the establishment in 1888 of the Bureau of Labor Statistics. After the decline of the Knights, the movement was continued by the AFL. The creation of the Department of Labor and Commerce in 1903, of which labor disapproved, intensified the struggle for a "voice in the President's cabinet," which culminated in 1913. (John Lombardi, *Labor's Voice in the Cabinet*, New York, 1942, pp. 1-7; Jonathan Grossman, "The Origin of the U. S. Department of Labor," *Monthly Labor Review*, March, 1973, pp. 3-7.)

typical of the conservative reaction to the appointment.[6] But organized labor regarded it as proof that Wilson intended to fulfill his campaign pledges. Gompers expressed a common feeling in trade union circles when he wrote to the president that the appointment marked

> ... the first time in the history of our government that a workman, truly representative of the human side of the rights, the interest and the welfare of the working people of America was the head of a great department in the government of the United States; the first time that a workman, representative of the workers, became a member of the cabinet of the President.[7]

Organized labor also greeted with enthusiasm the appointment of Louis F. Post, leading "single-tax" proponent, long-time friend of the labor movement, and liberal editor of *The Public*, the Chicago weekly that led the fight for municipal ownership, social reform, and the right of labor to organize. Wilson's refusal to yield to conservative pressure against Post's appointment as Assistant Secretary of Labor was hailed by the trade unions. Wilson's response to criticism of his designation of the pro-labor editor was that "he has enthusiasm for the right things."[8] The appointment of Charles P. Neill as Commissioner of Labor Statistics was also applauded by labor, especially since it was bitterly opposed by Southern anti-labor senators. Neill had conducted an investigation in 1907 of labor conditions in the Southern mills for the Department of Commerce, and his critical report on these conditions had infuriated Southern industrialists. Their rage, when Wilson nominated Neill, was to be expected, but, despite their opposition and that of the Southern senators, the appointment was confirmed by the Senate.[9]*

Even apart from the Secretary of Labor, several members of Wilson's cabinet were friendly to labor. Franklin K. Lane, Secretary of the Interior, had frequently advised the AFL on legal matters relating to the injunction abuse and was regarded by Gompers as a man who "had deep sympathy with the earnest aspirations of labor."[10] William Jennings Bryan, Secretary of State, had long enjoyed labor's confidence and support, and Secretary of the Navy Josephus Daniels was a close friend of William B. Wilson and had endorsed many of the pro-labor measures

*On the other hand, social workers and liberal intellectuals criticized Wilson for appointing three conservative labor leaders—John Lennon and James O'Connell, AFL vice-presidents, and Austin Garretson of the Railroad Brotherhoods—as labor's representatives on the United States Commission of Industrial Relations. The critics felt that the Socialist trade unions and the IWW should also have been represented. Gompers, however, insisted that only conservative labor be represented on the Commission and his view won out. (Father John S. Smith, M.A., "Organized Labor in the Wilson Era, 1913-1921," unpublished Ph.D. thesis, Catholic University of America, 1962, pp. 36-42.)

he had sponsored in Congress. Lindley M. Garrison, Secretary of War, was regarded by the United Mine Workers as a friend of labor. On the other hand, Secretary of Commerce William C. Redfield, Postmaster-General Albert S. Burleson, and Attorney-General James C. McReynolds were regarded as enemies of labor, and they soon proved themselves deserving of that designation. Still, Wilson's early appointments, like his inaugural address, seemed to hold out great promise for labor.

NO RELIEF FROM THE SHERMAN ACT

But the real test, as far as the AFL was concerned, was to come on labor's single most desired goal: relief from the Sherman Anti-Trust Act. During the campaign, Wilson had declared that his administration would guarantee labor's right to organize and had stated that on this fundamental issue, the law was "one-sided" and required revision. Moreover, he had indicated that he was opposed to the unrestricted use of injunctions in labor disputes. While he had failed to provide any details as to how he intended to carry out these pledges, the trade unions assumed that they could expect substantial aid from him in the struggle to exempt labor from the jurisdiction of the Sherman Act.

This aid, however, did not materialize. As soon as Congress convened in special session following Wilson's inauguration, the seventeen labor Congressmen introduced, with great anticipation, bills embodying the principles labor had up to that time sought unsuccessfully to have enacted. These included the Bacon–Bartlett Bill, the Clayton Anti-Injunction Bill, and the Clayton Anti-Contempt Bill. Under the provisions of the first of these measures, labor would be specifically eliminated from the Sherman Act's jurisdiction, and the issuance of injunctions in labor disputes would be strictly limited. Moreover, the bill defined "property" in a labor dispute in a manner that would make it impossible to construe it as the right to work or the right to carry on business. This constituted an important restriction on the ability of employers to use the courts to smash unions and break strikes by charging that organizing drives represented infringements on the rights of non-union workers to work and of employers to conduct their businesses.[11]

Passage of all three of these measures was blocked by the administration during the first session of the 63rd Congress. In spite of the Democratic Party's commitment in its 1912 platform and his own pledges during the campaign, Wilson refused to lift a finger in favor of any bill which proposed to exempt labor from the Sherman Act, or even to limit the issuance of injunctions in labor disputes.[12] The only concession labor received during the first year of Wilson's administration in this connection was the enactment of the Sundry Civil Appropriations Bill, with the Hughes rider attached, which prevented the use of any of the appropriated funds by the government to prosecute labor under the Sherman Act. But this concession was not won without a struggle, and it soon proved to be of little practical value.

No sooner was the bill re-introduced in Congress when the pressure from business groups to prevent its passage began. It was applied particularly to Wilson to influence him to follow Taft in vetoing the pro-labor rider should the bill, as seemed likely, pass both houses of Congress. Gompers was instantly alarmed. He did "not at all feel sure that he [Wilson] was in accord with labor's position on the issue." Unable to see the president in person because of his own illness, Gompers sent Wilson a thirteen-page letter outlining why labor felt the passage of the rider to be "a paramount issue." He denied that it represented "class legislation":

> Those rights we wish restored are those rights necessary to conducting the normal activities of labor organization. Labor organizations are formed to protect workers in their rights against the cupidity of employers and combinations of employers dealing in products created by labor. The right to strike, to withhold labor power, is essential to the maintenance of the freedom of the workers.[13]

Four days later, Wilson replied, thanking Gompers for having helped him "in thinking the problem through." He assured Gompers that he would give his letter the most careful consideration, "for I am sure you know my disposition in matters of this kind."[14]

Gompers felt relief—but only for the moment. The press reported that the NAM and other employers' associations were pouring protests into the White House urging Wilson to veto the rider on the ground that it was "class legislation of the most vicious sort."[15] The newspapers themselves supplemented the appeals with editorials urging veto of this "class legislation."[16] On April 25, 1913, the *New York Times,* which was regularly carrying editorials demanding the veto, reported gleefully that Wilson was weakening in the face of the pressure. Gompers, who was in the hospital recovering from a mastoid operation, immediately became worried again and sent Wilson a twenty-three-page letter "stating even more fully the reasons why labor urged approval of the bill." Again, Wilson assured him that he was grateful for his advice.[17] But this time,

Gompers' fears were not allayed by Wilson's assurances. He wrote to Morrison that further action was necessary to counter the NAM pressure for a veto, pointing out that James Kirby, the NAM president, had sent "scare" letters to employers all over the country urging them to flood Wilson with letters and telegrams demanding a veto. To offset this campaign, Gompers advised Morrison to "ask Senator Hughes of N. J. and Representative Hamil of N. J. to accompany you and Vice-President O'Connell to make a call upon President Wilson and seek to impress upon him the justice and urgency of his signing the bill." He continued:

> You should call his attention to the campaign of Kirby and the hostile press, etc. And also that we have not written or spoken to anyone throughout the country to even suggest that they write him to sign the bill; but if we had deemed that necessary could have . . . millions of workers and friends of justice throughout all parts of the country to literally swamp him with resolutions and petitions, that we rested our position upon what I had written him and the announcements we saw published that he would sign the bill. The President's attention should be called to the promises and declarations of his party and of the Progressive Party and also the history of the struggle for this measure as well as the British Trades Dispute of 1906.

Gompers concluded by noting that if the president refused to honor the pledges of his party and there was to be a fight, then "we might as well fight at once and in the open."[18]

Regardless of whether or not Gompers would have carried out his threat to break with the Wilson administration, there was not to be any need for "a fight." Wilson had already concluded that even if he signed the bill, there was no need to enforce it in a manner that would fulfill labor's expectations. Attorney-General McReynolds had made it clear at a conference held on April 12 that the proviso merely prevented the prosecution of trade unions *per se,* but did not prevent the prosecution of trade unions for acts which the Justice Department might regard as unlawful.[19] Wilson himself had written privately to the president of the Pennsylvania Railroad on April 22, after the latter had urged him to veto the rider, that the proviso applied only to a "single special additional appropriation" and did not restrict the Department of Justice from using money from the general fund, or "restrict its discretion as to the character of the suits which it is to bring."[20]

The bill passed both houses of Congress in mid-June, 1913, and Wilson, after holding it until the last possible moment, signed it. He accompanied his approval with a memorandum condemning the rider. If the labor proviso could have been separated from the rest of the bill, he wrote, he would have vetoed the item. In any event, he assured the rider's opponents not to be alarmed. The bill would not limit the actions of the Department of Justice in bringing suits whenever necessary. The actions of the Department would be determined by impartial judgment "as to the true and just meaning of the substantial statutes of the United States."[21]

In spite of this clear-cut repudiation of everything labor had hoped to gain from the bill, Gompers considered the signing of the measure "a decisive victory for the rights and protection of labor."[22] But events quickly proved otherwise and demonstrated that much more was needed to protect labor's rights in the face of the continued hostility of the courts toward unionism.

In April, 1913, Chief Justice Prentice of Connecticut decided that a union was responsible for any loss of wages caused by a closed-shop agreement which prevented a non-union worker from working at his trade. On May 5, 1913, the Court of Appeals of the District of Columbia sustained a lower court in finding Gompers, Mitchell, and Morrison guilty of contempt in defying the Bucks' Stove and Range Company injunction.* On December 18, 1913, the United States Circuit Court of Appeals for the Second Circuit, in a hearing on the Danbury hatters' case, affirmed the findings of the Hartford trial court that a conspiracy had been entered into, as alleged in the complaint. This decision resulted in a judgment of $252,130.90 being upheld against the 197 hatters' unionists.[23]

What Gompers described as "the culmination of judicial arrogance" occurred on December 23, 1912 and the victims were the United Mine

---

*On June 28, 1912, Justice Wright in the District of Columbia's lower court had again sentenced Gompers, Mitchell, and Morrison to jail—Gompers for twelve months, Morrison for six months, and Mitchell for three months. On the advice of their attorneys, the labor leaders appealed Wright's decision to the Court of Appeals, not on grounds of the right of boycott or the right to exercise free speech and press without the interference of injunctions, but mainly on the grounds that the statute of limitations barred any further prosecution of the alleged acts of contempt, and that the punishments meted out were cruel and unusual. Justice Van Orsdel of the Court of Appeals ruled that the statute of limitations did not apply, but he agreed that the punishment was unusual and excessive. He therefore reversed Wright's judgment and instructed him to impose sentences of thirty days for Gompers and $500 fine each for Mitchell and Morrison. (Washington *Herald*, June 29, 1912; May 6, 1913.)

The ruling was appealed to the Supreme Court and, on May 11, 1914, Justice Oliver Wendell Holmes read the high court's opinion. The court refused to rule on the basic issues involved in the case, but held that since all charges against the defendants were more than three years old, the judgment was reversed. Thus, after seven years of litigation, the Bucks' Stove and Range case came to its end. As Gompers commented, "The judiciary has refused to pass upon the great human issues involved in the case. The principles of justice have been lost in the maze of legalism." (*American Federationist*, June, 1914, pp. 483-86.)

Workers, who were attempting to organize the coal mines of West Virginia. The lower court, in the first decision in the *Hitchman Coal and Coke Co. v. Mitchell,* declared that the United Mine Workers' organization was an unlawful combination under the Sherman Act. The court based its decision on the aims and principles set forth in the union's constitution and on the union's avowed objective of organizing the entire mining industry. Although there was no evidence that any of the miners had voiced any threat against the coal company, each miner, by membership in the union, was held to be a co-conspirator with the union officers.[24] Not only were the unions restricted, by this decision, in using their economic strength to gain their demands, but their very existence appeared to be in question. As Norman J. Ware points out: "Thus, finally a trade union as such became unlawful, a condition that had never existed in the United States up to that time."[25]

On June 7, 1913, a few months after this sweeping decision, an indictment was brought against the leaders of the United Mine Workers under the Sherman Act for restraint of trade in seeking to unionize the West Virginia mines. The indictment was accompanied by a report, a portion of which also criticized certain mine operators for violating the law by entering into agreements with the UMW. But no indictment was returned against the coal operators. "Why?" asked Gompers. "Why is it that our laws may be perverted and interpreted to prevent those who toil from doing things necessary for their protection and betterment? Why is it men of wealth may with impunity break laws whose meaning is plain and unmistakable?"[26] Gompers did not answer his own question.

Although the indictment was dropped by the Department of Justice and never brought to trial, it provided proof that Attorney-General McReynolds had meant what he had said when he told a conference in April that the enactment of the Sundry Civil Appropriations Bill would not prevent the Department from prosecuting trade unions for acts which it considered unlawful.[27] Additional proof was provided in December, 1913, during the Colorado coal strike, when John P. White, Frank J. Hayes, and William Green were charged with a conspiracy in restraint of trade for attempting to form a monopoly of labor—in other words, for attempting to organize the non-union Colorado mines. Here again, the indictment was dropped and the case never brought to trial,[28] but labor was very much disturbed by press reports that the indictments in the West Virginia and Colorado strikes were regarded by Wilson as "vindication of his action in signing the Sundry Civil Appropriations Bill."[29] Regardless of how accurate these reports may have been, events since mid-June had demonstrated that the new law would not limit the Department of Justice's ability to act against unions under the Sherman Act. "It is necessary," Gompers wrote to Morrison when the United Mine Workers leaders were indicted in Colorado, "that extra efforts be made by AFL officers to secure enactment of laws which will exclude voluntary organizations of the wage workers from the provisions of the law, or any other bearing upon the subject matter."[30]

THE 1913 AFL CONVENTION

Gompers' letter was written on the eve of the 1913 AFL convention. The record of the Wilson administration since its inauguration was hardly designed to impress the delegates. To be sure, there were the appointments of William B. Wilson, Louis F. Post, and Charles P. Neill, and the passage of the Sundry Civil Appropriations Bill. But the president's reluctance to sign the rider to the latter measure had filled the trade unions with dismay and foreshadowed future difficulty in achieving permanent protection for labor from prosecutions under the Sherman Anti-Trust Act. Not a single piece of social legislation had been enacted, despite Wilson's emphasis on the need for such measures in his inaugural address; nor was there any legislation to limit lobbying by big business, in spite of the exposure of the nefarious practices of the NAM by both the press and Congress. And nothing had been achieved toward solving labor's most pressing problem—the exclusion of trade unions from the provisions of the Sherman Act.

Small wonder, then, that the agitation for an independent labor party was revived and grew to considerable proportions. This feeling was intensified by the disclosures during the summer and early fall of 1913 of the NAM's anti-labor practices. "Colonel" Martin M. Mulhall revealed that the organization had even been able to win over several of the members of Congress who had been elected with AFL support. James T. McDermott of Illinois, one of these "friends of labor," had been elected to four terms in Congress by the labor vote and carried a union card in his pocket, but Mulhall stated that "there had never been a lobbyist or a tool in Washington who was more subservient to the trust than this representative of the stockyards district of Chicago." The Congressional investigation substantiated Mulhall's statement. These disclosures gave new weight to the argument that the "reward-our-friends-and-punish-our-enemies" policy was an illusion, and the failure of the Wilson administration, which had been hailed by the AFL as a "friend of labor," to realize its bright promise added still further weight to the argument.

When the delegates assembled in Seattle for the 1913 AFL convention, the demand for a labor party was immediately voiced. And now, for the first time, the AFL leadership conceded that there was substantial merit to the call for a labor party; it merely argued that the time was not yet ripe to launch one. In response to the resolution calling for the establishment of an independent labor party, the Committee on Resolutions declared:

> . . . the time has not arrived when, with due regard to the economic movement still young and hopeful in organization a distinct labor party should be formed.
>
> We are confident that when our present political activities have suitably materialized, a new political party will be the logical result. . . .
>
> For the present we recommend a continuation and development of labor's non-partisan political position.[31]

Had the administration resorted to its usual tactic of denouncing the proposed labor party as a "Socialist plot" against unionism, the reaction of the delegates, sorely disappointed as they were by the feeble results of the "non-partisan political position," would have seriously challenged the leadership's control over the organization. As it was, Max Hayes, Socialist candidate for the AFL presidency and a leading exponent of the demand for a labor party, received 5,073 votes as against 11,974 for Gompers—the high point of the effort to unseat Gompers.[32]

THE AFL AND SOCIAL LEGISLATION

By the time the 1914 convention met, little had been achieved in the way of protective social legislation for labor. (Indeed, during the first three years of Wilson's administration, the La Follette Seamen's Act, adopted in March, 1915, was the only protective measure of any importance enacted, and no sooner had this measure been passed than the Department of Commerce began to subvert it by refusing to enforce it.)[33] Wilson, yielding to pressure from business groups, refused to support the major social reforms he had called for in his inaugural address, and without his support, there was no possibility of pushing these bills through Congress.[34] The AFL applied little pressure on Wilson to offset the influence of organized capital, for its attitude toward such legislation was the same as it had been in 1906—namely, that it would divert the attention of workers from the trade union movement and its organization to political activities. The purpose of laws, Gompers declared in 1914, should be only to "free people from the shackles and give them a chance to working out their own salvation"[35]—which was interpreted to mean that government should confine itself mainly to giving the trade unions a free hand in their organizing activities. The labor movement, Gompers continued, should resist the tendency of social reformers to attempt to expand the functions of government into areas from which it had been traditionally barred, especially in the economic and social spheres. As he put it:

> Whither are we drifting? There is a strange spirit abroad in these times. The whole people is hugging the delusion that law is a panacea. Whatever the ill or the wrong or the ideal, immediately follows the suggestion—enact a law. ... If wages are low, a law or a commission is proposed. Whether as a result of laziness or incompetency, there is a steady growing disposition to shift responsibility for personal progress and welfare to outside agencies. . . . Initiative, aggressive conviction, enlightened self-interest are the characteristics that must be dominant among the people, if the nation is to make substantial progress towards better living and higher ideals.[36]

Thus, at the 1912 AFL convention, a resolution demanding minimum wage legislation was killed by being referred to the Executive Council for study. The following year, the convention endorsed the Council's report which declared: "If it were proposed in this country to fix by law wages for men, Labor would protest by every means at its power. Through organization, the wages of men can and will be maintained at a higher minimum than they would be if fixed by legal enactment."[37] Naturally, nothing was said about the millions of workers who were not organized. During the hearings before the 1914 Industrial Relations Commission, Gompers emphatically voiced the Federation's opposition to minimum wage legislation for men, to the establishment legally of a maximum workday for men, and to state insurance for the unemployed. (The last demand was assuming increasing importance as a result of widespread unemployment arising out of the depression which had begun in the fall of 1913.) He informed the Commission that the increase in government powers was a "curb upon the rights, the natural development of the individual."[38]

Gompers took the same position on the question of compulsory health insurance. The American Association for Labor Legislation had made a complete study of the connection between the conditions of industry and illness; of the poisonous gases, dusts, germs, and miscellaneous irritants to which the worker is subjected, and the consequent results to his health of these surroundings; it had strongly recommended health insurance as the means for protecting workers from destitution when they succumbed to these illnesses for which industry had been proven responsible.[39] But Gompers and, indeed, the entire AFL Executive Council, rejected this carefully documented recommendation. "That the state should provide sickness for workers," Gompers declared, "is fundamentally based upon the theory that these workmen are not able to look after their own interests and the state must interpose its authority and wisdom and assume the relation of parent or guardian. There is something in the very suggestion of this relationship and this policy that is repugnant to a free-born citizen." In a flowery outburst, he cried: "For a mess of pottage, under the pretense of compulsory social insurance, let us not voluntarily surrender the fundamental principles of liberty and freedom, the hope of the United States, the leader and teacher to the world of the significance of this great anthem chorus of humanity, liberty."[40]

With this hostile attitude toward social legislation—an attitude shared by the NAM and other employers' associations—the AFL leadership was not unduly disturbed by the absence of any protective legislation for labor in the record of the Wilson administration for the year 1914,* especially when the year produced what seemed to be labor's greatest legislative triumph: the passage of the Clayton Anti-Trust Act, including Sections 6 and 20, which, in the eyes of the AFL leaders, secured for organized labor at long last relief from the Sherman Anti-Trust Act.

THE CLAYTON ACT

The AFL had hoped that by the time its 1913 convention met, the exemption of trade unions from the Sherman Act would already have been an established fact. But this, as we have seen, came to naught. Every measure aimed at achieving this goal that was introduced during the first session of the 63rd Congress had been blocked by administration opposition. When the second session opened in January, 1914, the AFL was again optimistic, for it was reported that Wilson was planning to incorporate labor's demands into his anti-trust program.[41] One can therefore imagine the feelings in AFL headquarters when Wilson appeared before a joint session of Congress on January 20, 1914, outlined his anti-trust program in a message of unusual detail which contained several assurances to the business community that it had nothing to fear

---

*The only reference to labor legislation in Wilson's message to Congress on December 2, 1913 was a request that it enact an employers' liability law for railroad workers.

from the administration—and failed to incorporate a single reference to labor's demands.[42] The feeling of anger was intensified when the *New York Times* reported on February 2, 1914 that the president had let it be known that he would veto any anti-trust measure that exempted labor from its provisions. Gompers, furious, announced that labor would go to the people for support: "Without further delay the citizens of the United States must decide whether they wish to outlaw organized labor."[43]

The threat failed to move Wilson. The deepening depression, notes Professor Link, was worrying the president, and he was concerned about convincing the business interests that they could count on the administration to relieve any tension between it and the business community. Hence, apart from his own personal lack of enthusiasm for labor's demands, the economic situation alone caused Wilson to take a firm stand against the proposal to exempt organized labor from the Sherman Act.[44]

By mid-March, 1914, four anti-trust measures had been introduced into Congress without a single provision in any of them embodying labor's demands.[45] But the Democratic members of the House and a number of Democratic senators were unhappy about the way things were developing. They knew that to adopt a new anti-trust law without granting labor some concessions would stimulate organized labor to intensified political activity in the elections of 1914, when many of them were up for reelection.[46] They would have been content to let the whole anti-trust program be abandoned and revived at the next session after the fall elections. But when it became clear that Wilson was going to insist upon the immediate passage of his anti-trust program, the Democratic members of Congress, with their political futures at stake, brought pressure upon the president to do something to fulfill the party's pledge to labor. Under these circumstances, a compromise was inevitable.[47]

On April 14, 1914, it was reported that Wilson would look with favor on the passage of anti-injunction and anti-contempt legislation by Congress. On the same day, Chairman Henry D. Clayton of the House Judiciary Committee announced that the Clayton Anti-Injunction and the Clayton Anti-Contempt Bills would be presented to the House for approval. He added, however, that the Bacon-Bartlett Bill, which labor especially wanted to see enacted, would not be reported out of committee.[48] The anti-injunction and anti-contempt bills were concessions to labor, but neither of them really touched on labor's primary objective— the exemption of labor from the provisions of the Sherman Act—which was embodied in the Bacon-Bartlett Bill. This latter bill, as we have seen, restricted the use of injunctions, but, in addition, specifically defined "property" in a labor dispute and definitely removed labor from the clutches of the Sherman Act.[49]

Another compromise was then effected. The anti-injunction and anti-contempt bills were to be combined into the Clayton Act, and even though the Bacon-Bartlett Bill was not to be included, a new section was to be added which, it was believed, would satisfy the AFL. It was based on the testimony Gompers had previously presented before the House Judiciary Committee in the course of the hearings on anti-trust legislation. In the course of his testimony, Gompers had asked the committee to recommend the passage of the Bacon-Bartlett Bill, but he had devoted most of his discussion to the need for asserting, through the proposed law, organized labor's right to existence. He made it appear that the assertion of this right was labor's basic demand. All that labor desired, Gompers emphasized, was the right to carry out its normal activities: "We do not ask immunity for any criminal act which any of us commit; we ask no immunity for anything; but we have the right to existence, the lawful, normal existence of a voluntary association of workers, organized not for profit, but organized to protect our lives and our normal activities." Thereupon, Gompers was asked by Representative Dick T. Morgan of Oklahoma if, instead of enacting the Bacon-Bartlett Bill, Congress were "simply to amend the Sherman Anti-Trust Law," the AFL would be satisfied. Gompers replied: "Substantially yes, insofar as that is concerned. . . ."[50]

When the various labor bills were combined into the Clayton Act, Gompers' passing reference to the need to enact the Bacon-Bartlett Bill was ignored, while his emphatic remarks about the need to assert labor's right to existence were used as the basis for Section 6 of the Clayton Act. At the time that this section was introduced in the House by Representative Clayton, it read: "That nothing in the anti-trust laws shall be construed to forbid the existence and operation of fraternal, labor, consumers, agricultural, or horticultural organizations under associations operating under the lodge system,* instituted for the purpose of mutual help, and not having capital stock or conducted for profit, or to forbid or restrain individual members of such orders or associations from carrying out the legitimate objects of such association."[51]

Gompers, proud that his testimony was serving as the basis for a new section of the proposed law, enthusiastically approved the provision.[52]

_____
*The words "under the lodge system" were later eliminated.

But wiser heads in the labor movement saw that it was extremely weak and in no way a substitute for the Bacon-Bartlett Bill. Although the AFL did not pick up the fight to include the Bacon-Bartlett Bill in the Clayton Act, it did demand that the words, "shall not apply to" be substituted in Section 6 for the phrase, "shall not be construed to forbid the existence and operation of."[53] But neither Wilson nor the House Judiciary Committee would accept this revision. For over a month, the tug-of-war continued. Wilson remained adamant in opposing any revision of Section 6; on the other hand, the AFL and the "labor Congressmen" demanded that nothing contained in the anti-trust laws "shall be construed to apply to labor organizations." In addition to Gompers, the letter was also signed by Morrison, the legislative representatives of the four railroad brotherhoods, and the representatives of the National Farmers' Union.[54]

This was, as later events demonstrated, the turning point in labor's long campaign for exclusion from the Sherman Act. The most effective pressure that labor could exert on any lawmaker was pressure from back home. One would expect, therefore, that the AFL would have followed up the letter to the congressmen with a flood of mail from union members all over the country—a deluge of letters from voters back home demanding that nothing contained in the anti-trust laws should be construed to apply to labor organizations. One would also expect the AFL to warn the Democratic members of Congress that the unions were prepared to collect on what they regarded as the heaviest political debt any Congress had ever owed to organized labor, and that its failure to fulfill the Democratic Party's pledge to labor would guarantee its opposition to their reelection in the fall. Finally, here was the time and the place for Gompers to reiterate his warning to the Democratic Party, made three years earlier, that "the time has come when we shall have a constructive, progressive, radical labor party, unless the Democratic Party shall perform its duty." There certainly was no better time to take concrete steps to prove that these were not just empty words.

But this is not what happened. The AFL did nothing to apply mass pressure on the members of Congress. Instead, on May 26, 1914, a compromise was reached. It consisted of adding to the end of Section 6 the phrase: "nor shall such organizations, or the members thereof, be held or construed to be illegal combinations or conspiracies in restraint of trade, under the anti-trust laws." In this manner, Section 6 was subsequently approved by the House.[55]

Why the Federation accepted this compromise is not clear. Perhaps the AFL leaders felt that Gompers' testimony before the Judiciary Committee weakened labor's ability to demand that the section be read "shall not apply to," since the compromise proposal affirmed what Gompers had insisted upon—the right of labor unions to exist. (As Representative Floyd of the Judiciary Committee pointed out on May 23: "We are doing what Mr. Gompers asked. We are taking them out from under the ban of law that would make them liable to dissolution. This is a bill of rights for labor."[56]) Perhaps the AFL really believed that the proposed compromise did exempt labor from the Sherman Act. (The Federation's legal advisors, including Judge Parker, assured Gompers that it did.) Furthermore, on May 27, 1914, Gompers assured the members of the AFL Executive Council that President Wilson, the House Judiciary Committee, and representatives of the Federation had agreed to accept the compromise as assuring labor of just such an exemption.[57]

But events immediately contradicted Gompers and demonstrated that Wilson and the Judiciary Committee had an entirely different interpretation of the section. Members of the committee told the House that the section merely legalized the existence of the trade unions.[58] President Wilson supported this interpretation. On June 1, 1914, he told newspaper reporters that the reason he had accepted the compromise was because "it strengthens the standing of labor unions and gives them in law, *what they were generally considered to have in fact, a clear right to organize for the common good of their members.*" But he took pains to assure the reporters that the provision did not exempt labor from prosecution under the Sherman Act. It simply meant that labor had the right to organize.[59] And this was the position Wilson was to maintain throughout the months during which the Clayton Bill was being debated in Congress. On July 13, he wrote: "The so-called labor exemption does not seem to me *to do more than exclude the possibility of labor and similar organizations being dissolved as in themselves combinations in restraint of trade.*"[60]

In short, when Gompers informed the Executive Council that Wilson and the House Judiciary Committee had agreed to accept the compromise as assuring labor exemption from the Sherman Act, he was engaging in wishful thinking. He had, as one student points out, been handed a "goldbrick" which he then proceeded to "gild."[61]

One can argue, as some defenders of Gompers' role in this crucial battle have, that the AFL president was correct in emphasizing the importance of obtaining a legal assertion of labor's right to exist, for a lower court had held in the *Hitchman* case that the mine workers' union was an illegal conspiracy and there was a danger that the courts might use this decision as the basis for new decisions to dissolve unions as illegal combinations.[62] But this threat had all but disappeared by May 29, 1914 when the Circuit Court of Appeals reversed the lower court in the *Hitchman* case.[63] Actually, Wilson was correct in stating that Section 6 gave the trade unions nothing they did not already have: *"what they were generally considered to have in fact, a clear right to organize for the common good of their members."* This right had frequently been rendered null and void by prosecutions of the unions under the Sherman Act, and the failure to remove labor from this possibility without any doubt in the future was to render Section 6 valueless. It is significant that during the debate over the Clayton Bill in the House, the only proposal that made any sense was the recommendation made by several representatives that Section 6 should be withdrawn and rewritten so that everyone could agree as to what it meant, and thus prevent any mistakes in the future as to its meaning. But this reasonable proposal received no support from the AFL and was voted down.[64]

Thus, the Clayton Bill passed the House in the midst of a basic disagreement over its meaning as far as labor was concerned. President Wilson, the Judiciary Committee, and a majority of congressmen insisted that Section 6 gave labor no more than the right to exist, while Gompers, the AFL Executive Council, the Federations' legal advisors, and a few congressmen maintained that it not only granted labor this right, but also exempted it from the Sherman Act. This confusion foreshadowed tragedy for the American labor movement in the years that lay ahead.

There was also disagreement over the meaning of Section 20 of the Clayton Bill. This section incorporated the Clayton Anti-Injunction and Anti-Contempt Bills. Several members of Congress pointed out that the injunction prohibition accomplished nothing because the section did not define a "property right" in a labor dispute as did the Bacon-Bartlett bill, and that the phrase "unless necessary to prevent irreparable injury to property, or to a property right, of the party making the application [for an injunction]," offered a loophole big enough for all open-shop employers to crawl through. There was also a good deal of dispute as to whether or not the section legalized the secondary boycott.[65]

Even before the final passage of the Clayton Act, it was clear to many authorities that the act did not remove the root of existing injustice. It did not, for example, prevent damage suits or clearly forbid injunctions against picketing and boycotts. Writing in *The Survey* of July 4, 1914,

Edwin E. Witte, a leading student of government–labor relations, while agreeing that the bill would prevent the dissolution of trade unions, expressed grave doubt over whether it would do anything else: "The acts enumerated in the bill are not ordinarily unlawful; but the combining to do these acts is unlawful when the intent is to injure an employer or non-union workman. The majority report of the Committee on the Judiciary states expressly that this section does not in any manner affect the law of conspiracy."[66]

A week after this statement appeared, Representative Edwin Y. Webb, who had replaced Clayton as chairman of the Judiciary Committee after the latter was appointed a Federal judge, confirmed Witte's interpretation. He maintained that the only thing done by the Clayton Bill was to place into statutory law "the rights of those organizations to exist and carry out their lawful purposes." Although labor had demanded an amendment that would have exempted it from the Sherman Act, the Judiciary Committee had not accepted this recommendation. The labor sections of the bill simply stated "the consensus of the judgments of the best Federal Courts. . . . There is nothing revolutionary or radical about it."[67]

But the AFL leadership remained adamant in its contention that "the section [6] would definitely and clearly exempt the organizations of laborers and producers from the civil as well as the criminal sections of the Sherman Anti-Trust Law."[68] Gompers exuded confidence as he wrote in the AFL's *Weekly News Letter* that the bill secured "for workers freedom of action for self-protection and for the promotion of their own interests." He had not the slightest doubt that the bill would fulfill labor's most optimistic hopes,[69] and stressed that, as far as organized labor was concerned, the problem was not to worry about the meaning of the bill but to make sure that it was not modified in the Senate. Immediately after the bill passed the House, Gompers warned all workers that they must be on guard to prevent powerful anti-labor interests from destroying the measure in the Senate. The AFL *Weekly News Letter* carried Gompers' message in its issue of June 6, 1914:

> Labor is now nearing victory at the end of a twenty-year fight. Every influence that greed and special privilege can assert will be used to defeat these labor measures in the Senate. Special privilege will not voluntarily yield its control over the making of law. . . . The victory is in sight, the fight is not yet won. . . .
>
> Every member of organized labor must make his Senators feel that he is personally deeply concerned that the labor section of the Clayton Bill shall be adopted by the United States Senate. Every member of the labor organiza-

tions should write his Senators immediately urging upon them the vital importance of this legislation to labor. . . .

Throughout the summer of 1914, AFL headquarters in Washington kept union workers in all parts of the country informed about the progress of the bill in the Senate. Editorials in the *American Federationist,* circulars, and leaflets urged union members to impress "upon their respective members in the Senate the imperative necessity of taking immediate and favorable action upon labor's needs and demands. Demand the bill as it passed the House." When particular senators indicated that they might vote against the bill, their names were dispatched in circulars to union members in their states with an appeal that letters, telegrams, and petitions be sent to them at once: "Respectfully and insistently request their support and vote for labor provisions of the Clayton Bill as they passed the House of Representatives."[70]

This insistent pressure won the admiration of labor's friends, but some progressive commentators noted that it would have been more useful if the AFL had begun this campaign while the bill was being discussed in the House and had made the demand for a clear affirmation of labor's exemption from the provisions of the Sherman Act the key to this drive.[71]

Although the AFL concentrated on getting the Clayton Bill passed in the Senate as it had been adopted in the House, Gompers offered Senator Albert B. Cummins of Iowa an opening section to Section 6 which read: "The labor of a human being is not a commodity or article of commerce." Cummins introduced this declaration as an amendment and was successful in getting the Senate to accept it.[72] He also made several other attempts to strengthen the labor sections and particularly to have the wording clearly exempt labor from the anti-trust act, but he was unsuccessful. Gompers, intoxicated over the wording of the opening declaration of Section 6 and entranced with the success in having the Senate adopt his statement, did little to rally labor support behind the other efforts to strengthen the labor sections.[73]

The conservatives, however, were not idle, and the bill as it passed the Senate contained modifications in the wording of both Sections 6 and 20 which made it even more acceptable to the business interests. The most important of these was the addition at various points of the words "lawful" and "lawfully." Thus, Section 6 was changed to read: " . . . or forbid or restrain individual members of such organizations from *lawfully* carrying out their legitimate objects thereof. . . ." And the injunction clauses of Section 20 were changed to read: " . . . or from recommending, advising, or persuading others by peaceful and *lawful* means so to do . . . or from peaceably assembling in a *lawful* manner, and for *lawful* purposes. . . ."[74] The *New York Times*, a bitter critic of the bill as it had passed the House, hailed these changes and asserted delightedly that if the "injunctive clauses are rightfully interpreted, labor which has thought the courts have chastised them with whips, will find that the statute chastises them with scorpions."[75] Daniel Davenport, general counsel of the open-shop American Anti-Boycott Association, who had characterized Sections 6 and 20 as passed by the House as "revolutionary and destructive," now observed gleefully: "In the shape in which it finally passed, it makes few changes in existing laws relating to labor unions, injunctions and contempt of court, and those are of slight practical importance." Former President Taft endorsed Davenport's interpretation in an address before the American Bar Association.[76] In its letter to bankers and industrialists, the National City Bank of New York assured its readers that the bill

> . . . did nothing more than recognize such combinations [labor organization] were not in themselves illegal combinations. It has never been seriously contended that they were, but the theory has been occasionally advanced in public addresses. Ex-president Taft, who while in the presidential chair, strenuously opposed all exceptions to the operations of the Sherman law, accepts this view of the new provision.[77]

On October 2, 1914, the Clayton Bill passed the Senate by a vote of 35-24, with only three Democrats voting against it. Thirteen days later, President Wilson signed the measure and sent the pen he had used to Gompers.[78] The new law was immediately hailed by the AFL as the decisive victory in labor's long fight for legal recognition and for protection against court assaults. "The labor sections of the Clayton Anti-Trust Act are a great victory for organized labor," exulted Gompers. "In no other country in the world is there an enunciation of fundamental principle comparable to the incisive, virile statement of Section 6. . . . The declaratatory legislation, 'The labor of a human being is not a commodity or article,' is the industrial Magna Carta upon which the working people will rear the structure of industrial freedom."[79]* He assured the Executive Council that this declaration was "the most important ever made by any legislative body in the history of the world."[80] So carried away was Gompers that he predicted that the "opening statement" alone would guarantee labor unions immunity

*The letterhead of the Order of Railroad Telegraphers carried the words on top: " 'The Labor Of a Human Being Is Not a Commodity or Article of Commerce'—Clayton Anti-Trust Law." (A. M. Simons Papers, Wisconsin State Historical Society.)

from future court attacks: "This declaration removed all possibility of interpreting trust legislation to apply to organizations of the workers and their legitimate associated activities."[81]

The joy at AFL headquarters was not shared by everyone in labor circles. Even as conservative a labor leader as Grand Chief Warren S. Stone of the Brotherhood of Locomotive Engineers doubted the value of the Clayton Act and asked ruefully if "the other side had fooled the unions instead of the unions fooling them."[82] Several trade union journals pointed out that, despite Gompers' boast to the contrary, the exemption of labor unions from prosecution under the British Trades Disputes Act of 1906 was much more specific and clear-cut than that in the Clayton Act.* The Socialists, agreeing for once with Grand Chief Stone, contended that "labor had been duped." The Party's *Washington Letter* reported that "astute legal minds in Washington completely realize that the amendment will not exempt the unions, but the politicians are delighted with the success of the game they have put across."[83] The AFL leaders dismissed this as "sour grapes," since, they contended, passage of the Clayton Act had disproved the Socialist argument that the Federation's political program would never net anything substantial for organized labor.[84] But the trade unions were disturbed by reports that Attorney-General T. W. Gregory was of the distinct opinion that the new law would not grant labor immunity from the Sherman Act,** and that President Wilson himself had asserted that the labor sections of the law were not designed to grant the labor organizations any privilege they did not already enjoy. Certainly, the fact that an open-shop mouthpiece like Daniel Davenport regarded the Clayton Act as granting labor only the most minimal concession and that "of slight practical value" was most disturbing, to say the least.

WHAT DID LABOR GAIN?

Unfortunately subsequent events bore out the truth of the open-shop spokesman's evaluation. There is not space enough here to list the

---

*As Sidney and Beatrice Webb point out, the British Act "explicitly declares, without any qualification or exception, that no civil action shall be entertained against a Trade Union in respect of any wrongful act committed by or on behalf of the Union." (*The British Labor Movement*, London, 1931, p. 606.)

**Attorney-General Gregory had written to Wilson on September 11, 1914, expressing the definite opinion that the law did not grant unions such immunity and that "the purpose of the section [6] is only to prevent such organizations from being dissolved because they or their members had committed unlawful acts, and to recognize the organizations as being in and of themselves lawful but not to grant them entire immunity from prosecution under the anti-trust law. . . ." (Woodrow Wilson Papers, Library of Congress.)

numerous judicial decisions which made a mockery of Gompers' high hopes, particularly since they occurred outside the scope of the present volume. Basically, however, it can be said that these hopes were wrecked by judicial interpretations made possible by the vagueness of the act, and that these interpretations were actually foreshadowed by many contemporary observers, apart from Gompers and the rest of the AFL leadership even before the courts decided the issue. The fact is that the leaders of the AFL bear a heavy responsibility for the years of suffering that lay ahead for American labor. Their failure to conduct a militant struggle to specifically exempt labor from the provisions of the Sherman Act and to mobilize labor to fight for this demand, especially when it was clear that with the elections of 1914 on the horizon, such a fight could have been won, opened the door to tragic consequences for the labor movement.* The acceptance by the AFL leadership, without a struggle, of the inclusion of such terms as "peacefully," "lawfully," and "in case where no irreparable injury would occur . . . " gave the courts the opportunity to destroy any effectiveness the Clayton Act possessed.** As early as 1917, in the Duplex Printing Press Company case, the court, in granting an injunction to the company, argued that "the emphasis placed on the 'lawful' and 'lawfully,' 'peaceful' and 'peacefully' . . . [in Section 20 of the Clayton Act] strongly rebutted a legislative intent to confer a general immunity for conduct violative of the Anti-Trust laws." In the same year, the Supreme Court decided in favor of the Hitchman Coal Company against the United Mine Workers, and the majority decision gave legal sanction to the "yellow dog" contract. This was followed by a widespread use of this anti-labor contract, despite the existence of the

---

*Norman J. Ware blames Gompers for the vagueness of the labor sections of the Clayton Act. (*Labor in Modern Society,* Boston, 1934, p. 347.) Dallas S. Jones also criticizes Gompers, but places the real blame for the vagueness of the act on President Wilson. ("The Wilson Administration and Organized Labor, 1912-1919," unpublished Ph.D. thesis, Cornell University, 1955, p. 182. *See also* his article, "The Enigma of the Clayton Act," *Industrial and Labor Relations Review,* vol. X, January, 1957, pp. 203-22.)

Father John S. Smith defends Gompers from the charge that he and [other labor leaders] were "duped by the administration and Congress," and that Gompers himself did not believe, as he announced publicly, that the Clayton Act really freed organized labor from anti-trust proceedings. (*op. cit.,* pp. 66-68.) It is certainly true that in his private correspondence, Gompers did not make the extravagant claims for the act that he did publicly. (*See* Gompers to David Kreyling, Mrs. Raymond Robins, and Frank P. Walsh, Jan. 19, Aug. 31, Sept. 15, 1915, *Gompers Letter Books.*)

**Stanley L. Kutler, however, contends that while the Clayton Act was very ambiguous and thus open to a wide variety of judicial interpretations, the conservative composition of the Supreme Court at the time, especially its anti-labor bias, doomed any possibility of achieving what labor hoped to gain. ("Labor, the Clayton Act, and the Supreme Court," *Labor History,* vol. III, Winter, 1962, pp. 19-38.)

Clayton Act, until it was declared unenforceable by the Norris–LaGuardia Act in 1932.

The AFL's belief that, by virtue of the Clayton Act, labor was no longer under the ban of the Sherman Act, and that strikes, boycotts, and picketing could no longer be obstructed by injunctions, proved to be unfounded. The only accomplishment labor could claim for itself was the recognition that unions, *per se,* were not illegal combinations in restraint of trade, a fact already acknowledged.[85] Apart from the right of trial by jury in contempt cases—sustained in November, 1924—labor's gains in the Clayton Act have been of slight importance. Writing in 1930, Felix Frankfurter observed:

> The position of labor before the law has been altered, if at all, imperceptibly. Common law doctrines of conspiracy and restraint of trade still hold sway; activities widely cherished as indispensable assertions of trade union life continue to be outlawed. . . . That the Clayton Act has defeated the hopes which inspired it, that its judicial application has revealed needs for further legislation, is written in recent Congressional history.[86]

From 1906 to 1914, the AFL leadership had persistently fought every attempt of American labor to have its own political party. The pattern of "reward-your-friends-and-punish-your-enemies" had been held out as the most effective way to achieve labor's political objectives. At the end of this eight-year period, Gompers defended his opposition to a labor party and pointed with pride to the record of achievement under the AFL's methods of political pressure.* "We have changed the control of our government from the old-time interests of corporate power and judicial usurpation," he wrote joyfully. There were, he enumerated triumphantly, the eight-hour law, child labor laws in the various states, improved safety regulations in industry, workmen's compensation acts in no fewer than thirty-five states—and, most important of all, the Clayton Anti-Trust Act.[87]

A careful study of these legislative successes casts serious doubt on Gompers' claims. For one thing, many of the laws passed in the states were the product of an alliance between the Progressive forces and the trade unions—an alliance frowned upon by the AFL leadership. Then again, the Wilson administration, in the period we have examined, acceded primarily to the minor demands of the AFL; its concessions on major matters were limited in both number and scope. And instead of the most important legislation which the AFL required—immunity from

---

*Referring to the period around 1914, John P. Frey declared: "He [Gompers] was reasonably satisfied with the results of his type of political action." ("Harvard University Seminar," May 11, 1948," John P. Frey Papers, Container 10, Library of Congress.)

prosecution under the Sherman Anti-Trust Act—it had produced the Clayton Act, an illusory promise which was never fulfilled. It was to take another twenty years before the trade unions received injunction relief through the Norris–LaGuardia Act. Almost half a century passed from the time agitation for such legislative amelioration was initiated until its achievement. In England, a single year of labor party agitation produced more effective legislation of this type than fifty years of the AFL's lobbying activities and political pressure methods.

Although the powerful machine control of the annual conventions made it impossible to secure convention approval of an independent labor party, the persistent demand for such action by organized labor made its influence felt in several ways. For one thing, it was an important influence in compelling the AFL leadership to abandon its anti-political action position and to begin, however inadequately, to mobilize labor's strength at the polls. Even a defender of Gompers concedes: "He only abandoned the principle of applying purely economic pressure when he was forced to do so."[88] By 1906, the AFL leaders knew that to continue to display indifference to political action was to surrender the field to the advocates of a labor party. In like manner, the pressure for a labor party helped impress upon the major parties the need to grant some of labor's legislative demands, lest the barriers erected in the AFL against a labor party be breached, and labor begin to operate as a truly independent force in American politics. When Gompers warned the Democratic Party that unless it "produced" for labor, a labor party would be organized, his words carried meaning only because of the existence of the pro-labor party forces within the AFL. In short, these forces prodded both the AFL to adopt more aggressive political methods and the major political parties, particularly the Democratic Party, to enact some of the legislation labor sought.

During the years that the AFL and its affiliates were involved in the political arena, seeking to achieve legislation to strengthen the trade unions and a better life for workers, they were also engaged in some of the most massive and bitter strike struggles in American labor history. While these were not the only significant strikes of the era—the IWW, as we have seen in a previous volume, conducted strikes of an unprecedented magnitude and militancy during these same years—they revealed that a very substantial section of workers who were members of the AFL were equally courageous, equally militant in facing the power of capital. We will see this illustrated in the following chapters in the strikes of street car workers, railroad shopmen, coal and copper miners, and workers in the ladies' and men's garment trades.

CHAPTER 6

The General Strike in Philadelphia—1910

On March 5, 1910, the front page of the Philadelphia *Public Ledger* carried the sensational news that a general strike had begun at midnight in support of the city's Rapid Transit Company carmen. This action of Philadelphia workers, it said, represented "an entirely new development in the history of combats between capital and labor in this country." Terming it "The Impossible Strike," the *Ledger* concluded: "This quaint conception of a whole people going on strike originated in Russia, where the people have little voice in the management of their affairs and as little political intelligence."[1]

Clearly, the leading Philadelphia paper was unaware of the fact that this was actually the second general strike in the City of Brotherly Love. The first occurred in 1835, when every group of workers in the city, skilled and unskilled, went on strike for the ten-hour day and thereby gave America its first general strike.[2]*

The origins of Philadelphia's second general strike go back to May 29, 1909, when a street car strike began after officials of the Philadelphia Rapid Transit Company refused to even receive a committee of the local branch of the Amalgamated Association of Street Car and Electric Railway Men of America, an AFL affiliate. Division 477's committee

---

*The first general strike in the modern sense took place in St. Louis during the Railroad Strike of 1877. (*See* David T. Burbank, *The Reign of the Rabble: The St. Louis General Strike of 1877*, New York, 1966, and Philip S. Foner, *The Great Labor Uprising of 1877*, New York, 1977, pp. 157–88.) Nevertheless, all newspapers called the 1910 general strike in Philadelphia the first in the United States, and the Socialist New York *Call* declared editorially: "The general strike of the wage workers of a great city is a decidedly new departure for the labor movement in America." (March 14, 1910.) This even ignored the New Orleans general strike of 1892.

was bringing with it the demands of the motormen and conductors for an hourly wage of 25 cents, the privilege of buying uniforms in the open market, a nine- or ten-hour day in place of the prevailing "swing run," in which the men had to put in from fourteen to eighteen hours, and recognition of the Amalgamated Association.[3]

When the company imported strikebreakers from New York and Boston, violence broke out. Cars were demolished and wiring and track were destroyed. The police arrested strikers wholesale. But the importation of strikebreakers and the harsh police brutality, coming on top of the popular hatred of the Transit Company for its generally poor service, financial mismanagement, and flagrant use of political influence, aroused widespread anger in Philadelphia, especially among the working classes. John J. Murphy, president of the Central Labor Union, issued the following ultimatum:

> If the Philadelphia Rapid Transit Company does not meet the demands of the trolley workers by Thursday night [June 7], a strike of all organized labor bodies of Philadelphia affiliated with the Central Labor Union, representing 75,000 men, will be called Friday morning. The present strike is only a beginning of the fight which will be waged by organized labor to emancipate the city of Philadelphia from the thraldom of capitalism.[4]

It was to take almost another year before the threat of a general strike in Philadelphia became a reality. But it was not needed in 1909, for the wide support for the car strikers produced a settlement. State Senator James P. McNichol, Philadelphia's Republican leader, met with C. O. Pratt, national organizer of the Amalgamated Association, after which Mayor John E. Reyburn urged the Philadelphia Rapid Transit Company to reach a settlement. On June 2, 1909, the workers gained a one-year agreement which included a wage increase from 21 to 22 cents an hour, a ten-hour day, the right to buy uniforms from five different clothiers, and recognition of the Amalgamated Association, with the company agreeing to meet with duly accredited union representatives to settle grievances.[5]

"The men are entirely satisfied with their victory," reported the New York *Call*. "The men are most pleased because it gives them a basis for future concessions. Their organization will now be firmly established so that when the contract expires they will be in a stronger position to secure improved conditions."[6] But satisfaction soon gave way to considerable discontent. The Philadelphia Rapid Transit Company, ignoring the terms of the strike settlement, established its own union—the "Keystone Carmen"—and not only met regularly with representatives of the company union, but gave its members the choice jobs and promotions.[7]

In December, 1909, the Amalgamated Association began negotiations for a new agreement. Ignoring the complaints that it had violated the existing agreement, the company turned down the request for a wage increase to 25 cents an hour. Instead, without consulting the union, it instituted a complicated welfare plan, including insurance and pensions. On January 3, 1910, two days after announcing the plan, the company discharged seven roadway employees of the elevated department who had announced that they were joining the Amalgamated Association and who criticized the welfare plan as a device designed to undermine the union and prevent a wage increase. When the Amalgamated Association asked for arbitration of their cases, the company refused to even consider the proposal.[8]

On January 18, by a vote of 5,121 to 233, the members of Division 477 adopted a "strike resolution," which declared that while the agreement adopted on June 8, 1909 had been "religiously observed by us," it had been "outrageously violated by the company." Among the violations cited were that the company had "instituted and encouraged another organization which creates dissension and discord"; had "discriminated against our members"; had "favored at all times employees antagonistic to our union"; had "refused adjustment for grievances"; had discharged "union employees from the elevated road after intimidating and otherwise endeavoring to prevent them from joining our union"; and had "refused arbitration." Therefore, the carmen resolved

> That we authorize our Executive Board to call a strike on the entire system of the Philadelphia Rapid Transit Company, and every department of the same at the most opportune time after complying with by-laws.[9]

The Philadelphia *Evening Bulletin,* after noting that the size and practical unanimity of the strike vote demonstrated "that the local union has a greater strength than the company's officials have given it credit for having," urged the PRT to take the decision seriously. But Charles O. Kruger, the company's president, responded by saying: "The strike vote will not change the attitude of the company the slightest."[10] Mayor Reyburn voiced his full approval of the company's position. "The street car employees are not union men or employees in the same sense that employees in an industrial establishment are," he warned. "They are semi-public functionaries, and they owe it to the public to recognize themselves in that capacity."[11] Evidently, in the mayor's eyes, the company owed no such allegiance or responsibility to the public.

The union did everything possible to stave off a strike. It even appealed for the intercession of State Senator McNichol, the political leader who had stepped into the breach the previous June and had helped achieve an agreement. But this time the company made it clear that it would not listen to any outsider. It reminded the men that if they struck, they would be debarred from participating in the company's welfare plan, which had already been put into effect.[12]

Informed by the Amalgamated Association that the company's tactics would inevitably cause negotiations to be broken off, AFL President Samuel Gompers sent an offer to President Kruger to have any issue that could not be mutually adjusted submitted to "arbitration by any impartial body of men." The union, he assured the PRT president, was prepared to go along, but Kruger merely thanked Gompers and told him that his good offices would not be needed since "the situation was adjusting itself."[13]

The arrogance of the company's response became clear on February 15, when Kruger informed the union's Executive Committee that the PRT would uphold the right of any of its employees to join or not join any union, and that the workers would be free to present their grievances to the company individually or as members of any organization they wished to represent them. As a result, negotiations were immediately broken off. With total indifference to these developments, the company, on February 19, discharged 173 men—all of them members of the Amalgamated Association—"for the good of the service." At the same time, an equal number of replacements were brought in from New York.[14]

The PRT had deliberately provoked a showdown with the Amalgamated Association, and within an hour after the men were discharged, Division 477's president and secretary, Peter Driscoll and F. B. Barrow, issued the order, authorized by the membership, calling the men out on strike:*

> Brothers! The company has yesterday and today discharged hundreds of our union men "for the good of the service." There is nothing whatever against the record of these men except that they belong to our union. They are among the best men employed by the company.

*The strike in Philadelphia was not the only major labor struggle in Pennsylvania early in 1910. On February 2, 1910, a three-man delegation, representing more than 700 skilled workers of the Bethlehem Steel Company in Bethlehem, Pennsylvania, were fired for presenting their grievances and demands. (A major grievance was that wage rates were too low and hours too long, and especially the company's refusal to pay time-and-a-half for overtime.) The company's action was followed by a strike which lasted for 108 days, involving both skilled machinists and unskilled laborers. On May 18, 1910, the strike ended without the workers having achieved any of their demands. (*See* Robert Hessen, "The Bethlehem Steel Strike of 1910." *Labor History,* vol. XV, Winter, 1974, pp. 3-18.)

The company has forced a lockout and you will instruct every union man to take his car into the barn at 1 o'clock this afternoon, February 19, 1910, and allow it to remain there until the company will sign an agreement with us guaranteeing 25 cents an hour and protecting us in our rights to belong to a union without being unjustly discriminated against.[15]

Subservient as always to the business interests, Mayor Reyburn joined wholeheartedly in the campaign to destroy the carmen's union. On the first day of the strike, several hundred strikebreakers arrived, and, under heavy police guard, they were hurried on special trolley cars to the barn at Frankford Avenue and Bridge Street.[16] The Philadelphia *North American* noted "the almost universal hatred which the public bears toward the traction company" and reported that the use of strikebreakers only served to increase the universal support for the strikers and the popular hatred of the PRT.[17] All over the city, cars were damaged, smashed, and burned. Stones were thrown at "scab" motormen and cars were hammered into junk by iron pipes. The police used their clubs freely in the Kensington industrial area and on Broad Street, where large crowds marched in protest against Reyburn's open alignment with management. In Germantown, 10,000 strike sympathizers clashed with police in a furious battle that raged for two hours. At the Baldwin Locomotive Works, strike sympathizers seized a street car, knocked the motorman senseless, and demolished the vehicle. When the police rushed to the scene, the workers hurled bricks at them, while from inside the Baldwin factory, nuts, bolts, and wrenches were flung at the officers. The police then opened fire indiscriminately, turning their revolvers against pedestrians and firing through the windows of shops at those who ran inside for protection. At the same time, firemen, who were called in by the police, directed heavy streams of water upon the people, even injuring women with babies in their arms.[18] "All this," warned the Philadelphia *Evening Bulletin,* "cannot be expected to quell the indignation which seems to be so generally manifest. It should be remembered that these people are Americans and they are not accustomed to Russian rule."[19]

In an effort to augment his police force, Mayor Reyburn issued a call for 3,000 citizens to do police duty. C. O. Pratt, the popular Amalgamated Association organizer, offered 6,000 union men "to perform such functions.... They are bonafide citizens of Philadelphia and will pledge themselves to preserve peace and order."[20] This offer, of course, was rejected, and Mayor Reyburn called in the Pennsylvania Fencibles, a private military and social organization. But the volunteers—many of whom were mere boys—were totally ineffective. Most of them had their coats torn off and their weapons seized by taunting crowds.[21]

Mayor Reyburn further infuriated the people of Philadelphia by ordering the arrest of Pratt and John J. Murphy, president of the Central Labor Union. Both were held in $3,000 bail on charges of inciting to riot and conspiracy. Reyburn then called upon Governor Stuart to order the entire state National Guard into Philadelphia. On February 24, 1910, the troops marched into the city, and the New York *Call* declared that Philadelphia was now "in the hands of the Cossacks."[22]

Although the Central Labor Union had at first promised only financial support to the striking carmen, Charles Hope, the CLU secretary had warned as early as February 20 that "if policemen and imported strikebreakers are used to any extent to run the trolley cars, the Central Labor Union may call a sympathy strike." Such a call, he predicted, would be assured of receiving an enthusiastic response: "As all union men know of the unfair treatment accorded the trolleymen, there is no doubt that all will respond to the call and strike in sympathy with those who have been oppressed."[23]

The following day, President Murphy revealed that a letter had been sent to every union affiliated with the CLU, asking if it was willing to join a general strike of sympathy with the carmen, and that already one-third of the unions had replied in the affirmative. Moreover, two independent bodies—the Allied Building Trades Council and the District Council of the Brotherhood of Painters, Decorators and Paperhangers of America, representing together 42,500 workers—had agreed to join the general strike if it were called.[24]

Church leaders and business men, the latter appalled at the potential effect that the threatened general strike would have on trade already suffering from the carmen's strike, pleaded with the Rapid Transit Company and the union to submit the dispute to arbitration. The union agreed, but the company refused. The threat of a general strike, it declared, was "pure bluff." "A general sympathetic strike," the company stated, "would break every employment contract in Philadelphia, which is something that even the most senseless labor leader would not do." As if to challenge the CLU to do its worse, the company served an ultimatum threatening dismissal for those who failed to return to work immediately.[25] Once again, Mayor Reyburn endorsed the company's policy. There was nothing to be alarmed about in a general strike by all trades," he told reporters. However, he went on, arbitration was no solution, for the union would only want to finish near future.

The entrance of the state troops guaranteed that the general strike would be called. "You can depend upon it," vowed John Murphy, "a general strike will take place. . . . The state police will be helpless. I want it understood that there are men in the northeast who can shoot as straight as any trooper who ever drew breath."[27] The first part of his fiery statement turned out to be correct. On February 27, the Central Labor union, the unaffiliated trades, and the Building Trades Council, meeting separately in the same building, voted to go on a general strike the following Saturday if the carmen's strike was not settled by that date. At first, the demand had been for an immediate general strike, but Pratt appealed for the delay so that further pressure could be put on the PRT to agree to arbitration, and, at the same time, to enable organized labor to marshal its forces more effectively. His argument prevailed, and after agreeing to the date, the three labor bodies passed a resolution which noted that the Philadelphia Rapid Transit Company had begun "a wholesale lockout of the union men, numbering hundreds, the only excuse being that they belong to the union," that since the carmen had been locked out, the company officials had conspired "with certain interests in City Hall and have clubbed, coerced, and arrested innocent men who were innocent of any crime whatsoever, have denied the citizens of this city their God-given and constitutional rights," and that the state police had been brought into the city "without any justification whatever, but ostensibly for the purpose of preserving order." Hence,

> Resolved, That we, the representatives of labor, in extraordinary convention assembled, do hereby determine that a general strike shall take place in protest against the high-handed action and arbitrary use of administrative power and that we pledge ourselves not to return to work until all rights have been recognized and complied with.[28]

To carry out the purposes of the resolution, President Murphy appointed a Committee of Ten made up of members of the CLU Executive Committee and the Building Trades Council.[29]

From cities all over the United States came wires of support for the vote taken in favor of the general strike should the company refuse to arbitrate. "250,000 union men in this city hail your action," wired John Fitzpatrick, president of Chicago's Central Labor Union, "and stand ready to join in a sympathetic strike against the traction powers." Andrew J. Gallaghe , secretary of the Central Labor Union of San rancisco, wired: "1 ,000 men in this cit·   ith you in any action u may take." Sar   el Devery, presid   entral Labor Union of   gton, D. C.   l·   ·' l: "Th   re taken by three labor bodies for a general strike was the greatest day Labor ever had in Philadelphia or any other city in America." "Stand your ground against the man-eating sharks of Philadelphia," read the telegram from Socialist Eugene V. Debs. "We are with you to a finish."[30]

When asked "why does your company discount the sympathetic strike talk even after the vote of the Central Labor Council and other labor bodies," Daniel T. Pierce, executive assistant to President Kruger, replied:

> Because we know that the real labor leaders are opposed to it. [T. L.] Lewis of the Mine Workers Union has plainly said so. Mr. Gompers, president of the American Federation of Labor, has refused to utter a word in favor of the proposition which, at one blow, would destroy whatever faith there remains in the value or desirability of contracts with trades unions.[31]

To check on the accuracy of this evaluation, the Philadelphia *Public Ledger* sent a telegram to the heads of various international unions, asking "whether you approve of the threat that all labor unions here strike in sympathy with the striking carmen. Also give views on the general strike."[32] Negative or qualified replies came from John T. Hayes, General Master Workman of the all-but-defunct Knights of Labor, who called a sympathy strike "a fool proposition"; from W. D. Mahon, international president of the Amalgamated Association, who said the entire matter was in the hands of local officials in Philadelphia; and from William D. Huber, president of the United Brotherhood of Carpenters and Joiners, who saw "no good" coming out of a sympathy strike. On the other hand, George Preston, secretary-treasurer of the International Association of Machinists, G. L. Blaine, secretary-treasurer of the Boot and Shoe Workers' Union, and Thomas B. Kramer, secretary-treasurer of the International Brotherhood of Blacksmiths, all favored a sympathy strike, Kramer put it most forcefully:

> I believe this to be as good a time as any other for the working people and their sympathizers to stand together in support of the men who have been forced to strike by this corporation that has grown rich, sleek and fat at the expense of the people of Philadelphia, and which seeks further to insult them by bringing into their city an imported system of gunnery and chasing them round like so many highway robbers. This means we must stand together in sympathy lest we be compelled to surrender that which we now enjoy.

Interestingly enough, J. J. McNamara, then still secretary-treasurer of the International Association of Bridge and Structural Iron Workers, took a more moderate position. He opposed a sympathy strike but favored, instead, "a strike of trackmen, linemen, powerhouse employees, etc., whose interests are identical with the striking carmen." As for the sympathy strike in a general sense, McNamara felt that organized labor must continue to make use of it "until the blacklist and other injustices of organized capital are abolished, either by strict and prohibitive legislation, or a better establishment of the feeling that is known as the 'Brotherhood of Man.'"[33]

Samuel Gompers refused to comment on the question of a general strike, but he did observe that the carmen's strike was "the result of a plot to destroy the men's union on the part of the Philadelphia Rapid Transit Company, and this conspiracy is being backed by the National Association of Manufacturers and every leading open-shop association in the country." There was justification for Gompers' assertion, for it was widely reported in the press that leading open-shop organizations were urging the PRT to stand firm against any concession to the union.

On March 1, 1910, while seven of the eight English-language papers of Philadelphia were pleading with the PRT to arbitrate and prevent a general strike,[34]* the company rejected a new appeal from a Churchmen's and Laymen's Committee and the United Business Men's Association, asking for arbitration and pointing out that the union had agreed to a proposal calling for the company to select two men, the union two men, and the four to select a fifth as an umpire in arbitration proceedings. President Kruger declared that there were only two issues at stake in the strike: "(1) the right of our employees to deal directly with us without the intervention of an organization controlled by outside men; (2) The right of this company to have the same freedom in hiring and discharging men that the men have in staying with or leaving the company." These rights, he maintained, were "fundamental and inalienable and do not submit themselves to any form of arbitration."[35] Mayor Reyburn immediately announced his full support for this position and declared that he would stand firm behind the PRT's refusal to arbitrate even if it meant his "political suicide."[36]

As a final concession, the union now agreed to have the authorities invoke the Act of 1893, which provided that the Court of Common

*The fact that seven of these papers favored arbitration was cited by them as an answer to the charge in *The Outlook* that Philadelphia newspapers were suppressing the truth about the strike because of "the domination of department stores." (Harold J. Howland, "The War in Philadelphia," *The Outlook,* vol. XCIV, March 5, 1910, pp. 523–24.) But the magazine refused to retract its charge and published an anonymous letter from Philadelphia supporting its position: "It is also a matter of common belief that at the present time strong pressure is being brought upon the press to suppress much of the news that may be damaging to the traction company or to the city authorities." (*Ibid.,* pp. 802–03. *See also* Philadelphia *Public Ledger,* March 17, 1910.)

Pleas, when appealed to, could appoint Boards of Arbitration in disputes between labor and capital. Up to that point, Pratt had rejected the idea of bringing the dispute "into the politically-directed courts." But, in an effort to achieve a settlement before the general strike went into effect, the union reversed itself. The concession, however, proved to be useless. The company would accept no arbitration of any kind and responded by merely extending to March 8 the deadline for taking strikers back if they applied for reinstatement as individuals.[37]

"I think myself a general strike is the only thing left, if recourse to the courts ... is refused by the PRT Co.," wrote Dora Lewis, a Philadelphia shirtwaist worker, to Agnes Nestor on March 4, 1910. "It is really a fight now for the existence of any union in the city and I think all the unions feel that."[38] Perhaps not all, but certainly the vast majority did. Convinced by now that no alternative was possible, the Central Labor Union took definite steps on March 2 to initiate the general strike, with a proclamation addressed to the "Trades Union Bodies of Philadelphia and Vicinity and Their Sympathizers." All workers, except those who furnished such absolute necessities as food, were requested to cease work at midnight, Friday, March 4, 1910. The proclamation emphasized the fact that the carmen were ready to accept arbitration, while the company, even though "a semi-public corporation, and, therefore, owing certain duties to the public not owed by private corporations," refused. It pointed out that events since the agreement of 1909 had proven beyond any doubt that the capitalists and a small group of "self-seeking politicians" in control of the Transit Company were "part of a larger group of capitalists and trust owners who hope to crush all organized labor by attacking and defeating it one group at a time." If ever the times called for organized labor to practice the principle of "an injury to one is the concern of all," the proclamation went on, it was at this particular moment. Hence, it was

> Proclaimed, That the time for action has arrived for all union workers and their sympathizers for the immediate assistance of the union street railway employees and the ultimate protection of all union employees and the working class will cease work on Friday at midnight, March 4, 1910, whether that is the regular stopping time or not, and remain on strike until further notice from the duly accredited representatives.

The proclamation was signed by the Committee of Ten representing the Central Labor Union and the Allied Building Trades of Philadelphia.[39] This committee also published a paraphrased version of the Declaration of Independence to justify the calling of the general strike.

After repeating the introductory paragraphs of the original Declaration, it stated: "The history of the Rapid Transit Company is a history of repeated injuries and usurpations, all having in direct object the establishment of absolute tyranny over the carmen." Then, after listing the oppressions heaped upon the carmen by the company and stating that petitions for redress "have been answered only by repeated injuries," the alternative Declaration of Independence* declared:

> We, therefore, the representatives of 150,000 toilers appealing to the Supreme Judge of the World for the rectitude of our intention, do, in the name and by the authority of organized and unorganized labor, declare that the demands of the striking carmen are founded upon right and justice and for the support of this declaration, with a firm reliance on the protection of Divine Providence and the abiding faith in the spirit of fairness of the American people and particularly the citizenship of Philadelphia, we 150,000 toilers unitedly pledge to each other our lives, our fortunes and our sacred honor.
>
> An adherence to the letter and spirit of the above declaration would soon render the United States of America as free of oppressive corporate influence, intimidation and corruption as St. Patrick rendered Ireland of snakes.[40]

Estimates varied as to how many workers walked off their jobs on March 4. Even those friendly to the strike complained that it was difficult to determine how many workers, organized and unorganized, abandoned their jobs, because no real information bureau had been set up from which the Committee of Ten could obtain a comprehensive view of the situation.[41] After the first day of the general strike, labor leaders placed the figure of those who had walked off their jobs at 100,000. The press, on the other hand, put it at between 48,000 and 50,000, while Director of Public Safety Henry Clay estimated the number to be no more than 20,000. But then, Clay was accused of owning $600,000 worth of traction stock, so his figure was generally discounted.[42] At any rate, a canvass by the *Public Ledger* and the *Evening Bulletin* indicated that textile industries, building operation, and garment-making firms were almost completely shut down, and that taxicab chauffeurs and cab drivers had quit work promptly at midnight, "many of them dumping fares into the streets far from their destination." On the other hand, firemen, engineers, electricians, and all classes of mechanics employed in the Rapid Transit Company's powerhouses, were reported to have "remained at their posts." Since the Committee of Ten had specifically

*For other examples of alternative Declarations of Independence used by American labor, *see* Philip S. Foner, *We the Other People: Alternative Declarations of Independence by Labor Groups, Farmers, Women's Rights Advocates, Socialists, and Blacks* (Urbana, Illinois, 1976.)

exempted bakers, milk and bread wagon drivers, and all others engaged in the delivery of household necessities from compliance with the strike call, "householders felt little, if any effect of the strike."[43]

The same newspapers, however, reported a great increase in the number of workers who joined the general strike on the second day. This was attributed to the house-to-house canvass by committees of workingmen and women urging their fellow workers who had failed to come out to join the strikers' ranks. "From early morning until late at night," the *Evening Bulletin* reported, "in groups of twos and threes, the strikers, sometimes accompanied by women, rang bells and begged the recalcitrants to join in labor's fight." The result was evident in the fact that unofficial estimates of the number on strike was now placed at between 100,000 and 125,000.[44]

The most specific breakdown of the number of men and women on strike in Philadelphia was made public on March 9, the fifth day of the general strike, by Charles A. Hope, secretary of the Committee of Ten. According to Hope, 139,221 workers were on strike, and they included, in addition to the 6,200 striking carmen, 40,000 in the building trades, 20,000 in the metal trades, 20,000 in the textile trades, 10,000 in the men's wear garment trades, and 9,000 in women's wear. Then there were workers in miscellaneous industries and trades, such as 105 insulators and asbestos workers, 210 cloth cap makers, 2,500 cigar makers, 1,000 shirtwaist and laundry workers, 151 piano movers, 347 confectionary workers, 468 pavers and rammers, 365 electrical workers, 410 waiters, and many other groups. Six thousand were reported out at the Baldwin Locomotive Works.[45] Conspicuously absent from the list of those on strike, however, were the men working in the PRT's powerhouses and the printers who were putting out the newspapers which published these statistics.[46]

Whatever the exact number of workers on strike at this time, the press did acknowledge that those who joined the general strike did so of their own free will and with a clear understanding of the issues involved. The *Public Ledger* interviewed fifty ordinary workers who had joined the general strike and published the following comments as typical. Alexander Ring, a carpenter (not, it was made clear, a Socialist), told the reporter: "The time has come when we must assert ourselves. Therefore I have quit and am doing my best to assert myself." Harry Benckert, a machinist, said: "I am striking because no man should be expected to spend his entire life slaving for capital." A. B. Du Bois, electrical worker, said: "This is a fight for ourselves—for organized labor. If the carmen lose this fight, all organized labor loses and goes to the wall. That's how I feel about it, and all the members of my local feel the same way." John Donnelly of the Plasterers' Union declared: "I voted to strike because I am a believer in unionism. Naturally, my sympathy is with the carmen, but this fight is not confined to that one union. It is an attack on organized labor, and threatens the life of every union in the country. We must win in this controversy or be wiped out by the capitalists." Finally, William H. Smith, an elevator constructor, said:

> Fair play—that's what we struck for—for the great American spirit of fair play. If you see a man getting hard knocks, don't you go to his assistance? Well, there's a conspiracy to beat down the carmen, a union of merchants' associations, newspapers, and so on, with the Rapid Transit Company, and there's nothing for the working men to do but to unite to support them. Every possible way was tried to effect a peaceful settlement. Now that's failing, we'll try another way—the strike.[47]

Eugene V. Debs, who paid a special visit to the city during the strike and addressed overflow crowds, was impressed by the class-conscious- ness of the workers who had quit work in sympathy with the carmen. He noted that the brutality of the Philadelphia police was deepening that class-consciousness, and, in general, that the strike was "making people think."[48] The point about police brutality was well taken. In the name of the General Strike Committee, the Committee of Ten requested the working people of Philadelphia to assemble in Independence Square on March 5 at 3 o'clock "to peaceably participate in behalf of the street carmen's union now on a strike."[49] Instantly, Mayor Reyburn issued a proclamation forbidding all assemblies until further notice.* But the workers insisted on attending the demonstration, and by 2:30 p.m., 20,000 of them were in or near Independence Square. Suddenly, mounted policemen began driving their horses savagely into the crowds, while automobile patrol wagons, crammed with heavily armed police, raced around the square, stopping here and there, while bluecoats leaped out and swung their clubs right and left. The mounted men, armed with long night sticks, then charged up and down Chestnut Street, scattering the crowd in which there were hundreds of women and girls seeking to escape from Independence Square. As the struggle between the police and the workers reached its climax, the bell in the belfry of Independence Square tolled the hour of three.[50]

*Mayor Reyburn even had his police ban the showing of John Galsworthy's play, *Strife*, at the Adelphi Theater on the ground that the performances might incite to riot. Evidently Galsworthy's message favoring arbitration of industrial disputes was too advanced for the mayor. Public pressure, in the end forced him to allow the play to be produced, and it was staged without incident. (Philadelphia *North American*, March 16, April 1, 2, 1910.)

Shortly after the brutal assault on the peaceful demonstrators, the Pennsylvania State Federation of Labor met in convention. On March 8, the enraged delegates unanimously adopted a resolution urging a statewide general strike "in case arbitration is further rejected by the Philadelphia Rapid Transit Company," and also calling on the American Federation of Labor to call a national strike. E. E. Greenawalt, president of the State Federation of Labor, was authorized to call a statewide general strike within eighteen days (or by March 26) if the PRT still refused to arbitrate by that date. However, all local unions in the state would first have to give their approval before final action was taken.[51]

The resolutions adopted by the Pennsylvania State Federation of Labor produced the first public statement by Samuel Gompers since the general strike in Philadelphia had begun. He refused to reveal whether or not he would approve of "the extension of the strike from Philadelphia to the state of Pennsylvania or to the country," maintaining that the answer to such a critical question should not be made public. "The forces arrayed against labor meet in secret and plan their schemes," he explained. "They take neither the public nor labor into their confidence. We will do the best we can to protect the rights and interests of the working people." Gompers then went on to denounce the PRT for rejecting arbitration and deliberately provoking the streetcar strike. He condemned Mayor Reyburn for not even trying to remain "impartial" and supporting the company in its refusal to arbitrate. Referring to the Independence Square meeting that had been banned by the mayor, he attacked the police for having brutally clubbed men, women, and children and treated American workers "as the Cossacks treat the Russian subjects, rather than as citizens are treated in the Republic of the United States." Finally, Gompers predicted that "while for the moment a corrupt gang such as obtains in Philadelphia may have the upper hand," this could not "last long, not in free America."[52]

This was Gompers' last public statement during the general strike, and whatever the AFL leadership may have planned with respect to a statewide or national strike remained a secret. But it was clear that without Gompers' endorsement, a statewide general strike would never be called, and it was also the opinion of a number of Philadelphia labor leaders that without the backing of a statewide strike, the citywide general strike would falter.[53] Indeed, the general strike had already begun to lose strength as more and more workers, once having made clear their sympathy for the trolley men, returned to work. On March 22, a large majority of the textile workers and the men of the Baldwin

Locomotive Works, both groups that were considered the backbone of the general strike, returned to work, vowing to contribute moral and financial support to the car strikers. By March 24, two days before the statewide strike was scheduled to go into effect if the company still refused to arbitrate, the idea of a general strike throughout the state was abandoned at a conference of Pennsylvania labor leaders. Speaking for the United Mine Workers, T. L. Lewis declared: "The Anthracite Mine Workers will respect their contract, which does not expire until March 31, 1912."[54]

Three days later, the Committee of Ten called off the general strike in Philadelphia, explaining: "This strike has been on for some five weeks. The Philadelphia Rapid Transit Company has had the united support of both the city and state governments, with all the power that their capitalistic friends can place behind them. Yet, with all this, they have been able to operate some 800 cars and that only a part of the time during the day, out of the 2,200 cars that would be in operation were the strikers at work." The PRT, it declared, was now facing bankruptcy, and "while the general strike has not yet secured a settlement of the carmen's dispute, we feel it has paved the way to bring that about." As of March 27, 1910, therefore, the general strike was officially over.[55]

But the car strikers vowed to keep on fighting until "an honorable settlement can be brought about."[56] The company, meanwhile, continued to operate with inexperienced strikebreakers with the result that the number of deaths from trolley accidents mounted. By the first week of April, the figure stood at twenty-seven fatalities, including fourteen children ranging in age from eighteen months to eleven years.[57] In its final presentment, the March grand jury took note of this situation and urged: "In view of the number of deplorable deaths and accidents that have occurred recently in this city, apparently through the inefficient operators of our street cars, this Grand Jury would recommend that as a safeguard to the public, the Philadelphia Rapid Transit Company be compelled to employ only efficient men to run their cars."[58] However, the recommendation was ignored, as was an appeal by the United Business Men's Association to the State Railroad Commission to investigate trolley deaths in Philadelphia. On April 10, the Central Labor Union voted to prosecute the mayor and the Rapid Transit Company officials on the charge of manslaughter because of the number of persons killed in trolley accidents. But nothing came of this either.[59] In fact, the only action taken occurred when two of the strikebreakers were sentenced to a year's imprisonment each because, through reckless of operation of cars, they had run down and killed two men. "It would have been more just," editorialized the New York *Call*, "had the heads of the trolley company responsible for that strike, been sent to jail. . . . They are undoubtedly morally responsible for the deaths and destruction that occurred."[60]

On March 29, the Philadelphia *Public Ledger* noted a new development in the trolley strike: "With the calling off of the sympathetic walkout and the consequent return to work of a great majority of the allied workers yesterday and today, all interest in the trolley strike has now centered upon the means by which the wives, daughters and women friends of the carmen plan to help them in their fight against the transit company." Three weeks earlier, several hundred women had met near each of the nineteen car barns operated by the company, and, after hearing a presentation of the issues involved in the strike, had organized a women's auxiliary of the carmen's union and elected Luella Twining as president. Now that the general strike was called off, the women's auxiliary voted to hold parades in various parts of the city to raise funds and maintain public support for the strikers. C. O. Pratt hailed the decision and predicted that "the alignment of the women in the fight and their appreciation of the situation will do much toward helping the cause to final success."[61]

During the ensuing weeks, the women's auxiliary made headline news. First a storm broke out over the denial by Director of Public Safety Clay of a permit enabling the auxiliary to march to Independence Square. The ban was appealed to the courts and the newspapers featured President Twining's reply to the judge's question as to whether she was an anarchist. "No, but I am a Socialist," she answered. The auxiliary, she told the judge, had 5,000 members and they would all participate in the parade, holding sheets with which to catch money for the strikers. "There will be men in the parade," she added, "but only such as are needed to carry babies in their arms or push the baby carriages while the women collect funds. It will be primarily a women's demonstration." But there was no "women's demonstration," for the court upheld Clay's edict.[62]

However, the auxiliary did hold entertainments, bazaars, and other fund-raising functions, and its members went from store to store and door to door, soliciting funds "to keep want from the households of the striking carmen."[63] On April 14, the Philadelphia *Evening Bulletin* announced that the Rapid Transit Company had encountered "a new and unexpected obstacle" in its efforts to operate its street cars:

Heretofore, the company and the police have had to meet only the resistance of a throng of men and boys. But today when an effort was made to run the Jefferson and Master Streets line for the first time since the strike began, one hundred or so women stood in the way and for a time at least, both the Transit Company and the police were forced to retreat. A barrel of ashes had been placed on the track at the crossing which forced the car to stop. Then the bombardment by the women began. Stones, bricks, clubs, everything at hand were hurled against the car and windows from end to end were shattered in a jiffy.[64]

While striking carmen and their wives and daughters were continuing the battle so militantly, the terms of a settlement were being negotiated. On March 21, Mayor Reyburn wrote to PRT President Kruger: "The good of the City of Philadelphia demands that the present strike be ended. The efforts of various well-meaning committees and individuals from the outside have failed. It is time that this matter be settled by parties in interest, and both sides should be willing to make concessions for the public welfare." Reyburn urged the company to take "the first step toward peace" by outlining the terms upon which it "will take back into its service the men now on strike and conditions of service in the future." If he had such information, and the men were assured that they would receive "the same status as to wages, pensions, and death benefits as they would have had if their service had not been interrupted," he would urge acceptance. He was confident that "my recommendation will be followed."[65]

The same day, as if by prearrangement, the company submitted an offer to the strikers through Mayor Reyburn, which included a provision that all strikers would be taken back; the hours of work would be not less than nine hours nor more than ten hours a day; wages would be 22 cents an hour and would increase by 1 cent an hour annually until the wage of 25 cents an hour was reached; employees would be "free to join, or not to join any organization"; and the company would not discriminate among the various committees of its workmen "or favor or give any encouragement to one organization over another." The question of the 174 men whose discharge had precipitated the strike was to be discussed, case by case, by the company and a representative chosen by the strikers.[66]

However, nothing was said either about recognizing the Amalgamated Association or restoring the strikers to the positions they had previously held with their former rights. President Kruger simply added:

As to the matters requiring adjustment arising from the strike, I promise you on behalf of the company to accept in our service the motormen and conductors now on strike, without any discrimination, and to join them in attempting to promote harmony between all our employees and the officers and superintendents of the company.[67]

Rayburn presented the terms offered by the company to the "Employees of the Philadelphia Rapid Transit Company, Now on Strike" and recommended acceptance, adding his "promise that my personal and official influence will be exercised at all times for such an administration of these terms as will make this a lasting and satisfactory peace."[68] But the strikers had no confidence in any assurance from their anti-labor mayor, and they insisted that their union be recognized and that their former status and rights be restored upon their return to work. On April 5, therefore, the strikers rejected the company's offer. Thereupon, the Transit Company announced that its offer was withdrawn and was no longer to serve as a basis for a settlement.[69]

Meanwhile, John P. Mitchell and Dennis Hayes, AFL vice-presidents, acting at the request of Amalgamated Association President Mahon and with the support of the Federation's Executive Council, had been conferring with U. S. Senator Boise Penrose, boss of Pennsylvania politics, State Senator John McNichol, and PRT General Counsel John Ballard. However, their efforts broke down when the company insisted on recognizing the so-called "Keystone Union" and denying the members of the Amalgamated Association the seniority rights they had enjoyed before they went on strike. Under pressure from Mitchell and Hayes, the Amalgamated Association leaders agreed to waive their objection to the provision recognizing the "Keystone Union," but they insisted that they could not accept a settlement which "did not restore all members on strike to the exact positions filled by them before the strike was inaugurated." The company could have two months to work out the details for restoring the men to their former status. On this single point, however, the company refused to budge, and Penrose and McNichol advised the AFL vice-presidents that they had exhausted their ability to persuade the company to meet the union's sole remaining demand.[70]

However' with its losses amounting to $20,000 a day, and forced to apply for a $25 million loan from the city, the Philadelphia Rapid Transit Company decided to yield on the single point standing in the way of a settlement. The terms of the final agreement offered on April 15 provided: (1) that all men on strike were to be taken back by the company and to receive their former positions as soon as possible; those who were not immediately placed were to be paid at the rate of $2 a day until they could be placed; (2) wages were to be 23 cents an hour beginning July 1, and to be increased at a rate of 1 cent per hour every six months until the minimum reached 25 cents; (3) the company was to have the right to hear the grievances of an employee or association of employees and the men were to have the right to join any union or organization they wished, or none at all; (4) no agreement was to be signed between the company and its employees, but the terms of the offer were to be posted in the various car barns; (5) the cases of the 174 men whose dismissal had brought on the strike were to be left to arbitration by Charles Kruger and a representative of the carmen's union.[71]

This time, the Amalgamated Association leaders recommended acceptance of the company's offer and urged an end to the strike. At meetings of the carmen, Pratt told the strikers that the agreement represented a victory for them, arguing: "The company undertook to destroy our union, but they failed to accomplish that object." He was confident that once the men returned, they would get "fair treatment," since the company had learned that their employees could strike effectively. To be sure, the agreement permitted the company to receive committees of non-union men and to deal with the "Keystone Union," "but," he maintained "they will also treat with us." When asked by a number of the strikers what guarantee there was that this agreement would not be violated immediately in the same way that the 1909 settlement had been ignored, Pratt could only answer: "We have verbal promises from the officials of the company that these will be kept. The settlement, I think, will lead to a permanent peace between the men and the employers."[72]

The response brought angry shouts from the strikers, and it was clear that the agreement would not be automatically ratified. But Pratt did not wait for the vote; instead, he left immediately for Detroit to attend a meeting of the Amalgamated Association's National Executive Board. After his departure, the rank-and-file workers, by a close vote of 1,265-1,258, rejected the terms of the settlement. However, the Executive Committee of Division 477, "after carefully weighing the circumstances involved in our situation and the lack of decisive authority [the slim majority] in the referendum of our membership," and after consulting the National Executive Board in Detroit, accepted the proposal, ended the walkout, and directed "our members on strike to return to work."[73]

Thus, to cries of "Sell out! Sell out!" from the majority who had voted to continue the strike, an end came to what the *Public Ledger* called "a struggle so titanic that it attracted the attention of all vested interests in this country and abroad."[74]

A number of Philadelphia labor leaders derived some comfort from the fact that, as a result of the "titanic struggle," union membership in the city had increased. President Murphy of the Central Labor Union boldly claimed a "twofold increase in the ranks of unionism" and cited this as justification for the general strike.[75] Others pointed to the launching of a labor party in the city and state as a direct result of the strike and noted the resolution calling for the formation of the labor party, with its reference to "the present strike of the working people against the political transit combination, which, by reason of its political power, has this city in its grip. . . ."[76]*

To the IWW, the labor party was nothing more than a futile effort to obtain at the ballot box what Philadelphia labor had failed to gain through the general strike. That failure, it insisted, was the result of the refusal of many workers in AFL unions to support the general strike, instead remaining at work and upholding the sacredness of their contracts. "The men who worked in the powerhouses, furnishing juice, with which to run the cars," charged the *Industrial Worker*, official organ of the IWW, "did more to defeat the striking motormen and conductors than the scab who manned the car."[77] In sum, argued W. E. Trautmann, the IWW strike strategist, "a farcical general strike was pulled off, so as to discredit forever the general strike idea."[78]

However, Louis Duchez, another IWW theoretician, refused to view the general strike as a total failure. He pointed out that those workers

. . . who had come out in support of the car men have done more to teach themselves and the whole State of Pennsylvania class consciousness and solidarity than a whole trainload of literature. By breaking their agreements with their bosses, the "sacredness of contracts" has recieved a good jolt; open hostility between them and their employers has been stimulated; the struggle between themselves and the bosses will be fiercer than it has ever been before. The bosses will no longer be sure of them; militants will be "tabbed" and

*The new labor party in Philadelphia was born at a meeting of the delegates of all labor unions in the city, held in the Labor Lyceum on March 24. The party's platform called for public ownership of all public utilities and government ownership of telephone and telegraph lines; equal wages for men and women when the latter did the same kind of work; an eight-hour law for workers; abolition of the state constabulary; a graduated income tax on all incomes over $5,000 a year; direct election of U. S. senators; disfranchisement of all bribers, bribetakers, and corrupt political workers; and new laws on health and labor conditions. (Philadelphia *Public Ledger*, March 24, April 21, 1910; New York *Call*, April 22, 1910.)

"chopped off" as the occasion presents itself; in short, there will be a fight from now on.[79]

* * *

"The settlement, I think, will lead to a permanent peace between the men and their employers," C. O. Pratt had assured the strikers as he recommended that they accept the settlement and end the strike. Unfortunately, the "peace" that emerged was one in which there was no room for the Amalgamated Association. In December, 1910, Thomas E. Mitten, the new manager of the bankrupt company, instituted a cunning system of welfare capitalism, under which 22 percent of all passenger fares would be set aside for workers' wages until the pay scale reached 28 cents an hour; a welfare fund would be established, to which both the company and the employees would contribute, to provide sickness, death, and pension benefits; and grievances would be settled through a series of joint labor-management committees. Then, taking advantage of a split in the Amalgamated Association, Mitten announced that he would recognize the union if two-thirds of its members accepted his welfare plan. When the vote among the workers failed by a small margin to reach the needed majority, Mitten simply ignored the Amalgamated Association and announced that his plan was in operation.[80] Thus ended, for a good number of years, the presence of the Amalgamated Association of Street Car and Electric Railway Men of America on the Philadelphia Rapid Transit lines.

CHAPTER 7

The Shopmen's Strike on
the Harriman System, 1911–1915

At the turn of the twentieth century, four great Brotherhoods stood astride the railroad world. They represented engineers, firemen, trainmen, and conductors. On the other hand, there were thousands of other railroad workers who remained outside the Brotherhoods. They were the shop workers (machinists, boilermakers, blacksmiths, electricians, etc.), telegraphers, yard workers, clerks, and maintenance-of-way men. They were either grouped in unions within each craft or were entirely unorganized. Unlike the Brotherhoods, which remained independent, these unions were usually associated with the AFL.

In 1893, under the leadership of Eugene V. Debs of the Brotherhood of Locomotive Firemen, the American Railway Union was organized as an industrial union uniting all white workers, men and women, who served on the railroads in any capacity except superintendents and other high officials.* The ARU grew rapidly and won several of its early battles, but it was virtually destroyed in the 1894 Pullman Strike in

---

*Women were not only admitted to membership, but the American Railway Union insisted "that when a woman performs a man's work, she ought, in all justice, to have a man's pay." (*Railway Times,* June 5, 1894.)

Debs warned the ARU that its policy of excluding Blacks from membership, a policy he opposed, could lead to disaster, but the ban against Black membership in the ARU constitution was reaffirmed at its national convention in June, 1894 by a vote of 112 to 100. The stand taken by the ARU was a backward carry-over from the practices of all the Brotherhoods which denied membership to Blacks and attempted to drive them out of the railroad service. (Philip S. Foner, *Organized Labor and the Black Worker, 1619-1973,* New York, 1974, pp. 103-07.)

which it suffered an overwhelming defeat.* All efforts to unify the railroad workers thereupon ceased temporarily.

In 1898, Congress passed the Erdman Act which provided machinery for conciliation between the railways and their train service forces. However, the workers placed little faith in government methods. Contrary to the conservative leadership of the Brotherhoods, they had reached the conclusion that only through unified action could the railroad men win redress of their grievances.[1] In 1902, an advanced form of concerted action was tried in the West, when conductors and trainmen in that part of the country joined together to form the Western Association, which was to take in all the railroads west of a line drawn from Chicago to Duluth, Minnesota, and southwest from Chicago along a branch of the Illinois Central Railway.[2]

On June 24, 1902, the Association simultaneously presented identical demands to all the western railroads for increased wages and improved working conditions. The managers of the Union Pacific and Southern Pacific Railroads, admittedly surprised by the suddenness and force with which the demands were presented,[3] agreed to the proposed changes after some negotiations. The minor systems followed suit.[4]

Having won this initial victory, the Brotherhoods consolidated their position and made plans for the more extensive demands for which they were to contend five years later. In the interim, the western railroads had prepared themselves for future confrontations. When the conductors and trainmen presented new demands with reference to wages and working conditions in February, 1907, they had to contend with a united body of western railroads. A committee representing forty-two roads, with a total mileage of 101,500 miles, met a joint committee of conductors and trainmen,[5] and together they sought to negotiate the railroad workers' demand for an eight-hour day and a 15 percent wage increase. A month's negotiations failed to produce any definite agreement, and the Brotherhoods' representatives went back to their locals and took a strike vote.[6]

The balloting favored a strike, but the conciliatory elements within the Brotherhoods prevailed, and negotiations were resumed with the management committees in April. The unions lowered their demands to a 12.5 percent increase and a nine-hour day. The railroads countered with an offer of a 10.5 percent wage increase, but they refused to discuss the shortening of the work day. As a result of the deadlock, the chairman

*For the rise and decline of the American Railway Union, including the story of the Pullman Strike, see Philip S. Foner, *History of the Labor Movement in the United States,* vol. II (New York, 1955), pp. 247-78.

of the Interstate Commerce Commission and the Commissioner of Labor were brought in as mediators and they succeeded in effecting a settlement. Conductors and trainmen who had been employed on the basis of the twelve-hour day had their hours reduced to ten without any reduction in wages; those who were working on a ten-hour schedule were granted a 10 percent increase in pay. Other increases were, for passenger conductors, $10 a month; for baggagemen, $7.50 a month; and for brakemen and flagmen, $6.50 a month. All these increases were to go into effect without any increase in mileage. Employees on freight service were given a flat 10 percent raise. These wage increases exceeded the last offer of the railroad managers by $1.50 a month for each group. The government's mediation board also prescribed a ten-hour system for the railroad trainmen after sixteen consecutive hours of work.[8]

While these negotiations were going on, the conductors and trainmen were extending their system of cooperation to the east. The eastern territory was defined as being bounded on the west by the main line of the Illinois Central Railroad, and on the south by the Ohio River and the Chesapeake & Ohio Railroad. The remaining territory was included in the Southern Association in 1909.[9]

In 1908, the conventions of the Brotherhood of Locomotive Firemen and Enginemen divided the country similarly into three districts—the Eastern, the Western, and the Southern.[10] This cooperative association met with the same success as that of the conductors and trainmen. In 1909, Eugene V. Debs heaped scorn on these unity efforts of the Brotherhoods when he asserted caustically: "Taken in the aggregate, there is no division of the working class more clannish and provincial, more isolated from other divisions of labor's countless army, than railroad employees, the workers engaged directly or indirectly in steam railway transportation."[11] Still, as one student of railroad unionism points out, the concerted action movement from 1902 to 1909 had marked an important development: "The railroad workers who were gathered into such organizations had come a long way since the day when they were breaking each other's strikes, and submitting to management for want of strength and unity."[12]

Influenced by the success of the brotherhoods' concerted action, the shop craft laborers began to form federations on each of the several railroad systems. Systemwide negotiations had enormous advantages for the workers. They forced management to bargain with a coalition of unions instead of with each individual union. They also enabled workers in each craft to unite their demands and establish uniform standards.

These advantages were fully demonstrated in 1908, when the shop craft workers of the Southern Railway, the New Haven & Hartford, the Union Pacific, the Santa Fe, the Missouri Pacific, and the Canadian Pacific all formed federations and defeated management's efforts to cut wages and impose piecework. After these victories, system federations sprang up all over the United States.[13]

At its 1908 convention, the AFL took note of this trend toward federation and established the Railway Employees' Department (RED) for all workers associated with the railroads who were outside the Brotherhoods. Officials of this new organization were given the power to grant charters to any future federations.[14]

The general trend among railroad workers to unite and act together in a solid front against management inevitably came into sharp conflict with the employers' preference for dealing with a labor movement organized along conventional craft lines. This conflict reached its climax in the great strike of 1911 on the Illinois Central and Harriman lines, more popularly known as the Harriman System strike.

Illinois Central extended for more than 4,500 miles from Chicago to New Orleans, with a major branch that reached Omaha. The Harriman lines represented a network of railroads from Texas to Oregon and included the Union Pacific, the Southern Pacific, the Oregon Short Line, and the Santa Fe. Although both systems mained separate administrative staffs, the Illinois Central was a major part of Edward H. Harriman's railroad empire, since the Union Pacific held a controlling interest in Illinois Central stock.[15]

The nine craft unions representing the shopmen on both lines—blacksmiths, boilermakers, machinists, carmen, sheet metal workers, painters, steam fitters, railway clerks, and pattern makers—met in Salt Lake City on June 5, 1911 and formed a system federation. The new federation was headed by E. L. Reguin, a San Francisco machinist and an ardent Socialist. In the opinion of many shopmen, this step was long overdue. "With the passing of the year 1910," wrote Carl E. Person, who was to become a militant system federation official and editor, "the average man who understood the labor movement was convinced that the time of individual craft strikes was of the past. They could no longer deliver the goods."[16]

On July 1, all nine craft unions presented the same demands to management. The first was for recognition of the system federation as the collective bargaining agent for all the crafts. They also included a demand for discussion of a minimum wage, standardization of hours, overtime rates, a seniority system, and the elimination of piecework.[17] Since shop craft federations had already been recognized on a dozen other systems, the shopmen did not anticipate any unusual resistance, but management was out to destroy the movement before it developed any further. Both W. L. Park, vice-president and general manager of Illinois Central, and Julius Kruttschnitt, president and operating head of the Harriman lines, indicated their willingness to discuss economic issues with each individual union, but both declared their refusal to confer with the new federation. They made it clear that they would only bargain with the unions one at a time.[18]

The shop craftsmen had taken a major step toward interunion cooperation, and they were not prepared to retreat. Instead of separate contracts, with separate expiration dates, negotiated by the individual crafts, they were determined to win a system-wide contract. The railroad executives, on the other hand, were just as determined to block the movement for an all-inclusive bargaining union. Management feared that the movement among the shop craftsmen, coupled with the concerted action of the Brotherhoods, could lead the way to an eventual nation-wide federation of all railroad workers. The ghost of Eugene V. Debs' industrial union of railroad workers—the American Railway Union—had come back to haunt railroad management.

When the railroad corporations united to destroy the American Railway Union, the Railway Managers' Association had vowed that never again would such an industrial union of railway employees be permitted to rear its head in the United States.[19] To be sure, the System Federation only provided for joint bargaining by nine of the twenty-six crafts in the railroad industry and included none of those engaged in the movement of trains, but, as *Solidarity* pointed out: "The system federation becomes the embodiment of a higher form of union and therefore a potential if not actual menace to the employing class."[20] Soon, however, as we shall see, separatism among the railroad unions seriously weakened even the System Federation.

In the hope of avoiding a strike the heads of the craft unions in the System Federation continued to meet with the company administrations, but management stood firm in its refusal to recognize the Federation. To demonstrate that the workers were prepared to strike over this issue, the unions polled their members as to whether they wished to walk out solely over recognition. Ninety-seven percent voted "Yes." After this ballot, the union appealed to management for a last-minute conference.[21]

In September, 1911, Julius Kruttschnitt met in San Francisco with representatives of the shop crafts, who presented specific demands to the head of the Harriman lines: recognition of the System Federation, union shop apprenticeship regulations, a universal eight-hour day, with seven hours' work on Saturday and pay for eight, wage increases of five cents an hour for hourly men and proportionate raises for monthly workers, double time after midnight for day men and after noon for night men, the right of the unions to review cases of members discharged from their jobs, and the application of seniority in filling positions of foreman and gang boss. Kruttschnitt objected to all of the demands, and in particular to the recognition of the federation. This, he charged, would muster "the whole body of workers behind a demand by any one craft, encouraging unreasonable requests." The Harriman lines, he said, would "risk a strike rather than deal with a System Federation." Immediately, W. L. Park of the Illinois Central echoed Kruttschnitt's refusal to recognize the System Federation, even if it meant a strike.[22]

After the final rejection of the shop crafts' demands, the Illinois Central and Harriman lines posted notices in their shops warning that anyone going on strike would forfeit pension rights and that no striker over thirty-five would be rehired. Even before this, throughout the months during which negotiations were taking place, high fences and stockades were constructed around Harriman properties; cars and cabooses were fitted with bunks for potential strikebreakers; and big arc lamps were installed to light the yards at night. Meanwhile, arrangements for farming out repair work to lines that would not be struck were announced.[23] What Eugene V. Debs termed the "interminable delay" in ordering the strike enabled the employers to make adequate preparations for meeting the walkout.[24]

Still, the Executive Committee of the Machinists refused to sanction a strike on the grounds that the System Federation had not conducted the negotiations properly, but on September 26, they were overruled by the Machinists' convention. Four days later, the System Federation on the lines of the railroad empire created by Edward H. Harriman began its strike. The walkout was on a grand scale. In fifteen states, from the eastern end of the Yazoo & Mississippi Valley Railroad to the tip of the Oregon Short Line, from Chicago to New Orleans, from Memphis to Sacramento, Illinois Central and Harriman workers, acting like a trained, disciplined army, "took up their tools and started for home as soon as the time clock pointed to 10." Union leaders claimed that 35,000 workers in shops west of New Orleans had already answered the strike call, and that, together with the walkouts in other sections, the strike had achieved "an almost complete tie-up." Although this claim was an exaggeration, even the Illinois Central management conceded that about 63 percent of its shopmen in twenty-eight cities* had struck, while Harriman's chief of operations admitted that half the work force had walked out.[25]

The commercial, labor, and Socialist press were as one in recognizing that the significance of the strike could not be measured solely by the number of men who had left their work. It was the principle involved that made this strike so important. "The railway labor question is but one aspect of the general labor question," the *New York Times* emphasized. What was at stake was the fundamental issue of craft *versus* industrial unionism. For if the contracts of the railroad workers could be negotiated to expire simultaneously, these workers would be able to achieve, through federation, what no single union could hope to obtain for its membership. Essentially, the shopmen were applying to the "general labor question" the principles used by the railroads themselves to enhance their profits. As the Socialist New York *Call* pointed out:

> The Harriman lines, among the most powerful in this country, are themselves the result of the federation of lines that had been weakened through competition, and in some instances brought almost to the verge of disaster through their "individual efforts" at independence. But the present heads of these lines instantly realized that what had been good for them through the combination of separate roads into a federated system would not have the same beneficent effect if the various crafts employed on the roads were also federated into a system. . . . [For] if federation . . . of weak competing lines into a strong system has been good for the Harriman roads, then the organization of small, weak and often warring unions into federation . . . will be good for workers.

And Eugene V. Debs, speaking for the Socialist Party, declared: "This strike is for a vital principle; it is our strike as well as the strike of those who are on the firing line."[26]

"Without the slightest sign of violence, the strike of over 30,000 shopmen on the Harriman lines went into effect this morning," the *New York Times* reported on October 1. The same situation prevailed on the Illinois Central, it added, and the following day, it reported that "all

*The affected shops were in the cities of McComb, Vicksburg, and Water Valley (Mississippi); Cheyenne (Wyoming); Pocatello (Idaho); Kansas City; San Francisco, Los Angeles, Sacramento, San Luis Obispo, and Bakersfield (California); El Paso, San Antonio, and Beaumont (Texas); Chicago, East St. Louis, Matton, and Clinton (Illinois); Omaha and North Platte (Nebraska); Ogden and Salt Lake City (Utah); Portland (Oregon); also Las Vegas, New Orleans, Seattle, Memphis, and Denver. (*New York Times*, Oct. 1, 12, 1911.)

shops in the Harriman system were picketed peacefully by the striking workmen" and that "no violence was reported from any shop center." But it also reported ominously that "many strikebreakers were being held in readiness by the agency working in behalf of the railroads."[27]

The importation of large numbers of strikebreakers turned a peaceful strike into one of the most violent labor disputes of the period. Everywhere, mass picket lines were thrown around the barricaded shops in which the strikebreakers were housed. Women members of strikers' families joined the pickets. As policemen and armed guards escorted the strikebreakers to and from the repair shops, battles broke out. In New Orleans, coaches containing strikebreakers were attacked and the scabs mobbed as they were being conveyed to the docks where they were to be put to work. "Women were prominent in several of the mobs," one paper reported, "and took an active part in stoning the strikebreakers and the trains."[28] The strikebreakers broke away from the guards and quickly disappeared. But Illinois Central immediately brought in a large body of replacements. This time, the riot that followed took the lives of six men and injured over one hundred. A reporter described it as "one of the bloodiest on record in this section."[29] Even with the entire reserve force of the New Orleans police rushed into action, supplemented by U. S. deputy marshals and railroad detectives, the Illinois Central found it difficult to protect the strikebreakers, and it freely furnished shotguns to state and federal officials.[30]

"Quiet at New Orleans," Vice-President Park of the Illinois Central told reporters on October 6. But his statement was belied by reports from the city telling of pitched battles between strikers and police, company guards, and state and federal officials, as the men on strike tried to get at the strikebreakers.[31] Similar clashes were occurring in Mississippi towns all along the Illinois Central line. With civil governments unwilling or unable to protect their communities from violence by strikebreakers, the strikers and other citizens assumed these duties themselves. In Durant, Mississippi, strikebreakers attempted a general raid on the stores of the town. They were repulsed by the combined efforts of strikers and other citizens, but they did loot a number of Black people's homes, taking food and cooking utensils. In Winona, Mississippi, strikers and other citizens were on guard, and when the strikebreakers attempted to loot stores, they were driven back and forced to leave town.[32]

The violence in Mississippi reached its climax in tremendous battles in McComb City, an important railroad terminal and repair center. About

1,500 employees worked in the shops there, and almost all of them left their jobs when the shop crafts went on strike. With the Illinois Central clerks already on strike, practically all the employees were out.[33]

On the Monday following the start of the strike, the sheriff addressed a meeting of all the strikers, and an agreement calling for peaceful picketing and no violence by either side was reached. Despite the arrival of twenty-two U. S. marshals who posted a writ of injunction restraining strikers from trespassing or interfering with the railroad's business, the peace was maintained for several days.[34] Then a special train bearing strikebreakers *en route* to New Orleans brought an end to the peace. The *McComb City Enterprise,* friendly to the strikers, described the battle that followed:

> Tuesday evening a special train carrying about 450 alleged strikebreakers who were in reality a gang of hoodlums, probably picked up in the slums of northern cities, arrived in town and as soon as they hit the city limits, they began conducting themselves in an outrageous manner by cursing and throwing stones at the people along the right-of-way, and making insulting remarks and gestures at several ladies standing at the crossing. These same men raided stores and assaulted the citizens of Winona, Durant, and Brookhaven before reaching here, and after leaving McComb the same afternoon, a part of them demolished sheds in front of the stores of Osyka and raided the lunch counter at Hammond.

After the scabs had hurled stones at the citizens of McComb, injuring several of them, the train pulled out and headed for New Orleans. Then, as the account in the *Enterprise* continued,

> . . . one of the gang pulled his gun and began shooting at the men who had secured pistols and guns for self-protection as soon as they saw the class of human rubbish the railroad had brought into the town. As soon as the first shot was fired at them, the citizens along the track opened up with their guns and pistols, and the "brave men" who had demoralized the towns above here dropped to the floor of the cars like ducks taking to water. The *Enterprise* understands that seven of their number were killed and fifteen wounded. The daily press stated the next morning that not one of them was even injured.[35]

Actually, the three coaches carrying the strikebreakers were wrecked and a number of strikers and strikebreakers were killed and injured. A reporter for the New Orleans *Times-Picayune* wrote that when the train reached New Orleans, "it looked as if it had been through the Boer War."[36] Immediately after the gun battle, the Memphis National Guard was mobilized and the authorities ordered the entire Third Regiment to McComb.

When the troops arrived, they found the strikers "confident of ultimate victory," while the railroad continued to bring in strikebreakers and was "apparently making preparations for a long drawn-out fight."[37] As scabs continued to be brought in, a dynamite explosion was followed by a threat from union men and their sympathizers that they would blow up the entire $2 million complex of Illinois Central shops in McComb unless the strikebreakers were deported. In desperation, the governor, the county sheriff, and the commander of the state National Guard appealed to the railroad to remove the strikebreakers in order to prevent a massacre. Reluctantly, Illinois Central complied. The train carrying the strikebreakers pulled out with sixty National Guardsmen aboard, who received these instructions: "If any man aboard lifts a hand or makes a motion to hurl a missile, if any striker, strike sympathizer, or citizen makes a menacing demonstration . . . shoot and shoot to kill."[38]

But so furious were the people at the company and its strikebreakers that the soldiers were fearful that they might be attacked and overwhelmed. One paper reported:

> When the train pulled out of McComb, it seemed as if every one within a radius of fifteen miles of the town witnessed the departure. Hundreds of farmers, stirred by rumors of insults to women in other Mississippi towns, gathered with their shotguns and rifles, and the soldiers feared another outbreak.[39]

However, more strikebreakers were brought into McComb, and National Guardsmen, with fixed bayonets, guarded the Illinois Central buildings where the scabs were kept. So enraged was the community that the strikebreakers did not dare venture outside company property. Indeed, the special train of the Illinois Central president, scheduled to pass through McComb on the way to New Orleans, had to be rerouted across the entire state of Mississippi.[40]

McComb's mayor publicly acknowledged "the complete failure of all civil powers to keep peace," but instead of demanding the departure of all strikebreakers and a halt to bringing any new ones into town, he urged the governor to invoke martial law. But not even martial law was able to restore peace, and as long as the strikebreakers remained in McComb, the violence continued. In invoking martial law, the governor charged that the troubles in McComb emanated from "foreign agitators." But all reporters agreed that the strikers were long-time residents of the town and that public opinion "was overwhelmingly in support of the strikers."[41] Reverend W. A. Gill, a Baptist minister, was described as expressing the opinion of the majority of McComb's residents when he defended the strikers in one of his sermons. In affirming the right to strike, he asked: "Do we question the legal right of men to withhold their money when they deem it unprofitable to invest? Neither can we justly question the right of men to withhold their muscle when they were not getting a decent living out of it." "Labor," he declared boldly, "creates the wealth and then the heartless possessor of wealth uses the product of labor to deprive the laborer of his right to organize and thus protect himself." Turning to the specific issues in the strike of the shopmen, Reverend Gill noted that one of the railroad officials was reported to have said that the company "hoped to starve the strikers to a point of coming back as separate crafts." He continued:

> Now you know what that means. It means that if the Federated Crafts fail to bring the railroad company to a conference, they would handle the separate crafts about like a Tom cat would handle a mouse. You see they do not object to dealing with a separate union as long as they are not strong enough to demand decent wages. . . . But the days of industrial slavery are numbered.[42]

Such words were wasted on the authorities. A Mississippi judge issued a sweeping statewide decree aimed at all union members on strike against Illinois Central, forbidding them to congregate on or near railroad property, intimidate non-strikers or induce them to quit, or interfere with the Illinois Central's normal operations in any way. Similar sweeping restraining orders were handed down in Illinois, Louisiana, Texas, and Kentucky. So far-reaching was the judicial restraining order in Kentucky that the president of the System Federation observed angrily that it prohibited strikers "from doing almost anything except breathing. They could not even speak to a man that was working on the Illinois Central Railroad."[43]

Freedom of the press also came under attack if it was used in any way to help the strikers. One of the major difficulties faced by the shopmen was in overcoming the almost unanimous opposition of the commercial press. Seven weeks after the strike began, the McComb strike committee pointed to this problem in a "Notice to the Citizens of this Community and the Public in General." The notice was triggered by reports reaching the committee "from people living remote from points on the Illinois Central Railroad and from out in the country, sympathizing with us over the *loss* of the strike." The belief that the strike was over was quite understandable:

> In view of the fact that the newspapers are only publishing the railroad company's side of the question, we cannot blame the people for believing as they do. Being unable to get our side of the controversy before the public, through the press, we are compelled to adopt this method of reaching as many as possible so that we may let it be known that the strike is still on. . . .[44]

To meet this problem. Carl Person, a twenty-four-year-old System Federation official and Clinton, Illinois editor, began publishing a *Strike*

Bulletin. At first, copies were produced on a mimeograph machine that Person had salvaged from a junk heap. Workers all along the Illinois Central and Harriman lines quickly made the paper popular, and many of them contributed to it. Soon the *Strike Bulletin* was appearing regularly in printed form.[45]

On November 13, 1911, Person published a special edition of the *Strike Bulletin* called the "Grave Yard Edition." In announcing this "special," Person described it as "artistically illustrated with pictures of some 75 wrecks that have taken place on the Illinois Central and Harriman lines since the strike." Charging that railroad management had hired incompetent strikebreakers and allowed the equipment to degenerate dangerously, Person proclaimed:

> See the crash at Montz, La., the arrival of the Grave Yard Special in New Orleans with the dead and injured; the San Antonio Explosion; the Kinmundy Disaster; the Wreck of the Daylight Special; the Sunset Limited in the Ditch; the Shasta Express upon the Mountain Side; the Overland Limited in the Valley of Apple Cut; the Crash of the Fast Mail at Memphis; the Fall of Salt Creek Bridge; the Miracle at Cat Fish Creek, and half a hundred other pictures of RECENT WRECKS ON THE STRUCK ROADS.

Every striker was urged to order a bundle of the *Strike Bulletin's* "Grave Yard Edition" and place one in each business house in his city.* This would be the means of keeping passengers off the struck roads: "It will help us to drive a hard blow against the struck roads. It will be the means of winning this strike." Person promised to issue "half a million copies" of the "Grave Yard Edition" if the strikers did their part, and to

---

*Throughout the strike, literature was distributed to business men in the hope of winning their support. One leaflet headed "MISTER BUSINESS MAN" began: "Did it ever occur to you that the shopmen's strike on the Illinois Central and Harriman lines is a matter of considerable importance to you and your business? Between seventy-five and eighty-five percent of the men who came out on strike are men of family, many of them taxpayers in their respective localities, all of them honest and a credit to any community." Pointing out that such men were being replaced by the dregs of society, the leaflet asked the business men to consider whether such men could do as much for them and the community as the men on strike: "Do you think that the strikebreaker as a class will ever come up to the standard of our clean-cut American citizenship as represented by the men who were forced out on strike? Never in a lifetime, and we know that you know this to be a fact. Bums from the slums, booze fighters from weakness of will power or, worse yet, from natural inclination, and moral degenerates don't make desirable citizens in any community." The leaflet then struck a nativist and racist note, observing: "The introduction of foreigners on all the struck roads and negroes on the Illinois Central in particular, and all at lower wages, will not have a tendency to make your business prosperous." (Copy of leaflet signed by A. O. Wharton, a Machinist business agent, in *Carl Person Papers*, Collections of the Archives of Labor History and Urban Affairs, University Archives, Wayne State University, Detroit, Michigan.)

"advertise the dangerous condition of the struck roads from Maine to California."[46]

The "Grave Yard Edition," with its photographs of blazing train wrecks, wounded victims, coffins piled high, scalded children, and mangled bodies, attracted nationwide attention and not only kept passengers off the struck roads, but helped to drive down the value of the stock of the Illinois Central and other Harriman-controlled roads. But it also launched the persecution of Carl Person by the Illlinois Central. "A battle royal is going on in Clinton, Illinois," wrote journalist Floyd Gibbons, "between a twentieth century David and an up-to-date Goliath of the Super-Dreadnought type. The David is Carl Person, the fighting editor of the *Strike Bulletin*. The all-powerful Goliath is the Illinois Central Railroad Company."[47] First, company detectives descended on Person's office and ransacked his files, desk drawers, and letter books. Then railroad officials secured an indictment against Person for "circulating through the U. S. mails matters reflecting injuriously on the conduct of the Illinois Central Railroad and its officials." The crime carried with it maximum penalties of $35,000 and thirty-five years in prison. Accompanied by an Illinois Central detective, postal inspectors entered Person's office, arrested him and took him before the United States Commissioner in Bloomington, where he was released on bail.* In an appeal to the strikers and the labor movement in general, Person described his arrest and wrote:

> My arrest does not worry me a bit, but to carry on an effective fight until the end of the strike is what I am worried about, and in this the Grave Yard Edition will do more than anything else, and the Illinois Central knows it, and just because of this every effort should be made to put out as many of the Grave Yard Edition as possible. . . .
> The detectives were particularly interested in our subscription, and we hope we get the money to carry on the work, and we can only say that if we do not get the subscriptions to carry on the work, the Illinois Central will be more than satisfied, and if we do, it will cause them further inconvenience, and therefore if you want to do something to agitate the cause along send in subscriptions to the bulletin, and we will do the rest. . . .
> In conclusion I am yours for the effective fight, regardless of all their crooked detectives, the usurped power of their courts, or their rotten jails.[48]

The indictment and arrest were the least of the attacks upon the young militant editor. Person was physically attacked by three men who beat him severely and left him for dead on the sidewalk. He recovered, only to be attacked more viciously on the streets of Clinton by Tony Musser,

*The post office also regularly held up mailings of the *Strike Bulletin*.

the town's former police chief, who was known as the "giant Portuguese." The giant would have murdered the youth if a group of spectators had not finally pulled him away. "Blood from gashes on his [Person's] head streamed down his face and blinded his eyes," Gibbons reported. "The scalp was torn from his skull in several places."[49]

Musser was able to break way from his captors and he lunged again at Person, crying out that this time he would "get" him. The editor had recovered slightly during the brief respite, and, certain that his assailant was out to kill him, drew a revolver and shot Musser dead. He then surrendered to the police, who refused to accept bail for him and turned down his request that a photographer be admitted to take pictures of his condition for use as evidence. It was only six weeks later, after every trace of the attack had disappeared from Person's body, that a photographer was admitted. While the editor was in jail, the police raided the *Strike Bulletin's* office.[50]

Union leaders set up a Person Defense League, which was supported by both the Illinois and Chicago federations of labor. Convinced that his client could not obtain a fair trial in Clinton because the railroad completely dominated the city, Person's attorney, who was the chief counsel of the Railway Employees' Department, fought for and won a change of *venue* to Lincoln, Nebraska. On October 5, 1914, after twenty-three hours of deliberation and twenty-two ballots the jury returned a verdict of "not guilty." Following the trial, Person declared: "The fight to crush organized labor is doomed."[51]

On March 5, 1912, William H. Johnston, president of the International Association of Machinists, returned from an inspection of the strike situation on a number of the roads affected by the shopmen's strike, including the Illinois Central. He was pleased to report that he had found "the strike being handled effectively." The railroad companies, he announced, were "badly crippled," while the men on strike were "in good spirits, full of courage and determination." Johnson concluded his report on an optimistic note: "From most accurate data obtained, and with many startling facts before me, I am of the opinion that the companies will not permit such a drain upon the resources to continue for an indefinite period."[52]

Unfortunately, this is precisely what the companies did. Although they continued to suffer severe economic losses, they also refused to retreat from their adamant opposition to negotiations with the System Federation officials. In its 1912 annual report, the Illinois Central showed a loss of over $3 million in operating revenues, while its operating expenses rose by almost the same amount. The shopmen's strike, the *New York Times* noted in explaining the decline, "cut into the earnings from above and below," because it decreased the volume of business while it added to handling costs.[53]

Neither the governors of the states affected by the strike nor President Taft could persuade the companies to sit down with representatives of the unions.[54] The closest they came to a settlement was early in 1913, when union officials and the Illinois Central general manager met secretly under assumed names in Chicago. They agreed upon tentative settlement terms which were to be unofficial and unsigned, subject to ratification by higher officials on both sides. The agreement called for the reinstatement of all employees, restoration of the old contracts in effect prior to the strike, and a company promise not to discriminate against any striker unless he had damaged railroad property.

Although the System Federation leaders recognized that these terms were tantamount to total surrender, they hoped to use the tentative agreement as a means for reopening talks with management. But at the very first meeting, company executives refused to discuss the possibility of any additional concessions and quickly closed the meeting.[55]

To Carl Person, however, the entire deal reflected the desire of the top officials of the shopmen's unions to settle the strike on any terms. He denounced the project as the "Chicago Frame Up," charging that even if it were successful, it would have applied only to the Illinois Central and did "not include any settlement on the Harriman lines." He accused the union officials of having become "tools of railroad managers for the purpose of making a break in the ranks."[56]

*   *   *

From the outset of the shopmen's strike, the IWW had argued that only a general strike on the railroads could defeat the corporations. The strike was being prolonged, it said, not so much by the strikebreakers in the shops, but by the engineers, conductors, trainmen, firemen, and telegraphers, who continued to operate the trains and carry strike-breakers and passengers. The San Francisco IWW local put out a sticker reading:

> Railroad men
> No Scab So Despicable
> As a Union Scab.
> Tie Up the Road
> Use IWW Tactics.
> Solidarity Wins.

Solidarity reprinted the sticker and urged locals in the strike area to print their own. It also published a story about a railroad engineer who came into a division point restaurant and became indignant with the waitress for serving scab shopmen. She looked him straight in the eye and asked, "Who brought him here?"[57]

In mid-October, the morale of the strikers in Los Angeles was bolstered by the rumor that "a thousand members of the Los Angeles lodges of conductors, trainmen, engineers, firemen and telegraphers would strike November 2." The rumor was quickly denied by the Brotherhoods. Instead, with November came the McNamara confession, and the press used this as a further argument against the strike.[58] It was at this time that a little-known Swedish-born longshoreman in San Pedro wrote a parody on a current song hit to ridicule how one set of railroad workers was used to defeat the strike of their fellow workers. The song was "Casey Jones—The Union Scab," by Joe Hill.

In San Pedro, the entire crew of three hundred had walked out of the shops of the Southern Pacific line. Joe Hill's famous narrative ballad dealt with an engineer who "got a wooden medal for being good and faithful on the S. P. line," by continuing to run his train during the shopmen's strike. It told of the IWW sabotage of Casey Jones' engine, his trip to heaven, where he even "went scabbing on the angels," his descent into hell, and the ignominious tasks assigned him there:

> Casey Jones, the Devil said, "Oh, fine;
> Casey Jones, get busy shoveling sulphur;
> That's what you get for scabbing on the S. P. line."

The song was an immediate success. Printed on colored cards which were sold to help the strike fund, the song helped to maintain the strikers' spirits.[59] But at no time during its four-year duration did any operating union join the shopmen's strike. Indeed, it was not even possible to obtain the support of the nine shop crafts for a general strike on roads not affected by the strike as a means of forcing the railroad management of the Harriman System to settle on reasonable terms. A referendum was held in the summer of 1912 among the members of the nine shop crafts on the issue of calling a general strike to support the Harriman and Illinois Central strikers. A majority of 451 out of 13,826 votes cast opposed such a sympathy strike.[60]

Ironically, the vote on the general strike occurred shortly after the shop crafts affiliated with the AFL decided that the RED was not effective enough, a conviction that was strengthened by the Harriman strike. On April 15, 1912, two hundred delegates representing five railway shop crafts from the areas south and west of Chicago met in Kansas City and created a new association called the Federation of Federations. Its constitution provided for full-time, full-salaried executives elected directly in conventions by system federation representatives. While the constitution did not provide for an industrial union, it did supply a new agency for more effective collective action. When the RED adopted the Federation of Federations' constitution and officers, with only minor alterations, the AFL Executive Council chartered the new organization as the Railway Department of the American Federation of Labor.[61]

Carl Person charged that the officials of the nine crafts had manipulated the vote on the general strike in order to get a majority against sympathetic action. In the fall of 1913, as Strike Secretary of the Illinois Central System Federation, Person tried to get the new AFL Railway Department to conduct a vote among the shop crafts on the issue of calling a general strike. But not enough lodges supported Person, and on December 16, 1913, he wrote that "because of that, the Railway Department don't feel warranted in submitting a vote for a General Strike among its membership." He added bitterly:

> The main reason why we failed in getting action from sufficient lodges was due to the fact that the Grand Lodge officers were antagonistic against such action, and instructed their membership to pay no attention to the proposition we sent out, and therefore the lodges were afraid to give us their opinion relative to a General Strike proposition.[62]

As the shopmen's strike dragged on, the pressure of economic necessity mounted. A questionnaire sent to strikers revealed that the conflict had compelled 10 percent of them to seek charity, 12 percent to sell their furniture, and 50 percent to borrow money. Over 90 percent of the workers and their families moved from already low-rent dwellings to even cheaper ones, while 68 percent of the strikers' families broke up their homes.[63]

On March 12, 1915, the *Strike Bulletin,* deprived of funds to keep it alive, published its valedictory issue. On May 24, the Executive Council of the Railway Employees' Department met in St. Louis to decide on the next step to be taken in the shopmen's strike. The RED had collected a special strike fund to aid the strike, but after almost four years of struggle, the fund was totally exhausted. The shop craft unions had also exhausted their resources, and the machinists, the strongest among them, had found it necessary to seek loans from their local lodges. At the St.

Louis meeting, a majority of the presidents of six of the shop crafts —machinists, boilermakers, blacksmiths, railway carmen, sheet metal workers, and the railway employees' department—voted "that the strikes on the Illinois Central, Harriman Lines and Pere Marquette Systems are declared officially at an end on and after 10 a.m. June 28, 1915."[64]

After forty-five continuous months—from September 30, 1911 to June 28, 1915—the longest railroad strike in history, the shopmen had not achieved a single one of their goals. Moreover, many of the strikers were blacklisted in the industry and never regained their old jobs. On several of the lines, clerks were required to check all new employees hired for the shops to insure they were not union men at the time of the 1911 strike. If they were, they were not hired.[65]

However, the future was not as bleak as the strike's results might indicate. Although it had done nothing to aid the very strike which had led to its creation, the Federation of Federations did strengthen the System Federation movement among the railroad shopmen. As the new movement grew, many of the former scabs in the 1911 strike joined its ranks and became some of the most enthusiastic union men in the years that followed.[66]

CHAPTER 8

Revolt of the Miners:
West Virginia, 1912–1913

Despite years of organizing activity by the United Mine Workers, in 1912, thousands of coal miners still lived under conditions not far removed from medieval feudalism. The mine operators also owned the surrounding land upon which they erected company-owned dwellings and stores. To work in the mines, a laborer also had to live in a rented company home and do his purchasing at the company grocery and dry goods stores. The miner who protested "lost simultaneously his job, his dwelling and his right to remain in the community."[1]

Probably more than any other important mining state, West Virginia urgently needed effective organization to protect the lives and interests of her coal miners. Engaged in one of the most dangerous occupations, they had to endure short coal weights, payments in company scrip, poor housing, low wages, inadequate medical attention, a system of blacklisting, brutal company guards, and high company store prices which kept them constantly in debt. A state investigating committee found "in many instances an overcharge ranging from ten to twenty-five percent . . . at company stores." One student of the West Virginia mines concludes that for the miners "a system of peonage existed."[2]

When the miners did obtain some relief from the legislative bodies, the courts invariably wiped out their gains. The West Virginia courts denied the miners the right to be paid in cash and refused to uphold the law which prohibited the mine owners from selling to the laborers at a higher price than outsiders. The court stated that these laws represented "unjust interference with private contracts and business," and that they were an "insulting attempt to put the laborer under legislative tutelage," which was "degrading to his manhood" and "suppressive of his rights as a citizen of the United States."[3] So the companies continued to use the scrip system of wage payment and to compel their employees to trade at company stores.

In the summer of 1911, Theresa Malkiel, a Socialist organizer, visited the mine regions of West Virginia. She wrote in the New York *Call* of August 27, 1911:

> The company owns the shacks in which the miners live all along the line for about twenty miles, and when a man offends in the least, he not only loses his job, but has to move; the man cannot find shelter anywhere along the line nor any work even in the adjoining mines. If you bear in mind that the miner seldom sees any cash and has no means to go elsewhere, you can realize in what state of abject slavery the miners are kept. They are paid by the month and having no cash must buy the provisions from the company store and pay 100 per cent more for every article.... A miner, his wife and baby get a bill for groceries amounting to $45 per month, and they do not get enough to keep body and soul together."

A year and a half later, the conservative New York *Tribune* confirmed the accuracy of this report:

> If anywhere in the world men need organizing to protect their interests it is in the West Virginia mining district. . . .
> In the West Virginia coal fields the mine operators are the landlords, the local merchants—for the miners trade at the company stores—and they are very much of the local government so far as there is any in those mountains. Indeed, they have always been a large part of the state government, too. Each way the miner turns, he comes up against the employing corporation. When he rents a house it must be at the company's terms. When he buys food and clothing he must pay the company's prices. And when he seeks his legal rights it must be from the authorities that are likely to be subservient to the great local industries. *It is a species of industrial feudalism to which he is subjected.*[4]

Exercising their right of private ownership, the operators employed guards who would not permit union organizers to come near the mines and would not even allow meetings of the miners. The guards permitted no one to visit the mines or mine villages or "even to walk along the roads leading to the villages unless his business was known. Strangers were stopped and asked their business."[5] Organizing the miners was made still more difficult by the fact that towns were isolated and often inaccessible because of the rugged terrain, "each constituting a little world within itself."[6] Another factor retarding union growth was the ability of the anti-union employers to capitalize on race prejudice. The United Mine Workers adhered to the policy of organizing both white and black workers into the same local, and this was played up by the companies in order to create hostility to the union among white miners, most of whom were either native mountaineers or recent immigrants. The fact that many Afro-Americans were brought into the state from the South as strikebreakers, often without their knowledge, also increased racial friction and antagonism.[7]

The unorganized status of the mines in West Virginia constituted a threat to both the United Mine Workers and the stability of the industry. The state's coal companies competed in both the Eastern and Great Lakes markets. Because of the union, mid-western operators were paying higher wages and had been forced to eliminate many of the miners' long-standing grievances. In West Virginia, on the other hand, the company store, excessive docking, the absence of checkweighmen appointed by the miners, over-sized mine cars, and the longer hours of work—all enabled the operators to sell their coal at a lower price. This, of course, was a constant threat to the organized coal fields. Not only did the non-union status of the industry attract operators to West Virginia, but even those with UMW contracts made it a practice to own mines in the state, so that they could shift operations from the union mines whenever they were threatened with a strike.[8]

Although the union began its attempts to organize West Virginia as early as 1885, it made no headway worth mentioning. Nevertheless, beginning with 1898, at each union convention and joint state conference, the delegates pointed to the need to organize West Virginia and warned that the UMW would remain weak until this was accomplished. John Mitchell told the delegates to a convention: "You cannot be permanently safe, you cannot rest in security until West Virginia . . . [is] organized."[9]

In spite of the vigilance of both the operators and their guards, a widespread organizing campaign was begun in 1901 which produced about 80 locals with approximately 5,000 members. At this point, the UMW felt strong enough to call a general strike for statewide recognition, and on June 7, 1902, the strike call went out. More than 16,000 miners in the Kanawha, New River, Norfolk, and Western districts responded and walked out. But the miners were defeated in all but one section by a combination of the eviction of strikers from their homes, the repression by the mine guards and National Guardsmen, the use of strikebreakers and injunctions, and the arrest of their national organizers, including the legendary "Mother" Mary Jones* and Thomas Haggerty.

*"Mother" Jones was fifty years old when she took up the cause of labor and she soon became known as "Mother" from Arnot, Pennsylvania to Cripple Creek, Colorado. Her courage in labor struggles took on the quality of a folk legend. In the strike of 1902 in West Virginia, she was arrested and imprisoned, charged with inciting riots. An injunction had been issued to prevent her from speaking, but as usual, she defied the courts.

Although the miners of the New River, Norfolk, and Western districts lost their strike, those in the Kanawha section managed to win an agreement which included a nine-hour day, the election of checkweighmen to watch the weighing of the coal to see that miners received their fair weight, semi-monthly pay days, a reduction in the price of powder, the right to trade at non-company stores, and no discrimination in rehiring the strikers or for union affiliation. In addition, the "check-off" was included, and the coal companies agreed to collect dues owed by the miners to their union and to transmit them to the UMW.[10]

In 1904, the only organized mining district in West Virginia suffered a setback when a strike over the issue of the "check-off" ended in a defeat.[11] Nevertheless, the union, increasingly threatened by the expanding coal production in the state, persisted in its efforts to organize West Virginia. The work had to be conducted in secret, for union organizers were followed and assaulted by guards and detectives. Miners seen talking to organizers were immediately discharged and those who even discussed unionism were dismissed and blacklisted. A letter sent to general managers or superintendents by the notorious Baldwin–Felts agency of Bluefield, West Virginia, which supplied guards (actually thugs) in the coal district, read: "I give you below the names of miners discharged from the Crane Creek Coal Company a few days ago for talking unionism." One UMW organizer called the New River section "the most dangerous locality for an organizer of any place in the United States." John W. White, UMW president, declared bluntly:

> Our organization has not been able to protect representatives in the Commonwealth. They have been assaulted and they cannot go into the fields and explain to the miners the purposes of our union, without being in danger of their lives.[12]

Some organizers did manage to move through the state with the message that only through organization could the miners improve their conditions, raise their standard of living, and provide safeguards for their protection in the mines. Their activities brought some results, but by 1912, only 12,000 of the 76,000 miners in West Virginia belonged to the UMW, and of these, only 2,494 were paid-up members. Cabin Creek in Kanawha County was the only organized coal field in the state.[13]

On April 1, 1912, the contract in the organized Cabin Creek district expired. As the expiration date approached, the miners presented new contract terms which included wage scales based on the rates in adjacent coal fields or increases of 2½ cents per ton, a working day of nine hours instead of ten, payment of wages fortnightly in cash, improved sanitary conditions in the company houses, the employment of checkweighmen to represent the miners and to be paid by them, the right of miners to trade wherever they pleased without discrimination for not trading at the company store, a "more complete recognition of the union," including the "check-off system," and abolition of the mine guard system.[14]

The operators, fearing that granting the new demands would enable the union to strengthen its position throughout the state, refused to negotiate and withdrew recognition of the union. The Cabin Creek miners' answer came swiftly. On April 20, they walked off the job and closed down the mines.[15]

Since the strikers who lived in company-owned houses were described by the operators as having "no more rights than a domestic servant who occupies a room in the household of the employer,"[16] the mine guards proceeded to forcibly evict the miners and their families. Strikebreakers were imported, the company guard was increased, Baldwin–Felts detectives and guards were brought in, searchlights were mounted over the collieries, and machine guns were installed.[17] The UMW set up a tent colony for the evicted families at Holly Grove, about fifteen miles from Charleston, near the mouth of Paint Creek. By July, the strike had spread to both the Cabin Creek and Paint Creek districts as non-union miners voluntarily joined the walkout, bringing the total number of strikers to 4,000 and the number of companies affected to forty.[18]

The Cabin Creek–Paint Creek strike of 1912–1913 became one of the most violent labor battles in American history. The miners and their families were threatened, beaten, and murdered, and in self-defense, the miners armed themselves with guns, erected forts, and organized armed squads to protect their families and fight back.[19]

Throughout July, the miners and the Baldwin–Felts guards engaged in pitched battles. On July 26, in a battle at Mucklow, not far from Holly Grove, twelve men, mostly guards, were killed. Governor William E. Glasscock dispatched three companies of the National Guard to the district, and on August 16, he declared a state of martial law in the area. Ten days later, the governor appointed a commission headed by the Most Reverend P. J. Donahue, the Catholic Bishop of Wheeling, to study the dispute and make an impartial report to the state legislature.[20]

On August 1, the 80-year-old "Mother" Jones, always playing a leading role wherever coal miners were engaged in battle, addressed a meeting of six thousand people in Charleston held to urge Governor Glasscock to remove the mine guards. She stood on the steps of the capitol in her prim, black dress, embroidered with white lace, and with wisps of silvery hair curling around her forehead, and told the miners in a loud voice:

> Let me say to you, my friends, let me say to the governor, let me say to the sheriffs and judges in the state of West Virginia, this fight will not stop until the last d----- guard is disarmed. . . . I don't care how much martial law the governor of West Virginia proclaims. I have had martial law proclaimed in other states where I have worked more than once and I did not stop fighting. When they took the martial law off, I began at once and he had to bring the troops back. Can't you see how to do business? If they proclaim martial law, bury your guns. . . .[21]

Protests against the presence of special guards in the Kanawha Valley began to mount. On August 8, three thousand persons petitioned Governor Glasscock to drive out the guards. On August 21, "Mother" Jones presented the governor with a petition from the strikers which asserted that the armed guards had acted brutally toward miners and their families, had seized and searched citizens without warrant of law, and had denied the right of peaceable assembly and freedom of speech. The governor was urged to disarm the guards and to protect the miners' constitutional rights. After touring the area on August 30, the governor stated that the conduct of the mine guards was creating a real disturbance.[22] However, he still refused to remove them and, as might have been expected, the violence increased.

On September 2, Governor Glasscock again declared martial law in the mining districts along Paint Creek and Cabin Creek and again ordered out the militia. Military courts were instituted and National Guard officers began to try prisoners. Colonel George C. Wallace, the officer in charge of the Cabin Creek area, justified the action of the military commission in arresting and sentencing strikers to jail "on the theory that a state of war existed . . . and we were exercising our war powers."[23]

On September 14, Governor Glasscock proposed that the questions at issue be arbitrated, that the miners return to work pending arbitration, and that the mine guard system be abandoned, but that the operators be allowed to employ *bona fide* citizens of the county as guards. The UMW, financially strained by the strike, accepted the proposal, but the operators refused, declaring that they would never recognize the union even if this were recommended by the arbitrators.[24] All this time, the military courts were busy. Thirty-seven strikers were tried and thirty-two of them were sentenced to sixty days each in jail for "intimidating workmen who are employed in the struck mines." The governor approved the sentences. Shortly thereafter, the state courts upheld the right of the military to arrest and imprison violators of military rule.[25] While strikers were being sent to prison for violating military orders, the mine operators continued to evict the miners.[26]

In the middle of October, martial law was ended and nearly all the militiamen were withdrawn from the strike district. Immediately, the operators brought back the mine guards and stepped up the importation of strikebreakers. Immediately, too, clashes between strikers and the mine guards and strikebreakers again flared up. Armed strikers seized trains carrying strikebreakers to the mines and ordered the coaches conveying the scabs to be uncoupled before they would allow the trains to proceed. Gunfire was exchanged between strikers and guards protecting the trains carrying strikebreakers. Again the governor declared martial law, ordered four companies back to the strike region, and appointed another military commission. Soon strikers were being arrested by the militia and tried before the military commission, which imposed sentences in some cases as long as five years in the penitentiary.[27]

On November 27, the strike commission appointed by Governor Glasscock submitted its report, together with a transcript of several hundred pages of testimony heard during its sessions. The commission condemned the mine guard system as "vicious, strife-prompting and un-American":

> There emerges clearly . . . that these guards . . . recklessly and flagrantly violated, in respect to the miners on Paint Creek, respectively, the rights guaranteed by natural justice and the Constitution to every citizen, however lowly his condition and state. . . . We are, therefore, unanimously of the opinion that the mine guard system as at present constituted, should be abolished forthwith. . . .

Still, the commission concluded that the miners' living conditions were good compared with those in other coal fields, and that wages were not lower than those in other fields. However, it admitted that the miners were being overcharged at the company stores, and that "some injustice" had been done them by the system of "docking" their pay for work considered unsatisfactory. Blacklisting, which it conceded was widespread, was condemned as "repugnant to the genius of our institutions." The commission upheld the right of the miners to organize but asserted that the operators "do not resist this right as a general proposition, but their claim is that the peculiarly independent condition in West Virginia would render it ruinous and therefore impossible for them to recognize the union."[28] In making this judgment, the commission overlooked the fact that during its own hearings, attorney Harold Houston, representing the miners, has asked: "Is it part of the policy of the coal operators to prevent unionism of Cabin Creek?" This question produced the following reply from W. T. Knight, chief counsel for the Kanawha Coal Operators' Association: "Yes, the operators are opposed to organizations like the United Mine Workers of America."[29]

In its recommendations, the commission urged the enactment of legislation similar to the Canadian Disputes Act, a workmen's compensation act, and a reduction in company store prices.[30] However, little came of its report, since the right to belong to a union and have it recognized remained a matter of heated contention.

In mid-December all four companies of militia were withdrawn from the strike zone and civil law was restored. On December 23, Governor Glasscock granted "Christmas pardons" to seven of the twenty miners sentenced by the military commissions to imprisonment for from one to five years. The strike continued during the severe winter season. The union had removed 900 strikers' families from the strike area, but 600 still remained in the tent colonies.[31]

On the night of February 7, 1913, an armored train equipped with iron plate siding and machine guns—the "Bull Moose Special"—crept slowly toward the tent colony at Holly Grove and stopped outside the first line of tents. Volley after volley of shots poured into the ragged tents of the sleeping miners. Miraculously, there were only a few casualties. One miner was shot dead running away from his dwelling and the wife of another was wounded in her bed. Quin Martin, general manager of the Imperial Coal Company, not only boasted openly of the shocking attack on the tent colony, but was reported as saying: "We will go back and give them another round."[32]

The fury of the strikers was expressed in a poem written by a "Paint Creek Miner," which went in part:

> They riddled us with volley after volley;
>   We heard their speeding bullets zip and ring,
> But soon we'll make them suffer for their folly—
>   O, Buddy, how I'm longing for the spring![33]*

Three days later, the infuriated miners marched in protest to

*Ralph Chaplin, the IWW poet who was aiding the strikers, was the author of the poem. The miners waited for the spring when the leaves would come out and the leafless hills would no longer make them targets for enemy fire and expose them when they fired back. (Ralph Chaplin, *Wobbly*, Chicago, 1948, pp. 125-27.) Chaplin also wrote the famous "Solidarity Forever" during the strike.

Mucklow. They were met by a posse of armed guards and a battle began, and before it was over, twelve miners and four guards were dead. Governor Glasscock declared martial law for the third time, ordered six companies of militia to go to the strikebound counties, and reestablished the military commission.[34]

A wave of arrests of strikers and their leaders now followed. Nearly three hundred were arrested and tried by the military commission. On February 12, "Mother" Jones went to Charleston to consult the governor, but upon her arrival in the state capitol, she was immediately arrested. On the same day, Charles R. Boswell, Socialist editor of the *Labor Argus*, was arrested and charged with murder in conspiring against non-union miners and others.[35]

About 125 of those arrested, including "Mother Jones," were taken to Pratt and held for trial by the military court. UMW President John P. White complained:

> Martial law is used to deprive our representatives of all access to the civil courts, as under martial law no decision is rendered as to the guilt or innocence of these parties, and they are simply detained to keep them out of active work for the organization and to blacken the reputation of the individuals and the organization. It is noticeable that no coal operators or their representatives are subject to the proceedings of this court.[36]

The union leader's complaint was fully justified. All of the prisoners were civilians and the charges against them were for civilian offenses within the jurisdiction of the civil courts, which were open and functioning in the districts under martial law. The prisoners had been arrested on orders issued by military men, and not by civil warrants. They were to be tried without juries before courts-martial. In many instances, persons had been arrested outside the martial law zone, some even for offenses committed outside the zone.[37] As Robert S. Rankin notes in his study, *When Law Fails:* "In the history of the United States, martial law has never been used on so broad a scale, in so drastic a manner, nor upon such sweeping principles as in West Virginia in 1912-13."[38]

The famous IWW poet, Ralph Chaplin, writing as a "Paint Creek Miner," penned these lines about "Mother" Jones during her incarceration in Pratt:

> How they fear her, how they hate her—hate her kind
>   and timeworn face.
> How they rush armed mobs to meet her when she moves
>   from place to place.
> Bristling bayonets and sabers working shameless,
>   deep disgrace.[39]

Even while in military prison, "Mother" Jones was not inactive. She managed to smuggle out a letter,* hastily scribbled, to William B. Wilson, a UMW leader who had been a member of Congress and who was shortly to become Secretary of Labor in President Wilson's cabinet. After describing how she had been picked up on the streets of Charleston, thrown into an auto and brought twenty-two miles to the military prison, she urged Wilson to get her note to Senator William E. Borah, so that he could know the facts about what was happening in West Virginia. "When I get out I will give them H---," she concluded.[40] A few days later, after Senator Borah had introduced a resolution in the Senate demanding an investigation of the strike by the federal government, "Mother" Jones wrote to him and thanked him "in behalf of the crushed and persecuted slaves of the coal mines of West Virginia. . . . I am in confinement now for a week at the age of 80 years. I am a military prisoner. This is just what the old monarchy did [to] my grandparents 90 years ago in Ireland."[41]

Borah's resolution failed of consideration, just as had a resolution introduced in Congress on August 19, 1912 by William B. Wilson, then a member of the House of Representatives, asking for a Congressional investigation of the West Virginia strike situation.[42] Early in March, attorneys for the union applied to the circuit court for a writ of *habeas corpus* to achieve the release of the military prisoners. The petition was granted, and the circuit court ordered the military authorities to justify their actions. Sheriff Hall went to Pratt to serve the court's order on the members of the military commission and the judge advocate, but, as he stepped from the train, the provost marshal informed him that he would not be permitted to serve any papers in the military district. On March 12, the circuit court reversed itself and upheld the right of the military commission to try cases.[43]

A number of the prisoners, including "Mother" Jones, refused to acknowledge the right of the military courts to try them and declined even to put up a defense. John Brown, a Socialist miner and one of the prisoners, explained the reason for this stand in a moving letter to his wife on March 9, 1913, written at the military camp in Pratt:

> . . . As you have undoubtedly seen by the papers, Boswell, Batley, Parsons, "Mother" Jones, Paulson, and myself have refused to acknowledge the jurisdiction of the military court, and therefore are not putting up any defense. You, perhaps with others, do not see at this time the wisdom in such

*One of the militiamen who guarded "Mother Jones" was friendly to the strikers, and he arranged to have her slip her letters through a hole in the floor.

tactics, seeing that we are wholly at the mercy of this tribunal; but time will tell and justify the position we take.

If it was only myself personally that was concerned, I would, for the sake of gaining my liberty and being free to go to you and the children, go before this court and defend myself. Nor have I the least doubt in my mind that I would come clear. But, my dear, there are principles involved in this case infinitely deeper than the fate of any one citizen. If the capitalist class gets away with this, then CONSTITUTIONAL GOVERNMENT IS DEAD; AND JUSTICE FOR THE WORKING CLASS IS A THING OF THE PAST . . . .

If we let them get away with it, then in the future wherever and whenever the interests of the working class and the capitalist class reaches an acute stage, out will come the militia, the Courts will be set aside, and the leaders railroaded to the military bull-pens, and thence to the penitentiaries. Here lies the great danger. . . .[44]

The military commission went ahead with the trials and found "Mother" Jones and sixty others guilty of murder, conspiracy, and inciting to riot, and transmitted its findings to Governor Henry D. Hatfield, who had succeeded Governor Glasscock. In late March, the new governor released about 45 of the 65 persons who had been convicted by the military commission, conditioned on their good behavior. But "Mother" Jones was not released. "I know," she wrote to a friend on April 5 from the "Military Bastille," "they would let me go if I would go out of the State but I will die before I give them that satisfaction."[45] Among the prisoners released by Governor Hatfield were several UMW organizers who left the district immediately after a private interview with the governor.[46]

In May, 1913, a resolution was introduced in the Senate by Senator John W. Kern of Indiana calling for a Congressional investigation of the strike. (The UMW had sought such an investigation by the newly-formed Department of Labor, but Secretary William B. Wilson contended that since no appropriation had been made for the Department, it could not conduct an investigation.)[47] The night before the question came up in the Senate, Senator Kern received a telegram from "Mother" Jones, which had also been smuggled out of military prison. The next day, Senator Kern read the following before an astonished Senate and press:

From out of the military prison wall of Pratt, West Virginia, where I have walked over my eighty-fourth milestone in history, I send you the groans and tears and heartaches of men, women and children as I have heard them in this state. From out these prison walls, I plead with you for the honor of the nation, to push that investigation, and the children yet unborn will rise and call you blessed.[48]

The investigation was voted, and on June 11, the Senate sub-committee began its hearings in Charleston. In its report, the Senate group denounced the military rule and the imprisonment of miners as a denial of constitutional rights. But it also charged that the union's campaign was motivated by a desire to organize the West Virginia coal fields in order to render them less competitive with the organized areas.[49]

Even before the Senate hearings opened, however, the strike was in the process of being settled. Having failed to break the strike for over a year and being unable to operate the mines with imported strikebreakers because of the miners' resistance, the operators were ready for a compromise. On March 26, UMW President White offered a basis for such a settlement, which Governor Hatfield watered down and then offered to the operators in the middle of April. The proposed contract's terms were a nine-hour workday, the right to select a checkweighman, semi-monthly pay, and no discrimination against union miners.[50]

The operators and UMW officials accepted the compromise settlement, but the union leaders, as David A. Corbin points out, "apparently feared opposition from rank-and-file miners, for, instead of submitting the proposed contract to a referendum, as was usual in contracts involving wage disputes, they called a convention of selected miners' delegates to vote on the settlement terms."[51] Even then, considerable resentment was expressed because the governor's proposals did not include the miners' most important demands—elimination of the hated guard system, payment of the "Kanawha scale" of wages, the "check-off," and reinstatement of all strikers. Socialist delegates led the opposition to the proposed settlement, but after three days of debate, the delegates ratified the contract.[52]

Throughout the strike, West Virginia Socialists had felt that the UMW leadership was not doing enough to achieve victory, and now the Socialist press charged that the settlement was forced upon the strikers by the UMW national officers, whom they accused of collaborating with the state's coal operators and Governor Hatfield to end the strike just when the miners were in a position to win their original demands.[53]

As opposition to the proposed settlement mounted among the miners, most of whom agreed with the Socialists' criticism, Governor Hatfield began to fear that the new contract would be rejected by the men. He immediately issued an ultimatum ordering the strikers to return to work within thirty-six hours or be deported from the state. He then moved to stifle Socialist opposition to the settlement. The editor of the *Labor Argus*, a Socialist weekly published in Charleston, was jailed because he editorialized against the governor's proposals. The *Huntington Socialist and Labor Star* was visited by a mob of militiamen and deputies after it voiced opposition to the settlement; its offices and plant were wrecked, its type scattered over a wide area, and its staff arrested. Fred Merrick, editor of the left-wing Socialist paper, *Justice,* was arrested and jailed because he, too, criticized the governor's proposals. In this repressive atmosphere, it was not really possible to voice further opposition to the settlement.[54]

Although the strike was officially ended, many of the miners most active in the struggle were not rehired, martial law still prevailed, and strikers and activists, especially Socialist miners and Socialist editors, were still in jail. In May, 1913, the national committee of the Socialist Party protested to President Wilson that "a reign of terror, of officially protected lawlessness and monarchy" existed in the mining fields of West Virginia. It selected Eugene V. Debs, Victor Berger, and Adolph Germer, a young Illinois miner and UMW official, to go to America's "Little Russia" to investigate conditions there.* Debs and Germer departed immediately for West Virginia, arriving on May 17, but Berger was delayed until the 20th. After making a whirlwind tour of the area, interviewing miners, and observing conditions first-hand, the committee met on May 22 with Governor Hatfield. After the meeting, Berger reported, the governor

> . . . saw things differently and immediately took a strong hand in the matter. The jails and "bullpens" were thrown open and the prisoners have been freed. All this happened after an hour and a half of conference. . . . The governor promised that he would protect both the organizers of the miners and . . . of the Socialist Party. . . . He promised to repeal the martial law immediately and see to it that all the strikers got their jobs back.[55]

In its report, submitted to the National Committee of the Socialist Party on May 26, 1913, the committee exonerated Hatfield from much of the criticism directed at him in the Socialist press, blaming his predecessor, and reported that a "better understanding . . . between the United Mine Workers and the Socialist Party" would pave the way for a concerted political and economic organization of the entire state.[56]

Editors of the Socialist press in West Virginia bitterly condemned the

*David A. Corbin argues persuasively that the members of the investigating committee were eager to achieve full, cordial relations between the Socialists and the UMW leadership and thus would do nothing to upset the settlement worked out between the mine union leaders and Governor Hatfield. ("Betrayal in the West Virginia Coal Fields: Eugene V. Debs and the Socialist Party of America, 1912-1941," *Journal of American History,* vol. LXIV, March, 1978, pp. 997-98.)

committee's report for having "whitewashed" Governor Hatfield, and the *Industrial Worker* sharply attacked Debs for having knifed "the struggling and outraged miners in the back." Samuel Gompers, too, denounced the "clean bill of health" given to the governor.[57] In reply, Debs cited the fact that shortly after the committee had arrived in West Virginia, sixty Socialist miners were released from military prison, martial law was revoked, the suppressed Socialist papers were permitted to resume publication, and assurance was received from Governor Hatfield that "free speech, free assemblage and the right to organize should prevail. . . ." When this was proved to be more fancy than fact, Debs charged his critics, especially the West Virginia Socialists, with seeking to undermine the United Mine Workers in order to open the door for the IWW to move into West Virginia and take over the organization of the miners. Scholars who have studied the controversy, however, have rejected Debs' charges.[58]

In the end, the rank-and-file miners did win a better contract. Refusing to accept the Hatfield compromise settlement, the miners in Paint Creek and Cabin Creek renewed their strike. Secretary of Labor William B. Wilson then appointed a commission of mediation and conciliation, which began negotiations on June 5 with UMW national officers, who had been forced to comply with the rank-and-file rejection of the settlement, and the operators. Unable to count any longer on the governor to issue another proclamation of martial law or to otherwise intimidate the miners, the operators were compelled to make new concessions. On June 18, Secretary Wilson wired John P. White: "Settlement of West Virginia strike arrived at today, subject to ratification by West Virginia miners." The new settlement included several of the miners' original demands, such as the "check-off" and a wage increase. The miners went back to work on July 1, and on July 15, in convention, they ratified the new agreement by a vote of two to one.[59]

Unfortunately, the mines in West Virginia still remained largely unorganized. In 1912, at the beginning of the strike, the UMW's strength represented three percent of the miners of West Virginia. In 1915, the figure stood at only five percent.[60]

CHAPTER 9

Revolt of the Miners: Colorado, 1913–1914

On April 21, 1914, in the quiet of the afternoon, a telephone lineman was making his way through the ruins of a tent colony in southern Colorado. He lifted an iron cot covering a pit under one of the tents and found the blackened, swollen bodies of eleven children and two women. The news was flashed to the world, and the tragedy was given a name: the "Ludlow Massacre." All told, twenty-one persons, including the eleven children, lost their lives in one of the most shameful episodes in all of American history.[1]

The tragedy was the central event in a 14-month strike of members of the United Mine Workers of America against the management of the Colorado Fuel & Iron Company, which took a toll of sixty-six lives. It was a battle against conditions which today seem to belong to the Middle Ages, but which were typical of many industrial communities in America on the eve of World War I. But in none did the conditions more resemble those of medieval feudalism than in the Rockefeller-dominated coal fields of southern Colorado.

In 1902, John D. Rockefeller, Sr. bought control of the Colorado Fuel & Iron Company and the Victor Fuel Company, the two major producers in the southern fields, and made them part of Rockefeller's industrial empire. Colorado Fuel & Oil produced 40 percent of the coal dug in Colorado and dominated coal and iron production activities in the Southwest. In 1911, Rockefeller, Sr. turned over his interest in the corporation, which amounted to 40 percent of the stock, to his son, John D. Rockefeller, Jr., who made major policy decisions from his office at 26 Broadway in New York City. John R. Lawson, the most important leader of the 1913–1914 strike, in testimony before the Commission on Industrial Relations, characterized the absentee owner, Rockefeller, as "invested with what is virtually the power of life and death over 12,000 men and their families, for the isolated nature of the coal industry lends itself to absolutism unknown in other activities. . . ."[2]

The situation was made even worse by the fact that both J. F. Wellborn, president of Colorado Fuel & Iron, and L. M. Bowers, its superintendent, maintained their offices in Denver, two hundred miles from the mines. Responsibility for the mining area fell to E. H. Weitzel, whose office was in Pueblo, fifty miles north of the area.

Colorado Fuel & Iron owned twenty-seven mining camps, including all of the land in these camps, the houses, the saloons, the schools, the churches and other buildings located within the camp environs, and the huts in which the miners lived and for which they paid exorbitant rents. A miner could be summarily evicted, since he had signed a lease agreeing that it could be terminated on three days' notice, and that he and his family could be immediately dispossessed. As a result, if a miner aroused the company's anger, this could bring about not only the loss of his job, but eviction from his home as well.

No words can adequately describe the contrast between the wild beauty of the Colorado countryside and the unspeakable squalor of these mining camps. The miners' huts, which were usually shared by several families, were made up of clapboard walls and thin-planked floors, with leaking roofs, sagging doors, broken windows, and old newspapers nailed to the walls to keep out the cold. Some families, particularly the Black families, were forced to live in tiny cubicles not much larger than chicken coops.[3]

Within sight of the huts were the coke ovens, the mine tipple, and the breaker house, with thick clouds of soot clogging the air and settling on the ground, effectively strangling any shoots of grass or flowers that tried to keep alive. Wriggling along the canyon walls, behind the huts, was a sluggish creek, dirty-yellow and laden with the slag of the mine and the refuse of the camps. Alongside the creek the children played, barefoot, ragged, and often hungry.

The miners received their wages, such as they were, in company scrip, which was discounted when coverted into cash; they traded in company stores, where they paid excessively high prices. They received treatment from a company doctor, whose fees were deducted from their wages whether they were sick or well. They worked in mines which were notorious for their lack of safety precautions and in a state which had a grim record of fatal accidents. In 1912, the year preceding the strike, the rate of fatal accidents for the entire nation was 3.15 for each million tons of coal mined, while in Colorado, the rate was 11.86. The high accident rate in the Colorado mines was aggravated by the absence of any workman's compensation law in the state. The surviving widow and children of a mine accident victim were left to wage a relentless struggle against poverty.[4]

Each mining camp was a feudal domain, with the company acting as lord and master. It had a marshal, a law enforcement officer paid by the company. Teachers were chosen and paid by the company. Company officials were appointed as election judges. Company-dominated coroners and judges prevented injured employees from collecting damages. The "law" consisted of the company rules. Curfews were imposed. Company guards—brutal thugs armed with machine guns and rifles loaded with explosive bullets—would not admit any "suspicious" stranger into the camp and would not permit any miner to leave. It is not difficult to imagine the condition of the miners—the serfs—in such a community. Most of them were immigrants representing twenty-one nationality groups—Greeks, Italians, Croatians, Russians, Serbs, Montenegrins, Bulgarians, Poles, etc.—all equally held in contempt by the operators and their agents.[5]

On paper, Colorado had an excellent code of laws for the protection of workers. But in reality the will of the operator was the law. The operators prohibited the miners from appointing their own coal checkweighmen with the result that they were robbed of from 400 to 800 pounds in each ton; they paid their workers in company-printed scrip instead of legal currency, so that the average daily wage of $1.60 had a purchasing power of about one dollar; they worked the miners for more than eight hours a day; they prohibited them from patronizing stores of their own choice and compelled them to buy at company stores, where prices were often twice as high as elsewhere; and they forced the miners to vote as the foremen directed—all in open defiance of the law. The truth is that neither state, county, nor federal law counted for much in the feudal domain dominated by the Colorado Fuel & Iron Company. Reverend Atkinson of Colorado reported the following exchange in an interview with Colorado Governor Elias Ammons:

> Rev. Atkinson: Have you no constitutional law and government in Colorado?
> Gov. Ammons: Not a bit in those counties where the coal mines are located.

Rev. Atkinson: Do you mean to say that in large sections of your state there is no constitutional liberty?

Gov. Ammons: Absolutely none.[6]

In 1914, a report of the Commission on Industrial Relations stated: "Not only the government in these counties [Huerfano and Las Animas, coal counties], but of the state has been brought under their domination and forced to do the companies' bidding, and the same companies have even flaunted the will of the nation as expressed by the President of the United States." Little wonder, then, that one student of the 1913–1914 Colorado strike describes it "not so much as a struggle for higher wages or other tangible advantages as a revolt against a political, economic and social despotism."[7]

In 1901, Colorado was organized into a district of the United Mine Workers of America. During the next two years, the union grew, as thousands of miners, unable to endure the deplorable conditions in the coal camps, looked to unionism as a solution. In September, 1903, local delegates voted to strike unless their demands were granted. These included an eight-hour day, semi-monthly pay, the abolition of payment in company scrip, a 2,000-pound ton instead of one of 2,400; and better ventilation in the mines. Only the demand for an eight-hour day was not required by statutes; in fact, in the main, the miners were merely calling for the enforcement of the state laws.

When the Colorado Fuel & Iron Company and the Victor Fuel Company refused to negotiate, the miners struck on November 9. Immediately, strikers' families were evicted from the company houses; union organizers were arrested; and strikebreakers were rushed in, protected by company guards and state troops. After the company guards had killed and wounded several strikers, many of the strikers acquired weapons in order to defend themselves. Finally, military rule was established, financed by the coal companies, railroads, merchants, and property owners. Military arrests followed, and between four and five hundred striking miners were rounded up by the state soldiers and armed guards and loaded into two trains. One was dispatched to Kansas and the other to New Mexico. The men were unloaded in the prairies and warned to keep away from Colorado. This massive state intervention on the side of the coal companies broke the strike, and in October, 1904, it was called off.[8]

Nothing was gained by the strike, but it did serve to intensify the anger and resentment among the miners and set the stage for an even bitterer struggle between the union and the coal companies, for between

1904 and 1913, not a single change took place to improve the conditions of the miners. Indeed, many of the strikers of 1913 had been brought into the area as strikebreakers in 1903. Yet so grim were both their working and living conditions that they, in turn, became the strikers a decade later.

After secretly organizing a recruiting campaign for two years, the United Mine Workers sent Vice-President Frank J. Hayes, John McLennon, president of District No. 15 (which included Colorado), E. L. Doyle, secretary of District No. 15, and John Lawson, executive board member, to Colorado. A policy-making committee was established, and in an effort to stave off a strike, attempts were made to get Governor Ammons to arrange a conference with the mine operators. These failed, as did an attempt by the Department of Labor to mediate the dispute. Early in September, 1913, acting on a request from the UMW for assistance in mediating the dispute, Secretary of Labor William B. Wilson appointed Ethelbert Stewart as mediator. Before going to Colorado, Stewart first went to New York City to enlist the aid of John D. Rockefeller, Jr., but he could not even get in to see him. Instead, he was told by a member of Rockefeller's staff that any decision with regard to the policy of the Colorado Fuel & Iron Company would be made in Colorado and that the New York office would not interfere.[9]

On September 15, 1913, at Trinidad, Colorado, 250 delegates from the state's mining camps opened their convention, singing:

We will win the fight today, boys,
We'll win the fight today,
Shouting the battle cry of union;
We will rally from the coal mines,
Shouting the battle cry of union.

Chorus:

The union forever, hurrah boys, hurrah!
Down with the Baldwins,* up with the law;
For we're coming, Colorado, we're coming all the way,
Shouting the battle cry of union.

Fed up with Colorado Fuel & Iron's refusal even to meet with union representatives, the miners demanded action. They were supported by the veteran labor organizer, 83-year-old Mother Jones, just released from jail for having helped the West Virginia coal miners in their fight against company feudalism. In an hour-long speech, she stirred the miners' spirit of revolt:

*The reference is to the strikebreaking Baldwin–Felts guards.

Rise up and strike. If you are too cowardly to fight, there are enough women in this country to come in and beat it out of you. If it is slavery or strike, why I say strike, until the last one of you drop into your graves. Strike and stay with it as we did in West Virginia. We are going to stay here in southern Colorado until the banner of industrial freedom floats over every coal mine. We are going to stand together and never surrender. When I get Colorado and Alabama organized, I will ask God to take me to my rest. I am going to force the operators to concede that human life is to be regarded above property life.

The convention voted unanimously to strike on September 23 for union recognition; a ten percent increase in wage scales; the eight-hour day; pay for "dead work" (timbering, removing fall, handling impurities, etc.); checkweighmen in all mines to be elected by the miners; free choice of stores, boarding houses, and doctors; enforcement of the Colorado mining laws; and "abolition of the notorious guard system which has prevailed in the mining camps of Colorado for many years." As in the case of the 1903 strike, nearly all of the demands were already on the statute books of Colorado but had been ignored by the company.[10]

Having learned through an effective spy system that the union's financial position was precarious and the UMW leaders did not really intend to go through with the strike, the Colorado Fuel & Iron Company did not take the strike vote seriously. On September 19, Superintendent Bowers informed the New York office that all the union officials really wanted was to obtain an interview with the operators in order to be able to boast "before the public that they have secured the principal point: namely, recognition of the union." Confident that the union was in no position to conduct an effective strike, the operators refused all further offers of mediation by the Department of Labor. E. M. Bowers informed Ethelbert Stewart, who had gone to Colorado in an effort to stave off a strike, that the company would never recognize the union. In a letter to Rockefeller, Bowers assured the absentee owner that the officials of the company "would stand by this declaration until our bones were bleached white as chalk in these Rocky Mountains." Rockefeller expressed complete approval of this course.[11]

While scoffing at the strike vote, the operators still took no chances. Even before the miners walked out, they ordered them out of the company houses into a bitter mountain winter. The UMW leased land just outside the company property, brought in tents from West Virginia, and set up tent colonies in Ludlow, Suffield, Forbes, Berwind, Starkville, La Veta, and seven other sites. On September 23, a scene of epic proportions was enacted in the coal mine district of southern Colorado. Between eleven and thirteen thousand miners—about 90 percent of the workers in the mines—gathered up their belongings and moved with their families to the hastily improvised tent colonies.[12]

The miners' wives and children tried to keep warm that winter, in temperatures as low as forty to fifty degrees below zero, by shoveling out from under four to six-foot snowfalls, while their men fought a bloody war against strikebreakers, company guards, and Baldwin–Felts detectives sworn in as deputy sheriffs. The Baldwin–Felts agency brought in a special automobile, with a Gatling gun mounted on top, which became known as the "Death Special." Its side armored, it roamed the countryside with several rifle-carrying detectives in the front seat, attacking the tent colonies indiscriminately. Day after day, mine guards, wearing deputy badges, fired at the strikers. On October 5, the operators shipped four machine guns into the strike zone. The miners threw up breastworks and dug pits under the tents to protect the women and children.

The machine guns were not just for show. A machine gun fired into women and children being evacuated from the Forbes tent camp. One miner was killed, a small boy was hit nine times but survived, and a young girl was shot in the face. On October 24, 1913, mine guards, wearing deputy sheriff badges as usual, fired into a group of strikers in Walsenberg and killed four of them.[13]

As the violence intensified, Governor Ammons ordered the National Guard into the strike zone. The militia arrived in Ludlow on October 31, 1913 and received a warm welcome from the miners. Even State Adjutant-General Chase, a long-time hater of trade unions, remarked on the friendliness of the strikers toward the militiamen. He wrote in his report:

> The parade of the troops of the Ludlow tent colony was memorable. The road for a half-mile or more between the point of detraining and the entrance to the colony was lined on either side by men, women, and children. Many of the men were in the strange costume of the Greek, Montenegran, Serbian, and Bulgarian armies; for the colony numbered among its inhabitants many returned veterans of the Balkan wars. The little children were dressed in white, as for a Sunday-school picnic. All carried small American flags and sang continually the Union songs. Through this line of men, women, and children the troops paraded infantry, cavalry, and field artillery. Flags were waved in welcome, and an improvised band of the strikers heralded our approach.[14]

Within a few weeks, however, the feeling toward the troops changed from friendliness to deep hostility. The thousand or so soldiers under Chase's command were literally strikebreaking agents of the Colorado Fuel & Iron Company. The company paid their salaries and the soldiers were quartered in company buildings and furnished with supplies by the company. Soon, the militia began recruiting mine guards to replace men released on the basis of hardship and business needs. The mine guards were in the favored position of receiving three dollars a day from the operators in addition to their one dollar as militiamen, both salaries paid by Colorado Fuel & Iron.[15]

On November 28, Governor Ammons, yielding to pressure, lifted the ban on the importation of strikebreakers from outside the state and ordered the militia to become the protective agent for the escort of the scabs into the mines. The source of the pressure for this step was spelled out by Superintendent Bowers in a letter to Rockefeller:

> Besides the bankers, the Chamber of Commerce, the Real Estate Exchange, together with a great many of the best business men, have been urging the Governor to take steps to drive these vicious agitators out of the state.
>
> Another mighty power has been rounded up in behalf of the operators by the gathering together of fourteen of the editors of the most important newspapers in Denver, Pueblo, Trinidad, Walsenberg, Colorado Springs, and other of the larger places of the state.[16]

In searching the miners' tents for guns, the militiamen robbed them and even raped some of the women. Strikers were thrown into jail without the slightest provocation and were held without any opportunity to prove their innocence. Mother Jones was arrested and held incommunicado for twenty days, with two armed sentries posted outside her prison door.

On January 22, 1914, there was a parade of women in Trinidad to protest the imprisonment of Mother Jones. At its head, an Italian woman carried the American flag. A troop of cavalry, led personally by General Chase, the commanding general of the militia, intercepted the marchers. When the parade reformed and started back to its initial point, a troop of cavalry, supported by foot soldiers, broke into the ranks of the women. A number of them were injured and eighteen were jailed. Not too long thereafter, militia cavalrymen destroyed the tent colony near Forbes and drove the inhabitants, including women and children, into a mountain snowstorm.[17]

After a careful investigation, a committee of four union men and Professor James H. Brewster of the University of Colorado found that the militia had tried to persuade strikers to go back into the mines; had escorted strikebreakers into the area; had frequently held strikers for long periods without filing any charges; had assaulted young girls; and had participated in robberies and holdups. After investigating the strike situation during February and March, 1914, the Congressional Subcommittee ones and Mining concluded that the National Guard had been guilty of many of the same offenses. Finally, George P. West, who investigated the strike for the U. S. Commission on Industrial Relations, noted that "the Colorado National Guard no longer offered even a pretense of fairness or partiality, and its units in the field had degenerated into a force of professional gunmen and adventurers who were economically dependent on and subservient to the will of the coal operators."[18]

Although criticism of the militamen's conduct did not seem to affect Governor Ammons, the state's precarious financial position resulting from the mounting costs in helping the operators break the strike did. Early in April, 1914, the governor withdrew the bulk of the National Guard from the strike zone. Only 35 men in Company B, formerly mine guards, were left. On April 18, a hundred deputies in the pay of Colorado Fuel & Iron were formed into Troop A of the National Guard and were sent to join Company B. The designated spot was a rocky ridge overlooking the thousand men, women, and children who lived in the tent colony at Ludlow, the largest colony of strikers.

The Ludlow colony was under the supervision of Louis Tikas, a Greek strike leader, who was loved and admired by men, women, and children alike at the colony because of his deep concern for their welfare and his keen understanding of the problems of the strike. A graduate of the University of Athens, Tikas wielded considerable influence over the immigrants in southern Colorado, and especially over the Greeks, the most militant element among the strikers in the Ludlow colony.

The two officers selected to take charge of the command at the Ludlow colony were well-fitted for the job assigned them by the company. One was Major Patrick Hamrock, a Denver saloonkeeper. But the dominant figure was Lieutenant Kenneth E. Linderfelt, a man especially hated by the strikers who was known to the colony's inhabitants as "Jesus Christ," since he had once told a striker's wife, "I am Jesus Christ and my men on horses are Jesus Christs—and we must be obeyed." On December 30, 1913, the powerfully-built officer came upon a teenage boy, the son of a striker, on a road near the colony. He promptly knocked the youth unconscious. Linderfelt had a special hatred for Louis Tikas, to whom he referred contemptuously as "Lou the Greek." One day, Linderfelt found Tikas alone, beat him brutally, and had him dragged to jail.[19]

April 19, 1914 was the Greek Orthodox Easter Sunday, and a group of Ludlow strikers were picnicking in a nearby meadow. It was one of the first sunny days of spring, and they were playing baseball. Over the hill from the north came five gunmen on horseback, rifles slung over their shoulders. They stopped near the players and one of them shouted, "Have your fun today! We'll have our roast tomorrow."

On the morning of April 20, Linderfelt approached the camp at Ludlow and demanded that Louis Tikas release an "unidentified person." After a search, Tikas met Linderfelt at the Ludlow depot and assured him that no such person could be found. Although Linderfelt later conceded that he "could not remember" the anonymous person's name, he and his armed guard companions bitterly denounced the Greek strike leader. Finally, Tikas retreated toward the camp.

Shortly thereafter, the quiet of the morning was shaken by an explosion. Rushing from their tents, the strikers could see columns of black smoke rising slowly from Water Tank Hill, where the militia was stationed. Major Hamrock, after talking with General Chase, had ordered the explosion of two dynamite bombs as a signal to the troops, who were armed with Springfield rifles and at least two machine guns.

For a little while, the countryside was unbearably still and tense. Then, exactly at 9 a.m., the dull clatter of a machine gun began and the first bullets ripped through the canvas of the tents. The clatter became a deafening roar as more machine guns went into action. Then the high-powered rifles of the militiamen joined in and poured a hail of explosive bullets into the tents. Five strikers and a 10-year-old boy were killed by gunfire early in the battle as militia bullets ripped through the tents.[21]

The men dashed from tent to tent to draw the fire and flung themselves into deep arroyos—ugly gashes in the Ludlow hills. Many of the women had been undressed when the firing began, but they ran crazily from tent to tent, hugging children to their breasts, seeking shelter. Fifty of the women were pregnant, and one of the mothers gave birth to a baby as she fled from the colony. Some of the women managed to run off into the hills and hide in nearby ranch houses. Others crawled with their children into the dark pits and caves which had been dug under a few of the tents. It was these dugouts which saved the strikers' families from total annihilation, for the colony was mercilessly raked by rifle and machine gun fire during the day. "The soldiers and mine guards," an eyewitness reported, "tried to kill everybody; anything they saw move, even a dog, they shot at."[22]

Had it not been for Tikas' rescue efforts, the Ludlow horror might have been even worse. Throughout the day, he and Pearl Jolly, the wife of a striker, moved from tent to tent, pulling the women and children out of their cellars and ordering them to move among the arroyos to the Black Hills, some two miles east of the colony. As Tikas was attempting to help a woman and two children escape from one of the cellars, he was captured by the troops. Linderfelt, who had threatened to "get" the union leader, now had his opportunity. Surrounded by his men, the burly lieutenant greeted his captive with, "Oh, it's you, you goddamn lousy red neck." Then, as Tikas replied, the lieutenant seized his army rifle by the barrel and brought the stock crashing down on the head of the defenseless prisoner with such force that the stock of the heavy gun was broken. Muttering that he had ruined a good rifle, Linderfelt turned and walked away. Three rifle bullets tore into Tikas' back, killing him. The terse report of the incident by the military board simply stated: "Lt. K. E. Linderfelt swung his Springfield rifle, breaking the head of the prisoner, Tikas."[23]

Two other union prisoners, among them James Fyler, the local union secretary, met their deaths in a similar manner. Both were shot deliberately by their captors.[24]

As the sun lowered behind the Black Hills on April 20, the firing of the guns decreased. The soldiers now moved slowly alongside the tents. They drenched the canvas with coal oil. At approximately 5:30 p.m., the southwest corner of the tent colony caught fire. At the same time, reinforcements for the militia in the form of deputy sheriffs arrived from Trinidad. Thus reinforced, Lieutenant Linderfelt led a raid on the stricken camp with the soldiers yelling battle cries as they ran. The screams of terrified women and children drowned out the war cries of the troops. When they reached the colony, the militiamen became a murderous, pillaging mob. The soldiers deliberately applied torches to the tents which had not yet caught fire. They looted and smashed their way through the miners' homes, systematically destroying what they were unable to steal.

On Tuesday morning, April 21, the sun shone down on a pitiful scene. The Ludlow tent colony, which had for seven months been the homes of the striking miners and their families, was now a miserable shambles. Here and there, an iron bedstead, a stove, a child's toy, and bits of broken pottery and glass marked the former site of a tent. It was then that a telephone lineman, going through the ruins, lifted a twisted iron cot that covered one of the larger pits and discovered the bodies of two young mothers and eleven children, ranging in age from three months to nine years. The coroner's jury which investigated the cause of the burning of the tent colony concluded that the cause of the deaths was "fire started by militiamen under Major Hamrock and Lt. Linderfelt, or mine guards, or both. . . ."[25]

"The number of fatalities at Ludlow may never be known for certain," concludes George P. McGovern in his study of the strike. But it is likely that thirty-two persons were either shot or burned to death. After a farcical trial, Linderfelt and others connected with the outrages were found guilty and "punished" by trifling changes in their eligibility for promotion.[26]

The story of the "Ludlow Massacre" was headlined in the press all over the country, although it sometimes received second place to headlines about the developing crisis with Mexico. Some papers tried to shift the blame from the company and its hired gunmen to the miners. Thus, the conservative *New York Times,* while referring to "crazily officered troops" and while describing the events at Ludlow as "worse than the order that sent the Light Brigade into the jaws of death, worse in its effects than the Black Hole of Calcutta," nevertheless reported: "Women and Children Roasted in Pits of Tent Colony as Flames Destroy It. Miners Store of Ammunition and Dynamite Exploded Scattering Death and Ruin." But the Denver *Express* put the blame where it belonged when it wrote: "Mothers and daughters were crucified at Ludlow on the cross of human liberty. Their crucifixion was effected by the operators' paid gunmen. . . . These dead will go down in history as the hero victims of the burnt offering laid on the altar of [the] Great God Greed."[27]

At the conclusion of a Ludlow protest meeting in Carnegie Hall in New York City, Upton Sinclair organized a demonstration in front of the Rockefeller office at 26 Broadway. Wearing bands of black crepe to symbolize the death of the Ludlow victims, he and four women began to walk silently back and forth in front of the Rockefeller headquarters. When the group was arrested and jailed for this "disturbance," Mrs. Sinclair and others continued the "mourning picket line."

At the head of New York's May Day parade that year was a delegation of "mourners" protesting the murder of the Colorado miners. Among the banners they carried were many with slogans denouncing Rockefeller, the most striking of which read "He uses Bibles in New York and Bullets in Colorado"—a bitter reference to Rockefeller's famous Sunday School sermons.[29]

From the United Mine Workers an appeal went out to all national and international labor unions in the country: "Will you, for God's sake and in the name of humanity, call upon your citizenship to demand of the President of the U. S. and both Houses of Congress to leave Mexico alone and come into Colorado and relieve those miners, their wives and children, who are being slaughtered by murderous mine guards."[30] And from Denver came a "Call to Arms," addressed to the unionists of Colorado and signed by the UMW officials and the secretary-treasurer of the Western Federation of Miners. It read:

> Organize the men in your community in companies of volunteers to protect the workers of Colorado against the murder and cremation of men, women, and children by armed assassins in the employ of coal corporations, serving under the guise of state militiamen.
>
> The state is furnishing no protection to us and we must protect ourselves, our wives and children, from these murderous assassins. We intend to exercise our lawful right as citizens to defend our homes and our constitutional rights.[31]

From coast to coast, there was a response to the appeal of the Colorado miners. Hundreds of mass meetings were held. Thousands of dollars were sent for arms and ammunition, and armed trade unionists were arriving in Colorado, when Federal troops, sent by President Wilson, came in.

The Ludlow tragedy had turned Colorado into a battlefield. As news of it spread, strikers in all parts of southern Colorado, joined by outraged laboring men and sympathizers, poured into the strike zone and struck back furiously against the wanton killings. The enraged strikers attacked company camps and mines throughout southern Colorado and even in the vicinity of Denver. Governor Ammons tried to stem the violence by ordering an additional six hundred militiamen to report to duty, but only about twenty-five percent of the men responded. At last, in desperation, the governor admitted that the situation was beyond his control and asked President Wilson for Federal troops. On April 28, Wilson declared a state of national emergency in Colorado and directed that Federal troops proceed immediately to the strike area.[32]

The Federal troops arrived in Colorado on May 2.* Soon, the mine

---

*United States regular army troops were also sent later that same year to Arkansas during the strike led by District 21 of the United Mine Workers against the Mammoth Vein Coal Mining Company in Sebastian County. The strike began early in 1914 when the company refused to renew its contract with the UMW and attempted to operate with non-union labor. The troops were sent in by the Secretary of War after pitched battles between armed union miners and company guards resulted in several workers being killed and the main mine almost totally destroyed. The federal troops were commanded by Major Nathaniel McClure, a veteran of the Colorado coal field wars. The strike ended in defeat. (Samuel A. Sizer, "'This is Union Man's Country,' Sebastian County 1914," *Arkansas Historical Quarterly*, vol. XXVII, Winter, 1968, pp. 306-29.)

guards and militia were withdrawn, strikers and deputy sheriffs alike were required to surrender their arms, and strikebreakers imported in violation of state law were compelled to leave. Thus the fighting ended.[33] But the strike dragged on while the operators showed not the slightest willingness to yield. In testimony before the House Committee on Mines and Mining and before the U. S. Commission on Industrial Relations, John D. Rockefeller, Jr. made this position crystal clear. After explaining that he had not visited Colorado for ten years and had relied completely for information about the labor situation on the word of the officials of the Colorado Fuel & Iron Company (a statement which the Commission on Industrial Relations later characterized as bearing no semblance to the truth),* Rockefeller gave his complete support to the company officials in Denver. He insisted, first, that the strike was simply the work of outside agitators and that the miners themselves had no legitimate grievance; and secondly, that the "open shop" represented a great American principle in defense of which no sacrifice was too great. When Congressman Martin Foster suggested that perhaps "the killing of people and shooting of children" might impel Rockefeller to inquire more carefully into the situation, the witness outlined his view of what was at stake in the Colorado struggle:

> We believe that the issue is not a local one in Colorado. It is a national issue whether workers shall be allowed to work under such conditions as they may choose. As part owners of the property, our interest in the laboring men in this country is so immense, so deep, so profound that we stand ready to lose every cent we have put in that company rather than see the men we have employed thrown out of work and have imposed upon them conditions which are not of their seeking and which neither they nor we can see are in our interest.

Congressman Foster asked if Rockefeller preferred that the violence continue rather than make an attempt to settle the strike, to which the witness replied, in effect, that only one thing could be done to settle the strike, and that was to unionize the camps, "and our interest in labor is so profound, and we believe so sincerely that interest demands that the camps shall be open camps, that we expect to stand by the officers at all costs." When asked by Congressman Foster if he would hold to that

---

*In its report, the Commission noted that "he [Rockefeller] followed step by step the struggle of his executive officials to retain arbitrary power, and to prevent the installation of machinery for collective bargaining, by which abuses might automatically be corrected, and he supported and encouraged this struggle in every letter he wrote to his agents." (63rd Congress, 3rd Session, *House Document 136*, Washington, D. C., 1915, *Report on the Colorado Strike Investigation*, p. 34.)

position "if that costs all your property and kills all your employees," Rockefeller replied: "It is a great principle."[34]

It was when he was questioned at the hearings of the Commission on Industrial Relations by its chairman, Frank P. Walsh, that Rockefeller's facade of upholding democratic principles in opposing unionism and of being so far removed from the events in Colorado began to crumble. Having examined the correspondence between the coal company officials and the Rockefeller office in New York, Walsh introduced concrete evidence that Rockefeller had fully supported the refusal of the company to negotiate with the union. It was clear from the correspondence that both the company in Colorado and Rockefeller insisted upon the unconditional surrender of the United Mine Workers.[35]*

The two government agencies that heard Rockefeller's testimony concluded that the strike could have been settled, but that "Rockefeller would rather spend the money of the company for guns, pay of detectives and mine guards and starve the miners into submission."[36] And that is how the strike finally ended—with the miners starved into submission. Early in September, 1914, President Wilson submitted to both sides proposals to end the strike, based on the recommendations of two presidential appointees—Hywel Davies and W. R. Fairley. The settlement called for the operators and miners to pledge themselves to a three-year truce based on six conditions: (1) that the mine labor laws of the state be strictly enforced; (2) the restoration of work of all striking miners who had not been found guilty of violating the law; (3) the prohibition of intimidation of either union or non-union workers; (4) the abolition of the mine guards; (5) the prohibition of picketing and parading; and (6) no suspension of work pending the investigation of any matter in dispute. Responsibility for enforcing the conditions was to be placed in the hands of three commissioners to be appointed by the president, and a majority decision of the commission was to be final.[37]

The miners accepted the proposal on September 16 at a convention in Trinidad, the site of the strike vote a year earlier. But the operators only accepted three of the proposals, rejecting two out of hand (2 and 6), and accepting the remaining one only if modified. They insisted they could

---

*When asked by Walsh if he should not inquire as to the responsibility of company officials for the Ludlow tragedy, Rockefeller replied: "Well, I think so long as I am undertaking to do the things that I think should be done I shall have to reserve the right to do them in the ways that seem to me best." Asked by Walsh if he did not feel moral responsibility for the violence, in view of the fact that the militia in the Ludlow killings were paid from company funds, Rockefeller answered: "I should have felt greater responsibility for the officers of the company if they had not used all means in their power to protect life and property." (*New York Times*, May 21, 1915.)

not restore to work all who had not been found guilty, since there were still 332 miners under indictment for murder and another 137 for other so-called crimes.[38]

As its final effort to break the deadlock, union officials agreed to hold a convention of the striking miners on November 19 for the purpose of calling off the strike, on condition that President Wilson would appoint a commission to arbitrate the dispute. The president quickly accepted the UMW proposal and appointed a special three-man commission of arbitration. Meanwhile, Federal troops patrolled the strike area, limiting the strikers' ability to picket or otherwise carry out strike duties. On December 10, 1914, a special UMW convention in Denver called off the strike. Federal troops began to leave Colorado on January 1, 1915, and by the tenth of the month, the state was again in complete control.

So, too, were the coal operators. After fifteen months, the strike had been crushed by a combination of guns, bayonets, and hunger. At least sixty-six men, women, and children had been killed. Not one militiaman or mine guard had been indicted for murder, but John R. Lawson, the leader of the strike against Colorado Fuel & Iron, was tried and convicted of murder.* The union had not won recognition.** Instead, a company union—the Industrial Representation Plan—was installed in the mining camps.[39]

The Industrial Representation Plan, worked out by McKenzie King of Canada in close cooperation with Rockefeller, went into effect at the Colorado Fuel & Iron coal mines in October, 1915 and in the company's Pueblo steel mills during the following year. Soon known as the "Rockefeller Plan," it represented the birth of company unions. It provided that the men at each mine should elect at least two representatives to serve for a period of one year. These men were to meet annually with an equal number of company officials, and at these sessions, they were given the right to discuss grievances or other matters of interest.[40]

As might be expected, the United Mine Workers denounced the plan. Nor was it alone. After a careful study, U. S. Commission on Industrial

---

*Lawson was accused of murdering John Nimmo, one of the deputies paid by the companies and appointed by the sheriff. No effort was made to prove that Lawson had fired the fatal shot. Commenting on his conviction, the Commission on Industrial Relations declared: "It is anarchism for profits and revenge, and it menaces the security and integrity of American institutions as they seldom have been menaced before." (*Report on the Colorado Strike Investigation*, p. 22.) Lawson's conviction was overturned on appeal.

**Although technically the Colorado strike was lost by the United Mine the mining camps, Joseph G. Rayback points out that the union itself showed a new spurt of life during the same period, as 150,000 miners joined its ranks. (*A History of American Labor*, New York, 1963, p. 258.)

Relations investigator George P. West agreed with the union that it was a company tool which offered the workers only the illusion of collective bargaining. The plan, he pointed out, embodied "none of the principles of effectual collective bargaining and instead is a hypocritical pretense of granting what is in reality withheld." It was a plan devised, not for the benefit of the employees, he declared, "but for the purpose of ameliorating or removing the unfavorable criticism of Mr. Rockefeller which had arisen throughout the country following his rejection of President Wilson's plan of settlement. . . ."[41]

It soon became clear that the plan provided no relief from many of the miners' most common grievances. The battle of the miners against the Rockefeller-dominated Colorado Fuel & Iron Company continued. In 1928, another strike broke out. The United Mine Workers was back again, this time for good. Later, the United Steel Workers of America organized the steel mills of Colorado Fuel & Iron.

Today, on the site of the "Ludlow Massacre," there stands a monument erected by the United Mine Workers. Annually, thousands of union-conscious motorists turn off the main highway between Trinidad and Pueblo to look at this shrine. On the monument is the inscription: "In memory of the men, women, and children who lost their lives in freedom's cause at Ludlow, Colorado, April 20, 1914." Some sing one of the songs written by the striking miners shortly after the outrage, called "The Ludlow Massacre," which went:

> Now folks, let me tell you a story
> About a terrible crime
> That was done in Ludlow, Colorado
> To men that work in the mine.
>
> Our children they were so hungry,
> Our wives were thin and worn;
> We were striking against a rich man,
> Meanest ever was born.
>
> John D., he'd stacks of money,
> John D., he'd stacks of gold;
> John D., he was warm in winter
> While mining folks went cold.
>
> He sent down his hired gunmen,
> They'd orders to shoot on sight,
> He sent down troops with helmets
> To break the miners' fight.

John D., he was a Christian,
John D., the psalms he sung;
But he'd no mercy in his heart,
He shot down young and old.

One night when all were sleeping,
All wrapped up in their dreams,
We heard a loud explosion,
We heard most terrible screams.

"Oh, save us from the burning flames,"
We heard our children cry;
But John D. laughed and shot them down
Right there before our eyes.

Folks the country over
And mining camps around,
Their hearts got sick with pity,
At what happened in our town.

It was a terrible thing to do,
It was an awful thing;
And mining men like me made up
This little song to sing.

To sing it to the people,
Poor folks that work and sweat,
What John D. did in Ludlow
They never should forget.[42]

CHAPTER 10

Revolt of the Michigan Copper Miners, 1913

During the years preceding World War I, militant mine strikes were not limited to the coal fields. The workers in the copper mines, too, had to battle conditions similar to those that caused the coal miners to revolt. Just as the Colorado Fuel & Iron Company dominated the southern Colorado coal fields and the entire economic, political, and social life of the community, so the Calumet & Hecla Mining Company completely controlled the copper mining area of the Kewlenaw Peninsula of Michigan. It produced 60 percent of the district's copper output and was the dominant employer, setting the prevailing labor policies.

C & H gained a reputation for paternalism by providing the miners with reasonably decent housing at nominal rents, in addition to free libraries, gymnasiums, and public baths. Medicines were also provided free, and there were other benefits as well.[1] But in the mines, the workers were at the mercy of arrogant and tyrannical petty bosses and of efficiency experts who watched their every move and called repeatedly for speed-up. Wages were low, barely averaging $2.50 to $3.00 per day, and the miners were subjected to numerous deductions from their wages which left them "in a continual state of impoverishment and debt." Many miners were able to make at best only $15 to $18 for a six-day week. Working hours were ten a day, but delays in transporting men underground added as much as one hour to the daily time spent below the surface. The result was that the so-called ten-hour day was in reality an eleven-hour day.[2]

Every aspect of the copper miners' lives in Michigan was dominated by the mine owners. Miners' children attended company schools, where they were taught by company teachers. The miners attended company churches and read a company-owned newspaper. They lived in company houses and were expected to buy at company stores. The company controlled the village, the county, and much of the state government.[3] While conceding that Calumet & Hecla had "done a great deal of welfare work," an investigator for the U. S. Department of Labor concluded: "Only one thing appeared to be lacking and that is the right of the workers to be free men in every sense of the word."[4] William D. ("Big Bill") Haywood, who knew copper mining conditions better than most, was much blunter. In August, 1910, he described the copper miners of Michigan as living "in a state of feudalism," and concluded that the "dominating influence of the company in all walks of life has bred servility on the part of the miners...." The "spirit of the slave" was not confined to any one of the many nationalities among the Michigan copper miners. It was evident among the English-speaking Cornishmen, the Irish or U. S. born, who usually held the better jobs in the mines, and the non-English-speaking Croatians, Slovenians, Poles, Italians, Austrians, and others of the thirty different nationalities in the mines. Although the Finns were "decidedly more progressive," and there was a local Socialist club, composed of members of the Finnish community, they, too, Haywood noted, were less militant in Michigan than their counterparts in the western mining camps.[5]

Still, Haywood did concede that the "wage slaves" in the Michigan copper mines were "awakening and organizing."[6] He was referring to the fact that although the miners had shown little interest in joining the Western Federation of Miners when it had sent organizers into the district in 1904, five years later, they themselves had requested the union to return. It did, and by the summer of 1913, the WFM had five locals in the area, with the greatest membership among the underground miners and the "trammers," the men who pushed the loaded tramcars to the lifts.[7]

But the mine owners were so confident that they had nothing to fear from unionism that they proceeded to arouse further discontent by discarding the two-man drill and replacing it with the one-man drill. A single man now had to set up a drill weighing from 135 to 150 pounds. The one-man drill, moreover, deprived the miner working alone of protection in case of an emergency as he had had before with a drill that required two men. Most miners bitterly called the one-man drill the "man killer" and the "widow-maker." It also made unemployment, since one man could now do what two had done before.[8]

Although the hard rock miners were ready to strike, the Western Federation of Miners urged a conciliatory policy. Pointing out that only about one-half of the underground men were organized, and less than that at Calumet & Hecla, the union recommended caution until a new organizational drive could enable it to take on the powerful copper barons of northern Michigan. But the rank-and-file miners called for action, and in mid-July, 1913, the WFM leaders sent an identical letter to each of the company's top officials, asking for a meeting to discuss "possibilities of shortening the working day, raising wages and making some changes in the working conditions." The letter asked for a reply by no later than July 21. Although the request did not spell out any specific demands and talked only in generalities, not one of the mining companies even acknowledged it, and one, the Quincy, returned the envelope unopened.[9]

Writing to President Woodrow Wilson, Secretary of Labor William B. Wilson observed: "When the miners selected a committee in order to present their grievances, their request was entirely ignored, not even a reply made to it. That precipitated the strike."[10] For the miners in Calumet, Houghton, and the other mining localities now only had one choice: to submit totally to the owners or to strike.

On July 21, 1913, the deadline passed, and on the following day, the miners met and called a strike for July 23. Their demands were for an eight-hour working day; a minimum wage of $3 a day for underground workers; an increase of 35 cents a day for those who worked above the ground; abolition of the one-man drill; and recognition of the Western Federation of Miners. Pickets were stationed at all the mines, and by the end of the first day of the strike, all twenty-one mines in the district were shut down and 16,000 miners were out.[11]

Although Sheriff James A. Cruse had sworn in extra deputies even before the strike broke out and had added loyal company officials on the day of the strike, he used the excuse of a number of brief clashes between the strikers and non-union miners to bring in the state militia. Arguing that the situation in the strike district was out of control, the sheriff appealed to Governor Woodbridge N. Ferris to immediately send in 2,000 National Guardsmen. Between July 24 and 27, the entire National Guard of Michigan arrived in the strike area. There were 2,334 men and 211 officers, all under the command of Brigadier General P. L. Abbey. In addition to the infantry, there were two troops of cavalry, one company of engineers, two ambulance companies, and three brass bands. They encamped on land belonging to the mine companies. The militiamen were armed with riot sticks, sabers, pistols, and Springfield rifles. They also had two automatic machine guns with them. It appeared that they were preparing for a real war, and indeed the Guard officers were convinced that the training their men would receive in the strike zone "would be of inestimable service in case hostilities break out between the United States and Mexico." In that event, the "Michigan troops would be the first sent to the front," because their strike service was "exactly the same as they would receive in the field in time of actual warfare."[12]

The mine operators were also busy bringing in armed men to supplement the state troops. Almost two thousand deputy sheriffs were sworn in, many of them in the employ of the mine companies, and a large number of strike-breaking detectives were brought in from New York City. These men were supplied by the notorious Waddell-Mahon agency, which billed itself as "an organization that specializes in labor disputes." So confident was James Waddell that his thugs and gunmen would break the strike that he sent out a circular to a number of large corporations, asking them "to watch the progress of the present strike, because we know it will be a triumph for law and order, a triumph for the mine owners, and will furnish still another evidence of the success we have always met in breaking strikes."[13]

To keep the mines open, a large number of strikebreakers were brought into Michigan. Many were engaged through the Austro-American Labor Agency in New York City and were recent German immigrants, few of whom could read English. They were not told that they were to act as strikebreakers and were unaware even of the existence of the strike. They were escorted into the strike area by deputy sheriffs and the National Guard. Some of them tried to escape and later testified that they were "held under guard as virtual prisoners and were not allowed to leave the bunkhouse."[14]

Dressed in their "Sunday best," with their wives and children at their sides, the strikers paraded every morning from the Miners' Union Hall to the mines and picketed peacefully outside the various shafts. Labor leaders from outside the area, including the aged Mother Jones and the young John L. Lewis of the United Mine Workers, joined the parades. At the head of every day's parade marched Anna Clemenc, wife of a Croatian copper miner, carrying a silk American flag. Known as "Big Annie" or "Tall Annie," she was in her early 'twenties when the strike began and she was hailed as "an American Joan of Arc" because of her fervent support of the strikers.[15]

Annie was attacked more than once by infantrymen with bayonetted guns, by cavalrymen with drawn sabers, and by Waddell-trained deputies with pistols and clubs. Their aim was to get her to drop the American flag she carried at the head of the miners' parades. But Annie stood her ground. "Kill me!" she once shouted to the infrantrymen and deputies as they tried to seize her flag. "Run your bayonets and sabers through this flag and kill me, but I won't move. If this flag will not protect me, then I will die with it." The attackers were forced to retreat. On another occasion, when two soldiers struck her with their bayonets—one on the wrist and the other on her breast—to force her to drop the flag she was carrying, she "raised the staff horizontally, letting its folds fall down in front, and said: 'Go ahead now, do your work, shoot me. I am willing to die behind the flag. If you don't respect the flag, I do.'" This time, "one of the soldiers, upon seeing that she was not to be scared and driven from the field, clubbed her over the shoulder with the stock." But a number of the strikers, seeing that she was in real danger, pushed her out of the soldier's path. In its description of the incident, the *Miners' Bulletin*, the strikers' organ, commented: "In recognition of the heroism of Anna Clemenc, Captain Blackman declared that she should have her head knocked off, a remark eminently worthy of this soldier."[16]

In September, the mine owners succeeded in securing an injunction against picketing and parading and any attempt to prevent the entrance of strikebreakers into the mines. Judge P. H. O'Brien of the Circuit Court dissolved the injunction, thereby bringing social ostracism upon himself and his family, but the Michigan Supreme Court promptly ordered it restored. The National Guard enforced the injunction, and those who attempted to disobey it were quickly arrested.[17]

One of those arrested was "Big Annie." In "A Woman's Story," published in the *Miners' Bulletin* of October 2, 1913, she described what had happened. She had met several workers who were going into the mines and had peacefully urged one of them: "O! George, you are not going to work, are you? Come stay with us. Stick to us and we will stick to you." "He stepped back," she added, "willing to comply with my request." At this point, the deputies came along, caught him by the shoulder and dragged him with them, saying: "You coward, are you going back because a woman told you not to go to work?" Eight or ten of the deputies pulled him along with them. A militia officer then said: "Annie, you have to get away from here." "No, I am not going," she shot back. "I have a right to stand here and quietly ask the scabs not to go to work." "A Woman's Story" continues:

I was standing to one side of the crowd and he said: "You will have to get in the auto." "I won't go until you tell me the reason." Then he made me get in the auto. I kept pounding the automobile with my feet and asking what I was being taken to jail for. The officer said: "Why don't you stay at home?" "I won't stay at home, my work is here, nobody can stop me. I am going to keep at it until this strike is won." I was kept in jail from six-thirty till twelve, then released under bond.

At about this time, Kate Richards O'Hare, the Socialist editor and organizer, visited the strike area. Her shocked report in the *National Rip-Saw* of December, 1913, entitled "War in the Copper Country," went in part:

> Though Michigan is a civilized, Christian state, with a constitution and statutes and a full corps of law enforcers and officials, I found that there was no law in the copper country except the will of the copper barons and that human life had no protection except that of a good strong arm and a handy club. Men could be beaten down, women assaulted and young girls forced to listen to the most degenerate and revolting language and the law of Michigan was dead and its enforcers were too busy protecting profits to take notice. . . .
>
> I stood in front of the court house and saw strikers, including men and women, driven into jail like droves of sheep into the shambles. Men were clubbed and beaten like wild beasts, and beautiful young girls dragged through the ranks of deputies, subjected to vile insults and jammed into jail, trailing their American flags behind them. As I watched them I thought of old Betsy Ross, and wondered if from that other side of life one may look back upon this one, what she thought of the depths to which her stars and stripes had fallen.

All this time, the mine operators were refusing to have any dealings with the Western Federation of Miners' officers or with anyone carrying a union card. Calumet & Hecla President Quincy A. Shaw refused even to leave Boston and come to Calumet to talk with the strikers. He preferred to let the armed gunmen and thugs from the Waddell agency do the talking for the company. One night, five of the gunmen surrounded a house in the small village of Seeverville and fired indiscriminately into it. Two men in the house were killed, two others seriously wounded, and a six-month old baby, held in its mother's arms, was grazed by a bullet. But even this was only the beginning. "Nowhere in the United States, not even in West Virginia," wrote James Lord after returning from Michigan, "have the mine owners with their hireling courts and soldiers and imported murderers, gone to greater lengths to defeat the just demands of the workers."[18]

As a result of public pressure, the gunmen in the Seeverville tragedy were arrested and later convicted of manslaughter. But these six men, and a deputy who shot a fourteen-year-old girl marching in a picket parade, were the only nonstrikers arrested during the strike. On the other hand, over 600 strikers were arrested, most on the charge of intimidating an officer or inciting a riot. Another 500 were arrested for violating the injunction against picketing and parading. As an investigator for the U.S. Department of Labor pointed out:

> When the strikers mistreated the men that went to work during the strike, they were arrested and fined, imprisoned or bound over. But when peace officers, deputy sheriffs, soldiers or Waddell men engaged in conflicts with the strikers and the officers were the aggressors in beating or riding down the strikers, there was no one to arrest the officers.

State officials and the U. S. Department of Labor made efforts to mediate the strike, but while the union accepted, the operators adamantly refused to meet with the WFM. The manager for Calumet & Hecla gave the typical company answer: "These men [the strikers] can find employment elsewhere. If they do not want to subscribe to the conditions that we impose, they are perfectly free to go to other places."[19]

In late November, a Citizens' Alliance was formed by local merchants and others who wished to help the copper companies drive unionism out of the district. Members were required to sign a pledge which read in part: "I believe the presence of the Western Federation of Miners is a menace to the future welfare and prosperity of this district, and that therefore in the interest of Law, Order and Peace, the Western Federation of Miners must go."[20]

Facing a cold winter with the prospect of eviction by their mine-owner landlords, some strikers gave up and returned to the mines. But the overwhelming majority held fast, although their bitterness found expression at times in violent attacks on strikebreakers. On a night early in December, 1913, three newly-arrived Canadian strikebreakers were killed by shots fired into the house at Painerdale where they were staying. Inflamed by the slayings and concerned about further losses in trade, the Citizens' Alliance began holding mass meetings demanding an end to the strike. Local merchants who were Alliance members now threatened to cut off all further credit to strikers.[21]

"Big Annie" Clemenc had earlier been arrested for assaulting scabs, tried for assault and battery, and found guilty. However, her sentencing was delayed until January, 1914.* Upon her release on bail, she and other strikers' wives formed a WFM women's auxiliary called the Women's Alliance, which sent appeals to unions in different parts of the country.

---

*In mid-January, she entered the county jail to serve her term.

Soon, clothing, candy, and other gifts for the strikers' children's Christmas party began to pour in. The Italian Hall in Red Jacket was obtained for the party. Three Christmas trees were set up and a local Santa Claus was hired. On the afternoon of December 24, seven to eight hundred people, including several hundred children, filled the second floor of the Italian Hall. Lunch was followed by the Christmas party. One by one, the children met Santa Claus, and each received a gift. Just as the party was about to break up, someone rushed into the hall and yelled "Fire! Fire! Fire!"

Panic ensued, and in a matter of seconds, the narrow staircase was jammed with children and adults, pushing, shoving, and screaming. People stumbled and fell, and soon the narrow stairway was jammed with bodies. Firemen, alerted by an alarm, rushed to the scene and began pulling children off the top of the pile. When it was over, sixty-two children and eleven adults were dead.

There had been no fire. But it was never determined by either the coroner's jury or a later Congressional investigating committee who it was that had cried out the tragic words or why he had done so. Charges that the guilty party had worn a Citizens' Alliance button on his coat were never substantiated. Editors of the Finnish language paper, *Tyomies,* issued an extra edition containing this charge and stated further that deputies had blocked rescue efforts while Citizens' Alliance members watched and cheered. The editors were promptly arrested on a charge of sedition for making these statements.[22]*

Woody Guthrie's moving ballad, "The 1913 Massacre," closed with this stanza:

The piano played a slow funeral tune;
And the town was lit up by a cold Christmas moon.
The parents they cried and the miners they moaned,
"See what your greed for money has done."[23]

As a shocked nation read the story of the Italian Hall disaster, offers of aid began to pour into the strike area. In a sudden burst of sympathy for the stricken families, Calumet & Hecla contributed $5,000 for their relief, and Citizens' Alliance members and other residents raised another $20,000 to $25,000. These funds were offered to strikers who had lost members of their families.[24] But the strikers called the relief funds "blood money," and when the delegation bearing them approached the homes

---

*Although no copy of *Tyomies* carrying the charges is available, the *International Socialist Review* (vol. XIV, February, 1914, pp. 458–59) published an English translation of the statements appearing in the Finnish paper.

of the bereaved families, they were told that the strikers and their union would take care of their own. WFM President Charles Moyer, who was in Hancock, backed these statements with one of his own in which, after indicating that it was not outside the realm of possibility that a Citizens' Alliance agent had raised the false fire alarm, he said that "the Western Federation of Miners will bury its own dead and the American labor movement will take care of the deceased."[25]

Labor and Socialist papers applauded both Moyer's statement and the stand taken by the stricken families. The Socialist *Milwaukee Leader* declared that the bereaved strikers, in rejecting the "charity" of the very men "who have been trying and are now seeking to starve them into the submission of the whipt slave... spoke as becomes men who are worthy to be free and who are worthy of the support of their fellow workers."[26]

The Citizens' Alliance, however, was enraged. An Alliance delegation visited Moyer in his hotel room in Hancock and demanded that he retract his charge against the Alliance and instruct the families to take what had been collected. When he refused, he was warned by Sheriff James Cruse that if he stuck to his position, the sheriff could no longer be responsible for his safety. No sooner had the sheriff left when Moyer and another union official were seized by a gang of armed men wearing Citizens' Alliance buttons, and were beaten and shot at. Moyer suffered a flesh wound. Bloody and beaten, he and the other union official were dragged out of the hotel, and the two were driven to the railroad station a mile away, where they were thrown into the night train bound for Chicago. Upon his arrival in Chicago, Moyer had to be hospitalized for ten days.[27]

"Moyer shot, slugged, and deported from Calumet district," read the next day's headlines. As far as the majority of the Michigan newspapers were concerned, Moyer got what he deserved. Everything that happened in the copper district "was absolutely the fault of outside agitators working among the foreign element," and Moyer, as president of the Western Federation of Miners, was the leading "outside agitator."[28]

The Houghton County grand jury was specifically charged by Judge O'Brien to investigate the kidnapping and shooting, but no one was ever indicted.[29]

On the Sunday after Christmas, mass services were held for the dead children and adults. Then, with 50,000 people in the procession, the funeral wound its way to the Lakeview Cemetery, two miles away. At the head of the long procession, carrying the same American flag she had borne so many times in the strikers' parades, walked Annie Clemenc, tears streaming from her eyes. At the cemetery, most of the victims were placed in two mass graves—one Catholic and the other Protestant. The graves were dug by the strikers themselves.[30]

On January 10, 1914, Secretary of Labor William B. Wilson made public a report on the Michigan strike by Walter B. Palmer, a Labor Department investigator. Affidavits by miners published in the report showed that "they had been forced into peonage." Calumet & Hecla, it was disclosed, had made "enormous profits" while paying the miners the lowest wages in the industry. Then, on January 12, the Chicago *Tribune* published material from Palmer's report which had not been included in Secretary Wilson's original statement. In it were stories of drunkenness among militiamen who had been allowed to wander around armed in this condition; of violence resulting in fatalities provoked by imported deputies; of lack of provisions for safety and sanitation in the mines; of work imposed on trammers in the mines which soon permanently disabled them; and of the fact that houses had been sold to employees by Calumet & Hecla built on leased ground, with one condition of the lease being that if the lessor "should cease to be an employee of the company by discharge or otherwise," he could be dispossessed and the company could take possession of his house and land.[31]

These disclosures revealed that "industrial feudalism" rather than "industrial paternalism" prevailed in the copper mines. They also produced a Congressional investigation, and for two months, a Congressional committee held hearings in the strike district, adding new information about the poor working conditions in the mines.[32]

But these disclosures had no effect on the employers, who made it clear that they would still have nothing to do with the Western Federation of Miners. Indeed, the union officials appeared to have given up all hope of winning the strike and even informed members of the Congressional committee that it was doubtful if further disclosures would do any good. All they wanted, they said, was for the employers to take back the remaining strikers without requiring them to give up their union membership.[33]*

As the hearings drew to a close, the union announced a cutback of strike benefits. From the outset of the strike, the WFM had furnished

*One committee member asked a WFM official: "Do I understand that you want to have the Committee make a report in which they would make no criticism of these alleged man-killing machines, unsanitary conditions in the mines, as to which there has been evidence introduced here that they are unhealthful; that a man could not live more than five or six or seven years? All those things to be relegated to the rear as mere incidents?" (U. S. Congress, Committee on Mines and Mining, *Conditions in Copper Mines of Michigan,* Senate Document No. 381, vol. VIII, pp. 113-14.)

strike relief, but it soon found that practically every striker needed such assistance. "The wages paid to the copper miners of the northern peninsula having been so low," the union noted, " . . . almost immediately after the declaring of the strike, many of those involved found themselves without visible means of support and began drawing relief." With assessments on the WFM membership providing less than half of the amount required, the union was compelled to borrow $25,000 from the United Brewery Workers and $100,000 from Illinois District No. 12 of the United Mine Workers. It was also helped by a liberal response to its appeals to organized labor, especially from the United Mine Workers, and it was able to sustain the copper miners of Michigan for nine months.[34]

By April 2, however, the union found that donations from most trade unions had dried up, while the United Mine Workers, with troubles of its own in Colorado and Ohio, could no longer send funds. The WFM Executive Board thereupon informed the strikers that relief would have to be reduced immediately, and that if they were willing to accept the serious reduction and continue the strike, the union would help to the best of its ability, but that not very much could be expected.[35]

On April 12, 1914, the remaining strikers took a vote and by a 3–1 margin, decided to end the strike. The WFM announced the results emotionally and dramatically to the entire union membership:

> Your striking members, after considering the situation, and while it was a cruel blow to them, and almost an impossible thing to do, yet, realizing the impossibility of continuing to supply their wives and little ones with the necessaries of life under the reduced relief, have, after fighting one of the most determined battles in the history of industrial conflicts in this country for a period of nine months, declared the strike at an end and will return to their employment under such conditions as they are able to secure.[36]

The union took some comfort in the fact that the strikers had "forced the copper magnates to concede that their claim for an eight-hour workday, an increase of wages and the regulating of working conditions was just." This was a reference to the fact that early in December, the companies had instituted an eight-hour day, raised wages, and announced the establishment of a grievance procedure. Although the men had been forced to renounce their union membership as a condition of getting their jobs back, the WFM proclaimed that with the concessions made in hours and wages, "their struggle has not been in vain."[37]

As far as the Western Federation of Miners itself was concerned, however, the strike in Michigan had brought only total failure. The union was eliminated entirely from the Michigan copper country,* and it was to take another quarter of a century before unionism would return to the district.[38]

*The Western Federation of Miners suffered another setback in 1914, this time in Butte, Montana, the union's original stronghold. A complicated struggle involving IWW intervention led to the union's collapse in Butte with a considerable loss of revenue.

CHAPTER 11

Revolt of the Garment Workers: I.
Uprising of the Waistmakers

On November 24, 1909, eighteen thousand waistmakers in Manhattan and Brooklyn, New York walked out of nearly five hundred shops. By the end of the day, over twenty thousand workers had joined the pickets. This great uprising served as a catalyst for workers in other branches of the industry. And it spearheaded the drive that turned the shells of unions into mass organizations, thereby laying the foundation for stable and lasting organizations in the women's and men's clothing industries and for the widespread unionization of women workers.

The manufacture of shirtwaists was a comparatively new branch of the garment trade which had developed rapidly after 1900, especially in New York and Philadelphia. By 1909, there were about six hundred waist and dress shops in New York City employing from thirty-five to forty thousand workers. About eighty percent of them were young women between the ages of sixteen and twenty-five, most of them unmarried, two-thirds of them Jewish, with a couple of thousand Italians and a few hundred Black workers. Men accounted only for about twenty percent of the workers, but they occupied the high-paying jobs that demanded special skill and experience.[1]

While dress and waistmakers experienced the typical inequities that were prevalent throughout the industry, working conditions in this segment of the industry were better than those in other branches. Since most of the shops had been set up comparatively recently, they were more sanitary than those in the rest of the industry. Most work rooms contained windows which provided adequate lighting. Wages, too, were generally higher than those in other branches of the trade. However, they varied both from shop to shop and within shops, depending on skill and on the system of work which prevailed. The latter, in turn, was determined by piece work, except for the more highly skilled workmen who represented only from fifteen to twenty percent of the labor force. Despite the fact that by the end of 1909, the industry was prosperous, wage rates had fallen steadily since the 1908 depression. Thus, early in 1908, a woman machine operator on waists could earn as much as $12 or $13 a week at piece rates, while late in 1909, she was lucky to make $9 or $10. In addition, workers received their wages directly from inside subcontractors who negotiated individually with the manufacturer.* This system inevitably created inequities in the pay scale. Some women received only $3 or $4 per week, while others, who worked directly for the manufacturer, received as much as $15 or $20 per week. As in other branches, wages fluctuated because of the seasonal nature of the industry. The workers' annual income was cut considerably by enforced idleness for three months of the year. One contemporary study found that the average weekly wage for the industry was $9, but since this was not for the entire year but only for the busy season, it brought the average down to only $5—and this was for 56 to 59 hours' work each week, with only the usual rate for overtime.[2]

The industry subcontractors—men who hired from three to eight girl helpers—exploited the very young girls through an oppressive system of apprenticeship. Workers were subjected to strict discipline: subcontractors and examiners levied fines for lateness and for sewing errors. "In the shops we don't have names," declared one waistmaker, "we have numbers." Manufacturers charged for needles and thread—often as much as $1.50 a week—as well as for electric power, for the chairs the workers sat on, and for the lockers in the shops—all at a substantial profit. They fined their employees half a day's pay for being a few minutes late, or for accidentally spoiling a piece of cloth. A ticket system prevailed under which a worker, after completing a task or piece, would receive a small tag, which was to be turned in at the end of a period in return for her wages. Most workers complained that the manufacturers deliberately made the tag or ticket very small, hoping that some of the

---

*Subcontracting was a variation of the traditional contracting system in the garment trades. Like the contractor, the subcontractor contracted with a manufacturer to complete a specified amount of work for an agreed-upon price. Like the contractor, too, he supervised a team of workers in completing the bundles of garments. Unlike the contractor, however, the subcontractor did not own a shop but worked in the manufacturers' large inside establishments. Subcontractors, not manufacturers, were responsible for paying their workers, and when manufacturers lowered rates, the subcontractors passed the decrease on to their teams of workers.

workers would lose them. And this is exactly what happened, and as a result, workers often received pay for only part of their work.

Because the industry operated on a piecework basis, the employer or his agent could easily show favoritism to "cooperative" workers by giving them larger bundles of work. To top it all off, the entire abusive system was characterized by tyrannical bosses, nagging, pettiness, espionage, favoritism, rudeness, and discourtesy.[3]

Local 25 of the International Ladies' Garment Worker's Union (ILGWU) had jurisdiction over the waistmakers. Although it had been founded in 1906 by seven young girls and six men, the local had failed to attract many workers. Just four weeks before the strike, the secretary-treasurer, organizer and walking delegate of the foundering union noted that the membership barely reached eight hundred workers who were described as irregular and unenthusiastic. Few of them had any knowledge of union organization. To be sure, members of the Women's Trade Union League had helped small groups of dressmakers learn the principles and practices of unionism and had convinced a group of them to affiliate with Local 25 in 1908.* However, men controlled the union, holding all the offices and eight of the fifteen positions on the executive board.[4]

Nevertheless, unrest had been building steadily and visibly for at least

---

*The Women's Trade Union League was founded in Boston's historic Faneuil Hall by a group of trade unionists and liberal professional social workers interested in the organization of women. (Among them were Mary Kenney O'Sullivan, formerly a general organizer for the AFL and William English Walling, a settlement house social worker.) Impressed by the accomplishments of the Women's Trade Union League of Great Britain in assisting in the organization of working women, the League's founders in America sought to solve three basic problems facing working women in this country: the unionization of women, the education of the unions to the need for organizing them, and the enactment of protective legislation for working women and children.

In 1904, state branches were formed in Illinois, Massachusetts, and New York, and by 1911, the League had grown to eleven branches. The New York League helped to organize more unions than any other League branch. From 1904 to 1912, it organized or helped to organize unions among the hat trimmers, embroidery workers, textile workers, bakery and confectionery workers, white goods workers, straw hat makers, laundry workers, shirtwaist workers, and paper box makers.

While women of independent means were important in the work of the national League and the state branches, working women emerged as important figures too—women like Rose Schneiderman of the cap makers, Emma Steghagen of the shoe workers, Agnes Nestor and Elizabeth Christman of the glove workers, Melinda Scott of the hat trimmers, Josephine Casey of the railway ticket takers, Stella Franklin of the department store clerks, Elizabeth Maloney of the waitresses, and Maud Swartz of the typographers.

For the origin and a brief history of the Women's Trade Union League before 1909, *see* Philip S. Foner, *History of the Labor Movement in the United States,* vol. III, New York, 1964, pp. 228-31.

a year before the uprising. Throughout late 1908 and 1909, walkouts became increasingly frequent in the large waist factories in the Washington Square area. Confrontations between manufacturers and workers over wage and piece rate cuts, subcontracting, and the practice of charging workers for electricity, needles, and other materials, became increasingly sharp.

In late July, 1909, the two hundred employees of the Rosen Brothers ladies' waist shop walked out on strike in protest against inadequate pay scales. During the strike, thugs assaulted pickets, and the police, obviously acting at the employers' request, arrested girls who shouted "scab" at strikebreakers. However, the strikers' perseverance brought results, for on August 26, Rosen Brothers capitulated. The victorious strikers gained full union recognition and a 20 percent wage increase.[5]

Early in September, the strike spread to additional shops and grew in intensity. One hundred and fifty young women walked out of the Leiserson factory, accusing their employer of paying starvation wages. The strike also spread to the Triangle Waist Company (which was to become nationally infamous in 1911 because of the tragic fire on its premises).* After the latter company's owners learned that a few of their employees had joined the union, they promptly locked out the entire shop of five hundred workers and advertised for replacements. The infuriated Triangle employees literally besieged Local 25's headquarters and signed up *en masse* with the union.[6]

Although some magistrates conceded that New York State law sanctioned the right to picket, all of them countenanced the arrests and beatings of the striking teenage girls. Every day, scores of pickets were fined or sentenced to the workhouse. On the other hand, the magistrates discharged entire contingents of thugs when they were arrested for assaulting young strikers, in spite of their criminal records.[7]

Despite the militancy of the strikers, it was clear that shop-by-shop strikes would not work, and that only by tying up the entire trade during the busy season could the workers gain their demands. On October 21, 1909, a general meeting of union members was called to discuss the possibilities of a general strike movement in the trade. The assembled delegates declared for a general strike, advanced a program demanding an immediate ten percent increase in wages and recognition of the union

*The fire at the Triangle Waist Company on Greene Street and Washington Place in New York City broke out on March 25, 1911. The bosses, Harris and Blanck, kept the factory doors locked during working hours and ignored the union's demands for improvements in these conditions. When fire struck, 500 girls, women, and men in the Triangle shop were trapped, and 145 workers, predominantly young girls, lost their lives.

by the employers, and appointed a committee to implement the strategy for a general strike.[8]

Even as the union leaders were displaying a reluctance to move, the striking girls of Local 25 received new moral and material support. The United Hebrew Trades, the central organization of Jewish unionists in the city, began a fund-raising appeal among trade unionists and succeeded in obtaining pledges from the working shirtwaist employees to give ten cents each on behalf of the strikers. The Women's Trade Union League of New York City, which had been helping the strikers from the outset of the walkouts, now established a corps of 48 volunteer pickets to assist the strikers. The volunteer pickets, generally women from the upper middle classes, accompanied pickets in order to prevent their unwarranted arrests. They, too, were attacked by the police on the picket line along with the strikers, and some were even arrested. But when the police learned that they were dealing with socially prominent women, they changed their tactics. When Mary Dreier, the League's president, was arrested by accident, and when her identity was discovered in court, she was quickly released and the arresting officer apologized humbly, asking: "Why didn't you tell me you was a rich lady? I'd never have arrested you in the world." Such obvious bias in favor of the rich was widely publicized by the WTUL and was contrasted with police outrages committed against the strikers, thereby arousing public sympathy for the girls. The police, in turn, grew resentful of the League's support of the strike and kept asking why educated women insisted on involving themselves with lower-class working women strikers.[9]

During the weeks of the shop strikes, about two thousand workers joined the union, and hundreds crowded the cramped union office daily with talk of a general strike. Now the union, too, began to consider calling a general strike. Because the New York WTUL had been active in assisting the workers in the Triangle, Leiserson, and Rosen strikes, and because any large undertaking would require the League's financial assistance, the union shared its deliberations with that organization. League leaders were enthusiastic and pledged their support. The two organizations rented Cooper Union for the evening of November 22 to discuss the question of an industry-wide walkout, as well as to protest actions of the struck companies and the police. Among the speakers scheduled to address the rank and file workers were Samuel Gompers, Mary Dreier, Meyer London, and Ernest Bohm, secretary of the New York City Central Federated Union.[10]

On the night of the meeting, Cooper Union auditorium was packed with an overflow crowd of shirtwaist workers, and several thousand girls had to be directed to other meeting halls in the general vicinity. For over two hours, as the tension in the auditorium mounted, the workers listened to one speaker after another urging caution and moderate action. Gompers reminded the audience that he always looked upon strikes as the method of last resort. He cautioned the workers against acting too hastily, adding, however: " . . . if you cannot get the manufacturers to give you what you want, then strike. And when you strike, let the manufacturers know that you are on strike. . . ." Wild applause followed this remark, but there was still no action for a general strike.

Then, after the audience had grown tired of hearing one moderate voice after another, a young working girl leaped to her feet, marched down the aisle and asked for the floor. The chairman was reluctant to grant her request, but the workers in the audience recognized her as one of the most militant rank and filers—Clara Lemlich from Leiserson's, where the workers had already been on strike for eleven weeks. They knew, too, that she had just returned from the hospital after having been brutally beaten on the picket line. The workers insisted that she be allowed to speak even though her name did not appear on the program. Barely five feet tall and not more than twenty years old, she spoke in impassioned Yiddish—the native tongue of the majority of the shirtwaist workers—and proceeded to berate the cautious speakers who had held the platform during the evening. She concluded: "I have listened to all the speakers, and I have no further patience for talk. I am one who feels and suffers from the things pictured. I move we go on a general strike!"

Instantly, the crowd was on its feet—women, men, and girls—cheering, stamping, crying approval. Chairman Feigenbaum called for a vote. Three thousand voices shouted their unanimous approval, waving hats, handkerchiefs, and other objects.

"Do you mean faith?" cried the chairman. "Will you take the old Hebrew oath?"

Three thousand right arms shot up, and three thousand voices repeated the Yiddish words: "If I turn traitor to the cause I now pledge, may this hand wither from the arm I now raise."

Meanwhile, messengers carried the news of the Cooper Union meeting to Beethoven Hall and the other halls where the waistmakers had gathered. There the strike vote was ratified just as enthusiastically,[11] and thus began the famous labor struggle which has become known as the

"Uprising of Twenty Thousand,"* and has been described as "women's most significant struggle for unionism in the nation's history."[12]

Both Local 25 and the WTUL were stunned by the waistmakers' response to the general strike call. At most, they had expected four or five thousand Jewish workers to strike.[13] Instead, on the first day, eighteen thousand shirtwaist workers came out in response to the strike call. Girls by the thousands stormed the small union office on Clinton Street to enroll in Local 25. Soon, nearly thirty thousand operators, cutters, pressers, and finishers were on strike. Although four-fifths of the female strikers were Jewish women, several thousand Italian and native-born U. S. women participated as well.

Many small waist manufacturers, unable to stand even a short interruption during the busy season, were soon parading to union headquarters to sign agreements with the union. These agreements included a provision for a union shop; a fifty-two-hour week; limitation of overtime work; equal division of work among union members; and a price list of changing styles to be fixed by conference between employer, employee, and union representatives. In addition, the employers promised to employ only contractors who used union labor; to furnish machines, needles, thread, and other supplies; and to allow a weekly check of their payroll by union officials. Any party violating the agreement would have to pay a $300 penalty. By the time the strike was hardly four days old, almost half the original twenty thousand strikers had won improved conditions, including union contracts, and had returned to work.[14]

Because many employers made quick settlements, Local 25 and the WTUL were optimistic that the strike would be short and spectacularly successful. But the employers who settled at once were those who could not afford a protracted work stoppage. The larger firms that dominated the industry were determined to fight it out to the bitter end. They formed the Association of Waist and Dress Manufacturers of New York and, on November 27, declared open war against the union, recruiting strikebreakers and vowing to hold against a settlement. A member of the Association warned that a trade agreement with the union was not "worth the paper it was written upon. . . ." The Association urged

*Estimates of the number of strikers range from the New York State Department of Labor Bureau of Mediation and Arbitration figure of 15,000 to Local 25's estimate of 40,000. The estimate of 30,000 is based on Helen Marot's calculation based on WTUL records. (Helen Marot, "A Woman's Strike, An Appreciation of the Shirtwaist Makers of New York," *Proceedings of the Academy of Political Science, City of New York,* vol. I, 1910, p. 122. The report on the strike in the *Annual Report 1909–1910 of the Women's Trade Union League of New York* is entitled "The League and the Strike of the Thirty Thousand," [New York, 1910, p. 11]).

employers who had signed agreements to repudiate them and warned that only manufacturers who opposed unionism would be eligible for membership in the employers' organization. "We insist upon the open shop," the president declared, "and from that stand we will not budge."[15] Thus, very early, the strike settled down to a protracted campaign of siege warfare against the larger firms. It required a good deal of spirit and devotion to unionism to maintain this siege. The winter of 1909–10 was exceptionally frigid and snowy in New York City. Many a frostbitten young picket was taken directly to the hospital or clinic. In addition, the ILGWU, then only nine years old, was not yet firmly established and had a scanty treasury, so that regular strike benefits were few and far between and the strikers were hard put to meet their rent and grocery bills. Actually, most of the original $60,000 strike fund and of the funds collected during the strike had to be used to pay the fines of girls convicted by biased magistrates.[16]

The members of the Association tried to break the strike by exploiting Jewish and Italian antagonisms and sought to drive a wedge between the girls by keeping Black workers on the job, by importing professional strikebreakers, or by arrangements with out-of-town plants, particularly in Philadelphia, to supply them with goods. But they depended primarily on brute force, arrests, and convictions.

By December 22, 1909, over seven hundred pickets had been brutally arrested; nineteen were sentenced to the workhouse on Blackwell's Island on charges of disorderly conduct and vagrancy, and the rest were fined. At Blackwell's Island, the young girls were thrown into cells with prostitutes, degenerates, and criminals.[17]

A magistrate summed up the prevailing attitude of the courts in these words: "You have no right to picket. . . . Every time you go down there you will get what is coming to you and I shall not interfere." Regardless of the evidence, or lack of it, the girls were usually convicted. When prosecutors failed to substantiate their charge that Nennie Bloom had assaulted a forelady, Magistrate Joseph Corrigan fined her $10 for disorderly conduct and stated that if more strikers appeared before him, he would send them to the workhouse. When one girl was tried for the offense of calling a strikebreaker a scab, the presiding magistrate told her: " . . . If these girls continue to rush around and cry 'scab,' I shall convict them of disorderly conduct. There is no word in the English language as irritating as the word 'scab.'" Another magistrate declared bluntly that while "the higher courts have held that strikers had the right to employ pickets and call names," he personally would forbid the right to picket.

Still another magistrate told a group of bruised and bleeding girls: "You are on strike against God and nature, whose prime law is that man shall earn his bread in the sweat of his brow." Members of the WTUL cabled this remark to George Bernard Shaw, who replied: "Delightful. Medieval America is always in the most intimate personal confidence of the Almighty."[18]

The cruel treatment of the girl strikers failed to dampen their spirit. "There never was anything like it," one union official declared in amazement. "An equal number of men never would hold together under what these girls are enduring."[19] It was precisely because women, who were not expected to take either their jobs or unionism seriously, were such militant strikers that the press expressed such amazement and devoted so much space to the waistmakers' uprising. The New York Women's Trade Union League, in its role as liaison between the strikers and the public, capitalized on the fact that the majority of the strikers were women. Members circulated detailed reports of police attacks on peaceful pickets and kept a careful tally of arrests. They described the callousness of police magistrates who sentenced young women to several weeks of hard labor for offenses as minor as yelling "scab" at strikebreakers. The League volunteered legal services in police courts, provided witnesses for arrested strikers, cross-examined those who testified, raised $29,000 in bail, and acted as a complainant at police headquarters. On December 6, the League established a strike headquarters. League leaders encouraged women whom the police had arrested to come in and report their experiences in detail. From these reports, they drew up rules for pickets designed to encourage safe and legal methods that would minimize the chances of arrest. League members distributed copies of the "rules" to all strikers so that they could study them daily.[20]

On December 20, the strike spread to Philadelphia. Leaders of Local 25 had suspected for some time that New York manufacturers were sending materials to Philadelphia for completion. ILGWU officials visited Philadelphia in November and early December and determined to halt the manufacture of goods destined for New York. However, the Philadelphia strike grew, basically, out of the same deplorable conditions that existed in New York. The conditions of the fifteen thousand waistmakers in Philadelphia were summed up in an interview with an eighteen-year-old waistmaker, who told a reporter for the *Public Ledger* that she had gone into the shops seven years earlier when she was only eleven years old. When there was plenty of work, she could sometimes earn as much as $9 a week, but in the summer she could not average more than $3, and some weeks she made so little as to have just enough to pay car fare. Some days she would earn only 30 or 35 cents. Then there were the petty exactions: two cents a week to pay for an outing sponsored by the proprietor every summer; 25 cents for a key to the closet; needles sold at four times what they cost; and the tyranny of some of the forewomen, who kept the girls at their machines all day long in the summer time, even when there was no work and they earned nothing. Excuses of illness made no difference: "She would keep you in if you were most dead."[21]

While only 3,500 of the workers belonged to Local 15, officials believed that conditions would lead the non-union workers to walk out if they called a strike. And so, demanding union recognition, a nine-hour day, a fifty-hour week, and uniform wages scales, the Philadelphia dress and waistmakers walked out in a general strike.[22]

The Philadelphia strike followed much the same course as that in New York: the waistmakers faced the same type of "gorillas" and police brutality, and the magistrates of Philadelphia were just as eager to sentence pickets to thirty days in the county prison as were their counterparts in New York. The Central Labor Union endorsed the strike, and many trade unions supported it. Throughout their fight, moreover, the striking girls were given support by leading society women and progressive-minded college girls.[23]

WTUL leaders Margaret Dreier Robins and Agnes Nestor (the latter president of the American Glove Workers' Union) hurried from Chicago to Philadelphia. They opened an office in the heart of the factory district where pickets could report and strikers could receive sandwiches and coffee. The youth and enthusiasm of the Jewish strikers amazed League members. Day in and day out, despite attacks by the "gorillas" and arrests by the police, they were on the picket lines. On January 14, 1910, the *Philadelphia Evening Bulletin* reported that a severe snowstorm had hit the city, and added: "Despite the storm, the pickets proved faithful to their duty today."

When Local 15's leaders disclosed that they would be willing to settle without achieving union recognition, they created an uproar among the strikers. The girls insisted upon including the union shop in the settlement, and Agnes Nestor supported their stand. "This sounds like a trick to get you back," she told the pickets. "Don't go into this thing blindly. We have plenty of money and can afford to wait." The *Public Ledger* called this "bravado," pointing out that "the treasury of the union is admittedly empty," but conceded that the Philadelphia "girl strikers still support the demand for the union shop enthusiastically."[24]

With their production virtually at a standstill as a result of the Philadelphia strike, and with practically every non-Association shop having settled with Local 25, the New York Manufacturers' Association was more inclined to seek a settlement. On December 23, a compromise was reached between the employers and the union officials. The employers conceded the demands of the workers for shorter hours, higher wages, and prompt consideration of an entire list of grievances, but refused to recognize the union or establish the closed or union shop. The work week would be reduced to fifty-two hours; there was to be no discrimination against union members; needles, thread, and appliances were to be supplied free by the employers, as far as practicable; equal work was to be given during the slow seasons; four paid holidays annually were to be granted; all shops were to establish wage committees; and all strikers were to be reemployed and no others were to be hired until this was accomplished. The Manufacturers' Association agreed that it would give consideration to any communications from any source concerning violations of the agreement and that it would welcome conferences about any differences that could not be settled between the individual shop and its employees. But the president of the Association stated that the manufacturers insisted on an open shop "and from that stand we will not budge."[25]

On December 27, the negotiated settlement was submitted to a vote of all union members. Since many of the girls working in non-Association, independent shops had earlier gained full union recognition, it was hardly to be expected that the strikers in the Association shops would settle for less. Addressing the strikers, Hillquit reminded them that the crux of their demands was union recognition:

> Collectively the waistmakers are strong, individually they are helpless and defenseless. If the employers were today to concede all the demands of the strikers, but be allowed to destroy or even to weaken the union, they could and would restore the old condition of servitude in their shops, within a very few weeks or months.

It came as no surprise, therefore, that the strikers overwhelmingly disapproved of the proposed settlement.[26]

After the rejection, the strike dragged on. While the enthusiasm of the strikers continued at a high pitch, and their determination to win a union shop inspired them to further sacrifice, funds ran low and many of the pickets depended on the WTUL soup kitchen for their meals. Meanwhile, the arrests continued and so did the fines, which ate up what little remained of the strike fund. Illness kept many of the girls confined to their beds while those who still picketed continued to shiver without winter clothing. League members also continued to picket, but their fur hats and coats stood out in sharp contrast to the clothing of the waistmakers. Still, they too suffered during the terrible winter. Vassar graduate Violet Pike, for example, reported daily for either picket or court duty. "Her hands deep in her pockets, her beaver hat a bit to the side and an angelic smile on her red lips," she was described as truly the "bravest of the brave, day in and day out shivering from cold and at times drenched to the skin."[27]

The climax of the New York strike occurred on January 2, 1910 at Carnegie Hall. Originally, several members of the Political Equality Association, led by Anna Shaw and Alva Belmont, had proposed a sympathy strike of all women workers in the city. But when this did not materialize, the Carnegie Hall mass rally was organized.[28] Placards hung throughout the concert hall proclaiming that "The workhouse is no answer to the demand for justice." Every seat was occupied, and the audience sat spellbound as speaker after speaker heaped accusations and recriminations upon the heads of New York's public officials. The sponsors had sold box seats to liberal clubs and organizations and netted a substantial amount for the strike fund. On the stage, in the front row, sat twenty strikers who had served sentences in the workhouse. The 350 young women who had been arrested by the police and fined by the magistrates filled the rest of the stage. Each girl wore a printed sash stating how the court had dealt with her, such as "Workhouse Prisoner," or "Arrested."

The high point of the evening came when, after her speech, Leonora O'Reilly led out Rose Perr. No taller than an average girl of ten years, with her hair braided down her back, she stood before the enormous gathering and told, in simple words, the alarming story of her arrest. The police had taken her to court as a witness because she had asked a police captain to arrest a "gorilla" who had slapped her companion. At the courthouse, she was suddenly accused of having assaulted a scab. Without any evidence furnished, the magistrate thereupon sentenced her to five days in the workhouse before she even had an opportunity to testify.

Hillquit praised the strikers for forming a powerful union practically overnight and fighting a gallant battle to maintain it. He declared that the strike had demonstrated how women permeated industrial life and proved how absurd it was for any man to say that women's place was in the home: "Let him remember the thirty thousand women strikers of one single industry in one city and let him remember that in the factories these women are treated with even less consideration than men." But these women he continued, had shown that they could fight for their rights with heroism. "Be of good cheer, your victory will be glorious," he closed to thunderous applause. At the conclusion of his speech, the audience unanimously adopted a resolution condemning "the conduct of the police in this case as an indefensible abuse of power," and denouncing the court actions against the strikers as examples of "a prejudiced and vindictive mind": "The office of Magistrate has been perverted into an instrument of persecution and oppression."[29]

Following the great Carnegie Hall meeting, the State Bureau of Mediation attempted to mediate the remaining questions in dispute between the union and the Association. While Local 25 was willing to discuss the open or closed shop, the Associated Dress and Waist Manufacturers' Association rejected the idea of even discussing the issue. Likewise, on January 11, the Association rejected the union's proposal, transmitted through the State Mediation Commissioner, for arbitration hearings by the Commission which would include consideration of the closed shop.[30]

And so the strike dragged on through the bitter cold month of January and into February. As strike benefits dwindled, hunger and deprivation became urgent problems. Then, too, the wealthy women's commitment to the strikers began to waver and diminish after the strikers rejected the settlement offered by the Association because it did not include union recognition.

By the beginning of February, with the strikers' resources nearing depletion and with the rich society women showing a growing coolness toward the struggle, the end was inevitable. The union was compelled to sign agreements with many of the larger shops without either recognition of the union or endorsement of the union shop. It was on this basis that the Triangle Waist Company settled with the strikers in the first week of February.

By the second week of February, almost the entire trade had resumed operation, and those unfortunate few strikers whose stubborn employers refused to sign straggled back to their shops without a contract. Finally, on February 15, even though the Association did not recognize the union, Local 25 officials declared the general strike at an end. The great uprising of the shirtwaist makers, which had begun with such fanfare, ended unceremoniously that day without any rejoicing.[31]

On February 6, the Philadelphia strike was settled through arbitration between Local 15 and the Philadelphia Manufacturers' Association.

Under the terms of the settlement, each side nominated two members to a Board of Arbitration, and these four chose a fifth impartial member. In the settlement, the employers were not permitted to make any charges for straps, needles, or any other part of the machines, unless they were willfully broken by the operator, and the hours of labor were reduced to 52½ per week. But both wages and the issue of the union shop remained to be arbitrated. The disappointed strikers, who had hoped for more, returned unhappily to their shops. But Agnes Nestor, before returning to Chicago, urged the waistmakers to "build up the union so that when the time comes to make another agreement, you will be in a position to get better terms."[32]

*   *   *

When the strikes in both New York and Philadelphia were over, the ILGWU was able to point with justifiable pride to definite gains made by the strikers. Women who had worked sixty or more hours a week before the strike in New York now had a guaranteed work week of 52 hours (52½ hours in those Philadelphia shops that had settled with the union), and in New York, they were to be paid time-and-a-half for overtime work. Workers no longer had to pay for power and materials, and other petty impositions had also been eliminated. Most importantly, nearly twenty thousand had joined Local 25 and ten thousand had become members of Local 15 during the strike.[33]

But the strike settlement had obvious limitations, and the waist-makers' contracts were weak. Because many manufacturers had to make individual settlements with the union, and because each shop determined its own piece-rate scale, neither conditions nor grievance procedures were standardized. As Hillquit had predicted, the failure to win a union shop opened the door to attempts by employers to restore previous conditions. Within months, waistmakers were coming to the WTUL to report violations, and shop strikes were becoming increasingly common. Unfortunately, a number of union leaders, instead of blaming this on the weaknesses in the settlement, attributed it instead to "the main illness of our Jewish organization—strike fever."[34]

Despite the strike's less-than-successful settlement, it did mark a turning point in the history of the union movement among women workers, as well as in the union movement of the garment industry. The strike of the women shirtwaist makers in New York City was both the largest and bitterest strike of women in the history of American labor struggles up to that time. During the eight weeks of preliminary skirmishing and the thirteen weeks of the general strike, the strikers had clearly demonstrated that workers who were usually regarded by leading officials of the AFL (and even by some of the ILGWU) as impossible to organize, could be united in effective economic action. In this struggle, young girls, most of them recent immigrants, working primarily at an unskilled trade, were able to gain from their employers, if not total victory, such important concessions as a 52-hour week, time-and-a-half for overtime, paid holidays, improvements in working conditions, and procedures for setting wages. Without either preparation or finances, the girls had walked the picket lines through the rain and snow, remaining solid in spite of beatings, arrests, fines, and jailings. They had laid the foundation for future gains. Their conditions and struggles had gained the attention of middle-class and well-to-do individuals in New York, and their strike marked the first time these individuals were actively involved in championing the cause of the working masses.[35] The strike pointed up for many New Yorkers the inadequacies of both their police department and the city's judicial system.* It awakened many in the city to a new awareness of the problems facing workers in general and working women in particular. "The great moral significance of the shirtwaist makers' strike," Morris Hillquit noted, "is that it helped awaken our dormant social conscience. The people of this city began to realize that society owes some duties to the toiling masses."[36]

Finally, the three months of picketing created a solidarity among the women workers and fostered a new awareness of what unity could achieve on the economic front. The girls had gained the understanding that together, they were a powerful force. As one girl phrased it: "This is not just a strike for self. Only by standing together can we get better conditions for all."[37]

Almost a quarter of a century later, an ILGWU veteran recalled that in the opening years of the century, "the waist and dress shops were the vilest and foulest industrial sores of New York and other big cities." And he went on: "Then came 1909. Then came the most heroic labor struggle in the history of the great city. Then came the beginnings of a strong and permanent organization in the needle trades. Then came the beginnings of decency in a vilely sweated industry."[38] These were true words. The impact of the women's strike in the waistmaking industry was a tremendous inspiration to the workers in the other branches of the industry and paved the way for the major advances in unionizing other garment workers.

*Shortly after the end of the strike, the New York City voters replaced Mayor McClellan with Mayor William Gaynor, who undertook a thorough housecleaning of the police department.

CHAPTER 12

Revolt of the Garment Workers: II.
Repercussions

Barely five months after the shirtwaist makers had returned to work, another and more extensive general strike paralyzed the ladies' garment trade. In July, 1910, some sixty thousand workers employed in the cloak and suit branch of the industry left their work benches *en masse* and marched to the picket lines.

In 1910, cloaks, suits, and shirts were manufactured in about 1,500 shops in New York City, employing approximately sixty thousand workers, of whom about forty thousand were Jewish and ten to twenty thousand were Italians. After 1890, partly because legislation outlawing "homework" had virtually ended sweatshops, many small shops had sprung up. The newer clothing factories used lighter, better, and more specialized machinery run by steam or electricity. But despite the disappearance of most sweatshops, factory conditions remained poor. Little provision had been made for adequate sanitary facilities; workers were still forced to buy their own sewing machines and to pay for repairs, oil, and thread; and inside subcontracting, which prevailed in most of the shops, created a chain of bosses whose common interest was in keeping wages down. In 1910, the average wage for operators was $15 to $18 a week, and for pressers, $14. Men worked for nine to nine-and-a-half hours a day during the slack season and for fourteen to sixteen hours a day when the shops were busy. In short, the cloakmaker's life, like that of the shirtwaist maker, was a bitter struggle for existence. For none was this truer than the female workers. Women held ten percent of the jobs in this branch of the industry. They played a minor role in cloak making, working primarily as "helpers" in the finishing departments, and earned the woefully inadequate wage of $3 to $4 per week.[1]

Unlike the waistmakers' strike, which had been spontaneous and haphazard, the cloakmakers' strike in the summer of 1910 was carefully planned. Unlike Local 25's leaders, the cloakmakers' officers had anticipated the strike, had prepared adequate funds, and enjoyed the full support of the International Union. Strike agitation had begun in August, 1908, and by the spring of 1909, about two thousand members had been recruited into the New York Joint Board of Cloak and Shirt Makers Unions. With the strike of the waistmakers, the movement for a general strike in the cloak and suit trade was ignited and membership in the Joint Board soared. In July, 1910, a secret ballot on the general strike issue showed 18,777 for striking and 615 against, and a committee decided on the following set of demands: union recognition, the 48-hour week, double time for overtime work, and the abolition of subcontracting.[2]

When the strike call was issued on July 7, about sixty thousand cloakmakers, six thousand of them women, walked off their jobs in what the press immediately termed "The Great Revolt." The Italians, who constituted about a third of the labor force in the industry and who had been involved in all stages of planning and executing the strike, joined the Jewish workers. Unlike the situation in the shirtwaist strike, which had little prior organization and in which the Italian girls were mainly strikebreakers, the Italians here were organized before the strike began.[3]

The cloakmakers began at once to negotiate with the smaller employers, who could not afford a long, drawn-out conflict and who rushed to arrange satisfactory agreements. But the larger manufacturers refused to yield. They were determined that under no circumstances would they grant the demand for union recognition and the closed shop. A number of the larger cloak manufacturers thereupon formed the Cloak, Suit and Shirt Manufacturers' Protective Association and pledged not to bargain with the Cloakmakers' Union.[4]

Like the shirtwaist makers before them, the cloakmakers soon had to contend with the Association's special policemen and thugs, in addition to the New York City police. All three groups joined forces in escorting strikebreakers into the struck shops. As in the shirtwaist makers' strike, too, magistrates regularly fined or sentenced pickets to the workhouse, while the police generally protected the thugs who were terrorizing the strikers. However, the Association was not satisfied with this, and it obtained a limited temporary injunction restraining the union from coercing any worker into leaving his work through the use of "force, threat, fraud or intimidation." The strikers promptly defied the injunction by mass picketing in the face of violence and clubbings by the police and the special guards hired by the employers.[5]

Even though women workers made up a small minority of the strike force, they quickly assumed important positions in the strike organization. For example, Dora Landburg, who had grown up in the cloakmaking trade, enthusiastically directed the strike headquarters, where she coordinated the picketing. In addition, she dispatched aid to those arrested strikers who requested bail.[6] In contrast to the shirtwaist strike, the WTUL played only a peripheral role in the cloakmakers' revolt, mainly because women made up only a small percentage of the strikers. But John Dyche, the ILGWU's national secretary-treasurer, having learned something from the girls' strike, requested help from the League and named Helen Marot and Leonora O'Reilly to the cloakmakers' strike committee. Every few days, Marot visited the headquarters of the settlement committee where the national officers sat in session. The union leaders appointed Marot and Schneiderman to negotiate a settlement with those manufacturers who employed female alteration hands. League members formed a milk committee which raised money and distributed 209,000 quarts of milk to strikers' children.[7]

After efforts by the State Bureau of Arbitration to mediate the strike had failed (the Association refused to enter into negotiations until the union agreed to state that it would not seek either recognition or the closed shop, which the union rejected),[8] A. Lincoln Filene, the Boston department store owner and a leading member of the Boston branch of the National Civic Federation, contacted Louis D. Brandeis and asked him to go to New York to help arrange a settlement of the strike. As counsel for the Boston cloak and suit manufacturers' association, Brandeis had helped to break a four-month general strike there in 1907 by obtaining injunctions against the union leaders.[9] Now he appeared in New York as a friend of labor but an enemy of the closed shop, one of the union's main demands. Under Brandeis' clever and persuasive maneuvering, Dyche and the majority of the strike committee agreed to eliminate the closed shop from the list of the union's basic demands. But the more radical of the union's executive officers, as well as the majority of the rank and file, declined to accept arbitration without some consideration of the closed-shop issue. In fact, the active personal intervention of Samuel Gompers was needed before indignant union leaders and members would agree to enter into a conference with the employers on July 28.[10]

The conference had little difficulty in coming to an understanding about the specific grievances of the cloakmakers, but it could make no headway on the closed-shop issue. At this stage, Brandeis put forward the formula of the "preferential union shop," which would bind an employer to give preference to an available union member in hiring, while still permitting him to hire non-union members and retain scabs. Brandeis did not invent the preferential union shop. Although Dyche thought the plan "too new," it had been promulgated as a union demand in the 1892 strike of the AFL teamsters, scalemen, and packers in New Orleans.[11] When the AFL was weak and fighting against the open-shop drive, it put forward the preferential union shop as a step toward the closed shop. By 1910, however, when the closed shop had been won in many contracts, acceptance of the preferential union shop represented a retreat.

Gompers, however, urged the union to accept it.[12] But with the *Jewish Daily Forward* denouncing the preferential shop as "the scab shop with honey," and with the *New York Call* urging the strikers to stick to their guns, Brandeis' maneuverings got nowhere. The mass of the workers rejected his proposal, and on August 3, the uniml amlaluded all joint conferences and renounced all offers of peace and arbitration, declaring: "The rank and file of our organization demand the closed shop. There can be no compromise on that score and if we were to accept any compromise, the rank and file would not abide by our decision."[13]

So vigorously did the strikers oppose any retreat on the closed-shop issue that members of the strike committee who favored the preferential shop were actually threatened with violence.[14] But when the strike leadership, bowing to the determined opposition of the rank and file, rejected the agreement proposed by the Association because it included the preferential union shop, Justice John W. Goff of the New York Supreme Court made the injunction against the strikers permanent. Goff labeled the strike a common law, civil conspiracy to obtain the closed shop and thereby to deprive non-union men and women of the opportunity to work and drive them out of the industry. The police were authorized to disperse all pickets, peaceful or otherwise.[15] "For the first time in the history of labor disputes in the state," observes Graham Adams, Jr., "an injunction not only permanently restrained men from peaceful picketing but also forbade them to interfere in any way at all with those who wished to work."[16]

Even Julius Henry Cohen, the attorney for the manufacturers, described the injunction as "the strongest one ever handed down by an American court against trade unionism," and the New York *Evening*

Post, which seldom favored the cause of labor in any strike, criticized Goff's injunction, commenting: "One need not be a sympathizer with trade-union policy as it reveals itself today in order to see that the latest injunction, if generally upheld, would seriously cripple such defensive powers as legitimately belong to organized labor."[17] Speaking for the AFL, Gompers called the decision another example of the "tyranny of the autocratic methods of concentrated capital and greed." The New York City Central Federated Union, in conjunction with the Socialist Party, organized a huge demonstration against this "judicial tyranny."[18]

Meanwhile, negotiations were continuing, and on September 2, the manufacturers presented a new proposal for a settlement with additional concessions. The strike committee, with the support of only two hundred hurriedly assembled shop chairmen and with a minimum of debate, ratified the first collective bargaining agreement in the industry. No public announcement was made of the agreement, nor were any public assemblies held before the ratification.[19]

The "Protocol of Peace," as the agreement was called, won for the workers, after nine weeks of bitter struggle, a 50-hour week, bonus pay for overtime, ten legal holidays, free electric power installation for machines, no home work, weekly pay in cash, not checks, limitations on overtime, a joint board of sanitary control to help clean up filthy shops, a committee of grievances and compulsory arbitration, with no strike or lockout permitted before arbitration, and price settlements to be made in each shop by negotiation. The settlement had tremendously important implications for unskilled women workers, since the agreement covered the wages and conditions of every worker in the trade, from the skilled tailors to the finishers.[20]

Despite these important gains, however, the settlement was a disappointment to many strikers, and a large number of the rank and file disapproved of it. One reason was that instead of the closed shop, there was "the preferential union shop." Furthermore, unlike the usual collective bargaining agreement, the Protocol had no time limit; it could run indefinitely but could be terminated by either side at will. As a concession, the manufacturers agreed to exert preference only as between one union man and another; non-union labor could only be hired when union help was unobtainable. The agreement also compelled employers to declare their belief in the union and in the ideal that all "who desire its benefits should share its burdens."[21]

But to many rank and file workers, all this was still only the "scab shop with honey," and they disapproved, too, of the no-strike clause and the provision for compulsory arbitration.[22] Responding to this criticism, the union's official journal declared:

> It is far better to strike for, and win recognition of our union, than an increase in wages, or decrease of hours, without the powerful organization needed to maintain the conditions once created. With such an organization, the possibilities of the future are unlimited.[23]

But events were soon to demonstrate that the union relied exclusively on the machinery of the Protocol and the good will of the employers to establish permanent industrial peace and failed to build a strong organization in order to enforce it. As a result, the employers were able to freely violate the terms of the Protocol.

* * *

The revolt in the garment trades next shifted to Chicago, where, on September 22, 1910, a small group of courageous women ignited the spark which led forty thousand unorganized clothing workers to strike. The uprising began when a few girls employed in shop No. 5 of Hart, Schaffner & Marx, the largest clothing factory in the city, walked off the job when their piece rate was arbitrarily cut from 4 cents to 3¼ cents a pair. One of these girls was Bessie Abramowitz, an immigrant from Grodno in White Russia, who had already been blacklisted in Chicago's clothing shops because of her militancy and was working at Hart, Schaffner & Marx under an assumed name. Under the leadership of Abramowitz and Annie Shapiro, twelve young women petitioned for a return to the old rate. When this appeal was rejected, they struck and sought help from the United Garment Workers, which had a small, male-dominated local of clothing cutters within the Hart, Schaffner & Marx plant. Uninterested in organizing young immigrant women, the elite local gave the strikers the "brush-off," whereupon the fourteen young women started to picket by themselves. At first, they received little support from other workers in the plant and it took three weeks of steady, day-by-day picketing by these fourteen determined strikers to convince the other workers that this was not just a lark, but a serious effort to redress their long-standing grievances. By the fourth week, other workers in the plant, realizing that the pickets were fighting for them as well, joined the fourteen women, and, by the middle of October, almost eight thousand Hart, Schaffner & Marx workers had walked out. The walkout gradually spread to other manufacturing houses until the entire industry was paralyzed.[24]

With the United Garment Workers indifferent to their struggle, the strikers appealed to the Chicago Women's Trade Union League and the Chicago Federation of Labor for assistance. Both organizations responded instantly. However, the WTUL's National Executive Board had just established a definite strike policy requiring that any union requesting League assistance had to include two League members on its strike committee. Pressured by the strikers, the UGW leadership agreed to this stipulation.[25] Thereupon the Chicago WTUL threw itself wholeheartedly into the strike. Members formed eleven separate committees to handle picketing, publicity, speakers, benefit meetings, public events, and relief. They established headquarters in the same building that housed the Chicago Federation of Labor offices.[26]

One of the original strikers explained why she and her colleagues had walked out:

> We started to work at seven-thirty and worked until six with three-quarters of an hour for lunch. Our wages were seven cents for a pair of pants, or one dollar for fourteen pairs. For that we made four pockets and one watch pocket, but they were always changing the style of the stitching and until we got the swing of the new style, we would lose time and money and we felt sore about it. One day the foreman told us the wages were cut to six cents a pair of pants and the new style had two watch pockets. We would not stand for that, so we got up and left.[27]

As in the New York strikes, the employers hired detectives and thugs and received the full support of the police. In fact, Chicago's police, long notorious for their brutality toward strikers, were even more barbarous than those in New York. By December, two of the strikers had been gunned down and killed by police bullets and many more had been injured by club-swinging members of the force. Arrests of strikers occurred daily, and members of the League's picket committee patrolled the streets in order to serve as witnesses for strikers arrested without cause. League members also joined the strikers' picket lines and reviewed the "Rules for Pickets" with the strikers each day before they went picketing with them.[28]

After forty thousand garment workers, ten thousand of them women, had walked off the job, the strikers received a crippling blow from their own union. Thomas Rickert, president of the United Garment Workers, was a conservative, old-line labor leader, interested in developing the union along craft lines. Skeptical of the value of unskilled immigrants to the union, he was eager to come to terms with the employers. In November, he announced an agreement with Hart, Schaffner & Marx, but it was unanimously rejected by the strikers, who declared it wholly unacceptable. Then League members and officials of the Chicago Federation of Labor learned that the UGW District No. 6's treasury was empty and that the union officers' offer to assist the strikers lacked any substance. In fact, the union had issued worthless vouchers to over ten thousand people. A joint conference of officials of the Chicago Federation of Labor, League leaders, and UGW officers managed to raise $700. They then proceeded to distribute $3 for each $5 voucher to the angry strikers.[29]

The strike revealed an extraordinary determination on the part of the strikers not to yield, in spite of hunger and cold. Jane Addams called it "a spontaneous revolutionary movement." The more brutal the thugs and police became, the more determined the strikers were to hold out until the strike was won.[30]

On November 5, Rickert reached an agreement with Hart, Schaffner & Marx for arbitration of all issues without union recognition. Once again, the workers rejected the proposal, and this time they made their hatred of the national officials so pronounced that Rickert had to leave the hall quickly by a back door. Thousands of striking cutters, trimmers, and spongers adopted a resolution stating that "we repudiate the action of . . . Thomas A. Rickert in signing any agreement without presenting the same for approval." Despite mounting violence against them (the final count was 374 strikers arrested and two killed), the workers, on December 8, again rejected an agreement that would have sent them back to work without union recognition. It took another five weeks of hunger, cold, and violence before the workers of Hart, Schaffner & Marx, on January 14, 1911, reluctantly agreed to go back to work and refer all issues to an arbitration committee. But the other thirty thousand strikers maintained their ranks solidly until, on February 3, Rickert and his lieutenants, without consulting the strikers, the WTUL, or the officials of the Chicago Federation of Labor, declared the strike over.

Workers returned to work without any agreement and with no method of adjusting the grievances that had driven them to strike. Those who had been the most militant of the pickets were refused employment when they tried to return to their former jobs. The 25-year-old Sidney Hillman, with Frank Rosenblum, Bessie Abramowitz (who later became Mrs. Hillman), and Sam Levin, had risen to leadership among the workers during the strike, and they recorded that the great majority of the strikers "were forced to return to their old miserable conditions, through the back door; and happy were those who were taken back. Many . . . were victimized for months afterwards. . . ." Members of the WTUL and the Chicago Federation of Labor who had worked tirelessly for a just settlement felt as betrayed as the strikers themselves.[31]

Only the Hart, Schaffner & Marx workers operated under a contract as a result of the strike. This contract, drawn up by Clarence Darrow, the famed labor lawyer, who had volunteered his services in defense of the strikers, and company attorney Carl Meyer, is historically regarded as the first major victory in the annals of men's clothing workers' unionism. It established a minimum wage for various departments in the factory, a 54-hour week, and time-and-a-half for overtime. It also presaged future occupational safety and health measures when it insisted that "all tailor shops be properly ventilated" and that "no sweeping of a character to raise dust in any of the shops be done during working hours." The agreement provided for overtime pay for extra work and initiated a permanent Board of Arbitration, composed of Darrow and Meyer, to hear and rule on future worker grievances.[32]

The Cleveland garment strike of 1911 followed the pattern that had emerged in New York and Chicago. Strikers—men and women alike—held out for ten long weeks to end low pay, unsanitary working conditions, inside subcontracting, and long and irregular hours. The strike began in June when 4,400 men and 1,600 women walked off the job demanding a 50-hour week, abolition of charges for supplies and electricity, elimination of subcontracting, union recognition, and a permanent joint wage committee composed of worker representatives, outside arbitrators, and employers, for the purpose of establishing a uniform wage scale. As it had in New York and Chicago, union recognition became a crucial factor, and as in the former two cities, middle-class women lent invaluable support, while WTUL organizers rushed to the scene to offer assistance.[33]

As in earlier strikes, too, the police came to the manufacturers' aid. But in Cleveland, they were even more brutal than elsewhere. The *Cleveland Plain Dealer* described an attack of the police on the girl strikers:

> They [the mounted police] galloped headlong at the crowd when they first appeared and the hundreds who blocked the street fled in terror. They swung their clubs when they reached the crowd and forced their way through, driving scores before them down the streets. Some girls who ran from them were chased for blocks. . . .

As the police carried the young garment workers from the strike scene in the patrol wagons, the women joined in song to keep their spirits high:

> All we ask is bail
> All we get is jail
> All that we want is to fight
> Until we get what is right.

At one of the factories, 45 girls were arrested at one time. No sooner were they jailed than one of the girls proposed that a meeting be held there in prison, and resolutions were adopted condemning the police. As one observer noted: "Girls who maintain this fighting spirit in police cells are not going to be easily beaten." Pauline Newman, who had been sent to Cleveland by the ILGWU to help the strikers, reported that "the spirit manifested by the girl workers in Cleveland" was an "inspiration" to the entire labor movement.[34]

Unfortunately, the strike failed. As it dragged on into October, the International's funds fell dangerously low, and the Cleveland manufacturers found New York and Chicago shops to fill their orders. In desperation, the ILGWU turned to the AFL Executive Council for assistance, pleading:

> For fourteen weeks the strikers have maintained their ranks unbroken. The strike has already cost over a quarter of a million dollars, almost all of which has been contributed by members and locals of the International Ladies' Garment Workers' Union. The Cleveland strikers are ready to keep up the fight until the principle of collective bargaining is recognized by the employers. Be prompt with your aid lest the employers starve us into submission.

But the AFL Executive Council remained deaf to the appeal. "And so," writes Elizabeth McCreesh, "despite the strikers' heroism and valuable support from sympathizers and union officials, organized manufacturers succeeded in halting the union movement among Cleveland's garment workers."[35]

Milwaukee's garment workers were more successful in their strike. There was a good reason for this. Of all the strikes of garment workers of the period, only the one in Milwaukee was not accompanied by police violence against and unjustified arrests and imprisonment of pickets. The chief reason for this difference was the election of Emil Seidel as Socialist mayor of Milwaukee on the eve of the strike, which broke out late in November, 1910. The police chief, a holdover from the previous administration, ordered the customary police brutality toward the pickets, whereupon Mayor Seidel addressed an official letter to him that went:

> Complaints have been made here that disemployed citizens have recently been subjected to abusive epithets and rough handling by policemen. Whatever may be the basis of these complaints, I want it understood that no man on the police force has the right to interfere with a citizen who is not violating the law. I expect you, as Chief of Police, to make clear to the members of your department that as long as a citizen is within his legal rights, he should not be manhandled or insulted. Officers tolerating such tactics and patrolmen prac-

ticing them will be accountable. Hoping that reports referred to will, on investigation, prove to be exaggerated.

Apparently the police got the message. Deprived of their usual allies, the manufacturers settled on December 9 on the basis of a 54-hour week, time-and-a-half for overtime, double pay for holidays, an open door to the employers, over the heads of foremen, with complaints of ill treatment, and the appointment of a committee representing workers and employers to discuss a new wage scale and the issue of union recognition.[36]

* * *

The next major battle in the clothing industry was fought by the New York fur workers.

In 1912, there were ten thousand workers in New York's fur manufacturing shops. About seven thousand of them were Jewish, practically all recent immigrants from Eastern Europe. The remainder included Germans, Greeks, Italians, French-Canadians, English, Bohemians, Slovaks, and other nationalities. About three thousand were women, mainly finishers. In April, 1904, the International Association of Fur Workers of the United States and Canada was organized, but the union's failure to organize the Jewish furriers led to its collapse and the surrender of its charter to the AFL early in 1911. At that point, however, the United Hebrew Trades initiated an organizing drive, and by the spring of 1912, three thousand of the ten thousand workers in the industry had been organized into three locals which affiliated with the AFL. With its enlarged membership and with $3,000 in its treasury, the union felt prepared for a major struggle with the employers.[37]

The need for changes in the working conditions in the fur trade made the union confident that there would be a positive response to its call. The poverty-ridden life of immigrant workers in New York City, with its low wages, horrible surroundings, long months of unemployment, and the constant struggle to earn a living, was nowhere better illustrated than in the case of the fur workers. The majority of the cutters, the aristocrats of the trade, earned about $12 a week. Operators averaged only about $6, and finishers, all women, only $5. Most fur workers worked 56 to 60 hours a week, and some even longer. They worked these incredibly long hours in filthy, disease-breeding sweat-shops, usually located in ancient, broken-down wooden tenements or in basements. In one or two small rooms, without even a pretense of ventilation, about twenty fur workers would labor. Stairs, hallways, rooms, and closets were packed with dust-saturated fur pieces and cuttings. Stench and dust blanketed everything. Hair, dust, and poisonous dyes ate at the workers' eyes, noses, skin, and lungs as they toiled at the bench or machine. In 1911, a New York State Commission conducted an investigation of sanitary conditions in fur shops. A special panel of doctors examined the workers. Two out of every ten fur workers had tuberculosis, and another two had asthma. The fingers of many workers were rotted by dyes. The skin on their hands had turned black. The commission reported that eight out of every ten fur workers were suffering from occupational diseases.[38]

Little wonder, then, that the newly-formed union was confident that there would be an enthusiastic response to its strike call.

The union began its preparations for a general strike in the spring of 1912, quietly preparing for action and framing a set of demands. These included union recognition, the closed shop, a nine-hour day (the 54-hour week), paid holidays, the abolition of home work and subcontracting, and a union scale of wages. On June 14, 1912, union members were balloted on the strike issue; the final tabulation showed an overwhelming favorable majority—2,135 for a general strike and only 364 against. Two days later, the union sent its demands to the manufacturers. The answer of the employers was swift. On June 19, the two employers' associations—the Associated Fur Manufacturers and the Mutual Fur Protective Association (the latter composed of about three hundred employers)—rejected the union's demands. The fur manufacturers were resolved to oppose union recognition and the closed shop, and the MFPA determined "not to enter into any contract, agreement or secret understanding that shall or may conflict with the principle of the open shop."[39]

On June 20, the strike call was distributed in the fur market. As was the custom in all garment strikes of the period, the strike bulletin was printed in red, and was known as the *Red Special*. Calling on the fur workers to "Arise to Battle," the *Red Special* declared: "Victory is positive. . . . The general strike starts today (June 20th) at 10 a. m. No one shall remain at work. Leave your shops as one man."

Exactly at the appointed hour, seven thousand fur workers in forty shops responded to the union's call. On the second day, 8,500 workers were out from five hundred shops—three-quarters of them Jewish and two thousand of them women. By the end of the first week, the strike was general in fact as well as in name. Only members of the German

Furriers Union remained at work until the fifth week, at which time they, too, joined the strike. With nine thousand workers out, the trade was completely paralyzed.[40]

With the entire trade at a standstill, the union leaders expected a brief, triumphant struggle. They felt that the employers had learned from the militancy and endurance demonstrated so recently by garment workers in their strikes. But it soon became evident that the fur workers were in for a long and bitter battle. Some small employers settled with the union during the first three weeks of the strike. The two employers' associations, however, were determined to fight to the end, and they were convinced that they could win by starving out the workers. The manufacturers would simply close their shops for three weeks, and on July 8, the shops would open for all workers to return under the old conditions.

There was some justification for the employers' confidence. After the first three weeks of the strike, the union's financial resources were approaching the vanishing point, and many of the strikers were faced with starvation and eviction. But the women pickets marched around the buildings that housed the fur shops, carrying signs in Yiddish and English that read: "Masters! Starvation is your weapon. We are used to starving. We will fight on 'til victory!" Carrying these signs, they struggled on day after day, going around the buildings from morning until night, with barely enough food to keep them going.

As July 8 approached, the eyes of all New York were on the furriers, and the question was asked: Would their ranks break? Nine thousand strikers gave the answer that morning as they walked the picket lines of the fur district. Every shop remained empty. The strikers had won the first test. The *Jewish Daily Forward* paid tribute to them in a front-page editorial:

> We have had many mass strikes, but the strike of the fur workers is a rare, golden chapter in the history of the Jewish labor movement.... The bosses thought that the sudden opening of the shops would bring the workers back. ... But the workers remained firm and united.... The morning sun saw the wonderful result of the common effort—one of the most memorable and heroic struggles in history.[41]

Nine times during the next ten weeks, the employers repeated their announcement that the shops would reopen. Each time, the strikers kept the shops closed by their militant demonstrations. "Not since the great 'Triangle protest march,'" wrote the *New York Call* on July 17, "was there a more impressive demonstration seen than the one of 9,000 fur workers which took place yesterday noon."

As in all of the previous garment strikes, except the one in Milwaukee, the fur employers unleashed gangsters against the workers, and the police protected the strikebreakers by clubbing and arresting the pickets. More than 800 strikers were arrested, including 250 women; 54 workers, 40 of them women, received workhouse sentences; and 215, over 60 of whom were women, suffered serious injuries at the hands of the thugs.* Despite these obstacles, the furriers remained steadfast. However, the union was compelled to issue an appeal to all sympathetic groups for funds. Fortunately, the response was generous. In order to aid the strikers financially, an aid committee was elected by the United Hebrew Trades. Rose Blank of the Women's Trade Union League and its delegate to the UHT, was chosen chairperson of the committee.[42]

Over $20,000 was raised through the *Jewish Daily Forward*. The Cloakmakers' Union, itself the recipient of contributions from the fur workers during its great strike, contributed $20,000, and the capmakers, $1,500. Special strike issues of the *Forward* and the *New York Call*, tag day collections, house-to-house canvassing, picnics, and theater benefits netted additional funds. Lodges of fraternal organizations contributed $1,000. Other AFL unions raised another $1,000. But not one cent of the $60,000 raised and spent by the union in the course of the strike came from the national AFL. When Morris Shamroth, a member of the strike committee, went to the AFL Executive Council in Washington seeking financial assistance, Gompers sent him back with the message: "Tell the strikers to let the world know they are hungry and keep up the fight."[43]

The tag days were operated by the army of women strikers. Rose Blank wrote later:

> Nothing stopped them. They went to saloons, restaurants, stores, amusement places and at dinner time, to shops. They stood the reprimands of their relatives, and even occasional insults. The girls were not disheartened; they kept on with their work.[44]

Chairperson of the two thousand women strikers was Esther Polansky. Russian-born, she had changed her trade from dressmaker to fur finisher and was so militant in helping to organize the union that she was selected as a member of the strike arrangements committee and then to head the women strikers. As chairperson, she won additional fame by her own example,

> ... because she herself never stopped considering when it was necessary to take down a shop or go up to a place where scabs worked. She never stopped

---

*Annie Tikolsky, who already bore two scars from police beatings in Warsaw, where she had organized textile workers, was "severely beaten and arrested many times" during the fur strike. (*Life and Labor,* vol. II, Dec. 1912, p. 361.)

before any danger. This the workers appreciated so much that not only did she win their admiration but also their willingness to sacrifice if she ordered them to do so.[45]

Toward the end of August, when the strike had been on for the better part of two months, negotiations finally got under way between the union and employer representatives. On August 22, at a specially arranged meeting of the strikers, the terms of a proposed settlement were read and explained. The strikers were granted nearly all of their demands, including union recognition; only the closed shop and the demand for a half-day on Saturday throughout the year were omitted from the proposed agreement. The work week was to include a half-day on Saturday during the first eight months of the year, but a full day on Saturday for the remaining four months.

Socialist Meyer London, the strikers' legal adviser, was cheered when he urged them to stick to their demands. So, too, was Samuel Gompers. The strikers overlooked the callous advice he had given them when they appealed for financial assistance and demonstrated their approval of his statement: "Since you have rebelled, which is a sign that you no longer want to stand for it, stay out and keep up your fight until your employers yield to your demands." The strikers then affirmed by unanimous vote that they would not return to their jobs unless the employers granted them the half-holiday on Saturday all year 'round, instead of simply for the first eight months.

Two weeks later, in the thirteenth week of the strike, victory was won. The strike ended on September 8 when the manufacturers acceded to the strikers' demand for the Saturday half-holiday. "The Fighting Furriers," as the *New York Call* labelled the strikers, also obtained a 49-hour week; overtime work only during the busy season, at time-and-a-half; ten paid holidays; the banning of homework; wages to be paid weekly and in cash; a permanent Board of Arbitration and a Joint Board of Sanitary Control; a standing conference committee to settle all disputes, with five from each side and with an eleventh and deciding member to be named jointly by both sides—*and union recognition*. The agreement was to last for two years.

"The power of unity and solidarity triumphed over the power of money, the power of police attacks and hunger and want," declared the *Jewish Daily Forward* in hailing the victory. It was an historical agreement, the best thus far achieved in the revolt of the garment workers, and the first collective agreement in an industry in which there was not even a national union. For the AFL charter to the International Fur Workers of the United States and Canada was not issued until July 1, 1913.[46]

*   *   *   *

During the opening weeks of 1913, the New York garment workers in both the men's and women's branches were participating in tremendous labor uprisings. At one time, more than 150,000 workers in the trade were on strike—men's tailors, white goods workers, kimono and wrapper makers, and shirtwaist makers. "The local needle industries," exclaimed the New York *Call* in some astonishment on January 13, 1913, "have been practically paralyzed by one of the most gigantic and general uprisings which Greater New York has ever witnessed."[47]

On January 6, 1913, approximately seven thousand white goods workers—nearly one-half of the workers in the trade—went out on strike, demanding a 20 percent increase in wages; a flat 54-hour week; the abolition of child labor, of the fining system, and of subcontracting; and recognition of the union and a closed shop. Once on the picket lines, the strikers encountered the usual indiscriminate arrests, and the employers' thugs beat up the young pickets, many of whom were little girls in short dresses and with hair down their backs. When WTUL members who accompanied the strikers on picket duty issued public protests against the employers' thugs, the bosses adopted a new tactic. Into the battle came the gangsters' "molls." They filled their pocketbooks with stones, and when a skirmish began, they swung their loaded bags against the pickets' heads. They also carried concealed scissors and at an opportune moment, they would cut the strikers' long braided hair. In addition, they dogged the strikers' steps, keeping up a steady barrage of obscenities and urging them to join their ranks, with promises of easy money and good times.[48]

But the picket lines held fast, and as the fifteen-year-old girls walked the lines, they sang the "Song of the White Goods Workers" to buoy their spirits:

> At last all New York's White Goods toilers
>   Just stopped the life of Slavery,
> And went to join the "Golden Soil"
>   Of the Union's Bravery.
>
> Now we're all doing our duties,
>   The spell of slavery to break,
> And the Boss's wife shall pawn the rubies
>   To get herself a Union Cake.

We're getting beaten by policemen,
With their heavy clubs of hickory
But we'll fight as hard as we can
To win "Strong Union Victory."[49]

As in the great uprising of 1909–1910, prominent society women took up the strikers' cause—although not this time in association with the WTUL—marching on the picket lines, holding benefit functions, assisting in police court, posting bond, and generally focusing public attention on the strikers' plight and their bravery. These women developed an enormous admiration for the white goods workers' courage and determination. Other prominent figures, too, took up the strikers' cause. Theodore Roosevelt paid a whirlwind visit to the strike scene and announced his shock over the girls' working conditions and the treatment the "future mothers of America" had received during the strike. Fola La Follette, daughter of the Progressive Senator from Wisconsin, picketed with the striking girls, along with college students from Barnard and Wellesley. Victor Berger, the Socialist congressman from Milwaukee, called for a federal investigation into clothing industry conditions. And New York City Mayor William Gaynor warned employers against the use of strong-arm methods. After League members and their striking colleagues had brought twenty-five cases of false arrest before Police Commissioner William Baker, the latter changed a number of officers and reprimanded others for their treatment of the young strikers.[50]

The white goods workers ended their strike on February 18, six weeks after it had begun, with an agreement that was negotiated with the assistance of Rose Schneiderman and Viola Shore, in which the Cotton Manufacturers' Association agreed to specified improvements in working conditions: hours were reduced from 60 a week to 52; charges for power and materials were abolished; subcontracting was ended in the Association shops; there were pay increases for both week and piece workers, plus extra pay for overtime, and four legal holidays annually with pay. In addition, the contract established a wage floor: no worker was to work for less than $5.00 a week. While the manufacturers refused to agree to a closed shop, they did consent to negotiate with shop chairladies whenever a disagreement occurred. The girls had hoped for a closed shop, and at one point during the six-week strike, the workers had voted to continue the struggle until such an agreement could be reached. However, the Association members would only accept the preferential union shop, agreeing to give union members preference when hiring.

While many girls raised violent objections to the settlement, claiming that it should have at least included a Protocol agreement, the majority eventually voted to accept the contract at an emotion-filled mass meeting.[51]

The women of Wrapper, Kimono, and House Dress Workers' Union, Local 41 walked out on January 8, 1913, and a week later, the leaders of Dress and Waistmakers' Union, Local 25 issued a call for their second general strike. The waistmakers' walkout, involving 25,000 waist and dressmakers, ended three days later, on January 18, with the acceptance of a protocol for the industry that provided for new wage scales, a 50-hour week, improved sanitary conditions, union recognition, and the establishment of arbitration boards to deal with workers' grievances.[52] The strike of the Wrapper, Kimono, and House Dress Workers' Union lasted longer. Amid desperate personal sacrifices, the women strikers refused to accept any agreement that did not provide for union recognition. On February 13, 1913, however, the manufacturers' association, feeling the pressure of public support for the strikers, signed a "Protocol of Peace" with Local 41.[53]

By the middle of March, 1913, every branch of the ladies' garment industry in the most important center of that industry—New York City—had contractual relations with the ILGWU which were based more or less on the cloakmakers' Protocol of 1910, and similar agreements were being signed in Boston and other centers. By year's end, these trade agreements covered 90 percent of the International's membership.[54]

The greatest of all the struggles in the wave of organizational strikes in the garment trades which began with the shirtwaist strike in 1909, was the New York general strike of more than 100,000 workers in the men's clothing industry. (Supporting men's clothing workers' strikes broke out also in Rochester, Buffalo, and Philadelphia.) Unorganized largely because of the indifference of the United Garment Workers' leadership, these workers had seen their wages falling while the cost of living rose. Then suddenly, realizing that the workers had been inspired by the struggles of the waistmakers, cloakmakers, and furriers, and were ready to fight, and that they had to give at least token support to their determination to achieve better conditions, the UGW leaders indicated a willingness to go along. On November 15, 1912, after a series of organizational meetings, the New York District Council of the union issued a call for "a general strike of the entire clothing industry of Greater New York," and predicted that out of it "a mighty tailors' union will be built up."[55]

When the tailors voted 35,786 for and only 2,322 against the general strike, the official call was issued for the walkout to begin on December 30. By the end of the first week, it was conceded that more than 100,000 workers were on strike in the largest of all the struggles in the garment trades that had begun with the shirtwaist strike in 1909. Of the 100,000 strikers, fully one-third were women, the majority of whom were Jewish and Italian, with Poles, Russians, Lithuanians, Greeks, Germans, Czechs, and other nationalities making up the rest.

On January 6, 1913, the union announced the beginning of mass picketing, headed by a picketing committee of ten thousand strikers, to secure the following demands: a general 20 percent wage increase; a 48-hour week; union recognition; extra pay for overtime; electric power for machines; abolition of tenement house work; and improved sanitary conditions in the shops. The significance of the last demand is indicated by the fact that Frances Perkins, executive secretary of the Committee of Safety (and in 1933 selected to be the first woman Secretary of Labor), described the workshops and factories of the clothing industry as "fire and death traps. . . . The lessons of the Triangle fire have not been learned by the employers. . . ."[56]

The workers did not have sufficient funds to provide sustenance for themselves and their families during New York's bitter winter. They faced the savagery of strikebreakers, thugs, and police. Daily reports read: "Blood flowed freely, skulls were cracked, ribs were broken, eyes blackened, teeth knocked out and many persons were otherwise wounded in a brutal assault on the garment strikers and pickets, not by the hired thugs and gangsters, but by the Cossacks, who comprise a part of the New York City police force." As in the past strikes, the judiciary did what it could for the manufacturers, and when the strikers defied state Supreme Court injunctions outlawing peaceful picketing, hundreds of them were arrested.[57]

The strikers' militancy, combined with mounting support from the public and from the labor and Socialist movements, forced individual firms to settle. On January 21, the Clothing Contractors' Association, speaking for itself and for the United Merchants' and Manufacturers' Association, agreed to enter into a conference with the UGW for the purpose of devising a means of settling the strike. At this point, UGW President Thomas Rickert stepped into the situation, and, as he had previously done in Chicago, disregarded both the strike leadership and the workers and accepted an agreement to end the strike. The strike leaders, bitter over this sell-out, rejected the settlement. But when, on the last day of February, the three largest associations of clothing manufacturers submitted a proposal for settling the strike, Rickert again ignored both the strike committee and the strikers and promptly accepted the offer. Under this latest proposal, the workers were to return to their jobs immediately pending an impartial investigation into the issue of reducing hours; the tailors were to obtain a general wage increase of $1 per week, with a proportional raise for piece workers; sanitary conditions would be somewhat improved; sub-contracting would be abolished; and there was to be no discrimination in the reemployment of the strikers. Even though there was not a word about union recognition in any form, the UGW officially proclaimed the walkout at an end.[58]

With the struggle already weakened by injunctions, police brutality, and arrests, the strikers were set back further when the *Jewish Daily Forward* suddenly reversed itself, lined up with Rickert, and urged the strikers to accept the settlement and return to their jobs. Then on March 7, with Rickert officially declaring the strike at an end, and with Mayor Gaynor, acting with Rickert's express authorization, ordering the police to disperse all remaining pickets, the strike faltered. On March 11, 1913, it ended. While the persistence and militancy of the workers produced a better agreement than either of the ones accepted by Rickert—the work week was reduced to 53 hours up to January, 1914, and to 52 hours thereafter for all but cutters, who were to enjoy a 50-hour week to January, 1914 and not more than 48 hours thereafter, along with a small wage increase—it was the only one of the garment strikes in which the final settlement did not contain at least some form of union recognition.[59]

However, the strike did encourage a number of workers in the trade to organize, and the underhanded, strikebreaking tactics of the UGW officials were to have important repercussions. Three days after the strike was ended, Isaac A. Hourwich wrote in *The New Review,* a left-wing Socialist monthly: "The work of building up a permanent organization of the tailors must now begin. If they are to profit by the lesson of this strike, they must rid themselves of boss rule (by Rickert and his henchmen)—if need be, by cutting loose from the national organization."[60] As a matter of fact, the strike paved the way for the 1914 rupture in the UGW and the resulting formation of the Amalgamated Clothing Workers of America, bringing with it a brighter future for all workers in the men's clothing trade.

For several years, two factions within the UGW had vied for power. Lager and Rickert, the UGW's top leaders, were enthusiastic advocates of Samuel Gompers' "pure and simple unionism." They ran the union on business principles and carried this concept so far that they made a private business of selling the union label, even to firms that operated with non-union workers and ran their shops and factories as they pleased. Frowning upon strikes and depending on the union label for their bargaining strength, the UGW leaders placed their main reliance on workers who lived in small communities and worked in large factories manufacturing overalls. A large section of their supporters were native American women, and Margaret Daly was the link between the conservative union leadership and these women, visiting each local annually to negotiate a new label contract.

The other faction of the UGW was made up of tailors and operators who worked in the large urban shops. A great majority of these workers were of immigrant origin, most frequently Yiddish-speaking Eastern Europeans. The U. S. born women in the small communities felt they had little in common with these workers in the urban centers, and the UGW leadership took advantage of this alienation by directing repeated sneering remarks at the non-English speaking tailors in the big cities. They even encouraged the women in several UGW urban locals to complain to the WTUL about the "fact that the Yiddish-speaking men were practically crowding out the women, who did not understand Yiddish." UGW officers made few attempts to organize the other urban centers, and when the tailors in the big cities struck, the leaders refused to acknowledge their strikes as legitimate. Then, when the workers refused to abandon the struggle, the UGW leaders invariably sabotaged the strike by arranging secret settlements.

The tailors in the UGW called for a new unionism that combined industrial unionism, class consciousness, and Socialism. While they wanted to change the entire structure of society, they also understood the need for waging the struggle for such immediate demands as higher wages, shorter hours, and better working conditions. They bitterly resented the corrupt class-collaborationist policies of the national and local officials, and were enraged by the irresponsible use of the label by these officials and by their intimate relationship with the manufacturers. Above all, they resented the fact that a minority of the membership—the overall makers—were being used by the autocratic leaders as a means of maintaining their domination of the union.[61]

In 1914, thirteen New York locals in the coat-making trade formed the United Brotherhood of Tailors. The New York tailors and related workers in Chicago, Baltimore, and Rochester now represented a clear majority of the total UGW membership, sufficient to control the approaching biennial convention and wrest the leadership from the conservative leaders. But Rickert and Lager were determined to remain in power regardless of the will of the majority of the membership. They therefore scheduled the convention to be held in Nashville, a site far removed from any of the large urban centers and a city administered by officials sympathetic to the UGW leaders. A few weeks before the convention, the union's auditor announced that a number of locals in New York and Chicago had fallen into financial arrears and were therefore ineligible to send delegates to the convention.[62]

However, the New York tailors had a full delegation of 107 of the 350 delegates present when the convention opened and distributed a leaflet appealing for their right to be seated. It concluded with a firm plea for unity: "Let us unite in order to fight our common enemy, *capitalism*, instead of picking suicidal quarrels among ourselves."[63] Rickert, however, brushed aside this and other attempts to compromise the differences between the two groups. He surreptitiously circulated a rumor that the Jews from New York were planning to subvert the union and turn it into an instrument of the Jewish people. Not a single delegate from New York received credentials.[64]

The excluded delegates moved to the balcony to witness the proceedings while others on the floor challenged the conservative leaders. Two women led the battle on both sides. Bessie Abramowitz, an authorized delegate from Chicago, worked tirelessly whipping up support for the excluded delegates. She shared the platform with fellow Chicagoans Frank Rosenblum and A. D. Marempietri as they addressed the convention and fought for the reinstatement of the 107 suspended delegates. Margaret Daly, a member of the union's Executive Board, lobbied for the conservative leadership. She spoke to the women delegates and sought to dispel any sympathy they might have for the suspended delegates, telling them that they were anarchists and Jews who were determined to disrupt the union. At a special meeting of women delegates which she called, Daly pictured the dissidents in the union as dangerous to the United States as well as to the UGW, and instructed the women to vote against the New Yorkers in the interests of their nation, their families, and their union.[65]

The convention finally split apart when the tailors from New York, Chicago, Baltimore, and Rochester—authorized and unauthorized delegates alike—left the convention hall and regrouped at their hotel. In the meetings that followed the rupture, the bolters declared themselves the properly convened union's legislative body, and elected new international officers. Bessie Abramowitz proposed Sidney Hillman, then serving in New York as clerk for the Cloak and Suit Protocol, as president. Once the convention designated Hillman, Abramowitz pleaded with him to leave his New York job and accept the presidency. She wired him: "Understand that personal pledges must cease when sister organization at stake. To become a martyr, I urge you to accept the office." Hillman eventually did accept.[66]

At the AFL convention in November, 1914, delegates appeared from both factions of the United Garment Workers, each claiming to represent the union. The fact that the anti-Rickert forces represented the great majority of the men's clothing workers was ignored by the AFL's Credentials Committee, which seated Rickert and his followers on the ground that they were the regularly and officially elected delegates of the union. Gompers promptly sent a circular to all locals of the United Garment Workers informing them that Rickert was the only president of the union, and that the organization he headed was the sole bona fide union of men's clothing workers affiliated with the AFL.[67] Ellen Gates Starr commented angrily:

> The hand which should have been the strongest and readiest to aid those brave and oppressed people who had rejected the existing leadership of the United Garment Workers was the one which shut off from them the most powerful sources of aid. . . . And why? Because a spirited body of people, unable to rid themselves, otherwise, of corrupt officials, had dared to secede in overwhelming majority and form a new and clean organization under honest and able leadership.[68]

The "new and clean" organization was formed at a special convention held by the insurgents in New York from December 26–28, 1914. Having lost in court the right to use the old union's name, the insurgents called themselves the "Amalgamated Clothing Workers of America," with Sidney Hillman of Chicago as president and Joseph Schlossberg of New York as general secretary. The union then represented forty thousand workers in the United States and Canada.[69]

The ideology of the new industrial union—a union born in militant struggle against the clothing employers and the bureaucrats of the UGW—was set forth clearly in the preamble to its constitution, which took note of the fact that there was "a constant and unceasing struggle" between those who owned the means of production and the class which had "nothing but its labor power." The union was characterized as "a natural weapon of offense and defense in the hands of the working class." Craft unions were called outdated, and only industrial unionism was considered able to meet the needs of the workers in the twentieth century. The preamble called for the eventual organization of the working class both economically and politically, and looked forward to the time when working class organization would "put the organized working class in actual control of the system of production and the working class will then be ready to take possession of it."[70]

REFERENCE NOTES

CHAPTER 1

1. Louis Adamic, *Dynamite: The Story of Class Violence in America,* New York, 1931, pp. 187-243; Grace Hilman Stimson, *Rise of the Labor Movement in Los Angeles,* Berkeley, Calif., 1955, pp. 366-419; Graham Adams, Jr., *Age of Industrial Violence, 1910-1915,* New York, 1966, pp. 1-24.

2 A glaring example of a history of American labor that ignores the McNamara case is Foster Rhea Dulles, *Labor in America,* New York, 1966. Brief discussions of the case are found in Selig Perlman and Philip Taft, *History of Labor in the United States,* vol. IV, New York, 1935, pp. 318-25; Philip Taft, *The AFL in the Time of Gompers,* New York, 1955, pp. 275-87; and Bernard Mandel, *Samuel Gompers,* Yellow Springs, Ohio, 1963, pp. 309-18.

3. See Philip S. Foner, *History of the Labor Movement in the United States,* Vol. III, New York, 1964, pp. 102-20; *Proceedings,* AFL Convention, 1912, pp. 292-93.

4. Luke Grant, *The National Erectors' Association and the International Association of Bridge and Structural Iron Workers,* Washington, D. C., 1915, pp. 159-66.

5. "Federal Industrial Commission Urged," *The Survey,* 27, Dec. 30, 1911: 1410.

6. Grant, *op. cit.,* p. 123.

7. *Proceedings,* AFL Convention, 1907, pp. 321-22; Stuart Reid, "The 'Open Shop' City of Refuge," *American Federationist,* 17, Oct. 1910: 896.

8. Frederick Palmer, "Otistown of the Open Shop," *Hampton's Magazine,* 25, Jan. 1911: 29.

9. Stimson, *op. cit.,* pp. 229-34; Ira B. Cross, *History of Labor in California,* Berkeley, Calif., 1935, p. 282.

10. Los Angeles *Times,* June 2, 28, 30, 1910.

11. *Ibid.,* July 17, 1910.

12. Stimson, *op. cit.,* pp. 345-46.

13. James Wilson to A. J. Berres, Secretary, Metal Trades Department, Los Angeles, Sept. 23, 1910, *American Federation of Labor Correspondence,* AFL-CIO Building, Washington. Hereinafter cited as *AFL Corr.*

14. Los Angeles *Times,* Oct. 3, 1910, and reprinted in Adamic, *op. cit.,* p. 210.

15. Stimson, *op. cit.,* pp. 372-73, 376.

16. George Gunrey to Frank Morrison, Los Angeles, Jan. 5, 1911, *AFL Corr.*

17. William J. Burns, *The Masked War,* New York, c.1913, pp. 46-49; "How Burns Caught the Dynamiters," *McClure's Magazine,* 38, Jan., 1912: 326.

18. Burns, *op. cit.,* pp. 137-41; "How Burns Caught the Dynamiters," p. 321; Ortie E. McManigal, *The National Dynamite Plot,* Los Angeles, 1913, pp. 87-88.

19. Burns, *op. cit.,* pp. 135, 319.

20. *Ibid.,* pp. 143, 153-55; McManigal, *op. cit.,* pp. 12-25, 34, 38.

21. Burns, *op. cit.,* pp. 148-210; McManigal, *op. cit.,* pp. 75-78.

22. Los Angeles *Times,* April 23, 1911.

23. Frank E. Wolfe, *Capitalism's Conspiracy in California: Parallel of the Kidnapping of Labor Leaders—Colorado—California,* Los Angeles, 1911.

24. *American Federationist,* Jan. 1912, pp. 21, 47; Samuel Gompers, *The McNamara Case,* Washington, D. C., 1911.

25. Samuel Gompers, *Seventy Years of Life and Labor*, New York, 1925, vol. II, p. 187.
26. *Literary Digest*, May 6, 1911, p. 868; The Conference of Executive Officers of the International Trade Unions with Headquarters in Indianapolis, *A Statement as to McNamara's Arrest*, dated Indianapolis, May 10, 1911, p. 3.
27. *American Federationist* 18, December, 1910: 32.
28. Philip Taft, *The AFL in the Time of Gompers*, p. 275.
29. George Gunrey to Frank Morrison, Los Angeles, February 10, 1911, *AFL Corr.*
30. Geo. Gunrey to Frank Morrison, Los Angeles, March 22, 1911, *ibid.*
31. Gompers to John Mitchell, Jan. 5, 1911, *ibid.;* Rowland Hill Harvey, *Samuel Gompers, Champion of the Toiling Masses*, Stanford, 1935, p. 125.
32. Reprinted in "Dynamite in Los Angeles (1910)," *Western Socialist*, No. 6—1966, p. 15.
33. Reprinted in *Literary Digest*, May 6, 1911, p. 868.
34. Ira Kipnis, *The American Socialist Movement, 1897-1912*, New York, 1952, p. 352; Socialist Party pamphlet, *Workers Rally to the Defense*, 1911.
35. *Industrial Worker*, July 20, 1911.
36. *Ibid.*, July 29, Oct. 5, 1911; *Solidarity*, May 6, 1911.
37. *The Public*, June 23, 1911, p. 583; Chicago *Daily Socialist*, June 19, 1911.
38. Clarence Darrow, *The Story of My Life*, New York, 1932, pp. 173–75; Charles Yale Harrison, *Clarence Darrow*, New York, 1931, p. 153; Harvey J. O'Higgins, "The Dynamiters: A Great Case of Detective William Burns," *McClure's Magazine* 37, August, 1911: 363; Taft, *op. cit.*, p. 28.
39. Taft, *op cit.*, p. 28.
40. *American Federationist* 18, June, 1911: 451–52; Samuel Gompers, "The McNamara Case," *ibid.*, pp. 438–39.
41. Copy of Appeal in *AFL Corr.*
42. Stimson, *op. cit.*, p. 394.
43. *New York Call*, Sept. 25, 1911.
44. Copy of script in *AFL Corr.*
45. *Los Angeles Times,* June 8, 1911; Burns, *op. cit.*, pp. 304–08; *Appeal to Reason*, July 1, 1911; Adamic, *op. cit.*, p. 233.
46. *New York Call*, Sept. 12, 1911; Burns, *op. cit.*, pp. 256–57.
47. William Dinger, Jr., Secretary, McNamara Defense Conference of Brooklyn, to Fellow Workers, *AFL Corr.*
48. *New Orleans Times-Democrat*, Oct. 5, 1911.

49. Gompers, *Seventy Years of Life and Labor*, vol. II, p. 187; *American Federationist* 19 March, 1912: 204; Mandel, *op. cit.*, p. 312; Philadelphia *Press*, Oct. 11, 1911.
50. Darrow, *op. cit.*, pp. 179–85.
51. *Proceedings*, AFL Convention, 1911, pp. 123-25, 138-40.
52. *New York Times*, Dec. 2, 1911; Burns, *op. cit.*, pp. 261–68; Irving Stone, *Clarence Darrow for the Defense: A Biography*, New York, 1941, pp. 273–74.
53. Lincoln Steffens, *The Autobiography of Lincoln Steffens*, New York, 1931, pp. 658–64; Harrison, *op. cit.*, pp. 159–60; Darrow, *op. cit.*, p. 179.
54. Steffens, *op. cit.*, pp. 670–71.
55. *Ibid.*, pp. 672–75; *New York Times*, Dec. 4, 1911.
56. Stimson, *op. cit.*, p. 403.
57. Steffens, *op. cit.*, p. 676; Harrison, *op. cit.*, pp. 163–66; Darrow, *op. cit.*, pp. 181–83.
58. Darrow, *op. cit.*, pp. 181–83; Steffens, *op. cit.*, p. 680.
59. Lincoln Steffens in Chicago *Daily News*, Dec. 2, 1911.
60. Steffens, *op. cit.*, pp. 684–88.
61. *Los Angeles Times*, Dec. 2, 1911.
62. *Ibid.*, Dec. 6, 1911; *The Public*, Dec. 8, 1911, p. 1242; Steffens, *op. cit.*, pp. 688–89.
63. *Los Angeles Times*, Dec. 6, 7, 1911.
64. Gompers, *Seventy Years of Life and Labor*, vol. II, pp. 192–93.
65. The entire statement appears in *The Public*, Dec. 15, 1911, pp. 1264–66.
66. *Literary Digest*, Dec. 16, 1911, p. 1135.
67. *Ibid.*, p. 1136; Chicago *Daily Socialist*, Dec. 9, 1911; *New York Call*, Dec. 7, 1911.
68. "Report of the McNamara Defense Fund of New York City, To the Trade and Labor Organizations and Branches of the Socialist Party of the City of New York," Tamiment Institute, New York University Library.
69. *Literary Digest*, Jan. 16, 1912, pp. 3-4.
70. Eugene V. Debs, "The McNamara Case and the Labor Movement," *International Socialist Review* 12, January, 1912: 397–400; McAlister Coleman, *Eugene V. Debs*, New York, 1930, p. 252n.
71. Richard Cole Searing, "The McNamara Case: Its Causes and Results," unpublished M.A. thesis, University of California, Berkeley, 1952, p. 14.
72. Herbert Shapiro, "The McNamara Case: A Crisis of the Progressive Era, *Southern California Quarterly* 61, Fall, 1977: 272–73.
73. George H. Shoaf, "Clarence Darrow and the McNamara Case," *American Socialist*, December, 1957, pp. 18–19. *See also* Robert Munson Baker, "Why the McNamaras Pleaded Guilty," unpublished M.A. thesis,

University of California, Berkeley, 1950, pp. 11–12.
74. San Francisco *Bulletin*, Dec. 2, 6, 27, 1911.
75. Steffens, *op. cit.*, p. 689.
76. *Industrial Worker*, Jan. 9, 1913.
77. *Solidarity*, Sept. 11, 1915.
78. *Plea of Clarence Darrow in His Own Defense to the Jury at Los Agneles, August, 1912*, Los Angeles & San Francisco, 1912.
79. Ella Winter and Granville Hicks, editors, *The Letters of Lincoln Steffens* (New York, 1938), vol. I, p. 282.
80. Lincoln Steffens, "An Experiment in Good Will," *The Survey*, Dec. 31, 1911, p. 1436
81. *The Survey*, Dec. 30, 1911, pp. 1430–31.
82. *Ibid.*, pp. 1414, 1420, 1425.
83. Adams, *Age of Industrial Violence*, p. 32.

CHAPTER 2

1. Introduction to *The Shame of the Cities*, New York, 1904, p. 5.
2. David Mark Chalmers, "The Social and Political Philosophy of the Muckrakers," unpublished Ph.D. thesis, University of Rochester, 1955, p. 18. *See also* C. C. Regier, *The Era of the Muckrakers*, Chapel Hill, N. C., 1932; Herbert Shapiro, "Muckraking in America," *The Forum*.
3. Leroy Henry Schramm, "Organized Labor and the Muckrakers, 1900–1912," unpublished Ph.D. thesis, Cornell University, 1972, pp. 46–47, 68, 96; Louis Filler, *Crusaders for American Liberalism*, New York, 1961, p. 99.
4. *International Woodworker*, May 6, 1906, p. 134; Schramm, *op. cit.*, pp. 171–72.
5. *The Arena*, vol. XXXIV, July, 1905, p. 92; *The Weekly Bulletin of the Clothing Trades*, Dec. 9, 1903; William E. Sackett, *Modern Battles of Trenton*, Trenton, N. J., 1914, vol. I, pp. 17–18.
6. Harry F. Gosnell, *Boss Platt and His New York Machine*, New York, 1924, pp. 88–89.
7. Alfred Henry Lewis, *Richard Croker*, New York, 1901, pp. 120–122; Alfred Henry Lewis, *The Boss and How He Came to Rule New York*, New York, 1903, pp. 35–36.
8. Richard Hofstadter, *The Age of Reform: From Bryan to FDR*, New York, 1955, chapters 4–5.
9. Gabriel Kolko, *The Triumph of Conservatism: A Reinterpretation of American History, 1900–1916*, New York, 1963, pp. 2, 285–86, 305.
10. James Weinstein, *The Corporate Ideal in the Liberal State: 1900–1918*, Boston, 1976.
11. Peter G. Filene, "An Obituary for the Progressive Movement," *American Quarterly*, vol. XX, 1970, pp. 20–34.

12. J. Joseph Hutmacher, "Urban Liberalism and the Age of Reform," *Mississippi Valley Historical Review*, vol. XLIX, September, 1962, pp. 231–41.
13. Irwin Yellowitz, *Labor and the Progressive Movement in New York State, 1897–1916*, Ithaca, N. Y., 1965, pp. 2–6, 128–44, 158–59.
14. New York *Voice*, Aug. 11, 1894.
15. James William Sullivan, *Direct Legislation by the Citizenry Through the Initiative and Referendum*, New York, 1893, pp. 103–07.
16. *American Federationist*, vol. I, pp. 9, 96, 173; vol. II, pp. 4, 47, 118, 202, 208, 277; J. W. Sullivan to Gompers, Aug. 24, 1898, *AFL Corr.*; Correspondence relating to conventions of Direct Legislation Leagues of New Jersey, Illinois, Missouri, and the National Direct Legislation League, 1894–1901, *AFL Corr.*; *Direct Legislation Record*, vol. I, May, 1894, p. 3.
17. *Direct Legislation Record*, vol. VIII, December, 1901, pp. 61–62; September, 1903, p. 59.
18. Stimson, *op. cit.*, p. 128; Albert H. Clodius, "The Quest for Good Government in Los Angeles, 1890–1910," unpublished Ph.D. thesis, Claremont College, 1953, pp. 32–33.
19. *Proceedings*, AFL Convention, 1901, p. 122.
20. *Ibid.*, 1902, pp. 225–26.
21. *Ibid.*, 1903, p. 32; *American Federationist*, January, 1904, p. 13; *Direct Legislation Record*, vol. VIII, June, 1902, pp. 29–31; December, 1903, pp. 79–80.
22. *Proceedings*, AFL Convention, 1903, p. 32; Geo. Bullock, Secretary, Executive Committee, Direct Legislation League of Missouri, to Gompers, March 3, 1899, *AFL Corr.*; *Direct Legislation Record*, vol. VIII, 1901, pp. 63–64; June, 1902, pp. 29–31; June, 1903, pp. 29–30.
23. "Proposing the Adoption of the Initiative and Referendum," 1904, *AFL Corr.*
24. *American Federationist*, July, 1904, p. 22.
25. *Proceedings*, AFL Convention, 1905, p. 78; Lancaster (Pa.) *Labor Leader*, April 8, 1905.
26. *Direct Legislation Record*, vol. I, May, 1894, p. 3.
27. Stimson, *op. cit.*, pp. 281–82; Los Angeles *Express*, Jan. 26, 1903; *Direct Legislation Record*, vol. X, March, 1903, p. 7; Clodius, *op. cit.*, pp. 32–33.
28. Stimson, *op. cit.*, p. 281; Los Angeles *Times*, April 24, 26, May 30, June 3, 6, 1904.
29. Janice Jacques, "The Political Reform Movement in Los Angeles, 1900–1909," unpublished M.A. thesis, Claremont College, 1948, pp. 32–36.
30. Stimson, *op. cit.*, pp. 285–86.

31. O. W. Johnson to Gompers, Phoenix, Arizona, July 21, 1910, *AFL Corr.*
32. "Labor's Declaration of Independence: Labor Party of Arizona," pamphlet, Phoenix, Arizona, 1910, copy in *AFL Corr.*
33. *Ibid.*
34. Arizona Republican, Aug. 14, 1910.
35. Leaflet issued by Executive Committee, Labor Party, copy in *AFL Corr.*
36. Arizona *Republican,* Aug. 25, 26, Sept. 6, 13, 1910.
37. *Ibid.,* Oct. 20, 1910.
38. *Minutes of the Constitutional Convention of the Territory of Arizona, October, 1910,* Phoenix, Arizona, 1910, pp. 45, 48, 60, 63, 107, 142, 155, 156, 157, 242, 273, 288, 341, 342; Arizona *Republican,* Oct. 30, Nov. 4, 5, 6, 1910.
39. *New York Times,* Aug. 12, 1911.
40. Paul G. Hubbard, "A Toledo Trade Union and the Arizona Constitution of 1910," *Ohio Historical Quarterly,* vol. XXIII, April, 1910, pp. 114–26.
41. *Ibid.*
42. *Ibid.*
43. Toledo *Union Leader,* Aug. 25, 1911; Hubbard, *op. cit.,* p. 126.
44. Oklahoma Department of Labor, First Annual Report, 1908, Oklahoma City, 1908, pp. 11–21.
45. Keith L. Bryant, "Labor in Politics: The Oklahoma State Federation of Labor During the Age of Reform," *Labor History,* vol. XI, Summer, 1970, pp. 261–63.
46. Keith L. Bryant, "Kate Barnard, Organized Labor and Social Justice in Oklahoma During the Progressive Era," *Journal of Southern History,* vol. XXXV, February, 1969, pp. 146–49.
47. Bryant, "Labor in Politics," pp. 257, 265–67; Bryant, "Kate Barnard," pp. 149–50; Frederick L. Ryan, *A History of Labor Legislation in Oklahoma,* Norman, Oklahoma, 1932, pp. 24–28.
48. Jersey City *Journal,* April 24, 1907.

CHAPTER 3

1. Foner, *op. cit.,* vol. I, pp. 122–23.
2. *Direct Legislation Record,* vol. VIII, June, 1902, p. 29.
3. Ella Winter and Granville Hicks, editors, *The Letters of Lincoln Steffens,* New York, 1938, vol. I, pp. 197–207; Philadelphia *Press,* Nov. 29, 1905; New York *Tribune,* Feb. 19, 1910; New York *Call,* Jan. 1, 1909; *The Public,* Jan. 12, 1907.
4. Gustavus Myers, *The History of Great American Fortunes,* New York, 1910, vol. I, pp. 236–37.

5. Philadelphia *North American,* Aug. 15, 1912.
6. Frederick Shaw, *The History of the New York City Legislature,* New York, 1954, p. 101. *See also University Settlement Studies,* vol. II, July, 1906, pp. 36–37 and John Collier and Edmund M. Barrows, *The City Where Crime is Play,* New York, 1914, pp. 2–3.
7. John D. Buenker, *Urban Liberalism and Progressive Reform,* New York, 1973; Amos Pinchot, *A Letter to the County Chairmen and Other Chairmen,* n.p., n.d., p. 15.
8. Jon M. Kingsdale, "The 'Poor Man's Club,': Social Functions of the Urban Working Class Saloon," *American Quarterly,* vol. XXV, October, 1973, p. 482; *Literary Digest,* Dec. 18, 1909.
9. James H. Timberlake, *Prohibition and the Progressive Movement, 1900–1920,* Cambridge, Mass., 1963, pp. 89–94; Allan Nevins, editor, *Letters and Journals of Brand Whitlock,* New York, 1936, vol. I, pp. 98–99.
10. Philadelphia *Press,* Aug. 10, 1902.
11. *The Letters of Lincoln Steffens, op. cit.,* vol. I, p. 207.
12. Philadelphia *Press,* Feb. 13, 1902; Chicago *Chronicle,* April 9, 1906.
13. Philadelphia *Press,* Feb. 13, 1902.
14. Samuel Prince to Gompers, Aug. 27, 1908; D. J. Conroy to Gompers, Oct. 24, 1908; Elias Kaufman to Gompers, Dec. 3, 1909; John N. Bogart to Gompers, Oct. 26, 1909; Joseph Dehan to Gompers, Dec. 30, 1902, *AFL Corr.;* New York *Call,* Jan. 13, 1910.
15. Disbrow, *op. cit.,* pp. 293–312.
16. *American Federationist,* October, 1895, p. 189.
17. Lincoln Steffens, *Up-Builders,* New York, 1909, pp. 3–46; Ranson E. Noble, Jr., "Early Years of the Progressive Movement in New Jersey," unpublished Ph.D. thesis, Princeton University, 1937, pp. 12–30; Ranson E. Noble, Jr., *New Jersey Progressivism before Wilson,* Princeton, N.J., 1946, pp. 12–14, 65–92.
18. James H. Rodabaugh, "The Reform Movement in Ohio at the Turn of the Century," *Ohio Archeological and Historical Quarterly,* vol. LIV, 1945, pp. 46–55.
19. James H. Rodabaugh, "Samuel M. Jones—Evangel of Equality," *The Historical Society of Northwestern Ohio, Quarterly Bulletin.* vol. XV, January, 1943, pp. 24–25, 44; Russel B. Nye, *Midwestern Progressive Politics: A Historical Study of its Origins and Development,* East Lansing, Michigan, 1959, pp. 173–78.

20. J. F. Mulholland, Pres. International Union of Bicycle Workers and Allied Mechanics, to Gompers, March 15th, '99, *AFL Corr.*
21. Toledo *Blade*, April 22, 1899.
22. Columbus *Dispatch*, May 15, 1899; James A. Cannon to Gompers, Columbus, May 15, 1899, *AFL Corr.; Direct Legislation Record*, vol. VI, September, 1899, pp. 70-71.
23. Printed petition in *AFL Corr.;* Samuel M. Jones "To the People of Ohio," July 29, 1899, printed circular, *ibid.*
24. J.F. Mulholland to Gompers, 8/5/'99, *AFL Corr.*
25. Samuel M. Jones to Gompers, Sept. 25, 1899, *AFL Corr.;* undated newspaper clippings, Toledo, Ohio, in *ibid.*
26. Chicago *Record*, Nov. 2, 1899.
27. *Ibid.*
28. Toledo *Blade*, April 25–May 14, 1901.
29. Ernest Crosby, *Golden Rule Jones, Mayor of Toledo*, New York, 1906; Rodabaugh, "Samuel M. Jones—Evangel of Equality," *op. cit.*, pp. 50-55.
30. *Letters and Journals of Brand Whitlock, op. cit.*, vol I, p. 12.
31. *Ibid.*, p. 38.
32. Brand Whitlock, *Forty Years of It*, New York, 1934, pp. 303-07; Donald G. Bahna, "The Pope-Toledo Strike of 1907," *Northwest Ohio Quarterly*, Summer, 1963, p. 118.
33. *Letters and Journals of Brand Whitlock, op. cit.*, vol. I, p. 87.
34. *Ibid.*, p. 121.
35. Cleveland *Plain-Dealer*, Feb. 6-7, 1901.
36. *Ibid.*, March 19, 1901.
37. *Ibid.*, March 26, 1901.
38. *Ibid.*, March 14, 1901.
39. Eugene C. Murdock, "Cleveland's Johnson: First Term," *Ohio Historical Quarterly*, vol. LXVIII, January, 1958, pp. 35-39.
40. *Journal of the Knights of Labor*, April, 1901, p. 4.
41. Cleveland *Plain-Dealer*, April 2, 4, 1903; Robert L. Briggs, "The Progressive Era in Cleveland, Ohio: Tom L. Johnson's Administration, 1901-1909," Unpublished Ph.D. thesis, University of Chicago, 1961, p. 139.
42. Cleveland *Plain-Dealer*, April 5, 10, 1903.
43. *Electrical Worker*, September, 1903, p. 53; Eugene C. Murdock, "Life of Tom Johnson," unpublished Ph.D. thesis, Columbia University, 1951, pp. 250-61.
44. Cleveland *Plain-Dealer*, Sept. 30, Oct. 3, 1903; Cleveland *Citizen*, April 6, 1901, Sept. 7, 1903.
45. Quoted in Murdock, "Life of Tom Johnson," p. 383.
46. Cleveland *Plain-Dealer*, May 2, 1908.
47. *Ibid.*, May 1, 1908.

48. *Ibid.*, April 29–May 2, 1908.
49. *Ibid.*, May 2, 3, 1908.
50. *Ibid.*, May 2, 1908.
51. *Ibid.*, May 16, 1908.
52. *Ibid.*, May 21, 1908.
53. *Ibid.*, May 17-30, 1908.
54. Tom Johnson, *My Story*, edited by Elizabeth J. Hauser, New York, 1911, pp. 280-82; *The Public*, June 12, 1908.
55. *The Motorman and Conductor*, January, 1909, pp. 35-36.
56. Cleveland *Plain-Dealer*, Oct. 12, 1909.
57. *Ibid.*, Oct. 14, 1909.
58. *Ibid.*, April 11, 12, 1911; Murdock, "Life of Tom Johnson," *op. cit.*, p. 448.
59. Cleveland *Plain-Dealer*, April 11, 1911. See also Eugene C. Murdock, "Cleveland's Johnson," *Ohio State Archeological and Historical Quarterly*, vol. LXII, October, 1953, p. 324.
60. *The Public*, May 5, 1906; Chicago *Chronicle*, April 9, 1906.
61. *The Public*, May 5, 1906. See also Wayne Urban, "Organized Teachers and Educational Reform During the Progressive Era: 1890-1920," *History of Education Quarterly*, Spring, 1976, pp. 41-42.
62. Ray Ginger, *Altgeld's America, 1892-1905*, pp. 262-74.
63. Chicago *American*, Sept. 22, 1903; *Direct Legislation Record*, December, 1903, pp. 68-69.
64. Ginger, *op. cit.*, p. 281.
65. Chicago *American*, Nov. 13-25, 1903; Ginger, *op. cit.*, pp. 275-76.
66. *Chicago's Vote for Municipal Ownership by an Impartial Observer*, pamphlet, New York Public Library.
67. *The Public*, May 26, 1906; Nick Alexander Komons, "The Reform Movement in Chicago, 1895-1910," unpublished Ph.D. thesis, University of Chicago, 1958, p. 340.
68. *Ibid.*, March 2, 1907.
69. Chicago *Daily Socialist*, Oct. 30, 1906.
70. *The Public*, March 9, April 7, 1906, March 16, 1907, March 12, 1908.
71. Philadelphia *Press*, Nov. 22, 1906. See also *ibid.*, Dec. 19, 1906.
72. New York *Journal*, May 2, 1896.
73. New York *American*, Dec. 21, 1904.
74. *Ibid.*, March 9, 16, 1905.
75. *Ibid.*, Dec. 19, 25, 1904.
76. *Ibid.*, Dec. 5, 15, 1904; Jan. 4, Feb. 3, March 6, 15, 1905.
77. *The Public*, Oct. 6, 1906.
78. Ferdinand Lundberg, *Imperial Hearst: A Social Biography*, pp. 103-04; James Allen Myatt, "William Randolph Hearst and the Progressive Era, 1900-1912," unpublished Ph.D. thesis, University of Florida, 1960, pp. 35-37.

79. W.A. Swanberg, *Citizen Hearst: A Biography of William Randolph Hearst*, New York, 1961, pp. 237–38.
80. Yellowitz, *op. cit.*, p. 201.
81. *The Public*, Sept. 29, 1906.
82. *New York Times*, June 25, July 16, Aug. 10, 1906.
83. *Ibid.*, Oct. 8, 14–15, 22, 1906; Melvyn Dubofsky, *When Workers Organize: New York in the Progressive Era*, Amherst, Massachusetts, 1968, *op. cit.*, pp. 339–40; Yellowitz, *op. cit.*, pp. 204–09.
84. August Belmont to Theodore Roosevelt, Sept. 20th, 1906, marked "Personal & Confidential," Theodore Roosevelt Papers, Library of Congress.
85. Theodore Roosevelt to Charles Evans Hughes, October 2, 1906, *ibid.*
86. *The Outlook*, November 10, 1906, pp. 21–22.
87. Eleanor M. Piller, "The Hearst-Hughes Gubernatorial Campaign of 1906," unpublished M.A. thesis, Columbia University, 1937, pp. 52, 64–68.
88. Charles Franklin Marsh, *Trade Unionism in the Electric Light and Power Industry*, Urbana, Illinois, 1928, p. 165; Buffalo *Courier*, June 11, 1900; *The Public*, Sept. 20, 1905, pp. 406–07; Detroit *Free Press*, April 29, 1913.
89. Stimson, *op. cit.*, pp. 306–07; Clodius, *op. cit.*, pp. 122–23, 250.
90. Marsh, *op. cit.*, pp. 165–66n.
91. Elizabeth (New Jersey) *Times*, April 21, 1906.
92. *New York Times*, July 25, 1906.
93. *Ibid.; The Public*, July 28, 1906; Gompers to A.F. of L. Executive Council, Dec, 21, 1906, *AFL Corr.*
94. *The Public*, April 14, 1906.
95. *Leather Workers' Journal*, vol. IX, October, 1906, p. 114.
96. Faulkner, *op. cit.*, pp. 85–88.
97. *Ibid.*, pp. 120–32.
98. Dewey W. Grantham, Jr., "The Progressive Movement and the Negro," *South Atlantic Quarterly*, vol. XLIV, October, 1955, pp. 461–77.
99. Alexander Saxton, "San Francisco Labor and the Populist and Progressive Insurgencies," *Pacific Historical Review*, vol. XXXIV, November, 1965, pp. 435–36; "Mayor Harper, The Recall and the Record," Los Angeles *Record*, Jan. 30, 1909.
100. Franklin Hichborn, *Story of the California Legislature of 1911*, San Francisco, 1911.
101. For conflicting interpretations of how much labor gained in California during the Johnson Administration, *see* George E. Mowry, *The California Progressives*, Berkeley, Cal.,

1951, pp. 45, 91, 92–93, 102, 103, 215, 295; Joseph Feldhammer, "Progressives in California, 1906–1911," unpublished M.A. thesis, University of California, Berkeley, 1927, pp. 100–08, and John L. Shover, "The Progressives and the Working Class Vote in California," *Labor History*, vol. X, Fall, 1969, pp. 584–601.
102. *American Federationist*, March, 1910, p. 224.
103. *American Federationist*, March, 1912, p. 217; June, 1912, pp. 459, 532–36; October, 1912, pp. 804–14; Fred Greenbaum, "The Social Ideas of Samuel Gompers," *Labor History*, vol. VII, Winter, 1966, p. 52.
104. Samuel M. Jones to Gompers, Sept. 25, 1899, *AFL Corr.*
105. Newark *Evening News*, April 4, 17, 1908.
106. Samuel M. Jones to Gompers, Sept. 25, 1899, *AFL Corr.*
107. Tom L. Johnson to Gompers, May 5, 1903, *AFL Corr.*
108. Edward F. Dunne to Gompers, Sept. 10, 1905, *AFL Corr.*
109. Pamphlet, *Mayor Jones and Public Ownership*, by Edward Wisner, copy in *AFL Corr.* with Gompers' notations.
110. Frank Morrison to A.F. of L. Executive Council, August 10, 1910, *AFL Corr.*

CHAPTER 4

1. *Proceedings*, AFL Convention, 1909, pp. 143–48.
2. Kenneth W. Hechler, *Insurgency: Personalities and Politics of the Taft Era*, New York, 1940, pp. 21–22.
3. *Ibid.*, pp. 45–46.
4. Frank Morrison to John Mitchell, April 27, 1910, *AFL Corr.* and *JMP.*
5. *Congressional Record*, 61st Cong., 2nd Session, vol. XLV, part 8, pp. 8657, 9223–24; *House Report 113*, p. 23.
6. Gompers to W. A. White, July 15, 1910, *GLB.*
7. New York *Call;* Feb. 12, 1910.
8. *Ibid.*, March 8, 1910; Chicago *Tribune*, March 9, 1910.
9. New York *Tribune*, March 11, 1910.
10. New York *Call*, March 23, 24, April 22, 1910; Philadelphia *North American*, April 11, 1910.
11. *New York Times*, Aug. 15, 1910.
12. Indianapolis *Star*, Jan. 31, 1910.
13. Booklet, published by A.F. of L., 1910; Circular, Nov. 2, 1910, *AFL Corr.*
14. Cleveland *Citizen*, July 23, 1910.
15. Seattle *Union Record*, Oct. 1, 1910.
16. *Proceedings*, A.F. of L. Convention, 1910, p. 121.
17. *New York Times*, Oct. 20, 1910.

18. A.F. of L. *Weekly News Letter,* April 8, 1911.
19. Indianapolis *Star,* Feb. 21, 1911.
20. Gompers to A.F. of L. Executive Council, March 3, 1911, *AFL Corr.*
21. A.F. of L. *Weekly News Letter,* April 8, 15, 22, 1911.
22. *Ibid.,* May 10, 1911.
23. *American Federationist,* June, 1912, pp. 460-61.
24. Gompers to A.F. of L. Executive Council, May 17, 1911, *AFL Corr.*
25. *Legislative Achievements of the American Federation of Labor,* Washington, D.C., 1916, pp. 10-11.
26. *American Federationist,* March, 1912, p. 217; June, 1912, pp. 459, 463, 535-36.
27. Circular entitled "Labor Planks Submitted to the Democratic Convention, 1912," issued by A.F. of L., *AFL, Corr.*
28. National Conference of Charities and Correction, *Proceedings,* 1912, pp. 376-94; *The Survey,* vol. XXVIII, August, 1912, pp. 668-70.
29. *American Federationist,* October, 1912, pp. 804-14.
30. *Ibid.*
31. Gompers, *Seventy Years of Life and Labor,* vol. II, p. 279.
32. From Gompers' notes on his speech before the Platform Committee of the Democratic Convention, 1912, *AFL Corr.*
33. Gompers to A.F. of L. Executive Council, June 12, 1912, *AFL Corr.*
34. *Democratic Text-Book, 1912,* pp. 24-26.
35. Gompers, *Seventy Years of Life and Labor,* vol. II, p. 279.
36. W.D. Jamieson to Frank Morrison, Des Moines, Iowa, February 2, 1912, containing appeal of A.F. of L. unionists in Des Moines, *AFL Corr.*
37. Michael Kraus, *The Writing of American History,* Norman, Oklahoma, 1933, p. 432.
38. Woodrow Wilson, *History of the American People,* New York, 1902, vol. V, pp. 140-41, 239-40, 266.
39. *Ibid.,* pp. 124, 164-65.
40. *Ibid.,* p. 127.
41. *Ibid.,* p. 300.
42. Ray Stannard Baker, *Woodrow Wilson, Life and Letters,* New York, 1933, vol. III, p. 70; Arthur S. Link, *Wilson: The Road to the White House,* Princeton, New Jersey, 1947, pp. 112, 127; *Ms.* of Baccalaure address, Woodrow Wilson Papers, Library of Congress, Manuscripts Division.
43. Link, *op. cit.,* pp. 112, 127.
44. Dallas L. Jones, "The Wilson Administration and Organized Labor, 1912-1919," unpublished Ph.D. thesis, Cornell University, 1956, pp. 15-16; James Kerney, *The Political Education of Woodrow Wilson,* New York, 1926, pp. 16-17.
45. Link, *op. cit.,* p. 127.
46. *Ibid.,* pp. 158-59.
47. Wilson to George Harvey, July 16, 1910, George Harvey Papers, Library of Congress, Manuscripts Division.
48. Wilson to Edgar Williamson, Aug. 23, 1910; pamphlet published by the Democratic State Auxiliary Committee, n.d., in Wilson Papers, Library of Congress, Manuscripts Division.
49. Link, *op. cit.,* p. 160.
50. Handbill published by the Progressive Voters League, Camden, New Jersey, 1910, copy in Wilson Papers, Library of Congress, Manuscripts Division; Jones, *op. cit.,* pp. 23-24.
51. Jones, *op. cit.,* p. 32; Newark *Evening News,* Oct. 1, 1910.
52. Newark *Evening News,* Oct. 24, 1910.
53. Jones, *op. cit.,* pp. 32-33.
54. *Democratic Text-Book, 1912,* pp. 273-74.
55. *New York Times,* March 13, 1913.
56. Gompers, *Seventy Years of Life and Labor,* vol. I, pp. 543-44.
57. Link, *op. cit.,* pp. 382-86; *Democratic Text-Book, 1912,* pp. 273-74; Jones, *op. cit.,* p. 43.
58. Gompers, *Seventy Years of Life and Labor,* vol. II, p. 279.
59. *See* George E. Mowry, *Theodore Roosevelt and the Progressive Movement,* Madison, Wisconsin, 1946, Chapter I; John Chamberlain, *Farewell to Reform,* New York, 1933, p. 266.
60. The text of the platform is in Theodore Roosevelt, *Progressive Principles,* New York, 1913, Appendix.
61. Bella Case La Follette & Folla La Follette, *Robert M. La Follette,* New York, 1953, vol. I, p. 258.
62. *Cf.* Everett (Washington) *Labor Journal,* Sept. 24, 1910, and Seattle *Union Record,* Oct. 1, 1910.
63. *La Follette's Weekly Magazine,* Sept. 10, 1910; Bella Case La Follette & Folla La Follette, *op. cit.,* Vol. I, p. 524; Jerome S. Auerbach, "Progressives at Sea: The La Follette Act of 1915," *Labor History,* vol. II, Fall, 1961, pp. 348-49.
64. Bella Case La Follette & Folla La Follette, *op. cit.,* vol. I, p. 447; A.F. of L. *Weekly News Letter,* April 8, 15, 22, May 13, 1911.
65. Carl Painter, "The Progressive Movement in Indiana," *Indiana Magazine of History,* vol. XVI, September, 1920, p. 189; *Papers of Edward P. Costigan Relating to the Progressive Movement in Colorado, 1912-1917,* edited by Colin B. Goodykoontz, Boulder, Colorado,

1914, p. 179; Sophie J. Eisenstein, "The Elections of 1912 in Chicago," Unpublished MA Thesis, Univ. of Chicago, 1947, p. 21.

66. New York *Herald,* Nov. 2, 1910; *New York Times,* Nov. 7, 1910.

67. Richard Hofstadter, *The Age of Reform: From Bryan to FDR,* New York, 1955, p. 64.

68. *Literary Digest,* Oct. 12, 1912, p. 607; *Miners' Magazine,* June 6, 1912, p. 11.

69. *Cf.* New York *Herald,* Nov. 26, 1912 for list of campaign contributions.

70. Theodore Roosevelt, *Progressive Principles,* pp. 301-02; Theodore Roosevelt *A Charter of Democracy,* Ohio, 1912, p. 9; *The Outlook,* July 27, 1912, p. 661.

71. William E. Walling, *Socialism As It Is,* New York, 1912, p. 18.

72. Mowry, *op. cit.,* pp. 271-72.

73. George E. Mowry, "The South and the Progressive Lily White Party of 1912," *Journal of Southern History,* vol. VI, May, 1940, pp. 237-47.

74. *New York Times,* Sept. 12, 1912.

75. Jones, *op. cit.,* p. 72.

76. Gompers, *Seventy Years of Life and Labor,* vol. I, p. 544.

77. *American Federationist,* August, 1912, pp. 623-28.

78. John W. Kern to Gompers, August 10, 1912, *AFL Corr.*

79. Gompers to John W. Kern, Sept. 16, 1912, *AFL Corr.*

80. *American Federationist,* October, 1912, pp. 807-14; A.F. of L. *Weekly News Letter,* Special Campaign Issue, no date, *AFL Corr.*

81. New York *World,* Aug. 2, 1912.

82. Link, *op. cit.,* p. 488.

83. Alpheus T. Mason, *Brandeis: A Free Man's Life,* New York, 1942, pp. 429-32.

84. Alfred Lief, *Brandeis: The Personal History of an American Ideal,* New York, 1946, p. 238; Milton J. Nadworny, *Scientific Management and the Unions, 1900-1932: A Historical Analysis,* Cambridge, Mass., 1955, pp. 38-39.

85. Mason, *op. cit.,* p. 377; Louis D. Brandeis, "Labor and the Trusts," *Collier's Weekly,* vol. XLIV, September 14, 1912, p. 8.

86. *New York Times,* Sept. 19, 1912.

87. New York *World,* Oct. 30, 1912, Woodrow Wilson, *The New Freedom,* New York, 1912, p. 259.

88. Boston *Globe,* Sept. 27, 1912.

89. Wilson, *The New Freedom,* pp. 19-20, 28-29.

90. Ray Stannard Baker, *The Public and Private Papers of Woodrow Wilson,* vol. II, p. 468; *Harper's Weekly,* vol. LVI, October 26, 1912, p. 8.

91. *Address of Louis D. Brandeis delivered before the Convention of the American Federation of Labor, Massachusetts branch,* September 18, 1912; *La Follette's Weekly Magazine,* vol. IV, October 12, 1912.

92. Copy in *AFL Corr.*

93. Copy in *AFL Corr.*

94. Gompers, *Seventy Years of Life and Labor,* vol. II, pp. 282-83.

95. *New York Times,* July 7, 1912.

96. *American Federationist,* October, 1912, pp. 801-04; November, 1912, pp. 889-94.

97. New York *Tribune,* Aug. 1, 1912.

98. Link, *op. cit.,* p. 514.

99. Jones, *op. cit.,* p. 52, Eisenstein, *op. cit.,* p. 93.

100. Gompers Collection, Book I, Index Card #37, "Press Statements and Interviews," Economic Division, New York Public Library.

101. U.S. Congress, House Committee on Judiciary, *Hearings on Trust Legislation,* 63 Cong., 2nd Sess., p. 15.

CHAPTER 5

1. *Proceedings,* A.F. of L. Convention, 1912, pp. 285-86.

2. Gompers, *Seventy Years of Life and Labor,* vol. II, p. 294.

3. Jones, *op. cit.,* p. 79.

4. *New York Times,* March 5, 1913.

5. Frank Morrison to Woodrow Wilson, March 7, 1913, *Woodrow Wilson Papers,* Library of Congress.

6. *New York Times,* March 9, 1913; *Literary Digest,* vol. XLVI, March 29, 1913.

7. Gompers to Woodrow Wilson, January 28, 1916, *Woodrow Wilson Papers,* Library of Congress and *GLB.*

8. Woodrow Wilson to Senator James A. Reed, June 13, 1913, *Woodrow Wilson Papers,* Library of Congress; Jones, *op. cit.,* p. 95.

9. John Lombardi, *Labor's Voice in the Cabinet,* New York, 1942, pp. 166-67.

10. Gompers, *Seventy Years of Life and Labor,* vol. II, p. 316.

11. Frankfurter and Greene, *op. cit.,* pp. 155-57.

12. Arthur S. Link, "The South and 'The New Freedom,'" *South Atlantic Quarterly,* Vol. LII, October, 1954, p. 319.

13. Gompers to Woodrow Wilson, March 14, 1913, *GLB* and *Woodrow Wilson Papers,* Library of Congress; Gompers, *Seventy Years of Life and Labor,* vol. II, p. 294.

14. Wilson to Gompers, March 17, 1913, *Woodrow Wilson Papers,* Library of Congress and *AFL Corr.;* Gompers, *Seventy Years of Life and Labor,* vol. II, p. 295.

15. *New York Times,* May 21, 1913.
16. *Literary Digest,* vol. XLVI, March 29, 1913, pp. 694–95.
17. Gompers to Woodrow Wilson, April 30, 1913; Wilson to Gompers, May 6, 1913, *Woodrow Wilson Papers,* Library of Congress; *GLB* and *AFL Corr;* Gompers, *Seventy Years of Life and Labor,* vol. II, p. 295.
18. Gompers to Frank Morrison, May 20, 1913, GLB.
19. *New York Times,* April 13, 1913.
20. Wilson to Samuel Rea, April 22, 1913, *Woodrow Wilson Papers,* Library of Congress; Jones, *op. cit.,* p. 132.
21. *New York Times,* June 24, 1913.
22. *American Federationist,* November, 1914, pp. 967–68.
23. *New York Times,* April 22, May 6, December 19, 1913.
24. *Hitchman Coal & Coke Co. v. Mitchell,* 202 Fed. 512 (1912).
25. *American Federationist,* December, 1913, p. 827; *Proceedings,* A.F. of L. 1914, p. 105.
26. *New York Times,* June 14, 1913; *American Federationist,* January, 1914, p. 16.
27. *New York Times,* June 29, 1913.
28. *Ibid.,* Dec. 14, 1913.
29. *Literary Digest,* vol. XLVII, December 20, 1913, pp. 1214–15; Jones, *op. cit.,* p. 139.
30. Gompers to Frank Morrison, December 7, 1913, *GLB.*
31. *Proceedings,* A.F. of L. Convention, 1913, pp. 314–15.
32. *Ibid.,* pp. 323–26.
33. Jones, *op. cit.,* pp. 283–84.
34. Arthur S. Link, *Wilson and the Progressive Era, 1900–1917,* New York, 1954, pp. 59–60.
35. *American Federationist,* February, 1914, p. 114.
36. *Ibid.,* February, 1915, p. 113.
37. *Proceedings,* A.F. of L. Convention, 1912, p. 121; 1913, p. 163.
38. *United States Industrial Relations Commission Report,* pp. 7750–51.
39. *American Labor Legislation Review,* vol. I, June, 1911, pp. 5–123; October, 1911, pp. 7–96; vol. III, February, 1913, pp. 167–71; vol. IV, March, 1914, pp. 49–72.
40. Gompers to editor of the *New York Medical Journal,* Oct. 4, 1916, *GLB.;* Gompers' address before Conference on Social Insurance, Washington, D.C., Dec. 8, 1916, *Gompers Collection,* Book 2, Index Card #40, Economics Division, New York Public Library.
41. *New York Times,* Jan. 12, 1914.
42. *Ibid.,* Jan. 21, 1914.
43. *New York World,* March 1, 1914.
44. Link, "The South and 'The New Freedom,'" *op. cit.,* p. 319; Link, *Wilson and the Progressive Era,* p. 75; Jones, *op. cit.,* p. 149.
45. *New York Times,* March 17, 1914.
46. *New York World,* March 25, 1914; *New York Times,* April 8, 1914.
47. *New York Evening Post,* April 14, 1914.
48. *New York Times,* April 14, 1914.
49. Franfurter and Greene, *op. cit.,* pp. 155–67.
50. U.S. Congress, House Committee on the Judiciary, *Hearings on Anti-Trust Legislation,* 63rd Congress, 2nd session, vol. I, pp. 16, 26–27.
51. *New York Times,* April 15, 1914.
52. Jones, *op. cit.,* p. 155n.
53. *New York Evening Post,* May 26, 1914.
54. Copy of letter in *AFL Corr.*
55. *New York Times,* May 19, 24–27, 1914.
56. *Ibid.,* May 24, 1914.
57. Gompers to Judge Alton B. Parker, May 28, 1914; Gompers to members of A.F. of L. Executive Council, May 27, 1914, *GLB.*
58. *Congressional Record,* 63rd Congress, 1st Session, pp. 9073–74, 9155–66.
59. *New York Times,* June 2, 1914.
60. Woodrow Wilson to Charles R. Van Hise, July 13, 1914, *Woodrow Wilson Papers,* Library of Congress. *(My emphasis, P.S.F.)*
61. Mason, *Organized Labor and the Law,* quoted in Jones, *op. cit.,* p. 169.
62. See Gompers' testimony, U.S. Congress Senate, Committee on Interstate Commerce, *Hearings on Antitrust Legislation,* 62nd Congress, 1st Session, vol. II, p. 1757.
63. *New York Times,* May 30, 1914.
64. *Congressional Record,* 63rd Congress, 1st Session, pp. 9171–73, 9429.
65. *Ibid.,* pp. 9081–88, 9496, 9543, 9654–55.
66. Edwin E. Witte, "The Clayton Bill and Organized Labor," *The Survey,* vol. XXXIII, July 4, 1914, p. 360.
67. *New York Times,* July 14, 1914.
68. "Minutes of the A.F. of L. Executive Council, 1914," p. 583. *AFL Corr.*
69. Quoted in *Literary Digest,* vol. XLVIII, June 13, 1914, pp. 1423–24.
70. Gompers to Organizers of the A.F. of L., June 20, 1914, *GLB;* Circular Letter from A.F. of L., Washington, D.C., July 10, 1914, addressed "To Organized Labor, Ohio, Fellow Workers and Friends," *AFL Corr.; American Federationist,* October, 1914, p. 556.
71. *Literary Digest,* vol. XLVIII, July 22, 1914, p. 1762.
72. Gompers, *Seventy Years of Life and Labor,* vol. II, pp. 295–96; *Congressional Record,* 63rd Congress, 1st Session, pp. 14590–91.
73. Jones, *op. cit.,* p. 182.
74. *Ibid.,* pp. 183–84.

75. *New York Times,* Oct. 11, 1914.
76. *Ibid.,* June 12, Oct. 25, 1914; Daniel Davenport, "An Analysis of the Labor Sections of the Clayton Anti-Trust Bill," *Central Law Review,* vol. LXXX, January 15, 1915, pp. 46-55; William Howard Taft, "Address of the President," *American Bar Association Reports,* vol. XXXIX, October, 1914, pp. 359-85.
77. National City Bank of New York, *Letter,* November, 1914.
78. Gompers, *Seventy Years of Life and Labor,* vol. II, p. 298.
79. *American Federationist,* November, 1914, p. 224.
80. Gompers to members of A.F. of L. Executive Council, September 3, 1914; Gompers to William B. Carey, October 15, 1914, *GLB.*
81. *American Federationist,* October, 1914, pp. 886-87.
82. George James Stevenson, "The Brotherhood of Locomotive Engineers and Its Leaders, 1863-1920," unpublished Ph.D. thesis, Vanderbilt University, June, 1954, p. 287.
83. Norman J. Ware, *Labor in Modern Industry,* Boston, 1934, p. 34.
84. Gompers to A.F. of L. Executive Council, October 15, 1914, *AFL Corr.*
85. Berman, *Labor and the Sherman Act,* pp. 102-03.
86. Frankfurter and Greene, *op. cit.,* pp. 197-98, 206.
87. *American Federationist,* January, 1915, p. 32.
88. Daniel Levine, "Gompers and Racism: A Strategy of Limited Objectives," *Mid-America,* vol. LXIII, April, 1961, p. 111.

CHAPTER 6

1. *See also* issue of March 5, 1910.
2. Philip S. Foner, *History of the Labor Movement in the United States,* vol. I, New York, 1947, pp. 116-18.
3. Philadelphia *Press,* May 28, June 1, 1909; New York *Call,* June 2, 1909.
4. *The Public,* June 6, 1909.
5. Philadelphia *Evening Bulletin,* June 2, 3, 1909; New York *Call,* June 3, 1909; "Philadelphia Strike and Settlement," *Motorman and Conductor,* vol. XVII, June, 1909, pp. 4-6.
6. New York *Call,* June 5, 1909.
7. Philadelphia *Evening Bulletin,* Jan. 11, 18, 1910.
8. Philadelphia *Public Ledger,* Jan. 7, 12, 15, 18, 1910.
9. Philadelphia *Evening Bulletin,* Jan. 19, 1920.
10. *Ibid.,* Jan. 18, 19, 1910.
11. *Ibid.,* Jan. 18, 1910.
12. Philadelphia *Public Ledger,* Jan. 29, 1910; Philadelphia *Evening Bulletin,* Jan. 29, 1910.
13. Samuel Gompers to Charles O. Kruger, January 23, 1910; Charles O. Kruger to Samuel Gompers, Jan. 24, 1910, and Gompers to Executive Council, A.F.L. of L. March 12, 1912, enclosing copies of correspondence, *AFL Corr.*
14. Philadelphia *Public Ledger,* Feb. 16, 17, 18, 19, 20, 1910.
15. *Ibid.,* Feb. 20, 1910.
16. Philadelphia *Evening Bulletin,* Feb. 21, 1910.
17. Philadelphia *North American* reprinted in *Literary Digest,* March 5, 1910.
18. Philadelphia *North American,* Feb. 23, 1910; *New York Times,* Feb. 23, 1910; New York *World,* Feb. 23, 1910; New York *Call,* Feb. 24, 1910; Philadelphia *Public Ledger,* Feb. 24, 1910.
19. Philadelphia *Evening Bulletin,* Feb. 21, 24, 1910.
20. *Ibid.,* February 21, 1920.
21. New York *Call,* Feb. 23, 1910; Graham Adams, Jr., *Age of Industrial Violence, 1910-1915,* New York, 1966, pp. 183-84.
22. New York *Call,* Feb. 25, 1910.
23. Philadelphia *Evening Bulletin,* February 21, 1910.
24. *Ibid.,* Feb. 22, 1910.
25. Philadelphia *North American,* Feb. 23, 24, 1910.
26. Philadelphia *Evening Bulletin,* Feb. 25, 1910.
27. *Ibid.,* Feb. 26, 1910.
28. *Ibid.,* Feb. 28, 1910; Philadelphia *Public Ledger,* Feb. 27, 28, 1910.
29. Philadelphia *North American,* Feb. 28, 1910.
30. Philadelphia *Evening Bulletin,* Feb. 28, March 3, 1910.
31. *Ibid.*
32. Philadelphia *Public Ledger,* Feb. 26, 28, 1910.
33. *Ibid.,* Feb. 28, 1910; Philadelphia *Evening Bulletin,* Feb. 28, 1910.
34. Philadelphia *North American,* March 1-3, 1910; Philadelphia *Evening Bulletin,* March 1-3, 1910.
35. Philadelphia *Evening Bulletin,* March 2, 1910.
36. *Ibid.,* March 3, 1910.
37. *Ibid.,* March 4, 1910.
38. Dora Lewis to Agnes Nestor, March 4, 1910, *Agnes Nestor Papers,* Chicago Historical Society.
39. Philadelphia *Evening Bulletin,* March 3, 1910.

40. Philadelphia *Public Ledger*, March 17, 1910.
41. "In Stricken Philadelphia," *Wilshire's Magazine*, April, 1910, p. 4.
42. Philadelphia *Evening Bulletin*, March 5, 1910; Philadelphia *Public Ledger*, March 5, 1910; New York *Call*, March 9, 1910.
43. Philadelphia *Evening Bulletin*, March 6, 1910; Philadelphia *Public Ledger*, March 6, 1910.
44. Philadelphia *Evening Bulletin*, March 6, 1910; Philadelphia *Public Ledger*, March 6, 1910.
45. Philadelphia *Evening Bulletin*, March 10, 1910.
46. Philadelphia *Public Ledger*, March 10, 1910. For a criticism of the failure of the printers to join the general strike, *see* "Good Union Men(?)" *Solidarity*, Oct. 1, 1910.
47. Philadelphia *Public Ledger*, March 7, 1910.
48. New York *Call*, March 8, 1910.
49. Philadelphia *Public Ledger*, March 5, 1910.
50. *Ibid.*, March 6, 1910; New York *Sun*, March 6, 1910; New York *World*.
51. Philadelphia *Evening Bulletin*, March 9, 20, 1910.
52. Gompers to A.F. of L. Executive Council, March 12, 1910, enclosing statement of March 11, 1910, *AFL Corr.*
53. Philadelphia *Public Ledger*, March 18, 19, 1910; Philadelphia *Evening Bulletin*, March 19, 1910.
54. Philadelphia *Public Ledger*, March 19, 20, 1910.
55. Philadelphia *Evening Bulletin*, March 28, 1910.
56. Philadelphia *Public Ledger*, March 20, 21, 1910.
57. Philadelphia *Evening Bulletin*, April 12, 1910.
58. Philadelphia *Public Ledger*, March 31, 1910.
59. Philadelphia *Evening Bulletin*, April 6, 11, 1910.
60. New York *Call*, June 6, 1910.
61. Philadelphia *Public Ledger*, March 29, 1910; Philadelphia *Evening Bulletin*, March 29, 1910.
62. Philadelphia *Evening Bulletin*, March 30, 1910; Philadelphia *Public Ledger*, April 1, 17, 1910.
63. Philadelphia *Evening Bulletin*, April 12, 1910.
64. *Ibid.*, April 14, 1910.
65. John E. Reyburn to Chas. O. Kruger, March 21, 1910, copy in *AFL Corr.*
66. Chas. O. Kruger to John E. Reyburn, March 21, 1910, copy in *AFL Corr.*
67. *Ibid.*
68. Philadelphia *Public Ledger*, April 4, 1910.
69. *Ibid.*, April 6, 1910.
70. John Mitchell to Samuel Gompers, April 2, 1910, *AFL Corr.*

71. Philadelphia *Public Ledger*, April 16, 1910.
72. *Ibid.*, April 17, 1910.
73. *Ibid.*, April 18, 1910.
74. *Ibid.*
75. Philadelphia *Evening Bulletin*, March 23, 1910.
76. Philadelphia *Public Ledger*, March 22, 23, 1910.
77. *Industrial Worker*, April 9, 1910.
78. W.E. Trautmann, *Why Strikes Are Lost: How to Win*, I.W.W. Publishing Bureau, New Castle, Pa., n.d., p. 10.
79. *Industrial Worker*, March 26, 1910.
80. Adams, Jr., *op. cit.*, pp. 186–87.

CHAPTER 7

1. J. Noble Stockett, *The Arbitrational Determination of Railway Wages*, Boston, 1918, pp. 12–13; Gerald G. Eggert, *Railroad Labor Disputes: The Beginning of Federal Strike Policy*, Ann Arbor, 1967, pp. 217–24.
2. Railway Conductors, *Proceedings*, 1903, pp. 18–21.
3. Edwin C. Robbins, *Order of Railway Conductors*, New York, 1914, p. 64.
4. Stockett, *op. cit.*, pp. 14–15.
5. *Railway Age Gazette*, April 5, 1907, p. 575; *Railroad Trainmen's Journal*, April, 1907, pp. 439–44.
6. *Railway Age Gazette*, March 1, 1907, p. 289.
7. *Ibid.*, March 29, 1907, p. 548.
8. *Ibid.*, April 5, 1907, p. 575; *Railroad Trainmen's Journal*, April, 1907, pp. 439–44.
9. *Railway Conductor*, April, 1907, pp. 397–98; Robbins, *op. cit.*, p. 64.
10. George W. Wark, "The Eastern Federated Board," *Locomotive Firemen and Enginemen's Magazine*, June, 1913, pp. 830–31.
11. Eugene V. Debs, "You Railroad Men," in *Wayland's Monthly* reprinted in *Industrial Worker*, April 29, 1909.
12. James William Kerley, "The Failure of Railway Labor Leadership: A Chapter in Railroad Labor Relations, 1900–1932," unpublished Ph.D. thesis, Columbia University, 1959, p. 32.
13. *Machinists' Monthly Journal*, vol. XX, April, 1908, p. 295; vol. XXI, April, 1909, p. 342; Adams, Jr., *op. cit.*, pp. 128–29.
14. *Proceedings*, A.F. of L. Convention, 1908, p. 242.
15. Edward C. Kirkland, *A History of American Economic Life*, 3rd ed., New York, 1951, pp. 353–55.
16. Carl E. Person, *The Lizard's Trail: A Story from the Illinois Central and Harriman Lines Strike of 1911 to 1915 Inclusive*, Chicago, 1918, p. 13.

17. *New York Times*, June 24, July 2, 1911; *Final Report and Testimony of United States Commission on Industrial Relations*, vol. X, pp. 9703–04, 9782. Hereinafter referred to as *Final Report and Testimony*.
18. *Final Report and Testimony*, vol. XI, pp. 9775, 9863.
19. Eugene V. Debs, "The Harriman Railroad Strike," *Chicago Socialist*, Oct. 10, 1911.
20. *Solidarity*, Oct. 14, 1911.
21. *New York Times*, Sept. 1, 2, 3, 5, Oct. 1, 1911; New York *Tribune*, Sept. 1, 5, Oct. 2, 1911; *Final Report and Testimony*, vol. X, pp. 9701–05.
22. *New York Times*, Sept. 20, 1911; *Final Report and Testimony*, vol. XI, pp. 9861–63.
23. *Final Report and Testimony*, vol. XI, pp. 9885–88; Robert Edward Lee Knight, *Industrial Relations in the San Francisco Bay Area, 1900–1918*, Berkeley and Los Angeles, 1960, p. 253.
24. Eugene V. Debs, "The Harriman Railroad Strike," *Chicago Socialist*, Oct. 10, 1911.
25. *New York Times*, Oct. 1, 3, 1911; *Final Report and Testimony*, vol. X, pp. 9786–88.
26. New Orleans *Times-Picayune*, Oct. 1, 1911; *New York Times*, Oct. 1, 1911; *Solidarity*, Oct. 19, 1911; New York *Call*, Oct. 2, 1911; Eugene V. Debs, "The Harriman Railroad Strike," *Chicago Socialist*, Oct. 10, 1911.
27. *New York Times*, Oct. 2, 1911.
28. *Ibid.*, Oct. 6, 1911.
29. New York *Call*, Oct. 6, 1911.
30. New Orleans *Times-Picayune*, Oct. 6, 7, 1911.
31. *New York Times*, Oct. 7, 8, 1911.
32. *Ibid.*, Oct. 9, 1911; New Orleans *Times-Picayune*, Oct. 8–9, 1911.
33. Donald Crumpton Mosley, "A History of Labor Unions in Mississippi," Unpublished Ph.D. thesis, University of Alabama, 1965, p. 71.
34. *Ibid.*, pp. 71–72.
35. *McComb City Enterprise*, Oct. 5, 1911; Mosley, *op. cit.*, pp. 72–73.
36. New Orleans *Times-Picayune*, Oct. 4, 1911.
37. *McComb City Enterprise*, Oct. 12, 1911; Mosley, *op. cit.*, p. 73.
38. *New York Times*, Oct. 5, 1911; New York *Call*, Oct. 6, 1911.
39. *New York Times*, Oct. 5, 1911.
40. New York *Call*, Oct. 5, 1911; *McComb City Enterprise*, Oct. 12, 1911; Mosley, *op. cit.*, p. 73.
41. *Machinists' Monthly Journal*, vol. XXIII, Dec. 1911, p. 1232; Mosley, *op. cit.*, p. 73.
42. *McComb City Enterprise*, Nov. 9, 1911; Mosley, *op. cit.*, pp. 76–77.

43. *Final Report and Testimony*, vol. X, pp. 9719–21, 9830; New York *Call*, Oct. 3, 1911; Adams, Jr., *op. cit.*, p. 136.
44. *McComb City Enterprise*, Nov. 30, 1911; Mosley, *op. cit.*, pp. 74–75.
45. Floyd Gibbons, "A Fight to a Finish: The Carl Person Case," *International Socialist Review*, vol. XV, August, 1914, pp. 72–73.
46. Copy of Circular in *Carl Person Papers*, Collections of the Archives of Labor History and Urban Affairs, University Archives, Wayne State University, Detroit, Michigan. Hereinafter cited as *Carl Person Papers*.
47. Gibbons, *op. cit.*, p. 72.
48. Carl Person to Dear Sir & Brother, April 12th, 13, *Carl Person Papers*.
49. Gibbons, *op. cit.*, pp. 74–75.
50. *Ibid.*, pp. 75–76.
51. *Ibid.*, p. 78; New York *Call*, Oct. 6, 1914; Adams, Jr., *op. cit.*, p. 138.
52. Official Circular No. 10, Wm. H. Johnston to the Order Everywhere, March 5, 1912, *Carl Person Papers*.
53. *New York Times*, Jan. 25, 1913.
54. *Final Report and Testimony*, vol. X, p. 9735; New Orleans *Times-Democrat*, May 10, 1912.
55. P. J. Conlon, "Memories of the Past," *Machinists' Monthly Journal*, vol. XXXV, Jan. 1923, pp. 21–22; Person, *The Lizard's Trail*, pp. 177–78.
56. Person, *The Lizard's Trail*, pp. 177–78.
57. *Solidarity*, Oct. 14, 1911.
58. Los Angeles *Times*, Oct. 14, Nov. 20, 1911.
59. Philip S. Foner, *The Case of Joe Hill*, New York, 1965, pp. 11–12.
60. Person, *The Lizard's Trail*, pp. 45–59.
61. "Federation of Federations, Official Proceedings," *Blacksmith's Journal*, vol. XIV, May, 1912, pp. 1–38; St. Louis *Post-Dispatch*, April 15–17, 1912.
62. Carl E. Person to Dear Sir & Brother, Dec. 16, 1913, *Carl Person Papers*.
63. *Final Report and Testimony*, vol. X, pp. 9832, 9838–39; *Railway Carmen's Journal*, vol. XXVIII, April, 1913, pp. 252–53.
64. *New York Times*, May 25, 26, 1915; Person, *The Lizard's Trail*, pp. 333–34.
65. Mosley, *op. cit.*, pp. 77–78; *Final Report and Testimony*, vol. X, pp. 9945–48.
66. Mosley, *op. cit.*, p. 78; P. J. Conlon, "Memories of the Past," *Machinists' Monthly Journal*, vol. XXXV, Jan. 1923, p. 22.

CHAPTER 8

1. Samuel Yellen, *American Labor Struggles*, New York, 1956, p. 206.
2. H. E. West, "Civil War in the West Virginia Coal Mines," *Survey*, vol. XXX, April 5, 1913, pp. 45–47; Stuart Seely Sprague,

"Unionization Struggles in Paint and Cabin Creeks, 1912-1913," *West Virginia History,* April, 1977, p. 188.

3. 33 West Virginia 179, 188.
4. New York *Tribune* reprinted in *Literary Digest,* April 5, 1913, p. 757.
5. Walter B. Palmer, "An Account of the Strike of Bituminious Miners in the Kanawha Valley of West Virginia, April, 1912 to March, 1913," pp. 2–3, typed *Ms.,* Records of Department of Labor, file 16/103, National Archives, Washington, D.C., (NA).
6. U.S. Coal Commission, *Report* in *Senate Doc. 195,* vol. I, p. 168.
7. Thomas Edward Posey, "The Labor Movement in West Virginia, 1900-1948," unpublished Ph.D. thesis, University of Wisconsin, 1948, p. 25.
8. Report of Industrial Commission, vol. XII, pp. 38, 74–76; United Mine Workers of America, *Minutes of 13th Annual Convention,* 1902, p. 41.
9. United Mine Workers of America, *Minutes of the 16th Annual Convention,* 1903, pp. 38–41; A.F. Hinrichs, *The United Mine Workers of America and the Non-Union Coal Fields,* New York, 1919, p. 119.
10. New York *Tribune,* June 12, 25, 27, Aug. 28, 1902; Charleston (W.Va.) *Gazette,* June 7, 1902; United Mine Workers of America, *Minutes of the 14th Annual Convention,* 1903, pp. 38, 42; Charles Bierne Crawford, "The Mine Workers on Cabin Creek and Paint Creek, West Virginia in 1912-1913," unpublished M.A. thesis, University of Kentucky, 1939, pp. 17–18.
11. Charles Phillips Anson, "A History of the Labor Movement in West Virginia," unpublished Ph.D. thesis, University of North Carolina, 1940, p. 117.
12. *Ibid,* pp. 118-20; *Proceedings of the Twenty-Third Convention, United Mine Workers of America,* 1912, vol. I, p. 922; Palmer, *op. cit.,* Appendix.
13. Palmer, *op. cit.,* pp. 1–2.
14. *United Mine Workers Journal,* June 27, 1912, p. 7.
15. U.S. Congress, Hearings on Senate Resolution 37, Report of Senate Sub-Committee on Education and Labor, *Conditions in Paint Creek District of West Virginia,* parts 1, 2 and 3, Washington, 1913, pp. 112–13.
16. U.S. Coal Commission *Report* in *Sen. Doc. 195,* vol. I, p. 169.
17. Palmer, *op. cit.,* p. 7; *United Mine Workers Journal,* Dec. 26, 1912, p. 2.
18. Palmer, *op. cit.,* p. 8.
19. *Ibid.,* p. 8; Ralph A. Chaplin, "Violence in West Virginia," *International Socialist Review,* vol. XIII, April, 1913, pp. 729-35.

20. New York *Call,* July 27, 1912; Evelyn L.C. Harris and Frank J. Krebs, *From Humble Beginnings: West Virginia State Federation of Labor 1903-1957,* Charleston, W.Va., 1960, pp. 72-78.
21. Charleston *Gazette,* Aug. 5, 1912; Crawford, *op. cit.,* p. 38.
22. Hearings on Senate Resolution 37, *Conditions in Paint Creek District of West Virginia, op. cit.,* p. 373; New York *Call,* Sept. 4, 1912.
23. Hearings on Senate Resolution 37, *Conditions in Paint Creek District of West Virginia, op. cit.,* p. 238.
24. *United Mine Workers Journal,* Sept. 19, 1912, p. 1.
25. New York *Call,* Sept. 13, 1912.
26. *United Mine Workers Journal,* Oct. 10, 1912, p. 1.
27. Palmer, *op. cit.,* pp. 12–13.
28. Commission Appointed by Governor William E. Glasscock, *Report of the West Virginia Mining Investigation,* 1912, pp. 59–60, 62, 74, 370-71.
29. Huntington *Advertiser,* Oct. 3, 1912; John L. Dunbar, "Two Periods of Crisis in Labor-Management Relations in the West Virginia Coal Fields (1912-13 and 1919-22)," unpublished M.A. thesis, Columbia University, 1946, p. 23.
30. *Report of the West Virginia Mining Investigation,* 1912, pp. 74–75.
31. *United Mine Workers Journal,* Jan. 23, 1913, p. 2.
32. New York *Call,* Feb. 11, 1913; *Senate Report 321,* 63rd Congress, 2d Session, I, p. 946.
33. "When the Leaves Come Out," By a Paint Creek Miner, Written during the West Virginia Strike, in "The Colorado Coal Strike, 1913-1914," pamphlets collected and presented by Miss Laurel Conwell Thayer, Indiana University Library. (*See also* Ralph Chaplin, *Wobbly,* Chicago, 1948, p. 127.)
34. *New York Times,* Feb. 10-11, 1913.
35. *Ibid.,* Feb. 12-14, 1913.
36. John B. White to W.B. Wilson, April 7, 1913, Records of the Department of Labor, File No. 16/13-B, NA.
37. Virginia Lee, "Political and Civil Liberties During Certain Periods of Emergency in West Virginia," unpublished M.A. thesis, Marshall College, Huntington, West Virginia, 1942, pp. 69–72.
38. Robert S. Rankin, *When Law Fails,* Durham, North Carolina, 1939, p. 85.
39. *International Socialist Review,* vol. XIV, June, 1914, p. 322.
40. Mother Jones to W.B. Wilson, Feb. 1913, Records of Department of Labor, CC: 20 16/13-H, NA.

41. Mother Jones to Senator Borah, Feb. 1913, copy, in Records of Department of Labor, CC: 20 16/13-H, NA.
42. William B. Wilson to T.W. Thompson, Washington, D.C., March 19, 1913, Records of the Department of Labor, 16/13, NA.
43. Palmer, *op. cit.*, p. 20; *New York Times*, March 13, 15, 1913.
44. Palmer, *op. cit.*, Appendix.
45. Mother to My dear friend, Military Bastille, Pratt, West Va., April 5th, 1913, Records of the Department of Labor, CC: 20 16/13-H, NA.
46. Palmer, *op. cit.*, p. 22.
47. William B. Wilson to John P. White, March 22, 1913, Records of the Department of Labor, 16/13, NA.
48. Mary F. Parton, *The Autobiography of Mother Jones*, Chicago, 1925, p. 162; Joseph Leeds, "The Miners Called Her Mother," *Masses & Mainstream*, March, 1958, p. 47.
49. *Senate Report 321*, 63rd Cong., 2d Sess., vol. I, pp. 12–20.
50. *United Mine Workers Journal*, April 3, 1913, pp. 1, 7; April 24, 1913, p. 4.
51. David A. Corbin, "Betrayal in the West Virginia Coal Fields: Eugene V. Debs and the Socialist Party of America, 1912-1914,-" *Journal of American History*, vol. LXIV, March, 1978, p. 992.
52. *Ibid.*
53. W.H. Thompson, "How a Victory was Turned Into a 'Settlement' In West Virginia," *International Socialist Review*, vol. XIV, July, 1913, pp. 12–17; Fred H. Merrick, "The Betrayal of the West Virginia 'Red Necks,' " *ibid.*, pp. 18–22; Corbin, *op. cit.*, pp. 992–93.
54. *New York Call*, April 30, May 10, 1913; *Industrial Worker*, May 15, 1913; *United Mine Workers Journal*, May 1, 1913, p. 1.
55. *Milwaukee Leader*, May 30, 1913.
56. *New York Call*, June 11, 1913.
57. Thompson, *op. cit.*, pp. 12–17; Merrick *op. cit.*, pp. 18–22; Mary E. Marcy, "The Hatfield Whitewash," *International Socialist Review*, vol. XIV, July, 1913, pp. 54–55; *Industrial Worker*, July 24, 1913; Corbin, *op. cit.*, p. 1001.
58. "Debs Denounces Critics," *International Socialist Review* vol. XIV, August, 1913, pp. 104–06; W.H. Thompson, "A Reply to Debs," *ibid.*, pp. 106–08; Corbin, *op. cit.*, pp. 1001–03.
59. William B. Wilson to John P. White, Washington, D.C., June 18, 1913, Records of the Department of Labor, file 16/013, NA; Wheeling *Intelligencer*, July 15, 1913.

60. U.S. Coal Commission Report, *Sen. Doc. 195*, vol. III, pp. 1051-52.

CHAPTER 9

1. New York *Tribune*, April 21, 29, May 10, 1914.
2. 64th Cong., 1st Sess., Doc. 415, Senate Commission on Industrial Relations, *Final Report and Testimony*, vol. VIII, Washington, D.C., 1915, p. 8006. Hereinafter cited as *Report of the Commission on Industrial Relations*.
3. *The Survey*, vol. XXXIII, Dec. 5, 1914, p. 246.
4. U. S. Bureau of Mines, "Coal-Mine Fatalities in the United States, 1870-1914," *Bulletin No. 115*, p. 159; *Report of Commission on Industrial Relations*, p. 6435; Eugene O. Porter, "The Colorado Strike of 1913-An Interpretation," *The Historian*, vol. XXXV, November, 1973, pp. 14–15.
5. *Report of Commission on Industrial Relations*, pp. 8022–23.
6. *Harper's Magazine*, May 23, 1914, p. 11.
7. *Report of the Commission on Industrial Relations*, pp. 7115–16; Yellen, *op. cit.*, p. 115.
8. George G. Suggs, Jr., "The Colorado Coal Miners' Strike, 1903–1904; A Prelude to Ludlow," *Journal of the West*, vol. XII, 1973, pp. 36–52; *Report of the Commission on Industrial Relations*, pp. 6447–48.
9. *Report of the Commission on Industrial Relations*, p. 8417; Porter, *op. cit.*, p. 3.
10. *United Mine Workers' Journal*, Sept. 25, 1913.
11. *Report of the Commission on Industrial Relations*, pp. 8418–20; Alvin R. Sunseri, "The Ludlow Massacre: A Study in the mis-employment of the National Guard," *American Chronicle*, January, 1972, p. 23; Monica Eklund, "Massacre at Ludlow," *Southeast Economy and Society*, vol. IV, Fall, 1978, pp. 27–28.
12. New York *Tribune*, September 24, 25, 1913.
13. *Report of the Commission on Industrial Relations*, pp. 6699–73; 63rd Cong. 3rd Sess., House Document 136, Washington, D.C., 1915, *Report on the Colorado Strike Investigation*, pp. 17–18.) Hereinafter cited as *Report on the Colorado Strike Investigation*.
14. Sunseri, *op. cit.*, p. 24.
15. *Report of the Commission on Industrial Relations*, pp. 6675–78; *Report on the Colorado Strike Investigation*, pp. 30–32.
16. *Report of the Commission on Industrial Relations*, p. 8607; Sunseri, *op. cit.*, p. 26; Suggs, Jr., *op. cit.*, pp. 8–9.

17. *Report on the Colorado Strike Investigation*, pp. 22–23; Sunseri, *op. cit.*, pp. 26–27; Porter's, *op. cit.*, pp. 8–9.
18. *Report on the Colorado Strike Investigation*, pp. 30–32; Sunseri, *op. cit.*, 26–27; Colorado State Federation of Labor, *Militarism in Colorado*, Denver, 1914.
19. *Report of the Commission on Industrial Relations*, pp. 7098–7101.
20. *Ibid.*, p. 6941.
21. *Ibid.*, pp. 6350–51; *Report on the Colorado Strike Investigation*, pp. 126–27.
22. *Report of the Commission on Industrial Relations*, p. 6893.
23. *Ibid.*, p. 6895.
24. *Report of the Colorado Strike Investigation*, p. 130.
25. *New York Times*, May 3, 1914.
26. *Report on the Colorado Strike Investigation*, p. 130; George P. McGovern, "The Colorado Strike, 1913–1914," unpublished Ph.D. thesis, University of Illinois, 1953, p. 282; W.H. Fink, *The Ludlow Massacre*, Denver, 1914, pp. 7–8.
27. *New York Times*, April 21, 23, 1914; *Denver Express*, April 22, 1914.
28. *New York Times*, April 29, 30, 1914.
29. New York *Call*, May 2, 1914.
30. Included in John P. White to Woodrow Wilson, April 21, 1914, Woodrow Wilson Papers, Library of Congress.
31. *Report of the Commission on Industrial Relations*, p. 871.
32. *Report on the Colorado Strike Investigation*, pp. 131–32.
33. Billie Barnes Jensen, "Woodrow Wilson's Intervention in the Coal Strike of 1914," *Labor History*, vol. XV, Winter, 1974, pp. 62–77.
34. *Congressional Record*, 63rd Cong, 2nd Sess., April 29, 1914, pp. 7440–41.
35. *Report of Industrial Commission*, pp. 7763–89; *New York Times*, Jan. 26, 28, May 21, 26, 1915.
36. *New York Times*, May 22, 25, 27, 1915.
37. *The Nation*, vol. XCIX, Sept. 10, 1914, p. 295.
38. *Ibid.*, Oct. 1, 1914, p. 397.
39. *New York Times*, Dec. 15, 16, 1914, Jan. 2, 11, May 2, 1915.
40. *New Republic*, vol. I, Nov. 17, 1914, p. 203; *The Survey*, Oct. 6, 1917.
41. *Report on the Colorado Strike Investigation*, p. 35.
42. John Greenway, "Songs of the Ludlow Massacre," *United Mine Workers Journal*, April 15, 1945, p. 5.

CHAPTER 10

1. Angus Murdoch, *Boom Copper*, Calumet, Mich., 1954, pp. 219–20.

2. 63rd Congress, 2nd Session, *Senate Document #38*, vol. VIII, "Strike in the Copper Mining District of Michigan," Washington, D.C., 1914, pp. 43–44.
3. William A. Sullivan, "The 1913 Revolt of the Michigan Copper Miners," *Michigan History*, vol. XLIII, September, 1959, p. 308.
4. U.S. Department of Labor, *Strike in the Copper Mining District of Michigan*, Washington, D.C., 1914, pp. 18–19. Hereinafter cited as *Strike in the Copper Mining District*.
5. William D. Haywood, "With the Copper Miners of Michigan," *International Socialist Review*, vol. XI, August, 1910, pp. 65–67.
6. *Ibid.*, p. 68.
7. Vernon H. Jensen, *Heritage of Conflict: Labor Relations in the Non-ferrous Metals Industry up to 1930*, Ithaca, N.Y., 1950, pp. 274–75; Sullivan, *op. cit.*, p. 307.
8. Doris B. McLaughlin, *Michigan Labor: A Brief History from 1918 to the Present*, Ann Arbor, Mich., 1970, pp. 80–81; *Strike in the Copper Mining District*, pp. 21–25.
9. Inis Weed, "The Reasons Why the Copper Miners Struck," *Outlook*, vol. CVI, January 31, 1914, pp. 247–51; Murdoch, *op. cit.*, pp. 219–20; *Strike in the Copper Mining District*, pp. 25–34.
10. W.B. Wilson to Woodrow Wilson, Jan. 21, 1914, *Woodrow Wilson Papers*, Library of Congress.
11. "The Copper Strike," *International Socialist Review*, vol. XIV, November, 1913, pp. 269–70; McLaughlin, *op. cit.*, p. 83; Jensen, *op. cit.*, pp. 276–78; Murdoch, *op. cit.*, pp. 221–22.
12. McLaughlin, *op. cit.*, p. 85; *Strike in the Copper Mining District*, pp. 28–32.
13. McLaughlin, *op. cit.*, pp. 84–85.
14. *Strike in the Copper Mining District*, pp. 62–65; Jensen, *op. cit.*, p. 281.
15. Clarence A. Andrews, "'Big Annie' and the 1913 Michigan Strike," *Michigan History*, vol. LVII, 1973, pp. 57–58. See also N.P. Cochran, "Annie Clemenc, An American Joan of Arc," *The Miners' Bulletin*, November 1, 1913, p. 1.
16. Andrews, *op. cit.*, pp. 58–59; "The Star Spangled Banner," *The Miners' Bulletin*, September 16, 1913, p. 1.
17. McLaughlin, *op. cit.*, p. 87; *The Public*, January 9, 1914, pp. 35–36.
18. *United Mine Workers' Journal*, reprinted in *Literary Digest*, December 6, 1914.
19. McLaughlin, *op. cit.*, pp. 88–89; *Strikes in the Copper Mining District*, pp. 38–41.
20. William Beck, "Law and Order During the 1913 Copper Strike," *Michigan History*, vol. LIV, 1970, p. 287.

21. *The Survey,* Nov. 1, 1913, pp. 127-28; Jensen, *op. cit.,* pp. 274-75; Andrews, *op. cit.,* p. 61.
22. Andrews, *op. cit.,* pp. 65-66; Murdoch, *op. cit.,* pp. 223-25; *New York Times,* Dec. 25, 26, 1913; *International Socialist Review,* vol. XIV, Feb. 1914, pp. 453-61.
23. John Greenway, *American Folksongs of Protest,* Philadelphia, 1953, p. 158.
24. *Chicago Tribune,* Dec. 26-28, 1913.
25. Andrews, *op. cit,* p. 66; McLaughlin, *op. cit.,* p. 91.
26. Reprinted in *The Literary Digest,* Jan. 20, 1914.
27. G.R. Taylor, "Moyer's Story of Why He Left the Copper Country," *Survey,* Jan. 10, 1914, pp. 433-35; *Chicago Tribune,* Dec. 29, 30, 1913, Jan. 1-4, 1914.
28. "Michigan Press on the Copper War," *The Literary Digest,* Jan., 10, 1914.
29. *The Public,* Jan. 9, 1914, p. 35.
30. Andrews, *op. cit.,* pp. 66-68; *New York Times,* Jan. 3, 1914.
31. *Chicago Tribune,* Jan. 12, 1914.
32. United States Congress, Committee on Mines and Mining, *Conditions in Copper Mines of Michigan,* Senate Document No. 381.
33. Ibid., vol. VIII, pp. 113-14.
34. "To the Membership of the Western Federation of Miners," April 13, 1914, copy in *AFL Corr.*
35. *Ibid.*
36. *Ibid.*
37. *Ibid.;* McLaughlin, *op. cit.,* p. 90.
38. Merle W. Wells, "The Western Federation of Miners," *Journal of the West,* vol. XII, 1973, pp. 33-34.

CHAPTER 11

1. Pearl Goodman and Elia Ueland, "The Shirtwaist Trade," *Journal of Political Economy,* 18 (December, 1910): 814-16; Louis Levine, *Women's Garment Workers,* New York, 1924, pp. 144-48; William Mailly, "The Working Girls' Strike," *The Independent,* 67 (Dec. 23, 1909): 1416-20.
2. Goodman and Ueland, *op. cit.,* pp. 817, 819, 820-25; Woods Hutchinson, "The Hygienic Aspects of the Shirtwaist Strike," *The Survey,* 23 (January 22, 1910): 541-50; Marian F. Scott, "The Spirit of the Girl Strikers," *The Outlook,* 94 (February 19, 1910): 394-95; Carolyn Daniel McCreesh, "On the Picket Lines: Militant Women Campaign to Organize Garment Workers, 1882-1917," unpublished Ph.D. thesis, University of Maryland, 1975, pp. 163-64; Nancy Schrom Dye, "The Women's Trade Union League of New York, 1903-1920,"

unpublished Ph.D. thesis, University of Wisconsin, 1975, p. 160.
3. Hutchinson, *op. cit.,* p. 547; Scott, *op. cit.,* p. 394; Constance D. Leupp, "The Shirtwaist Strike," *The Survey,* 23 (December 18, 1909): 383-86; Hyman Berman, "Era of the Protocol: A Chapter in the History of the International Ladies' Garment Workers' Union, 1910-1916," unpublished Ph.D. thesis, Columbia University, 1956, p. 72; *New York Call,* Dec. 16, 1909.
4. McCreesh, *op. cit.,* pp. 162-63. Levine, *op. cit.,* p. 149; *Proceedings,* Eighth Convention, ILGWU, 1907, p. 30; *Report and Proceedings of the Ninth Convention of the International Ladies' Garment Workers' Union, 1908,* (New York, 1908), p. 28; *New York Call,* Aug. 27, 1909; McCreesh, *op. cit.,* p. 166.
5. *New York Call,* Sept. 6, 8, 1909.
6. *New York Call,* Sept. 16, Oct. 12-20, 1909; Sue Ainlee Clark and Edith Wyatt, "The Shirtwaist Makers and Their Strike," *McClure's Magazine,* 36 (November, 1910): 70-86.
7. Secretary's Report, Women's Trade Union League of New York, November 11, 1909, *WTUL of New York Papers,* State Labor Library, New York City; Dyche, "The Strike of the Ladies' Waist Makers of New York," pp. 1-2; Dye, *op. cit.,* p. 159.
8. *New York World,* Nov. 23, 1909; *New York Call,* Nov. 23, 1909; Levine, *op. cit.,* pp. 153-54; Leupp, *op. cit.,* pp. 383-86; Scott, *op. cit.,* pp. 392-96; *Souvenir History,* p. 12.
9. McCreesh, *op. cit.,* p. 171.
10. Secretary's Report, Women's Trade Union League of New York, November 17, 1909, *WTUL of New York Papers;* Dyche, "The Strike of the Ladies' Waist Makers of New York," p. 2.
11. Mailly, *op. cit.,* p. 1419; *New York Call,* Nov. 23, 26, 27, 1909; Charles S. Bernheimer, *The Shirt-Waist Strike: An Investigation Made for the Council and Head Worker of the University Settlement* (New York, 1910), pp. 3-5.
12. Mailly, *op. cit.,* p. 1419; *New York Call,* Nov. 26-28, 1909; *New York Times,* Dec. 28, 1909; Graham Adams, Jr., *Age of Industrial Violence, 1910-1915* (New York, 1966), p. 106.
13. Leupp, *op. cit.,* p. 383; Women's Trade Union League of New York, *Annual Report, 1909-1910,* p. 14.
14. *New York Call,* Dec. 23, 1909; *New York Times,* Jan. 3, 1910.
15. *New York Times,* Dec. 21, 24, 1909, Jan. 4, 6, 7, 1910; Leupp, *op. cit.,* p. 384; *New York Call,* Nov. 25, 1909, Jan. 7, 1910; *Souvenir History,* pp. 13-14.

16. Mary Clark Barnes, "The Strike of the Shirtwaist Makers," *World To-Day*, 18 (March, 1910): 267.
17. *New York Times*, Dec. 17, 1909; Dye, *op. cit.*, pp. 165-66.
18. *New York Times*, Dec. 16, 1909; Minutes, Regular Meeting, Women's Trade Union League of New York, February 7, 1910, *WTUL of NY Papers;* Women's Trade Union League of New York, *Annual Report, 1909-1910*, p. 14.
19. *New York Call*, Dec. 23, 1909; *New York Times*, Dec. 4, 1909.
20. *New York Times*, Dec. 21, 1909. *New York Call*, Dec. 6, 1909; *New York Times*, Dec. 6, 1909; Theresa Malkiel, *Diary of a Shirtwaist Worker*, New York, 1910, p. 23; *Souvenir History of the Ladies' Waist Maker's Union*, pamphlet, N.Y., w.d., pp. 15-16.
21. *Philadelphia Public Ledger*, Feb. 5, 1910.
22. *Ibid.*, Dec. 8, 9, 10, 20, 21, 1909; *Philadelphia Evening Bulletin*, Dec. 9, 10, 20, 21, 1909; McCreesh, *op. cit.*, pp. 174-75.
23. *Philadelphia Evening Bulletin*, Jan. 7, 11, 12, 13, 14, 17, Feb. 1, 5, 1910; *Philadelphia Public Ledger*, Jan. 7, 13, 15, 21, Feb. 3, 1910; Mary Durham to Agnes Nestor, Feb. 6, 1910, *Agnes Nestor Papers*, Chicago Historical Society.
24. *Philadelphia Public Ledger*, Jan. 15, 17, 20, 1910.
25. *New York Call*, Dec. 27, 28, 1909; *New York Times*, Dec. 28, 1909.
26. *New York Times*, Dec. 28, 1909; Levine, *op. cit.*, p. 164; Morris Hillquit, "Speech to the Striking Waist Makers," *Morris Hillquit Papers*, State Historical Society of Wisconsin.
27. Malkiel, *op. cit.*, p. 55.
28. *New York Times*, Jan. 3, 8, 1910; *New York Call*, Jan. 3, 1910.
29. *Souvenir History*, p. 20; Malkiel, *op. cit.*, pp. 58-60; *New York Call*, Jan. 3, 1910; Morris Hillquit's speech at Carnegie Hall, January 2, 1910, *Morris Hillquit Papers*, State Historical Society of Wisconsin.
30. *New York Times*, Dec. 21, 25, 1909; Jan. 4, 5, 6, 11, 1910; Mary Brown Sumner, "The Spirit of the Strikers," *The Survey*, 23 (Jan. 22, 1910): 550-55; *New York Call*, Jan. 4, 11, 12, 1910; New York State Department of Labor, *Bulletin #43*, March 1910, pp. 35-43.
31. *New York Call*, Feb. 7, 15, 1910; McCreesh, *op. cit.*, p. 179.
32. *Philadelphia Public Ledger*, Feb. 7, 1910; *Philadelphia Evening Bulletin*, Feb. 8, 1910; Barbara Mary Klaczynska, "Working Women in Philadelphia, 1900-1930," unpublished Ph.D. thesis, Temple University, 1975, pp. 240-41.
33. Miriam F. Scott, "What the Women Strikers Won," *The Outlook*, 45 (July 12, 1910): 480-88; Dyche, "The Strike of the Ladies' Waist Makers of New York," p. 2; Berman, *op. cit.*, p. 103.
34. Max Katzman to Agnes Nestor, Philadelphia, May 17, 1910, *Agnes Nestor Papers*, Chicago Historical Society; International Ladies' Garment Workers' Union, *Proceedings of the Convention*, 1912, p. 69; Dye, *op. cit.*, pp. 178-79.
35. Women's Trade Union League of New York, *Annual Report, 1909-1910*, p. 11; Report of Summer Work, October 3, 1910, Women's Trade Union League of New York, *WTUL of NY Papers;* Dye, *op. cit.*, p. 172; "President's Address," Pamphlet, 1910, p. 8, File 300, *Leonora O'Reilly Papers*, Schlesinger Library, Radcliffe College; Samuel M. Gompers, "The Struggle in the Garment Trades—From Misery and Despondency to Betterment and Hope," *American Federationist* 20 (March, 1913): 189-90; James J. Kenneally, "Women and Trade Unions, 1870-1920: The Quandary of the Reformer," *Labor History*, 14 (Winter, 1973): 48.
36. Morris Hillquit, "Speech to the Striking Waist Makers, January 2, 1910," *Morris Hillquit Papers*, State Historical Society of Wisconsin.
37. *New York Call*, Feb. 6, 1910.
38. William M. Feigenbaum, "Memories of 1909—The First Dress-Makers' Revolt," *Justice*, Sept. 1, 1933, p. 9.

CHAPTER 12

1. Levine, *op. cit.*, pp. 168, 176; Berman, *op. cit.*, pp. 107-08; *New York Call*, July 8, 1910.
2. International Ladies' Garment Workers' Union, *Report of the Proceedings of the Tenth Annual Convention, June 6-11, 1910*, pp. 47-48, 71-72; *New York Call*, June 30, 1910; *New York Times*, June 30, 1910; Levine, *op. cit.*, pp. 180-81.
3. *New York Call*, July 8, 1910; Levine, *op. cit.*, pp. 172, 181; *Union Labor Advocate*, 11 (August, 1910): 12; Edwin Fenton, "Immigrants and Unions: A Case Study of Italians and American Labor, 1870-1920," unpublished Ph.D. thesis, Harvard University, 1957, pp. 496-97; ILGWU, *Proceedings, Tenth Convention*, pp. 49, 57, 94.
4. *New York Call*, July 12, 1910; *New York Times*, July 12, 1910.
5. *New York Times*, July 21, Aug. 12, 13, 14, 1910.

6. *New York Call,* July 15, 1910; Levine, *op. cit.,* pp. 192–93.
7. Helen Marot, "Secretary's Report, July 20, 1910, NWTUL Papers, New York; McCreesh, *op. cit.,* pp. 187–88.
8. *New York Call,* July 13, 21, 22, 1910; *New York Times,* July 13, 1910.
9. Report of the President, ILGWU, *Eighth Convention Report,* pp. 5–6; Hyman Berman, "Era of the Protocol: A Chapter in the History of the International Ladies' Garment Worker's Union, 1910–1916," unpublished Ph.D. thesis, Columbia University, 1956, pp. 48–49.
10. *New York Call,* July 28, 1910; Berman, *op. cit.,* pp. 126–28.
11. Foner, *History of the Labor Movement* 2: 200.
12. Gompers to Abraham Rosenberg, Aug. 4, 1910, AFL *Corres.*
13. *New York Call,* July 30, Aug. 4, 1910; Levine, *op. cit.,* pp. 186–91.
14. *New York Times,* Aug. 28, 1900; *New York Call,* Aug. 27, 29, 1910.
15. *New York Times,* Aug. 28, 1910.
16. Adams, Jr., *op. cit.,* pp. 115–16.
17. Reprinted in *Literary Digest,* Sept. 10, 1910, p. 372.
18. *New York Times,* Aug. 29, 31, 1910; *Weekly Bulletin of the Garment Trades,* 10 (Sept. 2, 1910): 4.
19. Berman, *op. cit.,* p. 151; Dubofsky, *When Workers Organize,* pp. 187, 194–95.
20. *New York Call,* Sept. 3, 1910; "The Outcome of the Cloakmakers' Strike," *The Outlook* 96 (Sept. 17, 1910): 99–101.
21. *New York Call,* July 4, 1910; Helen Marot, "A Moral in the Cloak-makers' Strike," *The Outlook,* 96 (Sept. 17, 1910): 99–101.
22. Berman, *op. cit.,* pp. 152–53; John Laslett, *Labor and the Left* (New York, 1957), Chapter 4.
23. *The Ladies' Garment Worker* 1 (Nov. 1, 1910): 2.
24. Women's Trade Union League of Chicago, *Official Report of the Strike Committee,* p. 6; McCreesh, *op. cit.,* p. 189.
25. Robert Noren, United Garment Workers, to Emma Stehagen, Oct. 9, 1910, National Women's Trade Union League, *NWTUL Papers,* Schlesinger Library, Radcliffe College, Cambridge, Mass.
26. Women's Trade Union League of Chicago, *Official Report of the Strike Committee,* p. 6; McCreesh, *op. cit.,* pp. 189–90.
27. Anderson and Winslow, *op. cit.,* pp. 38–39.
28. Women's Trade Union League of Chicago, *Official Report of the Strike Committee,* pp. 10–11.

29. *Ibid.,* pp. 13–14; Matthew Josephson, *Sidney Hillman, Statesman of American Labor* (New York, 1952), p. 54.
30. *Life and Labor,* February, 1911, p. 52.
31. *Chicago Daily Socialist,* Oct. 22–28, 1910; Amalgamated Clothing Workers of America, *Clothing Workers of Chicago, 1910–1922,* pp. 26–27; *New York Call,* Nov. 10, 1910; Matthew Josephson, *Sidney Hillman, Statesman of American Labor,* New York, 1952, pp. 41–57.
32. Anne S. Rivera, "Clarence Darrow for the Amalgamated," *The Advance,* May, 1974, p. 12; Alice Henry, "The Hart, Schaffner & Marx Agreement," *Life and Labor,* June, 1912, pp. 170–172.
33. *New York Call,* June 8, 1911; Levine, *op. cit.,* pp. 209–12.
34. *New York Call,* Aug. 6, 1911 (Sunday edition); *Life and Labor,* October, 1911, p. 307; Margaret Dreier Robins to Members of the Executive Board, *National Women's Trade Union League Papers,* Library of Congress.
35. McCreesh, *op. cit.,* p. 196.
36. Josephson, *op. cit.,* pp. 58–60; *The Public,* Dec. 16, 1910, pp. 1187–88; *Milwaukee Leader,* Dec. 11, 1910.
37. Philip S. Foner, *The Fur and Leather Workers Union* (Newark, N.J., 1950), p. 39.
38. *Ibid.,* pp. 24–26.
39. *Ibid.,* pp. 39–42; *New York Call,* June 15–22, 1912; *Jewish Daily Forward,* June 15–19, 1912.
40. Foner, *The Fur and Leather Workers Union,* pp. 42–43.
41. *Ibid.,* p. 44; *Jewish Daily Forward,* July 7–9, 1912; Rose Blank, "Strike of the Furriers," *Life and Labor,* December, 1912, pp. 160–61.
42. Foner, *Fur and Leather Workers Union,* pp. 46–47; Blank *op. cit.,* p. 360.
43. Quoted in Foner, *Fur and Leather Workers Union,* p. 48.
44. Blank, *op. cit.,* p. 360.
45. Foner, *Fur and Leather Workers Union,* pp. 44–49; *New York Call,* Aug. 22, 24, 25, Sept. 7, 8, 1912.
46. *Jewish Daily Forward,* Sept. 9, 1912; Foner, *Fur and Leather Workers.*
47. *New York Call,* Jan. 14, 1913; "Uprising in the Needle Trades in New York," *Life and Labor,* March, 1913, pp. 69–70; *New York Times,* Jan. 14, 15, 1913.
48. Harry Lang, *"62," Biography of a Union* (New York, 1940), pp. 93–99; Minutes of the Executive Board Meeting, Meeting of January 23, 1913, *Women's Trade Union League of New York Papers;* Rose Schneiderman, "The White Goods Workers of New York," *Life and Labor,* May, 1913, p. 134; McCreesh, *op. cit.,* p. 221.

49. "The Song of the White Goods Workers," original in *National Women's Trade Union League Papers*, Schlesinger Library, Radcliffe College, and reprinted in McCreesh, *op. cit.*, p. 216.

50. Minutes, Executive Board, Women's Trade Union League of New York, January 23, 1913, *WTUL of NY Papers;* Helen Marot, "What Can A Union Do For Its Members?" *New York Call*, Jan. 27, 1913; Nancy Schrom Dye, "The Women's Trade Union League of New York, 1903-1920," unpublished Ph.D. dissertation, University of Wisconsin, Madison, 1974, pp. 189-90.

51. Levine, *op. cit.*, pp. 229-30; Lang, *op. cit.*, p. 131; Schneiderman, "White Goods Workers of New York," *op. cit.*, p. 136; "Report of the New York League to the Biennial Convention of the National Women's Trade Union League," *Leonora O'Reilly Papers*, Schlesinger Library, Radcliffe College. Dye claims that the settlement did not mention either recognition of a preferential shop (*op. cit.*, p. 190). But all other authorities include the preferential shop in the agreement.

52. McCreesh, *op. cit.*, p. 223.

53. *New York Call*, Jan. 16-19, 1913; *New York Times*, Jan. 19, 1913; Levine, *op. cit.*, pp. 223-26; Berman, *op. cit.*, pp. 165-72.

54. Dubofsky, *op. cit.*, pp. 83-87; Levine, *op. cit.*, pp. 226-28.

55. Harry Best, *The Men's Garment Industry of New York and the Strike of 1913* (New York, 1913), pp. 14-15; *New York Call*, June 6, 1912; *The Weekly Bulletin*, May 31, 1912, p. 4; June 7, 1912, p. 4; October 25, 1912, p. 1; *The Garment Worker*, November 15, 1912, p. 1.

56. *New York Call*, Dec. 24, 30, 31, 1912; Jan. 5, 6-7, 8-12, 1913; *New York Times*, Jan. 8, 1913; *The Garment Worker*, January 17, 1913, p. 1; Best, *op. cit.*, pp. 16-18.

57. *New York Times*, Jan. 4, 1913; *New York Call*, Jan. 3, 14, 18, 23, 1913, and letter of A. Appelberg in *ibid.*, Jan. 22, 1913; *The Garment Worker*, January 17, 1913, p. 1.

58. *New York Call*, Jan. 1, 17, 22, 27, 28, 29, Feb. 3, 7. 10, March 1, 1913; *New York Times*, Jan. 15, 21, 27, 1913; *The Garment Worker*, January 24, 1913, p. 1; January 31,

1913, pp. 1-2; Best, *op. cit.*, p. 23; Letter Books, February 10, 1913, Socialist Party: Local New York, Tamiment Institute Library, New York University.

59. Best, *op. cit.*, pp. 20-25; Amalgamated Clothing Workers of America, *Fiftieth Anniversary Souvenir History of the New York Joint Board, 1914-1916* (New York, 1964), pp. 55-57; Dubofsky, *op. cit.*, pp. 79-82; *New York Call*, March 9, 12, 13, 1913; *New York Times*, March 2, 13, 1913; *The Garment Worker*, March 14, 1913, pp. 1-2; Algernon Lee Scrapbooks, Labor Struggles, 1913, Tamiment Institute Library, New York University.

60. Isaac A. Hourwich, "The Garment Workers' Strike," *The New Review*, March 15, 1913, pp. 426-27.

61. Charles Elbert Zaretz, *The Amalgamated Clothing Workers of America* (New York, 1934), pp. 73-90, 95-96; Earl D. Strong, *The Amalgamated Clothing Workers of America* (Grinnell, Iowa, 1940), pp. 2-7; Amalgamated Clothing Workers of America, *The Clothing Workers of Chicago, 1910-1922* (Chicago, 1922), pp. 76-77; Strong, *op. cit.*, pp. 8-10; *Documentary History of the ACWA, 1914-1916*, pp. 4-6.

62. Zaretz, *op. cit.*, p. 96; Amalgamated Clothing Workers, *The Clothing Workers* (New York, 1932), pp. 74-95; *Documentary History*, pp. 24-25.

63. Zaretz, *op. cit.*, p. 96; *The Clothing Workers*, pp. 74-95.

64. Zaretz, *op. cit.*, p. 97; Josephson, *op. cit.*, pp. 95-97.

65. Josephson, *op. cit.*, p. 99; McCreesh, *op. cit.*, p. 250.

66. *The Garment Worker*, October 23, 1914; p. 1; October 30, 1914, pp. 1, 4; Joel Seidman, *The Needle Trades* (New York, 1949), pp. 115-25; Warren R. Van Tyne, *The Making of a Labor Bureaucrat* (Amherst, Mass., 1973), p. 157.

67. Bernard Mandel, *Samuel Gompers* (Yellow Springs, Ohio, 1954), p. 166.

68. Zaretz, *op. cit.*, pp. 102-04; *Documentary History*, pp. 74-75.

69. *Documentary History*, pp. 74-75.

70. *Proceedings*, AFL Convention, 1915, pp. 144-46, 360-61.

INDEX

Abbey, P.L., 216
Abramowitz, Bessie, 246, 248, 263
Accidents, 197-98
Adamic, Louis, 7
Adams, Graham Jr., 7
Addams, Jane, 31, 40, 248
Advisory Initiative and Referendum, 46-47
Afro-American League (Los Angeles), 15
Agents provocateurs, 27-28
Alexander, George, 9, 11, 25
Allied Building Trades Council of Philadelphia, 148, 149, 152-53
Amalgamated Association of Iron and Steel Workers, 8
Amalgamated Association of Street Car and Electric Railway Men of America, 70-71, 72, 73, 143, 144, 145, 146, 147, 150-59, 161, 163
Amalgamated Clothing Workers of America, 260-64
American Anti-Boycott Association, 138
American Association for Labor Legislation, 89*n.*, 129
American Bar Association, 138
American Bridge Company, 7-8, 15
American Federation of Labor (AFL), demand in for independent labor party, 90, 119-20, 127-28, 142; Executive Council assumes responsibility for McNamara defense, 18-19; Executive Council emphasizes labor must depend primarily on economic action, 101; endorses Woodrow Wilson in 1912 election, 118; fails to rouse mass pressure on Congress, 133; hails Clayton Anti-Trust Act, 138-39; in Philadelphia general strike, 160; jubilant over labor's political victories, 99; leadership and the Progressive movement, 88-90; leadership condemns Arizona Labor Party, 90; leadership equates independent political action with So-

cialism, 90; leadership opposes social legislation, 100-01; machine domination of, 44*n.;* Metal Trades Department, 10; 1912 convention, 129; 1913 convention, 127-28; opposes compulsory health insurance, 129-30; opposes independent labor party, 128, 142; opposes social legislation, 128-30; organizes Ways and Means Committee to defend McNamara brothers, 18-19; political policies evaluated, 141-42; Railway Department, 180; Railway Employees' Department, 167, 179-80; refuses to aid fur strike, 254; rejects appeal of ILGWU, 250; supports direct legislation, 41-48; supports initiative and referendum, 45-47; supports McNamara brothers, 18-19, 21; supports United Garment Workers' leadership, 264; urges release from prison of J.B. McNamara, 29*n.*
American Federationist, 43, 45, 62, 137
American Federation of Musicians, 19
American Railway Union, 164-65, 168
Ammons, Governor, 200, 202, 203
Anti-Monopoly parties, 32
Appeal to Reason, 16, 28, 33-34
Arizona, 50-54
Arizona Constitution of 1910, 50-54
Arizona Constitutional Petition League, 53
Arizona Labor Party, 53-54
Associated Fur Manufacturers, 252
Association of Waist and Dress Manufacturers of New York, 232, 236, 238
Australian Ballot, 55

Bacon-Bartlett Bill, 122, 131, 132, 133, 135
Bagley, C.L., 19
Baker, Ray Stannard, 33, 34
Baker, William, 257
Baldwin-Felt guards, 186, 189-90, 200, 202